RENEWALS 458-4574

DATE DUE

GAYLORD			PRINTED IN U.S.A.

ISLAMIC TERROR

ISLAMIC TERROR

Conscious and Unconscious Motives

Avner Falk

PRAEGER SECURITY INTERNATIONAL
Westport, Connecticut · London

Library of Congress Cataloging-in-Publication Data

Falk, Avner.
    Islamic terror : conscious and unconscious motives / Avner Falk.
        p. cm.
    Includes bibliographical references and index.
        ISBN 978–0–313–35764–0 (alk. paper)
1. Terrorism—Psychological aspects. 2. Islam—Psychology. 3. Terrorism—Religious aspects—
Islam. I. Title.
[DNLM: 1. Islam—psychology. 2. Terrorism—psychology. 3. Motivation. 4. Unconscious
(Psychology) WM 460.5.U6 F191i 2008]
RC569.5.T47F35   2008
363.325—dc22   2008015609

British Library Cataloguing in Publication Data is available.

Library of Congress Catalog Card Number: 2008015609
ISBN-13: 978–0–313–35764–0

First published in 2008

Praeger Security International, 88 Post Road West, Westport, CT 06881
An imprint of Greenwood Publishing Group, Inc.
www.praeger.com

Printed in the United States of America

The paper used in this book complies with the
Permanent Paper Standard issued by the National
Information Standards Organization (Z39.48–1984).

10 9 8 7 6 5 4 3 2 1

Contents

Acknowledgments

I wish to acknowledge with thanks the valuable comments and suggestions of my old friend, colleague, editor, and mentor, Vamık Volkan. I also wish to thank my editor at Praeger, Debbie Carvalko, as well as Nicole Azze at Greenwood Press, and Christy Anitha and Kay Berry at BeaconPMG, for their skillful and helpful work on this volume.

Introduction: Infantile Terror and Adult Terrorism

This book is an interdisciplinary attempt, with psychoanalysis at its center, to understand one of the most striking, most dramatic, and most dangerous human phenomena of our time. It applies the insights of psychoanalysis along those of psychology, psychiatry, sociology, anthropology, and Islamic studies. The subject of this book being the psychology of Islamic terror, it also discusses the religion and culture of Islam, the psychology of religion in general and of Islam in particular, the Muslim family and the Muslim society from which the terrorists originate, and the psychological origins of the emotions that fuel terror, which, as we shall see, are not only rage, hatred and fear, but also, surprisingly, love and longing. The book also studies the psychology of those who wage a "global war on terror."

One of the basic ideas in this book is that one's attitude to terror and terrorism, as well as whether or not one becomes a terrorist, or whether one wages a "global war on terror," have to do with one's terrifying experiences, or personal terror, in one's infancy and childhood. This terror, which is first experienced in one's earliest relationship with one's mother, is symbolically expressed in fairy tales and myths about terrifying witches and female monsters. Further terror may be experienced in one's relationship to one's father, and also in various traumatic experiences occurring in one's young life. In addition to terror, there are feelings of helplessness, shame, humiliation, and boundless, overwhelming narcissistic rage.

This book discusses non-psychoanalytic theories of Islamic terrorism, which focus on its conscious aspects, and then the psychoanalytic ones, which focus on its unconscious motives. It has chapters on the origins and meaning of terror, on the psychoanalysis of love and hate, on the history and culture of Islam, on the sociology and psychology of the Muslim family, on religious and political terrorism, and on the special characteristics of Islamic terrorism. The last chapter discusses in psychological detail the cases of the terrorists Osama bin Laden, Ramzi Yousef, and Mohamed Atta, as well as that of the leader of the "global war on terror," George W. Bush.

The Meaning of Terror

The words "terror" and "terrorism" have several definitions, including the linguistic, academic, legal, and psychological. The *Merriam-Webster* dictionary tells us that the word *terror* derives from the Latin verb *terrere,* meaning "to frighten," and that it is akin to the Greek word *trein,* meaning "to be afraid" or "to flee," and to the Greek word *tremein,* meaning "to tremble." Terror, says the dictionary, has several different meanings: a state of intense fear, one that inspires fear, a scourge, a frightening aspect (as in "the terrors of invasion"), a cause of anxiety, an appalling person or thing, a terrifying political state (as in "the Reign of Terror" or simply The Terror), a violent or destructive act (such as bombing) committed by groups in order to intimidate a population or government into granting their demands (as in revolutionary terror).

It is no accident that a universally accepted legal definition of terrorism does not exist. "Cynics have often commented that one state's terrorist is another's freedom fighter" (United Nations Office of Drugs and Crime document on terrorism). In 1937, when the Nazi rulers of Germany practiced terror on their own people, the League of Nations attempted to adopt this internationally acceptable convention: "All criminal acts directed against a State and intended or calculated to create a state of terror in the minds of particular persons or a group of persons or the general public." This convention never came into existence. The United Nations has since grappled with the legal definition of terrorism. The United Nations Office of Drugs and Crime admits that "the question of a definition of terrorism has haunted the debate among states for decades" (United Nations Office of Drugs and Crime document on terrorism).

As its member states still have no agreed-upon definition, the United Nations cannot formulate a universal convention on terrorism to supplant its twelve piecemeal conventions and protocols on the subject. "The lack of agreement on a definition of terrorism has been a major obstacle to meaningful international countermeasures" (United Nations Office of Drugs and Crime document on terrorism). To solve the problem, the United Nations turned to Alex P. Schmid, a Dutch scholar in Terrorism Studies, who later became the head of the Terrorism Prevention Branch of the United Nations. In 1992 Schmid advised the UN Crime Branch, the predecessor of the United Nations Office of Drugs and Crime, to define terrorism as "the peacetime equivalent of war crimes." Schmid said that if the core of war crimes were deliberate violent attacks on civilians, hostage-taking, and the killing of prisoners in wartime, then the core of terrorism were the same criminal acts in peacetime.

In 1998 Schmid formulated what he called the "academic consensus" definition of terrorism:

> Terrorism is an anxiety-inspiring method of repeated violent action, employed by (semi-) clandestine individual, group or state actors, for idiosyncratic, criminal or political reasons, whereby—in contrast to assassination—the direct targets of violence are not the main targets. The immediate human victims of violence are generally chosen randomly (targets of opportunity) or selectively (representative or symbolic targets) from a target population, and serve as message generators. Threat- and violence-based communication processes between terrorist (organization), (imperilled) victims, and main targets are used to manipulate the main target (audience(s)), turning it into a target of terror, a target of demands, or a target of attention, depending on whether intimidation, coercion, or propaganda is primarily sought (United Nations Office of Drugs and Crime document on terrorism).

In 1999 the United Nations General Assembly adopted a resolution that "strongly condemns all acts, methods and practices of terrorism as criminal and unjustifiable, wherever and by whomsoever committed [and] reiterates that criminal acts intended or calculated to provoke a state of terror in the general public, a group of persons or particular persons for political purposes are in any circumstance unjustifiable, whatever the considerations of a political, philosophical, ideological, racial, ethnic, religious or other nature that may be invoked to justify them" (United Nations General Assembly Resolution 51/210).

To my mind, however, the academic and legal definitions of terrorism are less interesting than the psychological ones. In common usage, from which we have much to learn, the two most important meanings of the word "terror" are a profound fear, petrifying anxiety, panic, or mortal fright, and the acts of terrorists that inspire such fear. Psychologically, *sheer terror is the feeling of the overwhelming fear of death that infants and children experience when they are abandoned by their mother,* or the unbearable feeling of nonbeing that they have when their fusional mother cannot let them individuate from them and become separate human beings (Mahler et al. 1975). The other meaning of "terror" is "acts of terror," violent, murderous acts designed to sow terror in our hearts. The first use of the word "terror" was to describe state terror against the individual, as in the Terror of 1793–1794, during the French Revolution. In our own time, the word is usually used to denote individual terror against the state.

The word "terrorist" obviously comes from that second meaning of "terror," but it also has an intimate connection to the first: at least two American psychoanalysts who were born in Muslim families—the Turkish-Cypriot-born Vamık Volkan (born 1932) and the Indian-born Salman Akhtar (born 1946)—have found that many terrorists were themselves terrorized, abused, abandoned, neglected, shamed, humiliated, victimized, or otherwise traumatized during their early life (Volkan 1997, p. 160; Akhtar 1999). Since one man's "terrorist" is another's "freedom fighter" (Vaknin 2003), we need to be careful when using this term. The British-born American author, journalist, and literary critic Christopher Eric Hitchens (born 1949), a former leftist turned right-wing "neoconservative," had denounced the indiscriminate use of the word "terrorist" as a Medusa's head, which, unveiled, would "turn all discussion into stone [...] Whisk, whisk [...] and there goes history, there goes inquiry, there goes proportion" (Hitchens 1968, p. 68). The anti-theist Hitchens has published a book reviling religion as mankind's poison (Hitchens 2007).

Moreover, the word "terrorist" is ambiguous: it is used both to identify a person and to morally condemn that person. In 2004 Brian Hallett criticized the popular argument that terrorism was "the 'weapon of the weak' needed to wage an asymmetric war against the powerful" (Hallett 2004, p. 52). He claimed that a terrorist act can be distinguished from a common crime by two characteristics: his "theatrical aspect" of the act and his "delusional self-interest [...] masquerading as self-sacrifice" by which the terrorist justifies it (pp. 50–51). We shall examine the delusions of terrorists below. Hallett's argument contrasted terrorist acts with the Indian leader Mohandas Karamchand Gandhi's *satyagraha* (nonviolent resistance) from the point of view of political strategy as well as substantive values. He argued, for example, that Gandhi was more practical than Machiavelli, and that one needs to think about the meaning of "terrorism."

Political and religious terrorism, however, also have crucial psychological aspects. The American psychoanalyst Ana-Maria Rizzuto studied how we develop our image of an omnipotent Father God in our early life (Rizzuto 1979). Shortly after the September 1, 2001 tragedy in the United States, the Israeli-American-Jewish psychoanalyst Ruth Stein published a study of the leader of the terrorists, Mohamed Atta, which focused on his deep yearning for love from Father Allah (Stein 2002). We shall discuss this study, which throws a fascinating light on one of the worst scourges of our time, in detail below. The problem of terrorism involves both individual and collective psychodynamics. The Swiss-American-Jewish psychoanalyst Leon Wurmser believed that "one of the greatest contributions psychoanalysis can make in any debate is the idea of trying to understand the intra-individual, familial, and socio-cultural processes in terms of both conflict and complementarity—contending forces that clash, but also determine each other in circular ways and thus complement each other" (Wurmser 2004, p. 923).

The Psychology of Religion

Since the subject of this book is Islamic terrorism, Islam is one of the world's great religions, and Islamic terror is a case of religious terror, it is important for us to examine and understand religion from a psychological viewpoint. Religion is a fascinating and complex human phenomenon. While Sigmund Freud called it an "illusion," other psychoanalysts have thought that religion also has healthy aspects (Freud 1961; Volkan 2001a). All religions involve the belief in supernatural beings, whether they are gods, angels, ancestors' spirits, or other invisible creatures. Polytheistic religions like the ancient Greek and Roman ones, or the Hindu religion, involve the belief in many gods. Monotheistic religions involve the belief in one God, but they often incorporate or conceal the earlier polytheism.

The idea of many gods (or one God) in particular and religion in general have been the subject of psychological study long before Sigmund Freud called religion an "illusion," and for decades afterward (Starbuck 1897; James 1902; Coe 1916; Selbie 1924; Josey 1927; Dresser 1929; P. E. Johnson 1945; Fromm 1950; Grensted 1952; Zilboorg 1962; Bellah 1970; Oates 1973; Faber 1976; Byrnes 1984; Symington 1994; Black 2006). Freud's basic idea was that it was not God who created Man in his own image, as the Good Book says (Genesis 1:27), but rather the reverse: Man created God in his own image. Human beings, fearful of natural forces that they could not control, like the sun, the moon, the stars, oceans, mountain, and rivers, attributed human qualities to them and sought to appease them through worship and sacrifice. They also unconsciously projected upon them their own qualities, defects, wishes, and emotions.

Freud believed that religion was an illusion, a fantasy. In an unconscious process that Freud called *Übertragung* or transference, we transfer to our gods the infantile feelings that we had for our parents. Gods and demons do not exist—except in our own imagination: they are fantasies, unconscious externalizations of our inner images of our fathers, mothers, and ourselves, symbolic projections of our good and bad feelings. In fact, Freud called religion, with its numerous compulsive-looking rituals, "a universal obsessional neurosis." Freud had deep personal reasons for rejecting religion (Falk 1978; Yerushalmi 1991).

For at least two decades, Freud's ideas about religion were interpreted as anti-theist. Psychoanalysis was perceived as hostile to religion, and also as religion's rival for our hearts and minds. After World War II and the Nazi Holocaust, however, psychoanalytic scholars expanded and challenged Freud's theory of religion. Most of them claimed that Freud's ideas had been "reductionist" and that there was "much more" to religious belief than unconscious transferences, projections, and externalizations, such as the universal thirst for love and the quest for identity (Fromm 1950; Zilboorg 1962; Bellah 1970; Kristeva 1987; Jones 1993; Symington 1994; Blass 2004; Black 2006). Prominent psychoanalysts such as the Muslim-born Vamık Volkan have pointed out the psychological role of the idea of God in normal human development (Volkan 2001a).

James W. Jones, an American Christian theologian and psychotherapist, disputed Freud's view of religion as unconscious transference. Using examples from his own clinical cases, as Freud had done, Jones argued that religious experiences, doctrines, and practices reflect the "internalized interpersonal patterns" that are "our sense of ourselves" (Jones 1993). Jones believed that religion had great transforming power for its believers, both for good and for evil, as well as the power to terrify them. He thought that modern psychoanalysts had "moved on" from Freud's "rationalistic rejection of religion" and had prepared the ground for a richer and more nuanced understanding of the ways in which religion can be a two-edged sword, both to transform and to terrify us (Jones 2002).

Jones focused on the unconscious psychological process of idealization in religious belief. He believed that at the heart of every living religion was the idealization of people and objects. Such idealizations provide much of the transforming power of religious experience, which is one of the positive contributions of religion to psychological life. However, infantile idealization can also lead to religious fanaticism and terror. Drawing on the work of "relational" psychoanalysts, and combining it with his own "idealizational" theory, Jones developed a "psychoanalytically-informed" theory of the transforming and terrifying effects of religious experience—a subject that had been studied by his predecessor William James a century earlier (Jones 2002; James 1902).

During the 1980s many psychoanalysts, especially religious and Jewish ones, attempted to find "common ground" between religion and psychoanalysis (Smith and Handelman 1989). This quest for a "reconciliation" between psychoanalysis and religion has persisted. The Israeli Jewish psychologist Rachel Blass, however, examined critically this positive and conciliatory attitude toward religion that had become increasingly prevalent within psychoanalytic thinking and writing over the previous twenty years. She believed that this positive attitude had come from a change in the way psychoanalysts view the nature of religion and from its reassignment to the realm of illusion, making the passionate quest for "truth"—an issue central to both psychoanalysis and religion—irrelevant (Blass 2004, p. 615).

Blass thought that "the concern with truth"—more specifically, the truth of religious belief—played a dual role in the relationship between religion and psychoanalysis. While it underlay the opposition between psychoanalysis and religion, it was also the common ground between them. Blass believed that as Freud had developed his ideas regarding the origin of religious belief, the nature of this common ground was expanded and the dialogue between psychoanalysis and religion became more meaningful. At the same time, she felt that a meaningful dialogue between psychoanalysis and religion could only emerge through the recognition of their fundamental differences, not through their artificial "harmonization within a realm of illusion." She intended her study also as an attempt to recognize the fundamental differences that had been evolving within psychoanalysis itself concerning the nature of religion (Blass 2004, p. 615).

Two years later, the South African-born British psychoanalyst David Macleod Black edited a tome about religion in contemporary psychoanalysis. Black believed that since Freud had described religion as a universal obsessional neurosis and rejected it in favor of "science," the common wisdom held that psychoanalysts were hostile to religion. In fact, Black thought, "from the beginning" psychoanalysts had questioned Freud's rejection of religion. Black's contributors, who came from many different psychoanalytic schools, examined such questions as how religious stories carry or distort psychological truth, how religions "work" psychologically, what was the nature of religious experience, and whether there were any parallels between psychoanalysis and particular religious traditions (Black 2006).

Due to the explosion of violent religious terrorism, non-psychoanalytic scholars have also addressed the psychology of religion, but unfortunately some of them have done so in a nonprofessional and amateurish manner. The "rationalist" British evolutionary biologist Clinton Richard Dawkins has decried "the God delusion" and religions in general as the causes of all human trouble, and the British-born American scholar Christopher Eric Hitchens has called religion "mankind's poison" (Dawkins 2006; Hitchens 2007). Both Dawkins and Hitchens, however, have been criticized as shallow and infantile. The American theologian Eugene Brian McCarraher called Hitchens "an amateur in philosophy, an illiterate in theology, and a dishonest student of history," while the British critic Christopher Hart called Dawkins's ideas irrational and Hitchens's book "high entertainment," citing Dawkins's exclamation "How stupid our forefathers were! Those gullible Christian know-nothings!" (McCarraher 2007; Hart 2007) Hart felt that Dawkins had engaged in an "immature oedipal triumphalism." Hart's colleague Terry Eagleton criticized Dawkins's "rationalistic" and "obsessional" attitude to God, pointing out that Dawkins was just as obsessed with God as many crusaders against sexual freedom were obsessed with sexuality (Eagleton 2006).

Religious Terror and Academic Disciplines

The seemingly rational division of the human and social sciences in our universities and research institutes into single-discipline departments such as literature, psychology, sociology, history, political science, and anthropology may be seen as an unconscious defense known as "compartmentalization": it seeks to deal with the immense complexity of human affairs by dividing it neatly into departments or compartments, each of which deals only with one of its aspects. Salvador Dalí's famous paintings *City of Drawers* and *Giraffe on Fire,* with their drawers coming out of the body, purportedly try to expose the "hidden drawers" of the human heart. To me, they symbolize the compartmentalization of human affairs. We cannot understand human affairs from the viewpoint of a single discipline. To truly understand them, our human lives require an interdisciplinary and multidisciplinary undertaking.

As an example, let us examine the treatment of religious terror by sociologists and political scientists. While religious belief may or may not involve "a universal obsessional neurosis," as Freud believed, religious terrorist activity is considered by most experts to involve psychopathology. The complex and multifaceted phenomenon of religious terrorism has been studied by scholars from several different disciplines, including psychology and sociology. The American sociologist Mark Juergensmeyer pointed out that terrorist violence is only resorted to by *marginal groups* within the major human religions. He studied such groups within five religions: Christianity, Judaism, Islam, Sikhism, and Buddhism (Juergensmeyer 2000).

Within Christianity, Juergensmeyer studied reconstruction theology, the Christian identity movement, the abortion clinic attacks, the Oklahoma City bombing, and the violence in Northern Ireland; in Judaism, he studied Baruch Goldstein's massacre in Hebron's Tomb of the Patriarchs, Yigal Amir's assassination of Yitzhak Rabin, and Rabbi Meir Kahane's Jewish Defense League and Israeli *Kach* party; in Islam, the World Trade Center bombing and the *Hamas* suicide bombings; in Sikhism, the assassinations of Indira Gandhi and Beant Singh; and in Buddhism, the *Aum Shinrikyo* group and its sarin gas attack in the Tokyo subway. Juergensmeyer thought that in all those cases the fantasy of being part of a cosmic struggle between good and evil gave meaning to small groups of people who felt marginalized, deprived, or mistreated.

Religious terror, however, is not the only kind of terrorist illness to inflict our human species. Political terrorism is another variety, though the two are not always separate or distinguishable from one another. From September 1793 to July 1794, during the French Revolution, the left-wing Jacobin "Reign of Terror" killed numerous real and suspected noblemen, aristocrats, and "counter-revolutionaries." In July 1794 a right-wing *coup d'état* ousted the murderous *Comité de salut public* and replaced it with an equally murderous terror by royalist *chouans* and *Vendéens* in which real and suspected Jacobins alike were dragged into the streets and murdered.

Most historians agree that the first "white terror" occurred in France in early 1795. The Bourbons were the French royal family, and the name was derived from their white flag. The white terror was started by ultra-royalist and ultra-Catholic groups in southwest France calling themselves *les Compagnies de Jéhu, les Compagnies de Jésus,* or *les Compagnies du Soleil,* who planned a counter-revolutionary uprising to coincide with invasions of France by the United Kingdom in the west and by Austria in the east. Their antirepublican movement, however, was crushed by the young republican general Louis-Lazare Hoche at Quiberon in July of that year, and the Revolution triumphed until Napoleon Bonaparte became First Consul in 1799 and Emperor in 1804 (Falk 2006).

The second "white terror" occurred in 1815, after Emperor Napoleon's exile to Saint Helena and the restoration of King Louis XVIII to power in France. Frenchmen suspected of ties with the former republican government, or that of Napoleon, suffered arbitrary arrest and execution. Marshall Brune was killed in Avignon and General Ramel in Toulouse. These assassinations struck panic in the French population, terrorizing the Jacobin and *bonapartiste* electors into voting for the Bourbon royalists. Nearly 90 percent of the members of the first (and highly unpopular) *Chambre des deputés* of the Bourbon Restoration were ultra-royalists and ultra-reactionaries. The king himself called it *la Chambre introuvable* (the Inaccessible Chamber) and dissolved it the following year. The Chamber voted repressive laws, sentencing to death Marshall Ney and Colonel Labédoyère. Hundreds of people were given prolonged prison sentences and all the "regicides" (*conventionnels* who had voted for the death of Louis XVI in early 1793) were exiled from France.

Since then, the term "white terror" has referred to acts of political violence carried out by reactionary, monarchist, or conservative groups against their left-wing enemies as part of a counterrevolution. Often, such acts of terror were carried out in response to and followed by similar terror measures taken by the revolutionary side in a given conflict. In particular, during the twentieth century, in several countries, such as Germany, the term "white terror" was applied to acts of violence against real or suspected socialists and communists.

Like the sociologists, political scientists have also dealt with religious terror. Their efforts to explain it, however, were handicapped by their own ideology and by their neglect of the unconscious mind of the terrorists. The American political scientist James Kurth believed that there was a hidden connection between "American imperialism" and Islamic terrorism. As Kurth put it, "A dialectical and symbiotic connection, perhaps an escalating and vicious cycle, exists between the [growth of the American Empire and the growth of Islamic terrorism], and the world is about to witness a titanic and explosive struggle between them" (Kurth 2002).

While Kurth's apocalyptic scenario may not come about, the tragic U.S. war in Iraq, which has split U.S. public opinion, has involved incredible death and destruction. By early 2006, according to a report by the Nobel Prize–winning American economist Joseph Stiglitz and his colleague Linda Bilmes, the U.S. war in Iraq had cost over two trillion U.S. dollars, or $720 million per day of war, and the cost of the war *for one day* would have bought homes for 6,500 families or health care for 423,529 children (Bender 2006).

Another American political scientist, Monte Palmer, with his banker wife, Princess Palmer, have also tried to explain Islamic fanaticism and terrorism in Lebanon and the Israeli-occupied Palestinian territories (Palmer and Palmer 2004, 2008). Noah Feldman, an American-Jewish law professor, thought that the Palmers had put forth a "sensible and productive set of proposals for understanding Muslim extremism," and that they "analyze *jihadi* strategies with a nuanced common sense all too hard to come by in the sometimes sensationalist literature on the topic" (Feldman 2005). The Palmers, however, had a political agenda in their book: they wanted the U.S. government to "accept rule by Islamic parties dedicated to the establishment of an Islamic state" and to engage in political dialogue with them.

What Islamic parties did the Palmers have in mind? The Lebanese Shi'ite *Hezbollah* and the Palestinian Islamic *Hamas,* whom the Palmers called "radical-moderate" parties, and which, they said, unlike Iraq's Shi'ites and Turkey's Islamic Justice and Development Party, have pursued "simultaneous strategies of violence and political participation." In fact, those "parties" are constantly engaged in murderous terror against Israelis. The Palmers wanted the United States to "engage" with these "parties," because "efforts to eliminate them will only increase terrorism and push the United States into a war with Islam." Feldman thought that "it may be possible to negotiate with the radical-moderates on the condition that they abandon any active involvement in terror." The *Hezbollah* and *Hamas,* however, have shown no signs of abandoning terrorism: on the contrary, with Iran's support, they keep planning more.

In short, the efforts of non-psychoanalytic sociologists and political scientists, focusing as they do on the rational and conscious mind, however sincere or academically competent they may be, cannot in themselves suffice to explain Islamic or other religious terror. We need an interdisciplinary study, and we need to look at the unconscious mind.

POLITICS AND PSYCHOLOGY

Some rationalistic scholars defensively separate the political from the psychological and reject the very need for a psychological understanding of terrorism. After the tragedy of *9/11* (September 11, 2001), the respected American political scientist Michael Walzer concluded his attack on "left-wing excuses for terrorism" with a backhanded dismissal of psychology: "Maybe *psychologists* have something to say on behalf of understanding. But the only *political* response to ideological fanatics and suicidal holy warriors is implacable opposition" (Walzer 2001, p. 17). The correct reply to this dangerous splitting or black-and-white thinking was made by the late American psychiatrist John Edward Mack (1929–2004): "The proper place to begin our effort to understand (not to excuse), it seems to me, is with the question of causation. For no matter how loathsome we may find the acts of 'fanatics,' *without understanding what breeds them and drives them to do what they do in a particular time and place, we have little chance of preventing further such actions, let alone of 'eradicating terrorism' "* (Mack 2002, p. 174).

Mack distinguished three different levels of causation in the phenomenon of suicidal terrorism: the *immediate causes,* which include the "purposive actions of men who are willing to die as they destroy other lives"; the *proximate causes,* including the personal pain and the unhappy political, social, and economic conditions that breed such desperate acts; and the *deeper causes,* which derive from "the nature of mind, or consciousness itself." The immediate causes are obvious enough. The narcissistic rage and implacable hatred of the Palestinian Arab suicide bombers for their Israeli Jewish oppressors—as they see them—matches the "implacable opposition" of the political scientist to "ideological fanatics and holy warriors." Any journalist writing about the Middle East conflict will tell you about those immediate causes of suicidal terrorism: unemployment, despair, vengeance, and rage—all due to the Israeli occupation of Palestinian Arab lands and the deadlock in the Israeli-Palestinian negotiations.

Mack's "proximate" causes of suicidal terrorism are somewhat more complex. Here is how Mack described these historical, social, economic, and political causes of the conflict that have created the suicide bombers, citing the activist Indian writer Arundhati Roy:

> Listening to the pronouncements of President Bush and other American leaders in the weeks after the events of September 11th, one could get the impression that the rage that leads to the planning and execution of terrorist acts arises from a kind

of void, unconnected with history, without causation other than pure evil fueled by jealousy. Yet it is not difficult to discover that the present conflict has complex historical and economic roots. It has grown out of *the affliction of countless millions of people in the Middle East and elsewhere who perceive themselves as victims of the policies of a superpower and its allies that have little concern for their lives, needs, or suffering* [italics added], and of the actions of multinational corporations that, in the words of an Indian writer, "are taking over the air we breathe, the ground we stand on, the water we drink, the thoughts we think" (Mack 2002, p. 175).

Mack underscored this point: "For these millions, a figure like Osama bin Laden, who[m] we see only as the mass murderer that he is, can become a hero for moving beyond helplessness to action against the seemingly indifferent and invincible oppressor." But since the superpower that Mack had in mind above was obviously the United States, and since one of its allies was clearly Israel, was this wise psychiatrist, while seeking a psychological understanding of suicidal terrorism, identifying with—or taking the side of—what he saw as the millions of Palestinian Arab victims against their Israeli Jewish "oppressors"? Was the unconscious defensive process of *splitting* which this psychiatrist had detected in the political scientist operating in him as well?

Mack went on to explain why these "countless millions" of self-perceived Arab and Muslim victims of "American and Israeli oppression" adore terrorist masterminds like Osama bin Laden. Mack was writing *before* the U.S. invasion of Iraq:

> It is inconceivable that terrorism can be checked, much less eradicated, if these [proximate] causes are not addressed. This would require at the very least a reexamination of United States government policies that one-sidedly favor Israel in relation to the Palestinians (not to mention United States support of Saddam Hussein against Iran, before he started a conflict a few years later that continues to take the lives of tens of thousands of innocent Iraqi men, women, and children). It would require further help with the growing refugee problem and a turning of our attention to the toll that poverty and disease are taking in the Middle East and other parts of the globe (Mack 2002, p. 175).

While the difference between Mack's "immediate causes" and "proximate causes" of Islamic terror is not readily apparent, it would seem that by "proximate causes" he was referring to the "complex historical and economic roots" of this conflict.

The "deeper causes" of suicidal terrorism outlined by Mack comprise unconscious splitting, conflicting worldviews, dualistic thinking, and "augmenting dualistic thinking." The word "worldview" is a rendering of the German *Weltanschauung,* which literally means "looking at the world." Mack described a worldview as "a kind of mental template into which we try to fit events" (Mack 2002, p. 176). There are vast differences between the worldviews of the Israeli Jews and the Palestinian Arabs, who live in different psychological realities, and even more so between those of the far-right religious Jews and the fanatical Islamic terrorists (Falk 2004). Upon closer examination, however, one view may be a mirror image of the other. Mack contrasted the splitting, black-and-white view of the world as divided into good and evil, us and them, for-us or against-us, with the idealistic worldview of universal love and oneness which, he admitted, "has its own rigidities." Nationalism and religion augment dualistic thinking, the psychiatrist thought, although he did not use the psychoanalytic term of unconscious splitting (Mack 2002, p. 177).

To my mind, the trouble with the "deeper causes" proffered by Mack is that they are not deep enough. He repeatedly referred to "the nature of human consciousness" and to the need to change it if we are to "transcend the mind of enmity," but this psychoanalyst mentioned the unconscious mind only once in his entire study: "Although nationalists tend to resist looking at the harmful actions in their nation's history, they may, nevertheless, fear unconsciously that retribution for the crimes of the past lies just across the next border" (Mack 2002, p. 177). While this may be true, the unconscious mind of the nationalist in general and of the fanatical terrorist in particular harbors much more than this: murderous narcissistic rage against an engulfing mother and a punitive father, wishes for fusion with the early mother, the fear of this fusion, splitting, projection, externalization, and idealization. I shall examine all of these below.

Terrorists and Their Mothers

Some sociologists have boldly transcended the narrow boundaries of their discipline in studying religious terror. One of the perennial questions about terrorists is whether they have any particular and terrorist-specific family background. This question was addressed in a fascinating study by the German sociologist Klaus Theweleit (born 1942), who studied the "white terror" of the pre-Nazi *Freikorps* in early Weimar Germany, the precursor of Hitler's Nazis (Theweleit 1977–1978, 1987–1989). Before reviewing this study, let us take a brief look at the history of the *Freikorps*.

Political terror, rather than the religious variety, characterized Europe in the twentieth century. One of its early eruptions was the "white terror" of the *Freikorps* (free corps), the right-wing ultranationalist paramilitary organizations that sprang up all over Germany in late 1918 as traumatized German soldiers returned in defeat from the Great War of 1914–1918 (later renamed World War I). In 1919–1920 the *Freikorps* were the key paramilitary group in the German "Weimar Republic" (1919–1933), and they murdered their left-wing enemies on the streets of German cities. In 1933 this "white terror" was followed by the "black-and-brown terror" of Hitler's German Nazis, in which millions of Germans and tens of millions of non-Germans were murdered by 1945.

The *Freikorps* ranks swelled after Germany's humiliating defeat in 1918, when many German veterans felt disconnected from civilian and political life. They joined the *Freikorps,* which had been created by the king of Prussia in the eighteenth century, in search of the stability that they felt only a military structure could provide. Right-wing Germans, angry at their sudden and "inexplicable" defeat, joined the *Freikorps* in an effort to defeat the German Communists or to exact revenge from their enemies. They believed in the *Dolchstosslegende* (dagger-stab legend or stab-in-the-back myth), a popular conspiracy theory that attributed Germany's defeat in the Great War to domestic causes, denying the failure of its militarist policies.

The *Dolchstosslegende* proclaimed that the German public had failed to respond to its "patriotic calling" at the most crucial of times and that some treasonous Germans had even intentionally sabotaged the war effort and "stabbed their country in the back." From November 1918 to March 1919 there was great political upheaval in Germany. Some historians call this period the "German Revolution" and this term covers a series of events which led to the demise of the monarchy and the establishment of a democratic parliamentary republic called the "Weimar Republic," which lasted until Hitler took over Germany in 1933 and proclaimed the Third *Reich*.

The immediate cause of this German Revolution of 1918–1919 was the policy of the German Supreme Command and the tragic decision of the German Naval Command in the face of imminent defeat in 1918 to fight one last battle with the British Royal Navy. The German sailors mutinied in the German naval ports of Wilhelmshaven and Kiel. Within days their mutiny spread across Germany and led to the abdication of *Kaiser* Wilhelm II on November 9, 1918. The deeper and historical causes of this revolution of 1918 were the social and political tensions of the Second German *Reich*, created by the Prussian leader Otto von Bismarck in 1871, its undemocratic constitution, and the unwillingness or inability of its leaders to reform themselves and their institutions.

The far-reaching social and political goals of the German Marxist revolutionaries in 1918–1919 were foiled by the German Social Democratic Party (*SPD*) and by its leader Friedrich Ebert (1871–1925), the first president of Germany during the "Weimar" period. Like many other Germans, Ebert supported the monarchy and was furious when his colleague and rival Philipp Scheidemann (1865–1939), fearing a German workers' uprising, proclaimed the new republic from a *Reichstag* balcony upon the *Kaiser*'s abdication. Scheidemann became the first chancellor of the Weimar Republic, later succeeded by Ebert.

Like the other German middle-class parties, fearing an all-out civil war, Ebert did not wish to strip the old German imperial elites of their power, preferring to reconcile them with the new German democratic institutions. In this endeavor, he sought an alliance with the German Supreme Command and had the army and the *Freikorps* crush the Marxists by force. The ultranationalist *Freikorps* received considerable support from Weimar Germany's first defense minister, Gustav Noske (1868–1946), who used the *Freikorps* to crush the Marxist *Spartakusbund* (tragically named after Spartacus, the leader of the failed slave rebellion in ancient Rome) on the streets of Berlin and to murder its leaders, Karl Liebknecht and Rosa Luxemburg, in early 1919.

The *Freikorps* were also used by Ebert and Noske to defeat and annex the Bavarian Soviet Republic in 1919. Several *Freikorps* units fought in the Baltic, Silesia, and Prussia after the end of World War I in 1918, sometimes with significant success even against regular troops. They were officially disbanded in 1920, but some *Freikorps* members attempted to overthrow the German government in the Kapp-Lüttwitz putsch of March 1920, led by two disgruntled reactionaries. Ebert called a general strike to ensure that those who supported the putsch could not move around, and this doomed the putsch to failure. Kapp and Lüttwitz fled Berlin. In 1923 Adolf Hitler and the German war hero Erich Ludendorff staged the Beer-Hall putsch, which also failed. In 1933, however, Hitler became Germany's chancellor and *Führer* (leader), and the former *Freikorps* members became the first recruits to the Brown Shirts and Black Shirts, Hitler's Nazi army.

As we have seen, the German psychoanalytic sociologist Klaus Theweleit studied the psychology of the *Freikorps* members through their art and literature, through their letters, diaries, and autobiographies, focusing on their fear of women. Theweleit used the theories of the German-American psychoanalyst Wilhelm Reich (1897–1957) and those of the French "anti-psychiatrist" Pierre-Félix Guattari (1930–1992), as well as his wife's clinical-psychological experience. Theweleit examined the distorted images of women in the writings of *Freikorps* members, their letters, magazines, and novels. He found that the *Freikorps* members' images of women revealed a highly distorted view of personal and political reality (Theweleit 1977–1978, 1987–1989).

The common psychological process operating in these men was the unconscious defensive process of *splitting,* through which the infant defends itself against the anxiety produced by its irreconcilable good and bad feelings for its mother, and which is symbolically expressed in fairy tales like *Snow White,* where the heroine has an all-good mother who has died an all-bad adoptive narcissistic one who wants to kill her when she discovers that Snow White is more beautiful than she. The *Freikorps* men split their women into two types: the "white" mother, sister, or nurse, who was all-good but asexual, and the "red" one, who was highly sexual and all-bad. Due to their profound fear of their overwhelming mothers, Theweleit thought, many *Freikorps* members defensively reduced women to their vagina. In their Fascist approach to human life, the idealized "white" German Mother Nation was above the individual, while the "red" German Republic, symbolizing the bad, sexual mother, had to be destroyed.

Theweleit thought that the typical *Freikorps* male had experienced "ego dissolution" in his early infancy, due to his symbiotic infantile relation with his engulfing mother, that it had made him panic, and that as an unconscious defense against this overwhelming anxiety he had developed a "masculine body armor" in which he repressed his "feminine" traits and emotions, such as weakness, fear, softness, and guilt. The repetitive conditioning and brutal pedagogy in the *Freikorps* member's family had produced these negative self-perceptions, which were unconsciously projected onto the despised classes of society (such as Jews and Communists) and made to represent the chaotic forces of the collective cultural unconscious. Uncomfortably for us, Theweleit thought that this view was the core of a great deal of our own imagery and political self-perception. In his review of Theweleit's *Male Fantasies,* the American historian Paul Robinson offered the following summary of Theweleit's findings:

> *His central contention is that the Freikorps soldiers were afraid of women.* Indeed, not just afraid, *they were deeply hostile to them, and their ultimate goal was to murder them.* Women, in their view, came in only two varieties: Red and White. The White woman was the nurse, the mother, the sister. She was distinguished above all else by her sexlessness. The Red woman, on the other hand, was a whore and a Communist. She was a kind of distillation of sexuality, threatening to engulf the male in a whirlpool of bodily and emotional ecstasy. This, of course, was the woman the Freikorps soldier wished to kill, because she endangered his identity, his sense of self as a fixed and bounded being. In this manner Mr. Theweleit links the Freikorps soldiers' fantasies of women to their practical life as illegal anti-Communist guerillas: the Republic had to be destroyed because it empowered the lascivious Red woman, while it failed to protect the White woman's sexual purity. *Among the most interesting features of Mr. Theweleit's analysis is his examination of two distinctive elements in the fascist imagination: liquidity and dirt. He argues that aquatic and other liquid metaphors were associated in the minds of these soldiers with the loss of a firm sense of identity. Much of their literature speaks of Communism as a flood, a stream, or a kind of boiling or exploding of the earth— images [that] he shows to be associated traditionally with sexuality* (Paul Robinson 1987; italics added).

The preoccupation with female bodily liquids such as the amniotic fluid and menstrual blood in the writings of the *Freikorps* members betrayed the overwhelming role played in the minds of terrorists by their engulfing, overwhelming mothers. I shall examine this role in this book, as it is crucial to our understanding of Islamic terror.

The Nature of Islamic Terror

The "white terror" used by the German *Freikorps* members against their left-wing "enemies" was an example of political terror. The Islamic terror of our own time is a special case of religious terror. Is religious terror essentially different from the political variety? Is Islamic terror essentially different from the "white terror" or Nazi terror?

Islam is a special religion and culture, little understood by the "Western" mind. The word *Islam* is derived from the Arabic verb *aslama,* which means to accept, surrender, or submit (to the will of Allah). Thus, Islam means acceptance of and submission to Allah, and believers must demonstrate this by worshiping Him, following His commands, and avoiding the worship of any other god. The word *Islam* is given a number of meanings in the Qur'an. In some verses, the quality of Islam as an internal conviction is stressed: "Whomsoever Allah desires to guide, He expands his breast to Islam." Other Qur'anic verses connect the terms *islam* and *diin* (usually translated as religion): "Today, I have perfected your religion for you; I have completed My blessing upon you; I have approved Islam for your religion." Still others describe Islam as an action of returning to Allah than just a verbal affirmation of faith. In any event, Allah is the core of Islam. Like the traditional Arabian family, it is an autocratic and paternalistic religion, where the will of Allah, as interpreted by his Prophet and messenger Muhammad, is paramount.

Muhammad did not invent the god Allah. He made him into the only god of the Arabs. In pre-Islamic Arabia, *Allah* was used by the Meccans as the name of a creator-god, possibly the supreme deity of the Arabs (Qur'an 13:16; 29:61–63; 31:25; 39:38). Allah was not the sole divinity and the term was vague in the

Meccan religion. Allah had associates and companions, whom pre-Islamic Arabs considered as subordinate deities. The Meccans held that a kinship between Allah and the *jinn* (devil) existed (Qur'an 37:158). Allah also had sons, and the three local female deities, the fertility goddess al-Uzza (the mighty one), the goddess of fate Manat, and the moon goddess al-Lat, were his daughters (Qur'an 16:57; 37:149; 53:19–22). The Meccans also associated angels with Allah (Qur'an 53:26–27). Allah was invoked in times of distress (Qur'an 6:109; 10:22; 16:38; 29:65). Muhammad's father's name Abdallah means the "servant of Allah." There are entire encyclopedias devoted to the religion and culture of Islam (Martin 2004).

Due to its grave threat to world peace, world law, and world order, Islamic terror has been intensively studied by both "Western" and Muslim scholars at least since the 1980s, when the Lebanese extremist Shi'ite Muslim political group *Hezbollah* or Party of Allah began using it against its enemies, primarily Israel, and suicide bombings raised the global concern about radical Islam (Taheri 1987; Merari 1990; Abul-Jobain 1993; Pelletiere 1993; Langman and Morris 2002; Berman 2003; Morse 2003; Chesler 2004a; Mazarr 2004; Kushner and Davis 2004; Carter 2005; Shay 2005, 2006; Brewer 2006; Brigitte Gabriel 2006).

Can one define Islamic terror? One usually looks to a good reference work for such a definition. In our age of the Internet, the venerable *Encyclopaedia Britannica* has been supplanted by *Wikipedia,* the best online encyclopedia, which defines "Islamism" as

> a set of political ideologies holding that Islam is not only a religion but also a politi-cal system and its teachings should be preeminent in all facets of society. It holds that Muslims must return to the original teachings and the early models of Islam, particularly by making Islamic law (sharia) the basis for all statutory law of society and by uniting politically, eventually in one state; and that western military, economic, political, social, or cultural influence in the Muslim world is un-Islamic and should be replaced by purely Islamic influences.

Some scholars define "Islamism" as a more extreme ideology that holds that the whole world must be converted to Islam. The same reference work further defines "Islamist" terrorism as follows: "*Islamist terrorism* (also known as *Islamic terrorism* or *Jihadist terrorism*) is terrorism—an act of violence targeting non-combatants—done by a person or group identifiably Islamic, and/or to further the cause of Islamism as determined by the acts' perpetrators and supporters." Whether or not this simplistic definition is satisfactory depends on the view of its reader.

The National Counterterrorism Center, under the newly created Office of the Director of National Intelligence, is a U.S. government organization responsible for national and international counterterrorism efforts. In August 2004, during the "global war on terror," U.S. President George W. Bush had created the National Counterterrorism Center to serve as the primary organization in the U.S. government for integrating and analyzing all intelligence pertaining to terrorism and counterterrorism (mainly Islamic) and to conduct strategic operational planning against terrorists by integrating all the instruments of U.S. national power. Replacing the former Terrorist Threat Integration Center, the National Counterterrorism Center is housed in the Liberty Crossing Building in McLean, Virginia, a southern suburb of Washington, DC. In late 2004, the United States Congress codified the National Counterterrorism Center in the Intelligence Reform and Terrorism Prevention Act and placed it in the Office of the Director of National Intelligence. The authors of the *Wikipedia* gathered the following information from the U.S. National Counterterrorism Center about the geographical extent, incidence, and violence of Islamic terror:

> According to statistics gathered by the National Counterterrorism Center of the United States, Islamic extremism was responsible for approximately 57% of terrorist fatalities and 61% of woundings worldwide in 2004 and early 2005, where a terrorist perpetrator could be specified. Extremist acts have included airline hijacking, beheading, kidnaping, assassination, roadside bombing, suicide bombing, and occasionally rape. One of the most notable Islamist terrorist campaigns was the 9/11 attack on the United States. Less prominent Islamist attacks have occurred in France, Russia and China. France was the focus of terrorism in the mid 1990s from the Algerian civil war. Russia faced terrorist attacks stemming from its involvement in Chechnya (*Wikipedia* article on Islamist Terrorism).

Other countries, such as Egypt, Algeria, and Indonesia, had attempted to combat Islamic terrorism on their own turf, as it presented a direct threat to their own regimes. China, which has a large Muslim minority, mainly in its northwestern provinces of Xinjiang, Gansu, and Ningxia, and must deal with Islamic terrorism in these provinces, was also one of them. Their efforts, however, have not been very successful:

> In 1997 the Chinese government set up the Shanghai Cooperation Organization to combat radical Islamic movements in Central Asia. Islamist terrorist activity is usually referred to as *jihad* (struggle). Threats, including death threats, are often issued as *fatwas* (Islamic legal judgments). Both Muslims and non-Muslims have been among the targets and victims. Threats against Muslims are often issued as *takfir* (a declaration that someone or some thing considered Muslim is in fact an unbeliever). This is an implicit death threat as the punishment for apostasy in Islam is death, under traditional interpretations of *Shari'a* law (*Wikipedia* article on Islamist Terrorism).

The *Wikipedia* article lists many popular controversies around Islamic terror: whether the motivation of the terrorists is good or bad; whether they are murderers or freedom fighters; whether they seek self-defense or offensive expansion, national self-determination or Islamic supremacy; what targets of the terrorists or alleged terrorists are noncombatants; whether Islam condones terrorism, especially suicide murder; whether some attacks are Islamist terrorism, or only terrorist acts done by Muslims; how much support there is in the Arab and Muslim world for Islamic terrorism; whether the Arab-Israeli conflict is the root cause of

Islamic terrorism, or simply one cause; and so on (*Wikipedia* article on Islamist Terrorism). To me, the key issue is the psychological one: what is it about Islamic terrorists that causes religious believers to become murderous fanatics?

Since the 1990s, terror has been used as a weapon by many Islamic groups in several countries: the *Hezbollah* in Lebanon, the Palestinian *Hamas* and *Islamic Jihad* in Israel, the *Gama'a al Islamiya* (Islamic Group) in Egypt, the *Groupe islamique armé* (Armed Islamic Group) in Algeria, and the best-known Islamic terrorist group, *al-Qaïda*—supported for some years by the fundamentalist Islamic government of the Sudan and by the Taliban government in Afghanistan—all over the world (Crenshaw 2000, p. 412). In 1993 a few fanatical Islamists attempted to bomb New York's World Trade Center but failed. In 1998 Bin Laden's *al-Qaïda* blew up the U.S. embassies in Kenya and Tanzania. In 2001 the *al-Qaïda* suicide terrorists destroyed the World Trade Center with hijacked planes. In retaliation, the United States invaded Afghanistan and drove out the Taliban government, after which it invaded Iraq. The "global war on terror" has been going on ever since, and we shall discuss its psychological aspects below.

Historical and Sociological Explanations

A profound hatred of America, which they call "the Great Satan," and Israel, which they think of as "the Little Satan," seems to permeate the minds of Islamic terrorists. Shortly after the horrific tragedy of September 11, 2001, usually referred to by the shorthand of *9/11* (which, psychologically, may be a defensive abbreviation or euphemism), the American historian Paul Kennedy tried to put himself in the shoes of the Islamic terrorists:

> How do we appear to them, and what would it be like were our places in the world reversed [...] Suppose that there existed today *a powerful, unified Arab-Muslim state* that stretched from Algeria to Turkey and Arabia—as there was 400 years ago, *the Ottoman Empire* [sic]. Suppose this unified Arab-Muslim state had the biggest economy in the world, and the most effective military. Suppose by contrast this United States of ours had split into 12 or 15 countries, with different regimes, some conservative and corrupt. Suppose that the great Arab-Muslim power had its aircraft carriers cruising off our shores, its aircraft flying over our lands, its satellites watching us every day. Suppose that its multinational corporations had reached into North America to extract oil, and paid the corrupt, conservative governments big royalties for that. Suppose that it dominated all international institutions like the Security Council and the IMF. Suppose that there was a special state set up in North America fifty years ago, of a different religion and language to ours, and the giant Arab-Muslim power always gave it support. Suppose the Colossus state was bombarding us with cultural messages, about the status of women, about sexuality, that we found offensive. Suppose it was always urging us to change, to modernize, to go global, to follow its example. Hmm [...] in those conditions, would not many Americans steadily grow to loathe that Colossus, wish it harm? And perhaps try to harm it? I think so (Kennedy 2001; italics added).

Kennedy's suppositions, however appealing or convincing, were somewhat inaccurate. The Ottoman Empire was not "a unified Arab-Muslim state": it was primarily Turkish and Turkish-dominated. Even the medieval Muslim caliphate, which Kennedy did not mention, was not a unified empire: it was a group of independent Muslim caliphates, Sultanates, and principalities, and there were at least four different caliphates. In fact, there had never been "a powerful, unified Arab-Muslim state that stretched from Algeria to Turkey and Arabia"—except in the imagination of fanatical Islamic terrorists. In any event, Kennedy's empathic fantasies did not explain the profound irrationalities of Islamic terrorists: their gross distortions of reality, their portrayal of America and Israel as "the Great Satan" and "the Little Satan," their turning the Muslim mortal sin of suicide into an act of holy martyrdom, and their wishes to "re-create" an Islamic world empire that had never existed.

To explain this striking phenomenon, the American sociologists Lauren Langman and Douglas Morris combined the classical sociological theories of the German sociologist Maximilian Carl Emil Weber (1864–1920) with the "critical theory" of the Frankfurt School's Max Horkheimer and Theodore Adorno. In Langman and Morris's own words, they investigated "the interaction of *economic, cultural and political causes* and potential outcomes of Islamic terrorism" (Langman and Morris 2002; italics added). The word "psychological" was significantly missing from this statement: some sociologists overlook the crucial importance of emotional causes.

In the obsessive manner of academics, Langman and Morris did a great deal of classifying and enumerating. Historically, they wrote, Islam's decline had occurred through "three major internal moments: the limits to modernity, religious conservativism [sic], and *ressentiment* [the French word for resentment] of the West" (Langman and Morris 2002). Langman and Morris also thought that Islamic societies responded proactively to the rise of the West through "two strategies": Westernization and Islamic modernism, both of which have been strongly resisted. "In the 20th century, due to the internal suppression of secular political movements [. . .] puritanical fundamentalisms such as Wahhabism arose" (Langman and Morris 2002). Langman and Morris believed that Islamic terrorism could be explained without resort to depth psychology:

> Fundamentalisms in various religions explain reality by blaming social problems on the departure from religious morality and promise redemption via a return to an idealized community. In face of decline, colonization, and economic stagnation, *ressentiment* of the West became widespread in Islam. Fundamentalisms interacting with *ressentiment* may turn militant, as in the case of Al Qaeda. A war on terrorism is not likely to end terrorism. To solve the problem of terrorism requires addressing its roots: internal constraints, dictatorships sponsored by the West and the underdevelopment that results from neo-liberal globalization. We suggest terrorism will wane in the face of the evolution of modern Islamic public spheres that might challenge religious conservatism. In wake of 9/11 [the destruction of the World Trade Center by Islamic suicide terrorists on September 11, 2001], both

moderate and radical religious movements are likely to remain a basis for mobilizing alternative identities to globalization" (Langman and Morris 2002).

As we shall see, the problem with such "explanations" is that they leave the most important cause of Islamic terrorism, the unconscious psychological one, undiscussed. Once again, we can see the failure of single academic disciplines to explain religious terror.

Narcissistic Rage and Islamic Terror

In the fall of 2003, after the U.S. invasion and occupation of Iraq, Rami G. Khouri, the editor of the Lebanese newspaper *The Daily Star,* was invited to testify at a hearing of the United States Senate Foreign Relations Committee. The theme of the hearing was "Iraq—Next Steps: How can democratic institutions succeed in Iraq and the Middle East?" Note that for the senators, the question was "how," not "whether." They took it for granted that democracy could succeed and flourish in Arab and Muslim societies with no democratic traditions and with an authoritarian family and social structure. The following year, however, the Iranian-born scholar Amir Taheri wrote that democracy and Islam were incompatible, as the latter believed in rule by Allah and the mullahs: "To say that Islam is incompatible with democracy should not be seen as a disparagement of Islam. On the contrary, many Muslims would see it as a compliment because they believe that their idea of rule by God is superior to that of rule by men, which is democracy" (Taheri 2004). We shall discuss the controversial Taheri later in this book.

In 2004 the former U.S. President Gerald R. Ford (1913–2006) told the American journalist Bob Woodward, "I just don't think we should go hellfire damnation around the globe freeing people, unless it is directly related to our national security" (Woodward 2006a). It now seems that Taheri and Ford were right and that the United States Senate was wrong. "Democratic" Iraq has become the world's worst nightmare of Islamic terrorist violence and suicide murder (Enders and Sandler 2006; Mazzetti 2006). In 2007 and 2008, while U.S. President George W. Bush insisted that holding Iraq was vital to U.S. national security, Democratic and Republican leaders in his country publicly called for a U.S. withdrawal from Iraq.

Rami Khouri of Lebanon had made the following points to the United States Senate about the differences between the democratic culture of the United States and the nondemocratic culture of the Arab countries: Americans value *freedom* above all else, while Arab societies stress the *honor and dignity of the individual* more than his or her liberty. Honor and dignity are perceived as comprising the same range of values and rights that define democracy in the United States and the Western world—participation in political life and decision-making, a sense of social and economic justice, initial equal opportunities for all young people in their education and careers, and the rule of law applied equally and fairly to all in society. Americans organize their society primarily on the basis of the rights of the individual, while Arabs define themselves and their societies primarily through collective identities, such as family, tribe, clan, ethnic group, or religion. Americans tend to stress society's obligation to ensure the individual's rights to do as he or she pleases, within the limits of the law; Arabs tend to focus more on the obligation of the individual to fulfill his or her responsibilities to the family and society. The United States is a secular society, while religion plays a key public role in most Arab and Middle Eastern societies. The United States is predominantly an immigrant society with a short collective historical memory, while Middle Eastern cultures are indigenous and deeply defined by their historical memories and past experiences (Khouri 2003).

Shortly thereafter, the American political economist Marvin Zonis, an expert on Middle Eastern Muslim culture in general and on Iranian culture in particular (Zonis and Offer 1985; Zonis and Brumberg 1987; Zonis 1991; Zonis and Joseph 1994), disputed Khouri's ideas (Zonis 2003). Zonis thought that there was much more to the escalating violence in the Middle East than met the eye. Using the psychoanalyst Heinz Kohut's "self-psychology" (Detrick and Detrick 1989), Zonis had this to say about Middle East societies:

> When the commitment to dignity and honor are combined with the devastating failures of Middle Eastern states, the result is a profound and widespread feeling of *humiliation* and the deepest of *narcissistic wounds.* The narcissistic humiliation has generated powerful [narcissistic] *rage. That rage is the characteristic emotion of many in the Middle East;* an emotion that seems palpable to anyone who has dealt with its people. The rage of Middle Easterners is omnipresent and directed at the Jews and the United States, in particular, and the West, in general, and increasingly to their own leaders. *What has been the outcome of these failures and humiliation? The turn to Islam.* This has been facilitated by Middle Eastern rulers. Take Saudi Arabia, for example. Thousands of princes and princesses live high off the oil wealth while millions of Saudis go without jobs and without income. Providing neither economic well being nor political democracy, the Saudis need to find a way to legitimate their rule (Zonis 2003; italics added).

The psychoanalyst Heinz Kohut (1913–1981) had described narcissistic rage as "the need for revenge, for righting a wrong, for undoing a hurt by whatever means, and a deeply anchored, unrelenting compulsion in the pursuit of all these aims, which gives no rest to those who have suffered a narcissistic injury—these are the characteristic features of narcissistic rage in all its forms and which set it apart from other kinds of aggression" (Kohut 1972, 1978, pp. 637–638). The political economist Marvin Zonis applied Kohut's description to the mind of Islamic terrorists: "I would argue that those committing violence against the United States in Iraq have different ideological and political justifications for their actions. But psychologically their justifications are driven by [personal] rage, the rage generated by deep narcissistic wounds. Narcissistic rage knows no boundaries and no limits" (Zonis 2003).

Boundless narcissistic rage is a key to our understanding of Islamic terrorists. When using the term "terrorist," however, it is important to note the caveats of two American psychoanalysts who came from Muslim societies: the Turkish-Cypriot-born Vamık Volkan and his Indian-born colleague Salman Akhtar. They have pointed out that originally the term "terror" was used for state intimidation of civilians, that one man's terrorist is another's glorious martyr, and that terrorism is also a way of belonging to a group, which is emotionally vital to the terrorist (Volkan 1997, pp. 156–167; Akhtar 1999). Volkan pointed out the paradox inherent in "ethnic terrorism": in the Palestinian case, for example, innocent Palestinian people are victimized by the fanatics in order to verify the victimhood of the terrorists' ethnic group (Volkan 1997, p. 159).

Ethnic and Islamic terrorism have to do with the age-old Muslim notion of the *dhimmi.* For many centuries, under the rule of Islam, the Jews (and Christians) in the Muslim world were treated as *dhimmi* (protected people), second-class citizens who had to bow their head before any Muslim (Bat Ye'or 1985, 2002). By Muslim *Shari'a* law, a *dhimmi* is a person of the *dhimma,* a one-sided "pact" dictated to non-Muslims by the authorities of their Muslim government, under which they are "protected" by the authorities in return for paying the *jizya* capital tax. This status was originally made available only to non-Muslims who were "the People of the Book" (Jews and Christians), but was later extended to include Sikhs, Zoroastrians, Mandeans, and, in some areas, Hindus and Buddhists. The status of *dhimmi* applied to millions of people living from the Atlantic Ocean to India from the seventh century until modern times.

In 1839, an edict called the *Hatt-i Sharif of Gülhane* was put forth by Abdülmecid, the Ottoman Sultan and Caliph of the Muslims, that, in part, proclaimed the principle of the equality of all Ottoman subjects regardless of religion. Part of the motivation for this was the desire to gain support from the British Empire, whose help was desired in an Ottoman conflict with Egypt. In 1856 another edict was issued by the Sultan and Caliph, called *Hatt-i Humayan,* which came about partly as a result of pressure from and the efforts of the ambassadors of England, France, and Austria, whose respective countries were needed by the Ottomans as allies in the Crimean War. It again proclaimed the principle of the equality of Muslims and non-Muslims, and produced many specific reforms to this end. For example, the *jizya* tax was abolished and non-Muslims were allowed to join the Ottoman army. This was a major psychological blow to fundamentalist

Muslims for whom the *dhimma* was a basic tenet of their religion which supported their feeling of superiority and honor.

Ethnic terrorism, which was rampant in the "ethnic cleansing" during the Bosnia war in the 1990s, may be viewed as a form of racist evil. "Evil" as such is rarely studied by psychoanalysts (Hering 1997), while aggression and sadism are. The British psychotherapist Joseph Berke has studied "malice", while the American psychoanalyst Carl Goldberg has studied "malevolence" (Berke 1988, 2006; Goldberg 1996). Goldberg's study anticipated some of the large-scale evil that was to follow five years later. At the beginning of the twenty-first century, the world discovered a new kind of evil: the murderous narcissistic rage of the fundamentalist Islamic *jihadis* of *al-Qaïda.*

Studying the psychology of Muslim terrorism, Berke and his American-Israeli colleague Stanley Schneider thought that the abolition of the *dhimma* was a "big blow" to many fundamentalist Muslims, and that "ethnic pride was and remains a powerful emotional current among contemporary Muslims. It is impossible to comprehend current Arab-Western, Arab-Jewish, indeed, Arab-non-Arab, conflicts without taking into account the enforced subservience of non-Muslims, 'the dhimmis,' and the psychic wounds, still unhealed, that followed the abolition of 'dhimmi' status by the late Ottoman sultans." These scholars believed that

> according to the "Law" of Islam, the "dhimmis" included Jews, Christians, Armenians, Druses and Copts, but not pagans, who remained roughly equivalent to "untouchables". In Muslim society, the "dhimmi" were second-class citizens, allowed to live in Muslim territory and tolerated, but subject to a Koranic poll tax and many other disadvantages. These included the requirement to wear special clothes or badges, the prohibition from bearing arms or riding horses and inequality before the law. No matter what his accomplishments, every Muslim could feel superior to a "dhimmi", and could abuse him as he saw fit (Berke and Schneider 2006).

"Ethnic terrorism" may be paradoxical, but is also very real. Moreover, paradoxically, in some places, such as in Bosnia-Hercegovina, "Muslim" is an ethnic rather than a religious designation. Another vital point, made by the political psychologist Jeanne Nickell Knutson (died 1982), is that many terrorists are people who have themselves been victimized or terrorized in their early life (Volkan 1997, p. 160). Recognizing the feelings of shame and humiliation in the mind of the terrorist is vital to its understanding (Twemlow 2005, p. 958).

Islamic fundamentalism has been studied by several scholars, but none of them were psychoanalysts (Hiro 1989; Choueiri 1990; Davidson 1998; New 2002; C.G. Gunderson 2004). Assuming that Zonis and Kohut were right, what are those deep narcissistic wounds, those early rejections, losses of love, injuries to self-esteem, feelings of shame, humiliations, and other emotional wounds which provoke such "endless resentment" or "boundless narcissistic rage" in fanatical Islamic terrorists that they are prepared to commit suicide murder? While we in "the West" may ask ourselves, "Why do the Islamic fundamentalists hate us so much?" Zonis (2003) asked a different question: "Why are the Muslim fanatics so prodigious at hating?" Why can they not love as much as they hate? What is it about their families, their early-life relationships, early mothering, fathering, or sibling rivalries, or anything else in their infancy, childhood and adolescence that gives rise to such boundless narcissistic rage and hatred? This is what I set out to explore in this book.

The Narcissistic and Borderline Personality Disorders

Narcissism is evident in many terrorists' personality structure. Several psychoanalysts have found similarities between terrorists' personalities and the psychiatric descriptions of narcissistic and borderline personality disorders (Akhtar 1999; Vaknin 2003; Lachkar 2006; Piven 2006). A person suffering from a narcissistic personality disorder has a grandiose sense of self-importance, is often megalomanic or paranoid, is preoccupied with fantasies of unlimited success, power, brilliance, beauty, or ideal love, believes that he or she is special and unique and can only be understood by other special people, requires excessive admiration from others, has a strong sense of entitlement, takes advantage of others to achieve his or her own ends, lacks empathy for the feelings of others, is often envious of others or believes others are envious of him or her, and has an arrogance that annoys others (American Psychiatric Association 2000, pp. 714–718).

The borderline personality disorder is more severe than the narcissistic one, although they often overlap. Its many symptoms include anxiety attacks; frantic efforts to avoid real or imagined abandonment; a pattern of unstable and intense interpersonal relationships characterized by alternating between extremes of idealization and devaluation; identity disturbance, with markedly and persistently unstable self-image or sense of self; impulsiveness in areas that are potentially self-damaging (e.g., spending, promiscuous sex, eating disorders, substance abuse, reckless driving, binge eating); recurrent suicidal behavior, gestures, or threats, or self-mutilating behavior; affective instability due to a marked reactivity of mood; chronic feelings of emptiness; inappropriate, intense anger or difficulty controlling anger and rage (including frequent displays of temper, constant anger, recurrent physical fights); and transient, stress-related paranoid ideation or severe dissociative symptoms (American Psychiatric Association 2000, pp. 706–713).

In short, the borderline personality disorder is characterized by emotional instability, paranoid tendencies, "black and white" thinking, and turbulent interpersonal relationships. The British activist and writer Erin Pizzey has correctly called borderline patients "emotional terrorists" because they tend to terrorize those around them with their uncontrollable rage (Pizzey 1998). Psychiatrists describe the borderline personality disorder as involving diffuse ego identity and unclear boundaries of the self (the patient does not clearly distinguish between "me" and "not-me"), pervasive instability in mood, interpersonal relationships, self-image, ego identity, and behavior. This instability disrupts the person's family and work life, long-term planning, and the individual's sense of self. Borderline personality disorder seems to be more common among women than among men, and indeed Pizzey found that it is usually women who are the emotional terrorists in dysfunctional families. Most of those diagnosed with borderline personality disorder were seriously abused, terrorized, victimized, abandoned, neglected, treated ambivalently, or otherwise severely traumatized during their childhood (Masterson 1981, 2000; Akhtar 1992; Paris 1994; Dean 1995; J.G. Gunderson 2001; Kernberg 1975; Friedel 2004; Freeman and Fusco 2004; Fusco and Freeman 2004; Zananiri 2005).

The cases of political tyrants like Joseph Stalin of the Soviet Union (1878–1953), Adolf Hitler of Germany (1889–1945), Mao Zedong of China (1893–1976), and Saddam Hussein of Iraq (1937–2006) may serve to illustrate the connection between terrorism and the narcissistic and borderline personality disorders. All these dictators were professional state terrorists with their entire state apparatus following their orders. Their very names struck terror into the hearts of millions. All four had suffered highly traumatic childhoods, including physical and emotional parental abuse, feelings of rejection from birth, losses and abandonments, and their adult personalities were severely disturbed. The Polish-Swiss Jewish psychoanalyst Alice Miller had this to say about terrorist tyrants like Stalin, Hitler, Mao, and Saddam:

> In the lives of all the tyrants I examined, I found without exception paranoid trains of thought bound up with their biographies in early childhood and the repression of the experiences they had been through. Mao had been regularly whipped by his father and later sent 30 million people to their deaths, but he hardly ever admitted the full extent of the rage he must have felt toward his own father, a very severe teacher who had tried through beatings to "make a man" out of his son. Stalin caused millions to suffer and die because even at the height of his power his actions were determined by unconscious infantile fear of powerlessness. Apparently his father, a poor cobbler from Georgia, attempted to drown his frustration with liquor and whipped his son almost every day. His mother displayed psychotic traits, was completely incapable of defending her son and was usually away from home either

praying in church or running the priest's household. Stalin idealized his parents right up to the end of his life and was constantly haunted by the fear of dangers that had long since ceased to exist but were still present in his deranged mind. The same might be true of many other tyrants (Miller 1998, p. 584).

Indeed, Stalin was pathologically paranoid, even within his own family (Tucker 1973, 1990; Glad 2002; Miller 2005, pp. 28, 91). Like him, Adolf Hitler suffered the terror of parental abuse and psychic trauma as a child and from a severe case of borderline personality disorder as an adult (Erikson 1942, 1963; Langer 1972; Koenigsberg 1975; Stierlin 1975; Binion 1976; Waite 1977; Miller 1983, 1998, 2005; Bromberg and Small 1983; De Boor 1985; Burrin 1994; Schwaab 1992; Bursztein 1996; Chamberlain 1997; Victor 1998; Redlich 1999). The Austrian-American-Jewish psychoanalyst Friedrich Karl Redlich (1910–2004), who, like so many other Austrian Jews, had fled Austria for the United States after Hitler's annexation of that country to Germany in 1938, saw the *Führer* as a mercurial, paranoid fanatic who went to any lengths to maintain his popularity (Redlich 1999). Mao had suffered daily corporal and emotional punishment from his father as a child, and millions paid for it. Saddam, who had also been deeply traumatized as a child, suffered from "malignant narcissism," megalomania, and paranoid ideation (Post 1991, 2003; Glad 2002). He was more stable, if no less ruthless, than Hitler. The American writer Mark Robert Bowden saw Saddam's infinite vanity:

> The sheer scale of the tyrant's deeds mocks psychoanalysis. What begins with ego and ambition becomes a political movement. Saddam embodies first the party and then the nation. Others conspire in this process in order to further their own ambitions, selfless as well as selfish. Then the tyrant turns on them. His cult of self becomes more than a political strategy. Repetition of his image in heroic or paternal poses, repetition of his name, his slogans, his virtues, and his accomplishments, seeks to make his power seem inevitable, unchallengeable. Finally he is praised not out of affection or admiration but out of obligation. One must praise him (Bowden 2002).

In all those cases, the grandiosity of the self and the paranoid *unconscious* projection of one's "badness" on one's enemies were massive. Although most terrorists do not run states, some do. The cases of Hitler, Stalin, Mao, and Saddam are terrorist cases writ large. Alice Miller believed that the painful feelings of powerlessness and fear were so deeply etched into their *bodies* when they were children by the abuse they had suffered that they later murdered millions of people as adults rather than confront their own unbearable truth and experience those unbearable feelings. She also included Napoleon and Milošević in her list of tyrants (Miller 2005, pp. 28–29).

Are Terrorists Normal?

Despite the serious emotional disturbances from which political tyrants obviously suffer, there is still considerable debate among psychoanalysts and other scholars as to whether "ordinary" terrorists in general and suicide terrorists in particular act out of rational motives or out of a distorted and irrational perception of reality, whether they are emotionally disturbed or psychologically normal, and, if disturbed, whether they suffer from narcissistic or borderline personality disorder. The controversy is complicated by the fact that what "Western" psychiatry considers abnormal is often considered normal in the Arab world, and that what is considered normal behavior in one society may not be thought normal in another (Glidden 1972; Gaines 1992).

The American "self psychologists" Phillip Johnson and Theodore Feldmann discerned some "personality types" among terrorists (Johnson and Feldmann 1992). They believed that the study of terrorism and of the types of individuals drawn to terrorist groups was of great interest for forensic behavioral scientists, yet, although many studies had attempted to classify personality types and psychopathology in terrorist groups, the behaviorists had come to no consensus and developed no clear theoretical framework to explain the membership in these groups. On the other hand, they wrote, Kohut's self-psychology could provide such a framework. They thought that the terrorist group may be understood as serving a number of unconscious functions for its members, including a maternal one, all of which are designed to promote identity and self-cohesion. Such a formulation implies a degree of *narcissistic pathology* in many members. Johnson and Feldmann put forth a self-psychology formulation to explain the psychological function that membership in terrorist groups serves as an emotional rescue for "narcissistically vulnerable personalities."

Nonetheless, the American psychologist Clark McCauley believed that terrorists were normal people and that thirty years of research had found very little evidence that terrorists are suffering from psychopathology (McCauley 2002). The "psychohistorian" Lloyd deMause disagreed with McCauley, and DeMause's follower Joan Lachkar attacked McCauley's research as "preposterous" (DeMause 2002, 2006; Lachkar 2006). Confusing individual psychology with collective psychology, however, Lachkar, who had studied the psychopathology of "narcissistic/borderline couples" (Lachkar 1992), wrote about the Arab-Israeli conflict, "I tentatively diagnosed the Jews as having a collective narcissistic diagnosis, and [the] Arabs a collective borderline—very similar to couples."

While all terrorists may not have a borderline personality disorder, psychoanalysts have found that borderline patients tend to terrorize people, including their therapists, and that they have an *intrapsychic terrorist organization* with an over-representation of trauma in their backgrounds. Erin Pizzey and Salman Akhtar found an "inner terrorist" within the borderline mind (Pizzey 1998; Akhtar 1999). Akhtar thought that feeling acute terror is part of the terrorist's personal experience, who may share with the borderline patient a similar propensity for omnipotent denial, concrete thinking, psychotic transference enactments, and *an endless resentment about their impossible needs,* which of course cannot be accommodated by the objects of their love or hate or by their therapists (Twemlow 2005, p. 957). This "endless resentment" is what other scholars have called "boundless narcissistic rage" (Zonis 2003).

The questions of what normality and madness are, and whether terrorists are normal or emotionally disturbed people, have preoccupied several psychological scholars. Some "anti-psychiatrists" like the Scottish psychiatrist Ronald David Laing (1927–1989) believed that our world itself was insane and that "insanity is a perfectly rational adjustment to an insane world. Normal men have killed 100 million of their fellow men in the past 50 years" (Laing 1967). Whether the figure is correct or not, Laing may have overlooked the fact that most of this killing had occurred in wartime, under very special psychological circumstances. Human wartime behavior is arguably abnormal. It deviates markedly from peacetime norms and values. The irrationality and emotionality of war are a radical departure from accepted normal behavior. In the heat of battle, killing becomes the norm and is reinforced, even rewarded, by society.

The American terrorism expert Martha Crenshaw believed that terrorist behavior "displays a collective rationality" and that it is often effective in achieving its stated goals (Crenshaw 1998, p. 9). Her colleague Jerrold Post thought that "terrorists are driven to commit acts of violence as a consequence of psychological forces, and that their special psycho-logic is [unconsciously] constructed to rationalize [murderous] acts [that] they are psychologically compelled to commit" (Post 1998, p. 25). A third terrorism scholar, Ted Goertzel, thought that while all behavior is "a combination of rational and emotional responses, terrorists typically court death, torture, or imprisonment, and these self-destructive sacrifices are irrational" (Goertzel 2002a, pp. 97–98).

The Indian-born American psychoanalyst Salman Akhtar, who came from a Muslim family, found that the terrorist's mind is similar to that of the borderline patient, who also tends to terrorize those around him (Twemlow 2005, pp. 957–958). In studying a particular type of terrorist, the political assassin, I have found that these people are often late adolescents who suffer from severe psychopathology, especially borderline personality disorder (Falk 2001a). I have also found considerable psychopathology among Palestinian Arab suicide bombers (Falk 2004, pp. 159–173).

The American "terrorism expert" C.L. Ruby thought that terrorists were normal people (Ruby 2002). Ruby treated "terrorism" legally as defined by Title 22 of the United States Code: "politically motivated violence perpetrated in a clandestine manner against noncombatants." Experts on terrorism also include another aspect in the definition: the act is committed in order to create a fearful state of mind in an audience different from the victims. Whether or not an act is considered terrorism also depends on whether a legal, moral, or behavioral perspective is used to interpret the act. If a legal or moral perspective is used, the values of the interpreter are the focus rather than the act itself. Ruby thought that a behavioral perspective appears to be best suited for interpreting and reacting to terrorism.

Ruby thought that the terrorist attacks on the World Trade Center towers and the Pentagon have accentuated the threat of terrorism and that the attackers are popularly thought of as mentally deranged, evil individuals. He suggested that such an understanding is a misperception of these people and may interfere with an adequate response to prevent future attacks. Ruby reviewed the extant literature on psychological theories of terrorism and concluded that terrorists are not dysfunctional or pathological but rather that terrorism is basically another form of politically motivated violence that is perpetrated by "rational, lucid people who have valid motives." The only real difference between terrorism and conventional military action is one of strategy. Terrorists lack the necessary resources to wage war in furtherance of their political goals (Ruby 2002).

Similarly, the American anthropologist Scott Atran believed that suicide terrorists did not suffer from any serious psychopathology and were basically normal people (Atran 2003, 2004, 2006). In the West, this scholar said, we often misperceive suicide terrorists from the Middle East as crazed cowards who thrive in poverty and ignorance and are bent on senseless destruction. Atran thought that this was a serious misperception: suicide terrorists are neither poor nor ignorant; they have much to lose, and many of them are as educated and economically well-off as their surrounding populations (which is often poor and uneducated). This scholar thought that a first line of defense against suicide bombers was to get the communities from which they stem to learn how to minimize the receptivity of mostly ordinary people to recruiting organizations. Atran's controversial views are obviously not favorable to psychoanalysis.

Like Ruby and Atran, the young American political scientist Robert Pape offered rationalistic explanations for terrorism and tried to do away with psychological ones. Pape "collected" all the incidents of suicide terrorism around the world for the past two decades and then tried to "explain" suicide terrorism while ignoring its psychology and insisting that it had a rational "strategic logic":

> Suicide terrorism is rising around the world, but the most common explanations do not help us understand why. Religious fanaticism does not explain why the world leader in suicide terrorism is the Tamil Tigers in Sri Lanka, a group that adheres to a Marxist/Leninist ideology, while *existing psychological explanations have been contradicted by the widening range of socio-economic backgrounds of suicide terrorists.* [sic] To advance our understanding of this growing phenomenon, this study collects the universe of suicide terrorist attacks worldwide from 1980 to 2001, 188 in all. In contrast to the existing explanations, this study shows that *suicide terrorism follows a strategic logic, one specifically designed to coerce modern liberal democracies to make significant territorial concessions* (Pape 2003, p. 343; italics added).

It is not clear why the "widening range of socio-economic backgrounds of suicide terrorists" should contradict "existing psychological explanations." In any event, Pape also offered further rationalistic and non-psychological explanations for suicide terrorism which he thought did not require any psychological analysis:

> Moreover, over the past two decades, *suicide terrorism has been rising largely because terrorists have learned that it pays.* Suicide terrorists sought to compel American and French military forces to abandon Lebanon in 1983, Israeli forces to leave Lebanon in 1985, Israeli forces to quit the Gaza Strip and the West Bank in 1994 and 1995, the Sri Lankan government to create an independent Tamil state from 1990 on, and the Turkish government to grant autonomy to the Kurds in the late 1990s. In all but the case of Turkey, the terrorist political cause made more gains after the resort to suicide operations than it had before. Thus, Western democracies should pursue policies that teach terrorists that the lesson of the 1980s and 1990s no longer holds, policies which in practice may have more to do with improving homeland security than with offensive military action (Pape 2003, p. 343; italics added).

In a later book on the same subject, Pape argued that "foreign occupation" was the root cause of all suicidal terrorism (Pape 2005). Presumably, then, had the United States not occupied Afghanistan or Iraq, had Israel not occupied the Palestinian territories, or had Sri Lanka not "occupied" its own Tamil areas, there would have been no suicidal terrorism.

Even the American anthropologist Scott Atran, who, like Pape, had treated suicidal terrorism as normal, logical, and rational behavior, found "at least four critical flaws" in Pape's arguments: errors in sampling, conclusions that are both too narrow and too broad, that "rather than judging as Pape does the success of suicide tactics primarily by whether the sponsoring organization has helped to expel foreigners from its homeland, the broader strategic goal that suicide attacks seek may be to increase the sponsoring organization's political 'market share' among its own potential supporters, that is, to broaden its political base among the population and narrow popular support for rival organizations," and, finally, that "Pape's argument that suicide terrorism is unrelated or only marginally related to Salafi ideology employs an unfounded inference. Salafis believe that the *hadith* (oral tradition) and literal readings of the *Qur'an* are sufficient guides for social law and personal life" (Atran 2006, pp. 130–132).

Ruby, Pape, and Atran did not heed the caveat of the late psychoanalyst John Mack that "without understanding what breeds them and drives [the terrorists] to do what they do in a particular time and place, we have little chance of preventing further such actions, let alone of 'eradicating terrorism'" (Mack 2002, p. 174). Since even these rationalistic scholars, who do not accept the tenets of psychoanalysis about unconscious emotional motivation, cannot agree among themselves about the "logic" of suicidal terrorism, there must be more to it that meets the eye. In contrast to such simplistic "explanations," the Turkish-Cypriot-born American psychoanalyst Vamık Volkan, who came from a Muslim society, had a deeper view of suicidal terrorism (Volkan 2001b).

Volkan seemingly shared Atran's opinion about suicide bombers: "Suicide bombers are not psychotic. In their case, the fabricated identity fits soundly with the external reality, and, significantly, is approved by outsiders. Thus, future suicide bombers, like the Sabra and Shatila children at play in a team, by all outward indications are 'normal' and often have an enhanced sense of self-esteem" (Volkan 2001b, p. 209). However, Volkan's quotation marks around the word "normal" were not accidental: he observed that suicide bombers were "young people whose personal identity is already disturbed" and youths who seek an outer element to internalize in order to stabilize their unstable internal world. Furthermore, Volkan's colleague Salman Akhtar had found terrorists' personalities to be similar in structure to those of people with borderline personality disorder (Akhtar 1999). The heated controversy over the presence or absence of psychopathology in terrorists in general and in suicide bombers in particular is reminiscent of—and tied to—the controversy over the "Arab mind" itself, which we shall discuss below.

The Infantile Development of Terrorist Pathology

Like other psychological disturbances, the development of narcissistic and border-line personalities, which are among the best-known and most researched personality disorders, and the most prevalent among terrorists, begins in infancy. Margaret Mahler and her colleagues studied the separation-individuation process in infancy, which they called "the psychological birth of the human infant," the process by which he gains his separate, individual, and autonomous existence, self, and identity (Mahler et al. 1975). This process has several phases, including the *rapprochement* subphase. For our purpose, in order to understand the narcissistic and borderline personality disorders, which may characterize many terrorists, especially the suicidal ones, it is important to understand this subphase, which occurs at the age of seventeen to twenty-four months, and the *rapprochement crisis,* which is the crucial part of this subphase of child development.

The psychoanalysts Estelle and Morton Shane thought that in the early *rapprochement* subphase, the mother is no longer just home base for the child, but also a person with whom the child wishes to share his discoveries, wanting her interest and participation. His elation with locomotion wanes, and he shifts to a wish for social interaction with his mother and with other children. For both boys and girls, the discovery of anatomical differences produces a sense of their own bodies. For girls, the penis symbolizes what boys have that they cannot get, and for both sexes a claim to gender identity ensues. The child shows a characteristic negativity toward mother, which results both from a sense of expanded autonomy and more intense recognition of the father (Shane and Shane 1989).

In this subphase, the child reacts more strongly to mother's absence with increased activity, tension, and restlessness. Both responses indicate sadness, but the activity is seen as a *defense* instituted against that painful emotion of abandonment. The child can now cope better and can relate to substitute adults and engage in symbolic play to master the separation experience. The period of early rapprochement ends at about the age of eighteen months and appears to be a temporary consolidation and acceptance of separation; however, harbingers exist of impending crisis, including almost ubiquitous temper tantrums, vulnerability, rage, helplessness, recurrence of stranger reactions, and beginning loyalty conflicts between mother and others (Shane and Shane 1989).

As his awareness of separateness from the mother grows, the child has an increased need for the mother's love. This constitutes the basis for *rapprochement* —searching for a way back to the mother. During this period, the child has a strong need for optimal emotional availability of the mother. It is the mother's love of the toddler and her acceptance of his ambivalence that enables him to "cathect" his self-representation with neutralized energy. The father is of special importance also during this period. Shadowing and darting away are two behaviors characteristic of this *rapprochement* subphase and indicate the wish for reunion with the mother and the fear of re-engulfment. Concomitant with the acquisition of skills and perceptual cognitive capacities, there has been an increasingly clear differentiation of the intrapsychic representations of object and self; thus, the toddler must cope with the world of his own, as a small, helpless, separate individual, unable to command relief merely by feeling the need for it (Shane and Shane 1989).

The *rapprochement crisis* occurs from about eighteen to twenty-two months and is characterized by *conflicts* deriving from the desire to be separate, grand, and omnipotent, and yet have the mother fulfill wishes without having to recognize that help comes from the outside. The child's mood changes to one characterized by dissatisfaction, insatiability, temper tantrums, and, especially, ambivalence toward the mother. The mother is used as an extension of the self to deny separateness. *The mother, too, shows anxiety about separation,* and where the mother is dissatisfied with her child, or anxious about him, or aloof from him, the normal *rapprochement* patterns become exaggerated (Shane and Shane 1989).

During this period, the child shows a realization of his own limitations and relative helplessness. A new capacity for empathy and higher-level identifications develops. The child is especially aware of and sensitive to his mother's whereabouts. *Object constancy* is already achieved (Akhtar et al. 1996): the child can conceive of the mother leaving him and coming back, being elsewhere and found again, and that the mother will still be the same person, the same "object," rather than one that keeps changing. This is often reassuring; but children may still demonstrate difficulty in leave-taking from their mothers, with clinging behaviors and depression (Shane and Shane 1989).

Splitting as a defense mechanism is now possible. The child unconsciously splits the mother's internal image within himself into two: an all-good mother and all-bad one, as if he had two different mothers, the one a benevolent fairy, the other a malevolent witch. This is a common theme in fairy tales, such as *Snow White and the Seven Dwarves,* where Snow White has two mothers, one all-good but dead, the other a mean, narcissistic stepmother. Other people become the bad mother; the good mother is longed for, but exists in fantasy only, and the real mother becomes a source of dissatisfaction on her return, leading the child either to ignore the returning mother or to avoid her (Shane and Shane 1989).

If the rapprochement crisis is resolved, the child finds an optimal distance from its mother, exercising autonomy and sociability and avoiding the ambivalence that proximity to the mother might bring. By this age, children reveal less phase-specific behavior and more individual differences. Boys and girls seem very different for the first time, with boys being more disengaged from mother and girls being more engaged with her, demanding closeness in an ambivalent fashion and blaming her for their lack of a penis. Boys are less overly concerned with sexual differences (Shane and Shane 1989).

The developmental tasks for the child at the height of the separation-individuation struggle are enormous. Conflicts about oral, anal, and early genital drives all meet, and in addition there is *a need to renounce symbiotic omnipotence.* The belief in the mother's omnipotence, too, is shaken. Superego development begins with the intensified vulnerability to the threat of losing the object's love. Where development has been less than optimal, the ambivalence conflict in relation to mother that became discernible during the *rapprochement* subphase is unresolved, as revealed in rapidly alternating clinging and negativistic behaviors. These reflect an ambitendency not yet internalized. Excessive *splitting* may be revealed as well (Shane and Shane 1989).

How do we distinguish the narcissistic from the borderline personality? Apart from the clinical symptoms listed above, there are developmental differences. The psychoanalyst James Masterson thought that while the narcissistic personality is fixated at a developmental stage *before* the *rapprochement crisis* between the infant and its mother, and is therefore characterized by infantile grandiosity and omnipotence, the borderline personality is fixated in the rapprochement crisis itself, and "behaves as if all life were one long, unresolvable rapprochement crisis." In the narcissistic personality, the internal self and object (infant and mother) images are fused, whereas in the borderline personality, they are "split into rewarding and withdrawing part-units" (Masterson 1981, p. 29).

Nevertheless, borderline and narcissistic personality disorders have *the lack of object constancy* in common (Masterson 1981, 2000; Kernberg 1975, 2002). The American singer Jim Morrison's song *I can't see your face in my mind* is an example. Both he and his colleague Janis Joplin both suffered from borderline personality disorders and self-destructiveness, and both had very inadequate mothering. Narcissistic people tend to lose their friends because they unwittingly hurt them or upset them, and the injury of rejection by friends makes them withdraw into their own world (Vaknin 1999). We shall attempt to see whether these very serious psychological problems of narcissistic rage, borderline personality, lack of object constancy, and paranoia occur in fundamentalist Muslim families, and what they may have to do with Islamic terror.

Non-Psychoanalytic Theories of Terrorism

Islamic terrorism has been frightening and fascinating "Western" society, especially the United States, which has been trying to understand it. Psychoanalysis, however, which may be the key tool for this understanding, is a complicated and difficult discipline, and it deals primarily with painful emotions, which to some scholars is threatening. A few years ago my American colleague Chris Stout edited a four-volume work entitled *The Psychology of Terrorism,* in which over forty scholars set down their views on the subject (Stout 2002). Most of them, however, were non-psychoanalytic. In one chapter, the American scholar Diane Perlman thought that she had discovered a simple "formula' for the "emergence of terrorism" in the form of a vicious cycle:

> Suffering → Desire for Compassion and Help → Reaching for Help → Help Fails → Dejection, Humiliation, Despair, and Rage → Transformation from Victim to Master of Fate → Compensation for Helplessness by Identification with Powerful Leader Who Stands Up to the Enemy → Evacuation of Suffering into Other Through Acts of Terrorism → Retaliation → More Suffering → Repeat Cycle (Perlman 2002, p. 23).

Perlman also thought that she also knew how to break the vicious cycle and reverse it, thereby "transcending" terrorism and healing the terrorists:

> Suffering → Desire for Compassion and Help → Reaching for Help → Help Responds → People Are Calmed, Non-Negotiable Human Needs Are Met → Conflict Is Contained → Repair and Healing → Progress → Cycle Reversed.

At the end of her chapter, the optimistic Perlman gave a list of 18 "strategies for transcending terrorism" by building a new world, which she believed to be "both available and affordable." They include eliminating starvation and malnutrition, providing universal health care, eliminating inadequate housing and homelessness, etc. (Perlman 2002, pp. 45–49). By contrast, the Israeli psychologist Nira Kfir believed that "terror can be a peak experience, elevating the individual from meaninglessness to total involvement. I argue that what appears to be an attempt to destroy the West is, in reality, directed to and intended to overtake the terrorist's homeland" (Kfir 2002, p. 156). From a psychoanalytic viewpoint, it may be pointed out, both the "West" and one's "homeland" can be symbols of the terrorist's split-off good and bad mother.

Three years later, the young British scholar John Horgan, a Senior Research Fellow at the Centre for the Study of Terrorism and Political Violence and a Lecturer in International Relations at the University of St Andrews in Scotland, published a book with the same title (Horgan 2005). Horgan's book has barely three pages on "psychodynamic accounts" of terrorism. In the same year, the American psychiatrist Jeff Victoroff reviewed critically the "state of the art" in the psychological theories of terrorism (Victoroff 2005). He gathered data and theoretical material from the world's unclassified literature. Victoroff found that multiple *theories* and some demographic *data* have been published, but very few controlled *empirical* studies have been conducted investigating the psychological bases of terrorism. He thought that the field is characterized by theoretical *speculation* based on *subjective* interpretation of anecdotal observations. Moreover, said Victoroff, most studies and theories fail to take into account *the great heterogeneity of terrorists.* Many practical, conceptual, and psychological barriers have slowed progress in this important field. Nonetheless, even at this early stage of terrorism studies, Victoroff thought, modifiable social and psychological factors contribute to the genesis of the terrorist "mind-set." Victoroff believed that psychological scholarship could possibly mitigate the risk of catastrophic attack by initiating the long overdue scientific study of terrorist mentalities.

As if to answer Victoroff's critique, the Stanford psychologist Bruce Bongar and his colleagues edited yet another book with the same title—*Psychology of Terrorism*—but without the definite article. The book has twenty-nine chapters, each written by another expert (Bongar et al. 2007). Though Bongar's book has a chapter on suicide terrorism, as does my book on the Arab-Israeli conflict (Falk 2004), it has none on Islamic terrorism, and none of the chapters is written by a psychoanalyst. It seems that Bongar and Victoroff both think that psychoanalysis is not "empirical" enough and that it is "theoretical speculation based on subjective interpretation of anecdotal observations."

Scholars from various non-psychoanalytic disciplines have tried to explain Islamic terrorism. For example, the romance-language scholar Eric Lawrence Gans had founded the discipline of "Generative Anthropology" (Gans 1985, 1993), and the American literary scholar Adam Katz sought to apply his theories to Islamic terrorism:

Islamic terrorism is part of a struggle for power within the Islamic world: the pur-
pose, in the wake of the stalling of the several decades long attempt to take power in
Islamic countries, is to shift the terms of the game by provoking massive American
retaliation which will in turn discredit pro-American regimes and facilitate the tak-
ing of power by Islamicists. On this account, the United States is first of all an actor
within the Arab and Muslim worlds, involved in an intracivilizational civil war.
(Between the Islamists and whom? "Moderate" pro-American governments? Proponents of liberal democracy?—which complicates things, of course, because this
side doesn't quite exist, we must act on the faith that our actions will create it.)
(Katz 2004–2005; italics added)

This subject obviously attracts a great deal of attention from scholars of many
disciplines. This book focuses on the very subject that was underplayed in
Stout's, Horgan's, and Bongar's books: the *psychoanalytic* views of *Islamic* terrorism. In this book, I shall often use the adjectives "fundamentalist" and "fanatical." The word "fundamentalist" originates in Protestant Christianity. Ironically,
over two decades ago, it was these very fundamentalist Christians who were waging a war of "holy terror" upon what most other Americans consider their fundamental liberties, values, and rights (Conway and Siegelman 1982). The word
"fundamentalist" has since been applied to Islam and to politics in the sense that
Webster's dictionary defines as "a movement or attitude stressing strict and
literal adherence to a set of basic principles." The word "fanatical" is defined
by *Webster's* as "marked by excessive enthusiasm and often intense uncritical
devotion." We shall see that in the case of Islamic terrorists, the two adjectives
often go together.

In the obsessive manner of many academic scholars, Rex Hudson sought to
classify terrorist groups, rather than explain their motives, as if by sorting them
into types he could somehow understand or explain them:

This study categorizes foreign terrorist groups under one of the following four des-
ignated, somewhat arbitrary typologies: nationalist-separatist, religious fundamentalist, new religious, and social revolutionary. This group classification is based on
the assumption that terrorist groups can be categorized by their political background or ideology. The social revolutionary category has also been labeled "idealist." Idealistic terrorists fight for a radical cause, a religious belief, or a political
ideology, including anarchism. Although some groups do not fit neatly into any
one category, the general typologies are important because all terrorist campaigns
are different, and the mindsets of groups within the same general category tend to
have more in common than those in different categories [...] *A fifth typology, for*
right-wing terrorists, is not listed because right-wing terrorists were not specifi-
cally designated as being a subject of this study. In any case, there does not appear
to be any significant rightwing group on the United States Department of State's
list of foreign terrorist organizations. Right-wing terrorists are discussed only
briefly in this paper (see Attributes of Terrorists). This is not to minimize the threat
of right-wing extremists in the United States, who clearly pose a significant terrorist
threat to United States security, as demonstrated by the Oklahoma City bombing on
April 19, 1995 (Hudson 1999, p. 18; italics added).

One of the world's leading experts on terrorism, Jessica Stern of the Kennedy School of Government at Harvard University, has also distinguished between many types of terrorists, many of whom she interviewed personally in daunting and dangerous circumstances (J. Stern 1999, 2003). Classification and categorization, however, cannot be a substitute for explanation and understanding. To truly understand the emotional origins of violent Islamic terror, we need to understand its unconscious psychological underpinning, such as the narcissistic rage that underlies the desperate act or the yearning for the love of Father Allah that fills the heart of the Islamic terrorist (R. Stein 2002). This is what this book is about. At the end of this book, we shall discuss in psychological detail the cases of Ramzi Yousef and Mohamed Atta.

Globalization and Islamic Terrorism

One of the "gods" or idols of our twenty-first century is globalization. The *Wikipedia* defines globalization as a process of increasing integration between "units" around the world, including nation-states, households, individuals, corporations, and other organizations. Most of us in the "West" believe that globalization is good for humanity, as it enhances the quality of life around the world. Others think that it mainly enhances the profits of multinational corporations. Some Muslim scholars believe that globalization has upset traditional Muslim society (Ahmed and Donnan 1994; Mohammadi and Saltford 2002; Ahmed 2003).

Globalization usually means the free movement of people, money, goods, and services across international borders. It is an umbrella term, covering economic, trade, social, technological, cultural, and political processes. Globalization also creates enormous economic, political, social, and psychological problems, all due to global corporate greed: the exploitation of child labor and cheap labor in the Third World, the uprooting of traditional societies, the destruction of forests and the pollution of the atmosphere, environmental pollution and global warming and climate change. In 2007, Al Gore and the Intergovernmental Panel on Climate Change shared the Nobel Peace Prize for their efforts to warn humanity against the perils of global warming. The Intergovernmental Panel on Climate Change was established in 1988 by the World Meteorological Organization and the United Nations Environment Program.

While the term "globalization" had been in use for some years, the German-born American-Jewish economist Theodore Levitt (1925–2006) was the first to use "globalization" in an economic context (Levitt 1983). Levitt thought that the new commercial reality of the 1980s was the emergence of global markets for standardized consumer products on a vast, previously unimaginable scale. He believed that technology, by making communication, transport, and travel available and affordable to the masses, drove the world toward a converging commonality. Well-managed companies have moved from customizing items for wealthy customers to offering globally standardized products that are advanced, functional, reliable, and low priced. They benefit from enormous economies of scale in production, distribution, marketing, and management (Levitt 1983). A proactive form of globalization is emerging, spawned by international corporations that wish to loosen trade restrictions. It is the global financial firms that have been the most eager proponents of this expansion. A group of advocates from different parts of the world had been pushing for an integrated global society as envisioned in the Globalist Manifesto which is the foundation of globalism ideology. Globalization is supposed to have shaken up the traditional Muslim world and put it under siege (Ahmed and Donnan 1994; Mohammadi and Saltford 2002; Ahmed 2003). Yet the idealist Globalist Manifesto, created in the Philippines, is a paean to peace and prosperity. It paints an idealized picture of our world. It is wishful thinking at its most glaring:

Someday, this world will be peaceful, united, educated and prosperous. There will be no war, no poverty, and no discrimination. A world able to protect itself from global warming, over consumption, nuclear disaster, pollution, acid rain, ozone layer depletion, and AIDS. A world that is able to practice sustainable development, protection of environment and responsible parenthood. There is a world future where there will be no national boundaries, no racial discrimination, nor religious fanaticism. Because every human being is a child of God, everyone is equally important and deserves to enjoy human rights, freedom, happiness and prosperity. The citizens of the world have the duty to act towards this vision, in wherever, whenever, and whatever they can within their status in life. As soon as possible, and through a democratic consensus of all nations via global plebiscite and a drafting of a global constitution through an international constitutional convention, the goal of the citizens of the world is to set up a single and unified global government with police powers, powers to tax, and has the power of eminent domain. This task is arduous and long, but there is no justification for any armed solution in pursuance of this vision. Diplomacy should be the only way. The global government will have judicial, executive, and legislative branches; a government-financed two-party system from the global presidency down to village level; with one monetary system, civil service system, electoral system and an economic system grounded on free enterprise. A global president, vice-president, a chamber of hereditary leaders and a chamber of territorial representatives will be popularly elected. The territorial divisions of the world will have governors, vice governors, and territorial representatives who will also be popularly elected. The cabinet heads of the global government and as well as that of the geographical divisions should come from the popularly elected representatives of the territorial divisions. The formation of the Global Government consists of ten stages: (1) Information drive and leveling-off using the Globalist Manifesto. (2) Formation of the critical mass of global advocates from every corner of the world. (3) Formation of the International Global

Government Organizing Committee. (4) International Convention to Draft the Global Constitution. (5) International Plebiscite on the Global Constitution. (6) Formation of the global two-party system. (7) Election of the Global President, Vice-President, Territorial Representatives, and International Council of Hereditary Leaders. (8) Appointment of the Global Cabinet from among the Territorial Representatives. (9) Formation of the Global Seat of Government, Armed Forces and Central Bank. (10) Managing the world towards lasting peace and prosperity. This manifesto should be advocated worldwide to kings, queens, heads of the states, heads of the government, diplomats, military leaders, educators, scientists, church leaders, business leaders, personalities, thinkers and everyone. Leaders from all over the world would advocate this vision and one of them should become the founding president of the global government with the rest as the founding fathers. You could be one of them (Various Web sites).

The Globalist Manifesto reminds one of the Communist Manifesto of 1848, and of how communism became one of the world's most tyrannical political systems. Not surprisingly, perhaps, the Globalist Manifesto emerged in third-world Asia, in the classroom of a Master of Development Management class at the Center for Development Management of the Asian Institute of Management, one of the leading business graduate schools in the Filipino town of Makati City. The manifesto was secretly posted in the class bulletin board without the permission of the professor and drew lots of violent reactions. Some compared it to the vision of the Beatles, the popular British singing band in the 1960s. The manifesto was adopted by the class and was published on their Web site in 2003. With the help of Dean Poch Macaranas and Associate Dean Edel Guiza of the Center for Development Management, the Asian Institute of Management class spearheaded the formation of the International Movement of Development Managers.

The Globalist Manifesto movement serves two official functions: it is the alumni association of the Asian Institute of Management's graduates from all over the world who took the Master of Development Management program, and it is also an independent global network, doing economic projects for many global firms. But its chief function, in my view, is psychological: like Bertrand Russell's idealized vision of World Government (Russell 1961), it paints a rosy picture of what human life could be like on our planet, denying the enormous problems that globalization has created and that human nature and the human family contain within them.

The emergence of the "anti-globalization" movement is a testimony to this rosy denial. According to the *Wikipedia,* the term "anti-globalization" is commonly ascribed to the political stance of people and groups who oppose globalization in its current form. "Anti-globalization" is considered by many to be a social movement, while others consider it to be an umbrella term that encompasses a number of separate social movements. In either case, participants are united in opposition to the political power of large global corporations, as exercised in trade agreements and elsewhere, which they say undermines the environment, labor rights, national sovereignty, the third world, Islam, and other concerns. Most of the people who are labeled "anti-globalization," however, reject this term, preferring to describe themselves as members of the Global Justice Movement, the World Social Forum, the "alter-globalization" movement and a number of other terms.

The twenty-first-century conflict between the globalization and the "alter" globalization movements reminds one of the twentieth-century one between socialism and capitalism. It has the psychological flavor of inter-generational and class conflict, of individualistic antiestablishment people fighting the establishment. The anti-globalization movement has staged protest demonstrations at the meetings of establishment institutions like the World Economic Forum, the World Trade Organization, the World Bank, the International Monetary Fund, and the G8, among others. The World Social Forum is an annual meeting held in January of each year by members of the anti-globalization movement to coordinate world campaigns, share and refine organizing strategies, and inform each other about movements from around the world and their issues. It meets in January because that is when its "great capitalist rival," the World Economic Forum, meets in Davos, Switzerland, because of the logistic difficulty of organizing a mass protest in Davos, and in order to try to overshadow the coverage of the World Economic Forum in the world's mass communication media. We shall further discuss the difficult relationship between globalization and Islamic terrorism below.

The World Trade Center Tragedy

On September 11, 2001, a horrific mass murder of thousands of innocent people was committed by a group of fanatical Islamic suicide murderers, led by Mohamed Atta, in the United States. This horror is referred to as "9/11." That morning, the nineteen Islamic terrorists affiliated with *al-Qaïda* hijacked four commercial U.S. passenger jet airliners. Each team of hijackers included a trained pilot, who had ironically been trained in the United States. The hijackers crashed American Airlines Flight 11 and United Airlines Flight 175 into the Twin Towers of the World Trade Center in New York City. One tower collapsed within an hour of being hit, followed shortly thereafter by the other. A third airliner, American Airlines Flight 77, crashed into the Pentagon building in Arlington County, Virginia. Some passengers and flight crew members on the fourth aircraft, United Airlines Flight 93, attempted to retake control of their plane from the hijackers; that plane crashed into a field near the town of Shanksville in rural Somerset County, Pennsylvania. In addition to the nineteen hijackers, almost *three thousand people died;* another twenty-four were missing and presumed dead.

The formerly unthinkable tragedy became a frightening reality. One scholar wrote that "The violence of the attacks against the Twin Towers and the Pentagon has revealed an abyss of terror that is going to haunt our existence and thinking for years and perhaps decades to come" (Borradori 2003, p. 21). Others thought that "All acts of terrorism make the commonplace unsafe, unreliable [...] When ordinary reality can no longer be relied on to be only what it seems, it becomes uncanny [...] The boundaries between real and unreal falter when the unthinkable happens" (Coates et al. 2003, pp. 25–26).

The Swiss-American-Jewish psychoanalyst Leon Wurmser believed that hatred and anxiety underlay the tragedy:

> The terrorist acts of 9/11 [September 11, 2001] (and similar ones all over the globe) reveal depths of hatred and hint at buried, but *virulent anxiety in the perpetrators* that originate in personal, societal, cultural, and historical humiliation and shame, and a loss of self-respect and dignity. The aggression unleashed is ascribed to varied external motives, but at the same time *the resentment is an inner force of enormous destructivity,* as if to cry out, "Injustice has been done to us. We are the victims. Everything is permissible to redress the balance of justice" (Wurmser 2004, p. 912; italics added).

Wurmser's "resentment" is an understatement for "narcissistic rage."

Helping the traumatized survivors and other victims of the tragedy in psychotherapy and psychoanalysis has not been easy either: "Terror has the potential to induce, in both partners of the analytic dyad, primitive affective states" (Cancelmo et al. 2003, p. 9). Some scholars thought that "one can begin to think of trauma and human relatedness as inversely related terms. The greater the strength of the human bonds that connect an individual to others, and the more those bonds are accessible in times of danger, the less likely it is that an individual will be severely traumatized and the more likely it is that he or she may recover afterward" (Coates et al. 2003, pp. 3–4).

In Europe and the rest of the world, however, there were not only cries of horror and sympathy for America but also some expressions of joy and delight at America's "downfall." The Israeli scholar Dan Diner thought that "America is a counter-world to Europe" and thus serves as a projection screen for all those images and metaphors that are the opposites of the European self-image, specifically for "the dark sides of modernity." It is this "anti-modernistic reaction formation" that is now gripping large parts of traditional societies caught up in "globalization." Already at the time of the Enlightenment, there were "fantasy formations of decay coming from America" (Diner 2002, pp. 16–18).

There were, therefore, apart from expressions of horror, compassion, and solidarity, worldwide reactions of *Schadenfreude* to the catastrophe of *9/11:* "America is guilty, America has been punished—for its crimes, for its riches, for its 'way of life' [...]" (Diner 2002, p. 164). Prominent representatives of European culture expressed their "amazing joy in view of the destruction of the superpower, or more exactly: in view of its self destruction, of its suicide as work of art." So wrote the French scholar Jean Baudrillard (1929–2007) in *Der Spiegel.* After describing the catastrophe in "poetic" words, Sibylle Tönnies added that "this image evokes a majestic feeling," while the German composer Karlheinz Stockhausen (1928–2007) celebrated it as the "greatest work of art" ever (Wurmser 2004, pp. 919–920).

The Northern Irish Liberal Democratic politician John Thomas Alderdice (born 1955) was trained as a psychiatrist and psychotherapist, served as Speaker of the Ulster parliament, and is now Lord Alderdice of Knock in the British House of Lords. He thought that Islamic terrorists "see themselves as righting some terrible wrong, some humiliation, some deep disrespect that has been done [to] them, their community or their nation and they in their weakness are, with great courage and risks to themselves, embarked on the heroic task of righting that wrong" (Cancelmo et al. 2003, p. 14). This echoes Heinz Kohut's definition of narcissistic rage as "The need for revenge, for righting a wrong, for undoing a hurt by whatever means, and a deeply anchored, unrelenting compulsion in the pursuit of all these aims, which gives no rest to those who have suffered a narcissistic injury" and with Marvin Zonis's ideas on the same subject.

The terrorism expert Jessica Stern, who had interviewed religious terrorists all over the world, also found that rage at past humiliations was the key emotional factor in religious terrorist behavior:

> My interviews suggest that people join religious terrorist groups partly to transform themselves and to simplify life. *They start out feeling humiliated, enraged* that they are viewed by some Other as second class. They take on new identities as martyrs on behalf of a purported spiritual cause [. . .] *they enter a kind of trance, where the world is divided neatly between good and evil, victim and oppressor* [. . .] a sense of transcendence is one of many attractions of religious violence for terrorists, beyond the appeal of achieving their goals (J. Stern 2003, pp. 281–282; italics added).

The "trance" mentioned by Stern is the result of the unconscious *splitting* mechanism so well known to psychoanalysts.

Stern believed that terrorists are powerfully attracted by the seemingly absurd "appeal of purifying the world through murder" (Stern 2003, p. xxix). The psychoanalyst Leon Wurmser agreed with her that "Conflicts about values and authority, about guilt and shame, about the sense of justice and injustice—superego issues— go through the studies on terrorism like a red thread. As in Greek tragedy, *a single value is pursued to the exclusion of everything else,* especially empathy, thereby eliminating all moral ambiguities and dehumanizing the adversary—all in the service of an ideal: 'the appeal of purifying the world through murder.'" (Wurmser 2004, p. 918).

The Swiss psychoanalyst Arno Gruen thought that "behind all terrorism and violence stands *an inner emptiness* because no identity could be formed which would have been rooted in compassion and the sensibility for his own pain and the pain of the other. Instead of such a fundament, an identity structure arises that is based solely on identifications with authorities and obedience" (Gruen 2002, pp. 137–138, translated from German into English and quoted in Wurmser 2004, p. 918). Leon Wurmser added that

> The loveless and cruel attitude of caregivers is being taken over by the child. What is his own is being split off as something foreign. Instead, *revenge is taken on the supposed weakness of the other* (their pain, their tenderness, their femininity, their affects altogether), *which basically is one's own weakness. Violence becomes a source of feeling alive.* Albert Speer described the greedy, even delirious joy with which Hitler watched movies of the burning London, of the firestorm over Warsaw, and of exploding convoys and grew ecstatic imagining the cataclysm of New York (Wurmser 2004, p. 918; italics added).

The Muslim Brotherhood and Al-Qaïda

Before examining other psychoanalytic theories of terrorism, let us take a look at the history of the Muslim Brotherhood, and of Osama bin Laden and his *al-Qaïda* organization, the perpetrators of the *9/11* (September 11, 2001) tragedy. People in the "West" are not always knowledgeable about these two groups, and often have misconceptions which are furthered by the mass communication media.

While we call a suicide murderer a "terrorist," fanatical Muslims see him as a *shaheed* (martyr) for the glory of Allah and Islam. *Al-Qaïda* is neither the first nor the only Islamic organization fighting "Western influence, domination, colonialism, imperialism and exploitation." Its spiritual parent may be the Muslim Brotherhood, a worldwide Islamist movement founded in 1928 by the Egyptian social and political reformer Hassan al-Banna, which has spawned several religious and political organizations in the Middle East dedicated to the credo: "Allah is our objective, the *Qur'an* is our Constitution, the Prophet [Muhammad] is our leader, *jihad* is our way, and death for the sake of Allah is the highest of our aspirations." As stated on its charter and its Web site, the Muslim Brotherhood believes in the existence of the global Muslim *ummah* or nation (an Arabic word derived from *umm* meaning "mother"), and seeks to install an Islamic *khilafah* or caliphate (the religious-political government of the nation of Islam) across the Muslim world (or the whole world, as some say) through stages designed to Islamicize targeted Muslim-majority nations by all lawful means available.

Since its inception in 1928 in Egypt, and throughout the world, except in few places like Israel and its "Occupied Palestinian Territories," the Muslim Brotherhood has ostensibly given up violence and adopted political means to achieve its goals. This position has caused disputes within the movement, which have led to the formation of more radical groups such as the *al-Gama'a al-Islamiyya* (the Islamic Group) and *al-Takfir w'al Hijra* (Excommunication and Migration). The fiery young Osama bin Laden, while studying at a Saudi university, was impressed by professors with strong ties to the Muslim Brotherhood but disagreed with their nonviolence. Among its members was Muhammad al-Qutb (often anglicized as Kuttub), an Egyptian Muslim scholar who wrote dozens of books in Arabic about Islam and then fled to Saudi Arabia, where he became a professor of Islamic studies (Qutb 1968).

Muhammad al-Qutb's elder brother, Sayyid al-Qutb (1903–1966), wrote one of the Muslim Brotherhood's key tracts about *jihad* (Qutb 1953, 1977, 2006). A "Western" writer has called Sayyid al-Qutb "the philosopher of Islamic terror" (Berman 2003). Following traditional Muslim thinking, Sayyid al-Qutb called the pre-Islamic history of the Arabs the *jahiliyyah* or "dark ages," believing that the Arabs had lived in ignorance before Islam. Al-Qutb thought that the Muslim world had reverted to the *jahiliyyah* because it had abandoned the traditional Muslim *Shari'a* law. Consequently, all the states of the Muslim world that are not Islamic are illegitimate, including his native Egypt (*Wikipedia* article on Sayyid Qutb).

Sayyid al-Qutb wrote that rather than rule by a pious few or through democratic representation the Muslims should resist any system where men obey other men as un-Islamic and a violation of the *hakamiyya* or Allah's sovereignty. A truly Islamic polity would have no rulers, not even theocratic ones, since Muslims would need neither judges nor police to obey Allah's law. The way to bring about this freedom was for a revolutionary vanguard to fight the new *jahiliyyah* with a twofold approach: preaching, and abolishing the organizations and authorities of the current benighted system by "physical power and *jihad*." For his pains, Sayyid al-Qutb was arrested, given a show trial, and hanged in 1966 along with six other Muslim Brothers (*Wikipedia* article on Sayyid Qutb).

The Arabic word *jihad* originally meant "struggle," a personal struggle in devotion to Islam, especially involving spiritual discipline. It later became a synonym for a holy war waged on behalf of Islam as a religious duty. The idea and practice of "holy war" has been around for thousands of years before Islam in various religions. The ancient Israelites had a religious duty to make a genocidal war on the Amalekites. Many nations and religions have waged "holy wars" against those who believed in other gods or other social or political ideologies. In the Middle Ages, the Crusaders waged "holy wars" to liberate "the holy city of Jerusalem" and the "Holy Sepulcher" of Jesus Christ from the "Saracens," while the Muslims waged a *jihad* against the "Franks" and defeated them in 1187 at the Battle of Hattin, led by the Kurdish Muslim Sultan "Saladin" (Salah-ed-din al-Tikriti, 1137–1193), who, according to the Muslim chronicler Imad ad-Din al-Isfahani, who witnessed the scene, personally executed the Crusader leader Raynald de Chastillon. *Jihad* began in the seventh century of the Christian era as the Prophet Muhammad and the Qur'an enjoined all Muslims to *jihad* against the infidel (Bunyan 1752; Cheragh 1977; Dietl 1983, 1984; Laffin 1988; Hiro 1989; Von Rad 1991; J.T. Johnson 1997; P.L. Bergen 2001; New 2002).

The Muslim Brotherhood advocates the creation of a worldwide Islamic government, believing that Allah has set out a perfect way of life and social organization for all mankind in the Qur'an. It expresses its interpretation of Islam through a strict religious approach to social issues such as the role of women, but also believes that Islam enjoins man to strive for social justice, the eradication of poverty and corruption, and political freedoms as defined by the Islamic state. It has previously been and continues to be strongly opposed to colonialism, and was an important actor in the struggle against Western military and economic domination in Egypt and other Muslim nations during the early twentieth century. Their fantastic goal as stated by Hassan al-Banna was the doctrine of reclaiming Islam's manifest destiny: a Muslim caliphate, founded in the seventh century, that stretched from Spain to Indonesia.

The Muslim Brotherhood is one of the most influential movements in the Islamic world, and especially in the Arab world. The first Muslim Brotherhood was founded in Egypt by Hassan al-Banna in 1928, and Egypt is still considered the center of the movement; it is generally weaker in the Maghreb, or North Africa, than in the Middle East. Muslim Brotherhood branches form the main opposition to the governments in several countries in the Arab world, such as Egypt, Syria, and Jordan, and they are politically active to some extent in nearly every Muslim country. There are also "diaspora" branches in several nations in Europe and the United States, composed of Muslim immigrants previously active in the Brotherhood in their home countries.

In 1947 the United Nations General Assembly decided to partition Palestine between its Jews and its Arabs. The Jews were happy, but the angry Arabs rejected the UN Partition Plan out of hand. In 1948 the Palestinian Jews and Arabs fought a long and terrible war in which 10 percent of the small Palestinian Jewish population was killed and hundreds of thousands of Palestinian Arabs became refugees. The common Israeli version of this war (which Israelis call "the war of independence," "the war of uprightness," or "the war of liberation") is that the Palestinian Arabs left the country of their own volition. Most Arab historians and some Israeli ones claim that they were expelled. One "new Israeli historian" used the term "ethnic cleansing" about what his countrymen had done to the Palestinian Arabs in 1948 (Pappe 2006). This term, however, only became current in the 1990s, during the Bosnian war. During the war of 1939–1945, millions of people had been expelled from several European countries, and in 1948 expelling people from their homes during war was still common practice. The Israeli-born British historian Efraim Karsh claimed that Pappe and his colleagues had been "fabricating history" (Karsh 1997; cf. Falk 2004).

Between 1948 and 1949, shortly after the Muslim Brotherhood sent its volunteers to fight Israel in the war in Palestine, the conflict between the Egyptian monarchy of King Farouk (1920–1965) and the Muslim Brotherhood reached its climax. Concerned with the increasing assertiveness and popularity of the Brotherhood, as well as with rumors that it was plotting a coup, Prime Minister Nuqrashi Pasha disbanded the Muslim Brotherhood in December 1948. The organization's assets were impounded and scores of its members sent to jail. Less than three weeks later, the prime minister was assassinated by a member of the Brotherhood. This in turn prompted the murder of Hassan al-Banna himself, presumably by a government agent, in February 1949, when al-Banna was only forty-three years old and at the height of his career. King Farouk died of overeating at the age of 45.

The movement is immensely influential in many Muslim countries, and where legally possible, it often operates important networks of Islamic charities, guaranteeing it a support base among Muslim poor. However, most of the countries where the Muslim Brotherhood is active are ruled by undemocratic regimes. As a consequence, the movement is banned in several Arab nations, including Egypt, and the lack of a democratic system prevents it from gaining power through elections. Contrary to popular belief in the West, and unlike *al-Qaïda,* the Muslim Brotherhood normally does *not* pursue its goals through acts of violence or terror. However, the Brotherhood has advocated *jihad* and martyrdom to fight Israel and Zionism. The Brotherhood views militant acts and suicide bombings by the Palestinian Arab Islamic group *Hamas* (an acronym for the Arabic words *Harakat al-Muqawama al-Islamiyya* meaning Islamic Resistance Movement, which also means Zeal) as a legitimate struggle against Israel, despite its targeting of Israeli civilians (Boulby 1999).

The Muslim Brotherhood's writings in the Arab world and in the United States have argued that the murderous *9/11* (September 11, 2001) attacks were a proper response to murderous United States actions in the world. In the United States, the European Union, and throughout the Arab world, the Muslim Brotherhood is often regarded by experts as the source of modern jihadist terrorism. In 2005, the Arab columnist and former Kuwaiti official Dr. Ahmad al-Rabi wrote that "the beginnings of all of the religious terrorism that we are witnessing today were in the Muslim Brotherhood's ideology." The group is financed by contributions from its members who are required to allocate portion of their income to the movement. Most of these contributions come from members living in oil-rich countries, such as Saudi Arabia.

The Arabic word *al-Qaïda* (also rendered as *al-Qaeda*) has several different meanings, including "the law," "the foundation," and "the base." *Al-Qaïda* is an armed Sunni Islamist terror organization with the openly stated objective of eliminating all foreign and "infidel" influence in all the Muslim countries, and, like the Muslim Brotherhood, reestablishing the Muslim caliphate. Some of the most prominent members of *al-Qaïda* are adherents of Wahhabism or Salafism, two extreme, militant and fanatical sects of Islam.

Wahhabism is named after its Arabian founder, Muhammad ibn Abd-al-Wahhab (1703–1792), who reintroduced *Shari'a* law to the Arabian peninsula, and was influenced by the writings of the Muslim scholars Ahmad ibn Hanbal and Ibn Taymiyya (1263–1328). Wahhabism is the dominant form of Islam in Saudi Arabia, Kuwait, and Qatar, as well as in parts of Somalia, Algeria, and Mauritania. The term *Wahhabi* is rarely used by the people it refers to, who prefer the name *Salafi* from Salaf as-Salih, the "pious predecessors" as earlier propagated mainly by Ibn Taymiyya, his students Ibn Al Qayyim al-Jawziyya, and later by Muhammad ibn Abd-al-Wahhab and his followers. Wahhabism is among the most conservative forms of Islam. Others have described the doctrine as inspiring violence and intolerance.

While Osama bin Laden, who, for all we know, may be dead, is recognized as *al-Qaïda*'s leader, the group's operations are decentralized, and many independent and collaborative *al-Qaïda* cells exist in multiple countries linked by a common cause: fighting the hated "infidel" and bringing back the rule of Islam as it was in its days of glory. Osama bin Laden's *al-Qaïda* has been linked to multiple acts of terrorism against U.S. interests in many countries. It is officially designated as a terrorist organization in the United States, the United Kingdom, Canada, and Australia. In my psychobiographical study of Osama bin Laden, I have shown that his hatred for "America" is linked to his narcissistic rage at his mother, who abandoned him at an early age (Falk 2001b).

A State of Denial

On July 10, 2001, two months before the *9/11* tragedy, George John Tenet (born 1953), the director of the United States Central Intelligence Agency, and his counterterrorism chief, Joseph Cofer Black (born 1950), met with Dr. Condoleezza Rice (born 1954), President Bush's National Security Adviser, to warn her of mounting intelligence about an impending terrorist attack on the United States. Tenet claimed that his assistant "Rich B." had predicted a "spectacular" terrorist attack against U.S. interests "in the coming weeks or months" and added that "Multiple and simultaneous attacks are possible." After the meeting, "Rich and Cofer congratulated each other," feeling that at last the CIA had gotten the full attention of the administration, and at a CIA update in late July, "Rich" dramatically predicted, "They're coming here!" Rice, however, gave the CIA officials "the brush-off," denying the vital importance of their intelligence for U.S. security. Five years later Dr. Rice denied former U.S. President Bill Clinton's allegations that the Bush administration had failed to pursue counterterrorism measures aggressively before "9/11" (Woodward 2006b; Tenet and Harlow 2007, pp. 145, 149, 150–153, 158).

Most Americans and many other people around the world, especially in the "West," were excited, even euphoric, when U.S. President George W. Bush announced the "global war on terror" less than nine months after "9/11." Bush had angrily announced, "I will not forget this wound to our country, or those who inflicted it. I will not yield. I will not rest. I will not relent in waging this struggle for the freedom and security of the American people." This war has also been called the "global war on terrorism," "war on global terrorism," "war on terrorism," and "battle against terrorism."

The officially stated goals of the "global war on terror" include preventing those groups identified as "terrorist" by the United States (largely focused on militant Islamist groups such as *al-Qaïda* and its affiliates) from carrying out attacks and posing a threat to America and its allies; "spreading freedom" and liberal democracy; and putting an end to state sponsorship of terrorism in so-called "rogue states" and "failed states," beginning with Operation Active Endeavor, NATO's response to the terrorist trafficking of weapons. It was followed with the 2001 American overthrow of the Taliban government in Afghanistan, which had sheltered elements of *al-Qaïda* and its leader, Osama bin Laden, and later with the U.S. invasion of Iraq and the overthrow of Saddam Hussein.

The American general Wesley Kanne Clark (born 1944), a former NATO commander, however, thought that the Bush administration was so focused on winning the war in Afghanistan and Iraq that it made inadequate preparations for occupation and reconstruction (Clark 2003). Clark argued that the administration had refused to seek legitimacy from the United Nations and NATO, or to build on the international sympathy manifested immediately after September 11, 2001. The unhappy result, Clark believed, had been a loss of focus on what he called the "real war" against terrorism, a neglect of U.S. domestic security, and an unwise concentration on preemptively challenging purportedly hostile states like Iran, Syria, and North Korea. The unfortunate practical consequences, Clark wrote, included a series of wasted opportunities in Afghanistan, a quagmire in Iraq, and the increasing isolation of a United States that uses war as a first option instead of a last resort. Clark called for a return to international cooperation combined with greater emphasis on a sound economy.

Richard Alan Clarke (born 1951), a former advisor on terrorism to four U.S. presidents, resigned from President George W. Bush's Senior Executive Service in 2003 to write his book on his former bosses' failure to deal with terror effectively. In early 2001, Clarke had sent a memo to Condoleezza Rice, Bush's National Security Advisor, with an urgent request for a meeting of the National Security Council's Principals Committee to discuss the growing *al-Qaïda* threat in the greater Middle East, as well as offering new strategies for combating *al-Qaïda* that might be adopted by Bush's new administration. Clarke later claimed that nothing was done about his memo. As we have seen, Rice similarly dismissed the CIA's warnings on July 10, 2001.

On March 24, 2004, Clarke began an exhausting twenty-hour testimony before the National Commission on Terrorist Attacks upon the United States, the official U.S. Commission investigating the tragic events of September 11, 2001 (Clarke 2004; Kean et al. 2004). Clarke claimed that on the day after the tragedy occurred, Bush had pressed him to assert that Saddam Hussein of Iraq had been in cahoots with *al-Qaïda,* which was not true. According to the Commission, Clarke had given the final okay for the members of the Bin Laden family living in the United States to leave the country and fly to Saudi Arabia on September 14, 2001, a request that had originated with the Saudi embassy. During the hearing, Clarke told the Commission that he did not know who within the Bush administration had formally presented the request to him. When pressed on this point, he said that it had either come from the State Department or from the Office of the White House Chief of Staff.

Clarke allegedly lied to the 9/11 Commission, saying that once the request came to him he refused to approve it, referring it to the United States Federal Bureau of Investigation. However, he later admitted that he alone had authorized the flight, telling reporters, "I take responsibility for it. I don't think it was a mistake, and I'd do it again." His testimony aroused great controversy. Conservatives within and without the Bush administration began a campaign of character assassination, vigorously attacking both Clarke's testimony and his tenor during the hearings. Some of the families of the September 11, 2001 victims supported Clarke, while others felt that he was self-aggrandizing and that his criticisms were misplaced. In an "Open Letter to America," one group of victim-family members accused Clarke of "politicizing 9/11 and further dividing America."

Michael Scheuer, the former head of the "Bin Laden Issue Station" at the United States Central Intelligence Agency, contradicted Clarke's testimony. When asked to respond to Clarke's claim that Scheuer was "a hothead, a middle manager who really didn't go to any of the cabinet meetings," Scheuer replied, "I certainly agree with the fact that I didn't go to the cabinet meetings. But I'm certainly also aware that I'm much better informed than Mr. Clarke ever was about the nature of the intelligence that was available against Osama bin Laden and which was consistently denigrated by himself and Mr. [George] Tenet [the former CIA chief]." Scheuer claimed that Clarke's "risk aversion and politicking" had hurt the U.S. hunt for Bin Laden prior to September 11, 2001. He asserted that he and his team had provided information on *ten different occasions* that could have led to the capture or death of Osama bin Laden, but that his recommendations to act upon the information had been turned down by Clarke and other senior intelligence officials. Despite this heated exchange, Scheuer agreed with Clarke, however, that the invasion of Iraq was a serious diversion from the war against *al-Qaïda.*

Robert Upshur Woodward (born 1943) is a well-known and respected American journalist, now the assistant managing editor of *The Washington Post.* In 1972 the young Bob Woodward and his colleague Carl Bernstein exposed the Watergate break-in scandal, a journalistic coup that led to Richard M. Nixon's resignation as president of the United States. After 2001, as U.S. President George W. Bush conducted his "global war on terror," Woodward believed that the Bush administration was denying the realities of Islamic terror (Woodward 2002, 2004, 2006b). For instance, in May 2006, based on information gathered by its Defense Intelligence Agency, the United States Department of Defense, also known as the Pentagon for the shape of its building, secretly informed the White House that "insurgents and terrorists retain the resources and capabilities to sustain and even increase current level of violence through the next year." The Pentagon predicted a more violent year in Iraq, contradicting the rosy statements of President Bush himself: only two days earlier, Bush had said that the

United States was at a "turning point" that history would mark as the time that "the forces of terror began their long retreat" (Woodward 2006b).

Woodward thought that through its "state of denial" the Bush administration had avoided telling the American public and Congress—and above all itself—the painful truth about its war in Iraq. Just two days after its secret report to the White House, the Pentagon told Congress that the "appeal and motivation for continued violent action will begin to wane in early 2007"—an obvious lie in view of its report to the White House. One of the chief deniers was the United States Secretary of Defense, Donald Henry Rumsfeld (born 1932), the architect of the Iraq tragedy, who in 2003, before the invasion of Iraq, had predicted a quick and easy victory. Andrew Hill Card (born 1947), the White House chief of staff, with the indirect support of other high administration officials, vainly tried for eighteen months to get Rumsfeld replaced. President Bush and Vice President Cheney refused (Woodward 2006b). Rumsfeld finally resigned in late 2006. At a press conference announcing the resignation and the nomination of Robert Gates to replace Rumsfeld, President Bush stated, "America is safer and the world is more secure because of the service and the leadership of Donald Rumsfeld."

In early 2005, at the beginning of Bush's second term as president, Stephen John Hadley (born 1947), who replaced Condoleezza Rice as Bush's national security adviser, had given the administration a "D" grade on implementing its own policies. In a secret report to Dr. Rice, the new Secretary of State, her counselor Philip D. Zelikow stated that, nearly two years after the invasion, Iraq was a "failed state." At Cheney's and Rumsfeld's urging, Henry Kissinger, the former Secretary of State under President Nixon, who was still haunted by his loss in Vietnam, became the most frequent visitor and Iraq adviser to President Bush, a hidden but potent voice in favor of the Iraq war.

Rumsfeld himself believed that the system of coordination among departments and agencies in the Bush administration was broken. In a secret memo of May 1, 2006, he stated, "the current system of government makes competence next to impossible." Woodward sought to answer what he saw as the core questions about the "global war on terror": What happened after the invasion of Iraq? Why? How did President Bush make decisions and manage a war that he chose to define his presidency? Was there an achievable plan for victory? Woodward's book covered President Bush's war-making from the first days that George W. Bush thought seriously about running for president through the recruitment of his national security team, the war in Afghanistan, the invasion and occupation of Iraq, and the struggle for political survival in the second term. As the title of his book implied, Woodward thought that, without knowing it, President Bush and his administration were in persistent and dangerous denial of reality, and that this denial would lead to catastrophe.

The Japanese-American journalist Michiko Kakutani thought that Woodward's unflattering portrait of George W. Bush in *State of Denial* was in stark contrast to "the laudatory one" that Woodward had drawn in *Bush at War* "which depicted the president—in terms that the White House press office itself has pur-veyed—as a judicious, resolute leader, blessed with the 'vision thing' [that] his father was accused of lacking and firmly in control of the ship of state" (Kakutani 2006, p. 1). Kakutani also believed that Woodward's ideas were not original. "Mr. Woodward's portrait of Mr. Bush as a prisoner of his own certitude owes a serious debt to [...] Ron Suskind [Suskind 2004], just as his portrait of the Pentagon's incompetent management of the war and occupation owes a seri-ous debt to Thomas E. Ricks [...] [Ricks 2006]. Other disclosures recapitulate information contained in books and articles by other journalists and former administration insiders" (Kakutani 2006, p. 2).

Woodward had a point, though. Bush's government is indeed denying the tragic reality of Islamic terror. The "global war on terror" is far from successful, to put it mildly. In late 2006, in the United States, the official bipartisan Iraq Study Group, led by the Republican former Secretary of State James Baker and by the Democratic leader Lee Herbert Hamilton, the president and director of the Woodrow Wilson International Center for Scholars and a member of the U.S. President's Homeland Security Advisory Council, made seventy-nine rec-ommendations to U.S. President George W. Bush, counseling a phased with-drawal from Iraq (Baker et al. 2006). Bush rejected them. Instead, in early 2007, he announced a "surge" of twenty thousand U.S. soldiers into Iraq, yet another unwise and tragic gamble. The popular general David Howell Petraeus (born 1952) was placed at the head of the new war effort. By that time, terrorist and "insurgent" attacks in Iraq were taking hundreds of lives daily. Critics of the "global war on terror" cite a long list of failures and damages: the exploita-tion of the "war" by the U.S. and other governments to pursue their long-standing geopolitical objectives, the reduction of civil liberties, the infringement on human rights, the misuse and obfuscation of language, the "crusading" war on Islam, the waging of a perpetual war, and many others.

The Futile and Tragic "Global War on Terror"

U.S. politics is usually divided into left-wing "liberal" Democrats and right-wing "conservative" Republicans. The name "neoconservatism" designates a popular right-wing American political grouping that includes both Republicans and Democrats (Muravchik 2007). Before the "surge" in the U.S. war in Iraq, American neoconservatives such as former United States Army Vice Chief of Staff General Jack Keane and the "military analyst" Frederick Kagan had been pushing for a "surge" for four years (Kristol 2007). Other American neoconservatives like David Frum (a former speech writer for U.S. President George W. Bush who had coined the phrase "axis of evil" for his boss) and Richard Norman Perle (a former United States Assistant Secretary of Defense) believed that the "war on terror" could be won with "a new commitment to security at home, a new audacity in our strategy abroad, and a new boldness in the advocacy of American ideals" (Frum and Perle 2003). The authors voiced strong support for President Bush's policies and initiatives, including the wars in Afghanistan and Iraq, and for his policy of preemptive strikes where there is a perceived threat.

Frum and Perle called for a more vigilant "self-policed" America, the use of national identity cards, unwavering support for Israel, a hard line with Iran, Libya, Syria, and Saudi Arabia, and indifference toward European governments that stand in our way. Their plan, described "with all the subtlety of a pit bull on steroids" (Kakutani 2004), called for the United States to forcefully overthrow the government of Iran, abandon support of a Palestinian state, blockade North Korea, use strong-arm tactics with China, disregard Europe as its ally, and sever ties with

Saudi Arabia. They called for a reform of the U.S. bureaucracy that had failed on September 11, 2001 and for a better enforcement of existing immigration laws.

In fact, the "neoconservative" Frum and Perle had little new to say. Most of their opinions and arguments had been debated daily in the U.S. mass communication media. They were highly partisan, treating former President Bill Clinton with contempt and George W. Bush with adulation. Four years later, even though their ideas were adopted, the "global war on terror" seems to have failed, and the experts on security and terrorism are ominously predicting worse to come (Williams 2004, 2005, 2006, 2007; Benjamin and Simon 2005). Even the American arch-conservative Patrick Buchanan thought that Frum and Perle's plan was a prescription for endless war (Buchanan 2004). Another perceptive reviewer wrote, "The authors are fond of hinting that 'most Americans' are unflinching, heroic opponents of evil like themselves. But I doubt that most Americans really want to inhabit the America—and the world—depicted here. Fighting an intelligent war on terror is one thing. But when you think about it, the endless, obsessive, solitary war they recommend looks strangely self-destructive—almost, one might say, like the mission of a suicide bomber" (Kamiya 2004).

In stark contrast to Frum and Perle, the Arab-American scholar Rashid Khalidi saw the U.S. and Israeli "war on terror" as a "terrorism trap" designed to avert attention from "the Palestinian and Lebanese struggle for freedom" (Khalidi 2006). The American statesmen James Baker and Lee Hamilton, as well as several respected American scholars, have pointed out the psychological futility of the "war on terror" and suggested alternatives to it. The American national security expert Michael Mazarr, now with the National War College, had this to say:

> [...] there is an inherently psychological character to the war on terrorism that remains poorly appreciated: The security threats the United States faces today have everything to do with the pressures of modernity and globalization, the diaphanous character of identity, the burden of choice, and the vulnerability of the alienated. That is not all that they have to do with, and the influence of psychological factors lies in a larger context of socioeconomic, cultural, demographic, and other realities. Yet those material issues become most relevant, and most dangerous, when they are breathing life into latent psychological distress (Mazarr 2004).

Quoting the American scholar Thomas W. Simons, an expert in Eurasian and Islamic studies, Mazarr suggested an "effective alternative" to the unsuccessful "global war on terror": offer the Muslims a new, alternative psychological identity in the modern world, one that combines Islam with modernity:

> The alternative to a largely military response—the alternative, in fact, to a "war" so named—is a strategy that lays engagement alongside deterrence, human development alongside special operations, multicultural outreach alongside border controls, and, most of all, positive identity entrepreneurs alongside [anti-] terrorist ones. It is a strategy that takes seriously the larger, more dangerous phenomenon of which extremist terrorism is merely a hint of what could come. *It is a strategy, as Thomas Simons has written, that takes as its centerpiece the strengthening and*

encouragement of the numerous and varied elements in the Islamic world trying to find a comfortable synthesis of modernity and Islam. "It may now be possible to break the linkage of modernity with Western domination that has afflicted the Islamic world for nearly two centuries," Simons suggests. "It may now be possible at last for Muslims to shape for themselves a modernity that is consonant with Islamic belief and Islamic authenticity [...] [S]uch syntheses of what is modern and what is Islamic are possible and achievable." They are, as well, the keys to a successful, truly strategic response to September 11 (Mazarr 2004, quoting Simons 2003; italics added).

Mazarr understood that the way the "war on terror" was conducted was self-defeating and was not achieving its intended results:

> A psychologically inspired war on terrorism would address the need for reform in a number of key countries, allied and otherwise—and address it seriously, directly, and in conversation with reformers in those nations. It would, inevitably, make efforts—knowing that they will be pinpricks, drops in the ocean—to substantially expand United States foreign assistance programs in the region by a factor of, let's say, 10 to 20. Every home, hospital, school, or farm built with American aid dollars will work its effect on the minds of a few, and perhaps more. Every young person drawn into hope for a better life and away from the temptation to terrorism will count as a victory of sorts. Finally, there is no substitute for attention at the highest levels—visits from the United States president and his cabinet, over and over and over again, to key countries in the Arab and Islamic worlds to explain our values and our intentions, to speak to anger and resentment, to try to understand and be understood (Mazarr 2004).

A year later, two other American international security experts warned of the coming Islamic terrorist attack on America and proposed "new ways" of dealing with it (Benjamin and Simon 2005). They believed that the United States was actually losing the "war on terror" and was unwittingly clearing the way for the next attack on it. The authors showed how the Islamic terrorist threat was evolving a broadening array of tactics, an army of new fighters, and, most ominously, a widening base of support in the global Muslim community. Benjamin and Simon thought that the jihadist movement had been galvanized by the example of September 11, 2001 and by the missteps of the U.S. government, which had consistently failed to understand the nature of the new terror. The Israeli government has also made similar mistakes.

Benjamin and Simon thought that if the "war on terror" was left on its current trajectory, much worse terror faced us in the near future. They believed that America had the capacity to stem the tide of Islamic terrorism, but that this would require "a far-reaching and creative new strategy," one that recognizes that the struggle has been over-militarized and that a campaign for reform in the Muslim world must be more than rhetoric and less than bayonets. They argued that America's increasing tendency to frame the conflict in religious terms had undermined its ability to advance its own interests. Was America equipped to do what was necessary to combat Islamist terrorism, or was it blinded by its own ideology? The answer to that question will determine how secure we will truly be, in the years and decades to come (Benjamin and Simon 2005).

The American-Jewish political scientist Ian Lustick believed that the United States-led "war on terror" was a psychological trap that America fell into and needs to get out of. Lustick thought that the first principle of terrorism is to understand that the weak win by exploiting the strength of the powerful. When the September 11, 2001 terrorists with box cutters hijacked American airliners, they transformed America's preeminent transportation system into a devastating weapon of attack. They also set a trap with the promise of revenge and security as the bait. The hijackers' biggest victory was to goad the U.S. government into taking the bait by unleashing the "war on terror." Lustick believed that the worry, witch-hunt, and waste that have ensued are destroying American confidence, undermining its economy, warping its political life, and isolating it from its international allies (Lustick 2006).

The U.S. mass communication media had given constant attention to possible future terrorist-initiated catastrophes and to the failures and weaknesses of the U.S. government's response. Lustick questioned the very rationale for the "war on terror." By analyzing the virtual absence of evidence of a terrorist threat inside the United States along with the motives and strategic purposes of *al-Qaïda,* Lustick showed how disconnected the "war on terror" is from the real but remote threat terrorism poses. He explained how the generalized "war on terror" began as part of the justification for invading Iraq, but then took on a life of its own. A whirlwind of fear, failure, and recrimination, this "war on terror" drags every interest group and politician, he argued, into selfish competition for its spoils. In short, the "war on terror" was irrational (Lustick 2006).

In a recent study of the U.S. strategy for dealing with Iran, a major supporter of Islamic terror, which was published in *The Washington Quarterly,* three scholars of the Iran Democracy Project at Stanford University's Hoover Institution found that the U.S. strategy in Iran had utterly failed to achieve its four objectives: to limit Iran's aggressive assertiveness in the region, halt Tehran's support for Islamic terrorism, promote Iranian democracy and human rights, and stop Iran from obtaining nuclear weapons (McFaul, Milani, and Diamond 2006–2007). They also found that the military "solution" of bombing Iran's nuclear installations envisioned by so many politicians and scholars was illusory. The well-meaning Stanford scholars made the following suggestions:

> Given past and present failures, we need a radically new approach. It is time for the United States to offer the Iranian regime a deal it cannot refuse. Washington should propose to end the economic embargo, unfreeze all Iranian assets, restore full diplomatic relations, support the initiation of talks on Iran's entry into the WTO, encourage foreign investment, and otherwise move toward a normal relationship with the Iranian government. In return, Tehran would have to agree to three conditions: a verifiable and indefinite suspension of activity that could feed into a nuclear weapons development program, including all enrichment of uranium, with a comprehensive and intrusive international inspections regime administered by the

International Atomic Energy Agency; an end to support for terrorist groups and activities, including training, intelligence support, and weapons shipments for Hizballah, Hamas, and radical Shi'ite militias in Iraq; and affirmation of basic human rights principles under international covenants and a recognition of the legitimacy of international and domestic efforts to monitor those conditions (McFaul, Milani, and Diamond 2006–2007, p. 126).

If the well-meaning scholars imagined that Iran's fanatically Islamic regime would accept their "rational" terms, then they may have overlooked the issues of pride, honor, and humiliation that permeates the thinking and emotions of Iran's leaders.

One of these three scholars has an intimate knowledge of Iran. Abbas Milani, the director of the Iran Democracy Project, is an Iranian-American with much experience on both sides. Milani was born in Iran in 1949 but immigrated to the United States in his youth. Living in California, the brilliant scholar graduated from Oakland Technical High School in 1966, earned his BA in political science and economics from the University of California at Berkeley in 1970 and his Ph.D. in political science from the University of Hawaii in 1974. Milani then returned to Iran, where he was an assistant professor of political science at the National University of Iran from 1975 to 1977, and was jailed for a year as a political prisoner. He was a research fellow at the Iranian Center for Social Research from 1977 to 1978 and lived through the fall of the Shah and the Islamic Revolution in 1979. He was an assistant professor of law and political science at the University of Tehran and a member of the board of directors of Tehran University's Center for International Studies from 1979 to 1987 when he returned to the United States for good.

As Milani well knows, *the issue of pride, honor, and dignity is crucial to Arab and Muslim culture.* Everything must be done to erase one's humiliations and to regain one's honor. Mahmoud Ahmadinejad, the highly controversial president of the Islamic Republic of Iran, who has called for Israel's destruction, denied the Holocaust of the Jews, pursued the development of a nuclear power program which can be used for military ends, supported Islamic terrorists everywhere, and has sworn to "humiliate the United States" and Iran's other enemies, seems preoccupied by the emotional issues of pride, dignity, shame, and humiliation. *It seems as if not being shamed or humiliated is more important to him than life itself, as if he is prepared to sacrifice millions of his countrymen to secure his country's pride and dignity.* The Iranian president clearly identifies himself with his country, as his many public pronouncements testify. If this is so, and if we wish to save our human civilization from destruction by an irrational and fanatical Islamic regime that is developing nuclear weapons, we must understand the mind of its president, as well as its culture.

In 1996 my Canadian colleague Blema Steinberg published an important book entitled *Shame and Humiliation: Presidential Decision Making on Vietnam,* showing how personal experiences of shame and humiliation deeply affect leaders' decision-making in international conflicts and may lead to disastrous and even cata-strophic consequences. A military attack on Iran's nuclear facilities by Israel or the United States would entail hundreds of thousands of casualties and untold destruc-tion and suffering, and may not even achieve its aim of destroying Iran's nuclear capability. If Ahmadinejad's need to repair his feelings of shame and humiliation by achieving his country's nuclear power is so deep and strong, then the only way to avert this very grave threat to our human civilization is to find a way to make him feel dignity and pride without resorting to such extremely dangerous measures.

Modern Iran is the natural successor to ancient Persia, a country and a civiliza-tion that have existed for several millennia. In an important article entitled "Misreading the Enemy" in *The Washington Post* of April 28, 2006, the American journalist David Ignatius pointed out that what matters most to Iran, and one of the chief reasons for its building its nuclear program, is respect and dignity, which in Muslim culture is honor or *sharaf.* He wrote:

> A word that recurs in radical Muslim proclamations is "dignity." That is not a political demand, nor one that can be achieved through negotiation. Indeed, for groups that feel victimized, negotiation with a powerful adversary can itself be demeaning. That's why the unyielding Yasser Arafat remained popular among Palestinians, despite his failure to deliver concrete benefits. He was a symbol of pride and resistance. Hamas, too, gains support because of its rigid steadfastness, and a strategy that seeks to punish pro-Hamas Palestinians into compromise will probably fail for the same reason. *The Muslim demand for respect isn't something that can be negotiated, but that doesn't mean the West shouldn't take it seriously.* For as the Muslim world gains a greater sense of dignity in its dealings with the West, the fundamental weapon of Iran, *al-Qaeda* and *Hamas* will lose much of its potency (Ignatius 2006).

The big question left unanswered by Ignatius, however, is whether and how the "West" can help the Muslim world, and above all Iran, gain a greater sense of dignity or "sharaf" that would make it desist from building nuclear weapons or engaging in murderous terrorist activity. For Muslims who suffer from a pain-ful sense of shame and humiliation, an insult to their honor or *sharaf,* the tradi-tional way of repairing that damage to their dignity is through humiliating those who they feel inflicted the shame and humiliation in the first place. And as Ahmadinejad perceives it, those who need be destroyed and humiliated are Israel and the United States.

On May 8, 2006, Iran's President Ahmadinejad sent a personal letter to U.S. President George W. Bush, ostensibly to propose "new ways" to end the dis-pute between Iran and the United States over Iran's continuing program to develop nuclear power. U.S. Secretary of State Condoleezza Rice and National Security Adviser Stephen Hadley reviewed the letter and dismissed it as a nego-tiating *ploy* and publicity *stunt* that did not address U.S. concerns about Iran's nuclear program. Had they read the letter psychologically, they would have noticed the striking recurrence of the themes of dignity and humiliation.

A few days later, at a meeting in Jakarta, Indonesia, Ahmadinejad said, "the letter was an invitation to monotheism and justice, which are common to all divine prophets." Scholars of Islam will tell you that for a fanatical Islamist like Ahmadinejad, "monotheism" is synonymous with Islam, that fundamentalist Muslims consider Allah the god of all people, and all people to be born Muslim but to be raised erroneously by their parents on other faiths. Some time later, Ahmadinejad sent a similar letter to Angela Merkel, the chancellor of Germany. Once again, the issues of honor, dignity, shame, and humiliation were paramount. In early 2007 Ahmadinejad scorned the UN sanctions imposed against his country for its nuclear program, telling an Iranian crowd that Iran had "humiliated the United States" in the past and would do so again.

My American colleague Stanley Renshon devoted much of his "Political Psychology" blog of May 10, 2006 to refuting Ahmadinejad's statements to Bush, himself the subject of a laudatory "psychobiography" by Renshon (Renshon 2004). It is amazing to me that Renshon ignored the crucial importance of the emotional issues of dignity and humiliation in the letter:

> It's not only that the letter is framed in *large religious and political terms* like "needs of humanity," "rational behavior, logic, ethics, peace, fulfilling obligations, justice, service to the people, progress, property, service to the people, prosperity, progress and *respect for human dignity,*" and calls on Mr. Bush to "follow the teaching of divine prophets." Words like peace, justice, progress and prosperity have many meanings of course. However, in Mr. Ahmadinejad's view they all lead in one direction—that Mr. Bush and the United States have, by their behavior both at home and abroad strayed from the path of virtue as defined by Mr. Ahmadinejad and reaped the just rewards of world hatred as a result.
>
> [. . .] And, along with *the grand but vague terms noted above* the letter is riddled with misinformation, misunderstanding and disingenuousness that makes it hard to follow much less fully understand [. . .] The issue is not the virtue of scientific progress in history, but Iran's apparent quest to develop nuclear weapons. I take Mr. Ahmadinejad's letter and views as sincere and that is precisely the problem. His list of grievances is laid at the door of a single villain—the United States. His motives and those of his country are pure, without guile, artifice, or self-interest [. . .] The letter is presumptuous and, because of its lecturing without any hint of real humility or perspective, insulting. But its real importance lies elsewhere. *The letter is a window into a mindset of a man whose piety easily slides into sanctimony. It is the mindset of a man who, in spite of the high-minded appeal to religious aspirations, treats the real world in decidedly black or white terms in which his word is the final judgment.* The question is not whether he is "crazy," a word the *Wall Street Journal* used in the title of an editorial about him. In the clinical sense, he is a sane as the leadership he represents, and that is our problem (Renshon 2006, May 10).

Well, Mahmoud Ahmadinejad may not be crazy by our ordinary "Western" standards, and certainly not by those of his own Iranian Muslim culture. At the same time, his preoccupation with the pride and dignity of his country, which, in his unconscious mind, is himself, and with inflicting humiliation on the enemy, is striking in his letter to Bush, as it is also in his letter to Angela Merkel. The words "humiliation" and "dignity" appear many times in those letters. And to the current president of Iran, the acquisition of nuclear power and nuclear weapons is the symbol of pride and dignity, the antidote to the unbearable shame and humiliation that he feels he or his country has suffered.

Whether, when, how, and why Mahmoud Ahmadinejad suffered painful feelings of shame and humiliation in his early life we do not know at this point. The biographies of his that are publicly available say next to nothing on this subject. All we are really told is that he was the fourth of seven children of a blacksmith in a village near Tehran, born in 1956. The next thing we know is that he is twenty years old and competing to get into a university. Iran itself boasts continuous millennia of self-rule, including by Cyrus the Great and Darius the Great, calls itself a great country and a great civilization, and ignores its humiliation by the "Western" powers. Yet Persia had suffered several defeats in its wars with Imperial Russia during the Qajar era (1781–1925), resulting in Persia losing almost half of its territories to Imperial Russia and to the British Empire via the treaties of Gulistan, Turkmenchay, and Akhal. Repeated foreign intervention finally resulted in Persia's constitutional revolution establishing the nation's first elected parliament in 1906 within a constitutional monarchy. During the twentieth century, the Pahlavi dynasty was a puppet regime for foreign powers. In summer of 1941, Britain and the USSR invaded Iran to prevent Iran from allying with the Axis powers. In 1953 the revolutionary Mossadegh regime was overgrown by a coup d'état led by the United States. Shame and humiliation by foreign powers were certainly inflicted upon Iran. Ahmadinejad sees himself as part of the 1979 revolution that overthrew the Shah and brought "dignity" to Iran.

On May 30, 2006 Ahmadinejad was interviewed by the German magazine *Der Spiegel* about a wide array of subjects, including soccer, Iran, Israel, the United States, the Holocaust, and nuclear weapons. The next day, in the *National Review Online,* the neoconservative American scholar Michael Arthur Leeden noted the repetition of the theme of "humiliation" in Ahmadinejad's answers to the *Spiegel* interviewers. His conclusions were ominous:

> "Why must the German people be humiliated today because a group of people committed crimes in the name of the Germans during the course of history?" [said Ahmadinejad]. The *Spiegel* journalist doesn't have the wit to ask Ahmadinejad why *jihadis* like him base their actions on events that took place centuries ago, and then have the *chutzpah* to condemn the Germans for feeling guilt about the actions of their parents. *The use of "humiliation" tells us a lot about the way the mullahs think about the world; they look at international events as a matter of domination or humiliation,* and he hammers away at this theme: "Saying that we should accept the world as it is would mean that [. . .] the German people would be humiliated for another 1,000 years. Do you think that is the correct logic?" *You can be quite certain that the mullahs are not going to accept anything less than the humiliation of the West, and Ahmadinejad's hatred for the Europeans oozes from every verbal exchange.* When the *Spiegel* interviewer asks him whether he

wants nuclear weapons, Ahmadinejad treats him with total contempt. If you know how to parse the language, you will see that he says "yes. Hell yes!" But instead of putting it in the context of the pursuit of Iranian national interests, he treats it as part of his hatred of the West: "In our view, the legal system whereby a handful of countries force their will on the rest of the world is discriminatory and unstable [...] there are a number of countries that possess both nuclear energy and nuclear weapons. They use their atomic weapons to threaten other peoples [...] What we say is that these countries themselves have long deviated from peaceful usage. These powers have no right to talk to us in this manner. This order is unjust and unsustainable" (Leeden 2006; italics added).

The next day Renshon echoed Leeden's observations in his "Political Psychology" post entitled "Iran's 'dignity' and the bomb." Wrote Renshon:

Reading through the recent *Spiegel* interview with Iran's President Ahmadinejad *the theme of being humiliated and meting out humiliation is invoked several times.* There are echoes of this theme in his development, and certainly in Iran's modern history, but it is the implications of these themes for Iran's quest for nuclear weapons that is my focus here. David Ignatius recently raised an interesting question about why the Iranian government wanted to develop a nuclear arsenal. He noted their "implacability" and attributed it to three sources: divisions in the ruling elite, their theocratic view that mandates from God can't be negotiated, and their elevation of "dignity" as an irreducible essential of the regime's goals (Renshon 2006, June 1; italics added).

Ahmadinejad's public pronouncements indeed betray his private feelings. He and Iran, as he perceives it, must avenge their own shame and humiliation and achieve pride, honor, and dignity by humiliating the "West." Destroy Israel, humiliate the United States, and Iran's dignity will be restored. U.S. President George W. Bush has warned that this would lead to World War III with its unthinkable toll of mass death and destruction. The sanctions are making Iran feel more isolated and humiliated. So we seem to have David Ignatius on the one hand searching for ways to give Iran and the entire Muslim world the "dignity" that they so badly crave, so as to make them desist from trying to achieve it through catastrophic violence, and Michael Leeden on the other hand saying that "the mullahs are not going to accept anything less than the humiliation of the West." Who is right?

Now this is a very important issue. *Is there any way for us to give Ahmadinejad and Iran the dignity and honor they crave so much, to undo their feelings of shame and humiliation, so as to remove their need to develop nuclear weapons, to destroy Israel and to "humiliate the United States"?* Can we avert the catastrophic missile-dominated showdown in the Middle East? Whatever the answer, it seems that David Ignatius was right: we are misreading the enemy. So long as the well-meaning scholars from Stanford, as well as many other well-meaning "Western" scholars and statesmen, fail to understand the depth of the emotional issues of honor and humiliation in the Iranian soul and in that of Ahmadinejad in particular, it is hard to see how this crucial issue that threatens the very existence of human civilization can be resolved.

One should also bear in mind the irrational but powerful psychological need for enemies that has been studied by my Cypriot-Turkish-born American colleague Vamık Volkan in his classic book on the subject (Volkan 1988). Enemies serve a wide variety of psychological needs and purposes. They enable us to unconsciously split off from our inner selves the painful aspects of ourselves and the painful emotions that beset us and externalize and project them upon our enemy. The enemy also reinforces our group cohesion. At the end of the Cold War, Georgi Arbatov, the director of the Soviet Institute for the Study of the U.S.A. and Canada, told American visitors to Moscow, "We are going to do a terrible thing to you: we are going to deprive you of an enemy." Arbatov was more psychologically perceptive about American politics than many leaders in Washington. Legend has it that in at least one Pentagon office there used to hang a sign that read: WANTED: A GOOD ENEMY.

During the term of office of U.S. President George W. Bush, such enemies have been found aplenty: Osama bin Laden and his *al-Qaïda*, the "axis of evil" including Iran, Iraq, and North Korea, and at times also Syria and Libya, the Taliban in Afghanistan, Saddam Hussein and the *jihadis* in Iraq, Hugo Chávez in Venezuela, and above all Mahmoud Ahmadinejad in Iran. They are all "good enemies" in that they are easy to hate and make themselves readily available as targets for the externalization of painful feelings about oneself. Having such enemies, and waging a "global war on terror," supposedly gives the United States a sense of purpose and cohesion. On the other hand, the United States is deeply divided on the war in Iraq, and perhaps even more so on what to do about Iran.

The Irrationalities of Islamic Terror

Organized warfare has characterized our species for the past ten to fifteen thousand years. The Italian psychoanalyst Franco Fornari (1921–1985), a follower of Melanie Klein (1882–1960), thought that war was the paranoid or projective "elaboration" of mourning (Fornari 1974). Our nation and country play an unconscious maternal role in our feelings, as expressed in the term "motherland." Fornari thought that war and violence develop out of our "love need": our wish to preserve and defend the sacred object to which we are attached, namely our early mother and our fusion with her. For the adult, nations are the sacred objects that generate warfare. Fornari focused upon *sacrifice* as the essence of war: the astonishing willingness of human beings to die for their country, to give over their bodies to their nation. Fornari called war the "spectacular establishment of a general human situation whereby death assumes absolute value." We are sure that the ideas for which we die must be true, because "death becomes a demonstrative process." We shall discuss Melanie Klein's theories of love and hate below.

The so-called "cold war" was a period of conflict, tension, and competition between the "capitalist" United States and the "communist" Soviet Union (and their allies), which lasted almost fifty years, from the mid-1940s until the early 1990s. The main U.S. allies were Western Europe, Japan, and Canada. The main Soviet allies were Eastern Europe and China (until the Sino-Soviet split). The rivalry between the two superpowers was played out in military coalitions, ideology, psychology, espionage, industry, technology, defense spending, the space race, a massive conventional and nuclear arms race, and many proxy wars. The term "cold war" was coined in 1947 by the American-Jewish financier-statesman Bernard Baruch (1870–1965) and by the American-Jewish journalist

Walter Lippmann (1889–1974) to describe the emerging tensions between the two former wartime allies. There never was a direct military engagement between the United States and the USSR, but there was a half-century of military buildup, and political battles for support around the world, including significant involvement of allied and satellite nations.

The United States and the Soviet Union had been allies against Nazi Germany, but the two sides differed on how to reconstruct the postwar world even before the end of World War II. Over the following decades, the "cold war" spread outside Europe to the whole world. The United States sought to "contain" communism and forged numerous alliances to this end, particularly in Western Europe, the Middle East, and Southeast Asia. Right-wing American politicians persecuted the American communists. From 1947 to 1957, the chief persecutor was Joseph Raymond McCarthy (1908–1957), a Republican United States Senator from Wisconsin. From 1950 to 1954, McCarthy aggressively investigated claims that there were Communist and Soviet spies and sympathizers inside the federal government.

As the Cold War escalated between the United States, the Soviet Union, and China, the United States went through a paranoid period of anticommunist tensions and suspicion. Many thousands of individuals were suspected of being spies or communists. Although the American Communist Party was never illegal under U.S. federal law, membership in the party or support of its goals was regarded by many as tantamount to treason. From 1950 Senator Joseph McCarthy became the most visible public face of anticommunism. The term "McCarthyism" was coined that same year to describe and condemn the senator's methods, which were widely seen as demagogic and based on reckless, unsubstantiated accusations and unreliable documents. Later the term was applied more generally to the anticommunism of the late 1940s through the late 1950s. Today, it is used even more broadly, to describe public attacks made on a person's character or patriotism that involve the sort of unethical tactics associated with McCarthy.

During the "cold war," there were repeated crises that threatened to escalate into world wars but never did: the Korean War (1950–1953), the Cuban Missile Crisis (1962), and the Vietnam War (1964–1975). There were also periods when tension was reduced as both sides sought *détente*. Direct military attacks on adversaries were deterred by the potential for massive mutual destruction using deliverable nuclear weapons.

The "cold war" supposedly ended in the late 1980s following the launching of Soviet President Mikhail Gorbachev's reform programs, *perestroika* and *glasnost*. The Soviet Union ceded power over Eastern Europe to the United States and was dissolved in 1991. Yet, sixteen years later, the "cold war" seemed to have revived with Russia taking the place of the former Soviet Union. The United States had proposed stationing a radar station in the Czech Republic and a battery of rockets in Poland to detect and shoot down hostile Iranian missiles. In 2007 Russia's autocratic and feisty president, Vladimir Putin, called a news conference in Moscow, publicly criticized the U.S. plans for an antimissile system in Central Europe, and warned that Russia would produce a "highly effective" response.

An angry Putin dismissed Washington's arguments about defending Europe from Iran and said that the U.S. antimissile system next door would "directly affect" Russia. "Our specialists don't think that anti-missile systems in Eastern Europe are aimed against terrorists or Iran. Can you really fight terrorists with ballistic missiles?" he said. Iran, Putin said, did not have long-range ballistic missiles, only medium-range one. "We are also thinking about how to ensure our external security," Putin added. "All our responses will be asymmetric but they will be highly effective." Putin said that Russia already had systems capable of overcoming U.S. missile defenses but promised a future generation of Russian weapons on which the U.S. missile defense systems "will have absolutely no effect." He did not give details. Putin complained about Washington's decision in 2006 to impose sanctions on Russian arms firms because of their sales to Iran and Syria. The real motive, he said, was to stop Russian arms firms from taking away business from their U.S. rivals.

Ian Lustick thought that, facing the threat of nuclear incineration during the "cold war," America had overcome its paranoid panic about the imaginary communist sleeper cells poised inside its territory to destroy the country, a panic fueled by the destructive hysteria of McCarthyism. Through careful analysis of the Soviet threat, Lustick wrote, the United States had managed to sustain a productive national life and achieve victory, despite the terrifying daily possibility of nuclear catastrophe. Lustick claimed that his book was inspired by that success. He wished to point the way forward, not toward victory in the "war on terror" but toward victory over it. The first and most difficult step toward that victory is to know the enemy. That also meant understanding how *al-Qaïda* was making the United States its own worst enemy (Lustick 2006).

Indeed, after the tragedy of September 11, 2001, the international wars and the "cold war" of the twentieth century were replaced by the "global war on terror." In response to what Americans call *9/11* (numbers may be less painful to recall than actual memories and images of the horrors), U.S. President George W. Bush declared the "war on terrorism" and divided the world into "either you're with us or you're with the terrorists." Such notions, however, are unrealistic (Alderdice 2002, p. 10). All the world's terrorists are not made of the same cloth, nor do they all have the same aims, nor are they interconnected, nor do they all know of one another, nor do they always work together. Lumping them all together into one monolithic group is dangerous black-and-white thinking (Falk 2004, pp. 118–129).

The American international affairs scholar Bard O'Neill has studied insurgency and terrorism around the world (O'Neill et al. 1980; O'Neill 1990, 2005). Substituting typology for explanation, O'Neill classified the various insurgencies by their ultimate goals, strategies, forms of warfare, the role and means of acquiring popular support, organizational dynamics, causes and effects of disunity, types of external support, and local government responses. O'Neill's follower Michael Carter studied Islamic terrorism in Southeast Asia and concluded that the "global war on terrorism" was basically sound. Examining the Southeast Asian terrorist groups based on O'Neill's classification, Carter found an ineffective, regional U.S. strategy, with deficiencies in regional diplomacy, economic reform, financial and judicial practices, and military organization. He recommended prioritized improvements in these areas, along with more efficient maritime control and customs procedures. Carter also found a lack of an effective regional information campaign against terrorism. He finally put forth "an effects-based counter-terrorism strategy needed to win in the Global War on Terrorism" (Carter 2005).

Unfortunately, O'Neill and Carter deluded themselves about the rationality of the "global war on terror." Like Lustick, the American national security expert Derek Reveron and the American political scientist Jeffrey Murer have pointed out the fallacy of the basic assumption of the "war on terror"—that there is a single enemy united around one principal cause, namely, a religiously motivated hostility to freedom and to the democratic American way. This single enemy does not exist. *Al-Qaïda* is but one of many disparate Islamic groups around the world (Reveron and Murer 2006, pp. vi–viii, xi–xxxi, 322–327).

Not only is the "war on terror" in its present form irrational and futile, it is also self-defeating and self-destructive. It causes many disparate Muslim groups, which have had little in common, to unite in a common cause with *al-Qaïda* against the United States and "the West." In 2006, for example, the civil war in Somalia, which had been raging for fifteen years, took a religious turn. The Islamic Courts Union, a militant group made up of various Somali religious clans and warlords and led by *Sheikhs* Hassan Dahir Aweys and Sharif Sheikh Ahmed, declared "holy war" on the government and invited foreign jihadists to join in on its side. At United States urging, neighboring Ethiopia, a largely Christian nation, claimed that the Islamists were meddling in its internal affairs by inflaming its own Muslim minority, and joined the war on the side of the "legitimate" Transitional Federal Government of the Somali Republic, formed in Kenya in 2004, with the tacit approval of the United States, which, supporting Ethiopia in its "global war on terror," claimed that the Islamists were part of *al-Qaïda* and were creating a terrorist state, using child soldiers, and committing unspeakable atrocities (Dealy 2006; Perry 2007).

The Somali Islamists, however, were not part of *al-Qaïda*. They had temporarily brought a semblance of law and order to the capital of Mogadishu and other parts of Somalia after fifteen years of no central government, lawlessness, and chaos under competing Somali warlords. They had also won support from many nations. During its attempted takeover of Somalia, however, the national security chairman of the Islamic Courts Union, a former warlord named Yusuf Siad Inda'ade, told an American news magazine reporter: "We believe [that] the war against terrorism is a war against Islam. Those who are making trouble are not based here. Bush is the mother and father of terrorism." With some hyperbole, the reporter wrote, "The Islamists' takeover [of Somalia] is a parable of *the unintended consequences of the United States's war on terrorism*" (Dealy 2006; italics added).

The Islamists, however, had not taken over Somalia. After the Ethiopian invasion they lost control of Mogadishu, which became chaotic and lawless again, and fled to the Somali provinces while the "civilized" world was still trying to figure out how to apply the lessons of Rwanda, Bosnia, East Timor, Kosovo, and the disastrous U.S. food mission to Somalia of 1992 to the present Somali crisis. While the Transitional Federal Government of the Somali Republic, led by the fifty-four-year-old Ali Mohammed Ghedi, tried to create a new semblance of law and order, as the Islamists had done, the latter vowed to wage *jihad* against Ghedi's "traitors." In 2008 the United States killed Aden Hashi Farah "Ayro," the alleged *Al-Qaïda* leader in Somalia. Another American news magazine reporter correctly observed that "[the war in] Iraq shows how *labeling an insurgency as linked to al-Qaïda can become self-fulfilling:* conflict pushes extremists to the fore and is a magnet for itinerant foreign jihadists" (Perry 2007; italics added).

My own country of Israel, a tiny land with a population of seven million souls, has made the same tragic mistake as the great United States. In its struggle against *Hamas, Islamic Jihad, Hezbollah,* and other jihadist groups seeking its destruction, Israel has joined the U.S. "global war on terror." Some Israelis think that by so doing, Israel risks pushing these Palestinian jihadist groups into *al-Qaïda*'s arms and making enemies of 1.2 billion Muslims worldwide. Nonetheless, General Moshe Ya'alon, Israel's neoconservative Defense Forces chief of staff from 2002 to 2005 (whom some Israelis blame for not having prepared his forces properly for a war with *Hezbollah* during his tenure, thus causing our 2006 military debacle against *Hezbollah* in Lebanon), has joined the chorus of U.S. neoconservatives calling for the "global war on terror." Ya'alon is now a scholar at the neoconservative Shalem Centre in Jerusalem.

On a visit to Australia in the fall of 2006, General Ya'alon said that "the West" must wake up and understand that it is fighting the "Third World War" against a movement of global jihadists. "We are under attack, we are in defense, they are on the offense so far," he said. Ya'alon added that Iran had become the headquarters of a global Islamic movement that wants to impose a strict form of Islam on the rest of the world, that "the West" should confront this threat through diplomatic and even military action if necessary, and that Iran and Syria must be held responsible for their support of militants in Iraq (*The Australian,* November 23, 2006).

The following month, when General Ya'alon was in New Zealand on a fundraising trip organized by the Jewish National Fund, an Auckland District Court Judge issued a warrant for his arrest for alleged war crimes arising from his role in the 2002 assassination of *Hamas* leader Salah Shehadeh in Gaza City, in which at least fourteen Palestinian civilians were killed, saying that New Zealand had an obligation to uphold the Geneva Convention, which outlawed the murder of civilian noncombatants. The New Zealand Attorney General, however, voided the judge's warrant after advice from the Crown Law Office that there was insufficient evidence against Ya'alon. The former Israeli chief of staff is an important player in right-wing Israeli politics.

By common "Western" wisdom, Ya'alon was right. Iran's Islamic government is seen by "the West" as a very dangerous one. Back in 1979 Iran had begun the showdown between militant Islam and the United States by taking hostage the entire staff of its diplomatic mission. The "Iran hostage crisis" lasted 444 days, from November 4, 1979 until January 20, 1981. With Iran under its new Islamic ruler, the *ayatollah* Ruhollah Khomeini, the "Muslim Student Followers of the Imam's Line" (proxies of the Iranian regime) captured and held hostage sixty-three U.S. diplomats and three other U.S. citizens inside the U.S. diplomatic mission in Tehran. The hostage takers released several captives, leaving fifty-three at the end. The United States, under President Jimmy Carter, launched a rescue operation, Operation Eagle Claw, which failed, causing the deaths of eight U.S. military servicemen. Some historians consider this crisis to have been a primary reason for Carter's loss to Ronald Reagan in his reelection bid in 1980 (Bowden 2006). The crisis also punctuated the first Islamic revolution of modern times. The crisis was ended by the Algiers Accords but Iran alleged that the United States had not fulfilled its commitments. Iran's rulers still call America "the Great Satan" and Israel "the Little Satan."

In 1989 the "Salman Rushdie Affair" drew the world's attention to the ominous power of fundamentalist Islam. Ahmed Salman Rushdie, born in 1947 in Mumbai (Bombay), India, is a British-Indian Muslim writer whose novels are set in the Indian subcontinent. He had achieved literary fame with his second novel, *Midnight's Children* (Rushdie 1981), which won the prestigious Booker Prize, and his ongoing literary output had continued to receive both critical acclaim and commercial success. Rushdie became best known, however, for the violent rage that his book *The Satanic Verses* (Rushdie 1988) provoked in the Muslim community. After death threats and a *fatwa* (Muslim religious ruling) the following year by the Iranian imam *ayatollah* Ruhollah Khomeini calling for his assassination, he spent many years underground, appearing in public only sporadically.

Nevertheless, the Israeli general may also have been wrong. Psychiatric scholars have shown that the "war on terror" was irrational (see below), and that a black-and-white, "us and them," good-against-evil attitude is a prescription for further war and destruction (Group for the Advancement of Psychiatry 1978, 1987). Some tendentious documentary films about Islamic terrorism such as Wayne Kopping and Raphael Shore's *Obsession: Radical Islam's War Against the West,* Quixotic Media's *Islam: What the West Needs to Know,* and Glenn Beck's *Exposed: The Extremist Agenda* tend to confuse "radical Islam" with moderate Islam and show them both as hell-bent on destroying Israel and America. Some documentaries deliberately compare "radical Islam" to Hitler's Nazism, ignoring all possible differences. They tend to reinforce our irrational black-and-white view of the world, support our unrealistic "war on terror," and distort our understanding of the complexities of the Muslim world (al-Tabari 1985–1999; Esposito 1992, 1999, 2002, 2003; Lewis 1995).

Bernard Lewis, "the dean of Middle East scholars," studied the "roots of Muslim rage" at the "West" and tried to explain Islamic terrorism from a rationalist point of view. Lewis believed that the Islamic world was locked in an internal struggle over how best to cure the ills of its societies: widespread poverty, extreme economic inequality, the prevalence of government by despotic rulers, and the inability to keep pace with emerging economies. The crisis of Islam concerned the choice the Islamic world faces between two diametrically opposed solutions. While some Muslims want the continued and peaceful spread of economic and political freedoms as a means to solve these problems, there are fundamentalist Muslim movements, such as Wahhabism (the variety of Islam prevalent in Saudi Arabia), which blame all of these ills on the modernization and Western influence that the Islamic world has embraced, and advocate a total rejection of the West and a return to traditional Islam (Lewis 1990).

Lewis thought that this rejection of the "West" by fundamentalist Islam expressed itself as violence against "Western" countries and interests, as well as violence against "impious" Muslim rulers who have adopted "Western" ways. The Islamic fundamentalists seek the establishment of states and societies based on Islamic law and traditional mores. Lewis believed that the outcome of this struggle between Western and anti-Western groups in the Islamic world would determine whether "the Islamic world" took its place alongside progressive countries in a global community or regressed into backwardness and intractable conflict with non-Muslim nations (Lewis 1990).

Is militant, fundamentalist, fanatical, or radical Islam, however, cohesive, global, monolithic, and unitary in purpose, is it identical with terrorism, and is it purely religious in nature? No, said the American political scientist Jeffrey Murer. To conceive of it as such, Murer said, can only hamstring international efforts to decrease terrorism around the world. "There is no single motivation shared by those we lump together as terrorists," said Murer. "We found that the insurgents who are using Islam around the world are doing so to mark their differences from the states they are opposing. These groups are primarily fighting local wars, asymmetrical wars of independence. Other than that, they have very little connection with one another" (*College News,* August 3, 2006).

A prime case in point, Murer said, is the "Free Aceh" movement in Indonesia, led by an Islamic group in Java that has been fighting for independence for decades—first against the Dutch, then against the native Indonesian government. The movement, Murer notes, is primarily interested in fighting colonization, not bringing down the West. "The danger," said Murer, "is that those pursuing the war on terror are treating the Free Aceh movement as internationally connected with bin Laden and ignoring its local orientation. This attitude, unfortunately, seems then to drive the creation of these international connections" (*College News,* August 3, 2006).

Nevertheless, in the name of the "war on terror," the United States invaded Afghanistan and Iraq, changed their regimes, and kept looking for the elusive Osama bin Laden and other *al-Qaïda* leaders, who were hiding in the mountainous tribal regions of Waziristan on the Afghan-Pakistani border. The United States changed Afghanistan, whose fanatical-Muslim Taliban government was providing safe haven to Osama bin Laden and *al-Qaïda* members, into a "democratic" country led by President Hamid Karzai. The Taliban, however, never gave up, and are fighting to regain power. In Iraq, the murderous regime of Saddam Hussein was toppled, and a "democratic" government set up, but countless murders and suicide murders have been and are being committed daily, not least by the government itself, with numerous "terrorists" targeting Americans as well as members of their own people of different Muslim sects. It is a terrible and tragic mess.

Israel has had its share of dealing with fanatical Islamic terror, including suicidal murder, from groups like *Hamas, Palestinian Islamic Jihad,* and the Lebanese *Hezbollah* for decades (Falk 2004, pp. 159–173; Van Evera 2006). Europe, which has some 18–20 million Muslim residents, mostly peaceful ones who had immigrated to find work and a new life, awoke to Islamic terrorism on March 11, 2004, when Islamic fanatics committed several bombing attacks on four commuter trains in the Spanish capital of Madrid. All four trains containing explosive devices had departed the Madrid railroad station at Alcalá de Henares after seven o'clock in the morning. At eight o'clock, emergency relief workers began arriving at the scenes of the bombings. The police reported "numerous victims" and spoke of fifty wounded and several dead. By 08:30 the emergency ambulance service had set up a "field hospital" at a sports facility at Daoiz y Velarde. Hospitals were told to expect the arrival of many casualties. Bystanders and local residents helped relief workers. By nine o'clock, the police had confirmed the death of at least thirty people.

That day a London newspaper reported receiving an e-mail message from a group affiliated with *al-Qaïda,* claiming responsibility for the attacks, and a videotape claiming responsibility was also found. The coincidence in timing of the attacks with elections in Spain inspired several politically focused speculations on the real identity of the perpetrators, with many initially suspecting the fanatical Basque group ETA. However the Interpol, the Spanish government, police, and judicial institutions agree that a fanatical Islamic *al-Qaïda* cell was the perpetrator. On April 3, 2004, in Leganés, near Madrid, several Arab militants suspected in the bombing blew themselves up rather than face capture, killing one *Grupo Especial de Operaciones* policeman and wounding eleven.

The United Kingdom, which has its own large Muslim community, mainly immigrants from its former colonies in South Asia and the Middle East, has been dealing with fundamentalist Islamic fanaticism for at least a decade. In 1997 the British Muslim writer Hanif Kureishi, who was born in southern England in 1954 to a Pakistani immigrant father and an English mother, published *My Son, the Fanatic,* a novel about a stable British Muslim family man whose life comes unraveled as his son becomes a fanatical Muslim. The book focused on the marginal world of Parvez, a Pakistani living in a grimy English city. Though he has been in England for twenty-five years, Parvez has risen no higher than cab driver. But his son, Farid, is engaged to the daughter of the local English police chief, much to the delight of Parvez and his traditional wife, Minoo. They believe the union will signal their final acceptance into English culture (Kureishi 1997).

Farid, however, unaccountably breaks off the engagement with the English police chief's daughter, and in his dismay Parvez confides in one of his regular passengers, a prostitute named Bettina. Gradually Parvez realizes that his son Farid has joined a fundamentalist and fanatical Islamic sect. Farid invites an exploitive *mullah* and his entourage to live in the family house, and it is not long before the group has taken control of the household, forcing Minoo to take refuge in the kitchen and swamping Parvez with debt. A visiting German businessman with a taste for cocaine and call girls hires Parvez's services not only as a cab driver but also as procurer—and his favorite partner is Bettina. In the course of sharing confidences, Parvez and Bettina are surprised to find that they have enough in common to form the foundation for a relationship. But Farid's fanatical Muslim sect has begun a campaign to drive the prostitutes, including Bettina, out of the neighborhood (Kureishi 1997).

While Kureishi's novel is as much about the classical Oedipal father-son struggle as about Islamic fanaticism, this novel was made into a film in 1998, and one of its reviewers thought that "*It doesn't matter that these things rarely happen in reality* because it's so tantalizing to wonder what it would be like to wake up to a new life—to wake up as a new person" (Tom Block on the *Culture Vulture* Web site). Alas, these things do indeed happen in reality, and often. Even before the 2001 *al-Qaïda* attacks in America, Great Britain was becoming obsessed with the "cultural stare-down" between its white, secular majority and its estimated 1.5 million "dark" Muslim immigrants.

Despite the so-called "global war on terror," led by the United States, by 2007 *al-Qaïda* was resurgent:

> Senior leaders of Al Qaeda operating from Pakistan have re-established significant control over their once-battered worldwide terror network and over the past year have set up a band of training camps in the tribal regions near the Afghan border, according to American intelligence and counterterrorism officials. American officials said there was mounting evidence that Osama bin Laden and his deputy, Ayman al-Zawahri, had been steadily building an operations hub in the mountainous Pakistani tribal area of North Waziristan. Until recently, the Bush administration had described Mr. bin Laden and Mr. Zawahri as detached from their followers and cut off from operational control of Al Qaeda. The United States has also identified several new Qaeda compounds in North Waziristan, including one that officials said might be training operatives for strikes against targets beyond Afghanistan (Mazzetti and Rohde 2007).

In addition to the extremely dangerous *al-Qaïda,* there is another fanatical Islamic group called *Hizb ut-Tahrir* (Party of Liberation) which may pose just as great a threat to "Western" civilization. *Hizb ut-Tahrir* is an Islamist political party whose goal is to establish a pan-Islamic caliphate (*khilafah*). The organization was founded by *Sheikh* Taqiuddin an-Nabhani (1909–1977), a Muslim judge (*qadi*) from Jerusalem, in 1953, when East Jerusalem was part of the Kingdom of Jordan. *Hizb ut-Tahrir* is dedicated to what it sees as the political unity of all Muslims via the reestablishment of the caliphate, the removal of what the organization considers to be neocolonialist Western control of Muslim lands, and a return to government based on Islamic law (*Shari'a*). In accordance with that, the party has called for all Muslims to overthrow their governments, and to declare *jihad* against Israel. It has called the suicide bombings in Israel "legitimate" acts of "martyrdom."

In this context, it is important to examine a basic irrationality in the minds of Islamic terrorists: the conversion of suicide in their Islamic belief from a cowardly sin to a heroic act of martyrdom. One Christian theologian thought that the basis for this belief was found in the Qur'anic verses, "And do not think that those who have been killed in the Way of Allah as dead; they are rather living with their Lord, well provided for" (Qur'an 3:169) and "Those who have emigrated and were driven from their homes, were persecuted for My sake, fought and were killed, I will forgive their sins and will admit them into [my] Gardens, beneath which rivers flow, as a reward from Allah" (Qur'an 3:195) (Chapman 2005).

The Qur'an, however, is full of contradictions, as are the Jewish and Christian Bibles and most other religious texts. Seeking a rational explanation for an irrational belief, Chapman thought that in Islamic law, suicide had always been regarded as a mortal sin, totally forbidden, but that the Sunni Muslims had recently been influenced by the tradition of martyrdom within Shi'ite Islam, and have come to believe that *suicide in the context of jihad* was permissible, and therefore a legitimate way of fighting against the enemies of Islam. But the belief in suicidal murder as an act of holy martyrdom is far more extreme than this. In fact, this contradiction is yet another indication that religious belief, especially the fanatical kind, has no regard for logic or rationality, and can always be bent and distorted to fit the emotional needs of the believer.

Hizb ut-Tahrir has a significant presence in forty countries, including European ones, with 5,000–10,000 "hard-core" members and tens of thousands of followers (A. Cohen 2003; Mayer 2004). Although membership is legal, its public activities were banned in Germany after a charge of spreading anti-Semitic propaganda, cotravening German law. The ban is currently subject to a legal challenge. *Hizb ut-Tahrir* is proscribed in Russia, Pakistan, throughout the Muslim states of Central Asia, and in almost every Arab country, but it is permitted to operate in the more liberal UAE, Lebanon, and Yemen. It survived proposed bans in Australia and the United Kingdom after clearance from the intelligence services and police. The British journalist Melanie Phillips thought that this was a huge mistake, as was the British government's decision to allow the fundamentalist Muslim Brotherhood to serve as its advisers on terrorism. She believed that Britain as well as the entire Western world were tragically denying the fact that since the *ayatollah* Ruhollah Musavi Khomeini (1900–1989) had taken over Iran in 1979, they were facing an Islamic enemy determined to wage war on them, defeat them, take over the world, and impose Islam on it (Phillips 2006, 2007).

The evolution of homegrown fanatical Islamic terrorism in the United Kingdom has received much attention from both experts and journalists. Dominique Thomas, a French consultant on Islamist terrorism, coined the neologism "Londonistan" to describe the new phenomenon (Thomas 2003). Thomas believed that London had become the foremost international base for fanatical Islamic terrorists. Two years later, Thomas summed up his views as follows:

> To understand how London acquired its position as Islamic fundamentalist clearing house, it's useful to retrace the origins of what has been dubbed "Londonistan." Between the late 1980s and the early 1990s, radical Islamist thinkers and militants began arriving in London. Mainly of Arab origin, some of them had passed through the Jihadist camps in Afghanistan and inherited part of that ideology—Jihadi Salafism, started in the 1980s by a Palestinian preacher Sheik Abdallah Azzam, considered the founder of al-Qaïda and a mentor of Osama bin Laden. Salafis adopt a fundamentalist literal interpretation of Muslim teaching from the Koran and other sacred texts. These preachers and their militants were seeking fertile and safe ground to continue their Jihadist causes in places like Bosnia, Chechnya, Kosovo and Kashmir. At the same time they began creating European networks of Jihadist Salafism. For other militants, the decision to set up in Western nations was based on the need to establish international and financial networks. Given that the British legislation was less restrictive than others, and there was a strong Arab-Islamic banking and media presence, London was an obvious choice. But Londonistan was also the product of the meeting between imported Jihadist ideology on one hand, and a segment of the British Muslim population which had become increasingly radicalised since the Salman Rushdie affair erupted in 1989. Londonistan is essentially divided into two distinct factions or schools of thought, the nationalists and the internationalists (Thomas 2005).

The United Kingdom, whose government had apparently denied the grave threat from within, received its rude wake-up call on the morning of July 7, 2005, when a series of coordinated suicide bomb blasts struck London's public transport system during the morning rush hour. Three suicide bombs exploded within less than one minute of each other on three London Underground trains. A fourth suicide bomb exploded on a London bus nearly an hour later in Tavistock Square. The suicide bombings killed fifty-two innocent people, the four homegrown fanatical Islamic suicide bombers, and also caused a severe, day-long disruption of the city's transport and telecommunications.

It was a major tragedy that became etched in the British people's minds. The French terrorism expert Dominique Thomas had this to say about the events:

> Whatever the motivations of the four young British Muslims believed responsible for the London bombings, their synchronised attacks have inevitably put the British capital in the spotlight as a centre of international Islamic extremism. Though initial investigations indicate the four may not be directly linked to global Jihad (Holy War) groups, their actions have compromised Britain's future role as an

ideological, financial and operative base for those who gravitate around the al-Qaïda terror network. It is possible that those who carried out the 7 July explosion in London may have been acting independently, deciding to act in the name of an ideology, promoted by those who endorse a global Jihad, without necessarily having a "central command." One thing is certain though. By striking so violently on British soil, the attacks run the risk of putting a definitive end to what London has become for radical Islamist groups—an international financial, ideological and strategic base for jihadist action around the globe. Their freedom of movement and action will in the future be substantially curtailed (Thomas 2005).

The hawkish British journalist Melanie Phillips, who borrowed the neologism *Londonistan* from Thomas, thought that the "curtailment" of the freedom of movement and action of British *jihadis* had not gone nearly far enough (Phillips 2006). In 2006 the British Home Secretary, John Reid, met with the Muslim community in London to urge Muslim parents to watch their children for signs of Islamic extremism. He said, "There is no nice way of saying this, but there are fanatics looking to groom and brainwash children, including your children, for suicide bombing." Reid was hoping that his warning would help Muslim parents stem the growth of homegrown British Islamic terrorism. But Reid overlooked the fact that one of the reasons young people become fanatics is precisely their complex and tortured relationships with their parents. Later, a public row erupted when UK Prime Minister Tony Blair and other politicians criticized the wearing of veils by Muslim women as a slap in the face to mainstream British society. In an interview with a journalist, the British Muslim writer Hanif Kureishi said, "It's an important debate about the relation between Islam and liberalism and the kind of society we want to make" (R. Johnson 2006). The problem of homegrown Islamic terrorism in the United Kingdom continued to preoccupy the world in late 2006 as British air traffic was halted due to Islamic terrorist plots to blow up in midair dozens of airliners flying to the United States with their many thousands of passengers.

Terror, Love, and Hate

To understand the mind of terrorists, we need to know what terror has to do with early infantile love and hate. We need to understand the psychological origins of love and hate, early infantile terror, and narcissistic rage, as well as their vicissitudes in the fundamentalist Muslim family, in order to understand Islamic terrorism. Love and hate are among the most important emotions that affect our lives, but they are highly elusive, complex, and multifaceted phenomena. They are puzzling and often tragic, and they may lead to violence and terror. Violent love may turn into violent hate. The word "lovesick" attests to love's psychopathological aspect.

What are we to make of the fanatical, blind, and self-destructive love of the young Spanish soldier for the gypsy *femme fatale* in Prosper Merimée's novella *Carmen* (and in Georges Bizet's opera of that title), which leads the hero to desert the army, become a criminal, and finally murder the woman he loves? And what are we to think of the teenager love in Scott Spencer's novel *Endless Love* (and in Franco Zeffirelli's film of that title), which leads the seventeen-year-old American boy to "accidentally" burn down the house of his beloved fifteen-year-old girlfriend and her family after her father tries to stop him from seeing her? Is the "unconditional love" preached by the Roman Catholic Pope Benedict XVI in early 2006 similar in any way to what most of us normally call love? And why did the same pope berate Islam and its Prophet Muhammad later that year, fanning the fires of rage and hatred of fanatical Muslims for "infidel" Christian "Crusaders" in the name of "love"?

FREUD'S THEORIES OF LOVE

During the first two decades of the twentieth century, the founder of psycho-analysis, Sigmund Freud (1856–1939), developed three different theories of love, which he often called by, connected with, or confused with, the Latin word *libido,* meaning "desire" (Freud 1905, 1910–1918, 1914; English versions Freud 1953, 1957a, 1957b, 1957c, 1957d). The American-Jewish psychoanalyst Martin Shlomo Bergmann (born 1913), son of the Czech-born Israeli Jewish philosopher Hugo Bergmann (1883–1975), labeled Freud's theories of love "love and genitality," "love and narcissism," and "love and object loss" (Bergmann 1988).

Freud's first theory of love, "love and genitality," published in 1905, made the discovery of infantile sexuality. Freud found that infants and children were not innocent, asexual creatures, but that they had a sexual world of their own. Freud also discovered the crucial importance of unconscious transference (in German *Übertragung*). He wrote: "*The prototype of every love relationship is the child sucking at his mother's breast. The finding of the love object is in fact a re-finding.*" For Freud, all love was "transference love." Freud looked at love as a "sublimation" of genital sexuality. He thought that love as well as sexuality was rooted in infancy. A person's first love object is the mother. The mother's breast provides the infant not only with nourishment but also a source of sexual pleasure which he will later on seek from his adult lover. For girls, the object of love is also first the mother but later becomes the father.

Freud saw adult love and sexuality as an extension (or rediscovery) of their early infantile forms. Later, Freud saw mature and healthy love as the coexistence of "two psychological currents," namely tender affection and sensuality. The former originates in the infant's awareness of the care and nourishment received from the mother, then from both parents, and the latter is related to "sexual energy," "sexual love," or "libido." Happy love is the fusion of these two currents. Separation of them and suppression of one or the other results in neurosis. When a man's affection and sexuality are for separate "love objects," a man may love his wife but be attracted to "lower" women sexually.

Freud thought that the sexual instincts or drives (*Triebe*) had a gratification-seeking aim. He believed that the inhibition of this aim can make sexual desire being transformed into affection in long-term relationships such as marriage. Freud stated that it is "very usual for directly sexual impulses, short-lived in themselves, to be transformed into a lasting and purely affectionate tie; and the consolidation of a passionate love marriage rests to a large extent upon this process." For Freud, intimacy and companionate love were due to the inhibition of passion.

Later, in his second theory, "love and narcissism," Freud realized the importance of self-love or narcissism in the development of love from infancy to adulthood. *Narcissism, however, can be healthy or pathological, benign or malignant, normal or abnormal. Much depends on how it develops in our early life.* Later still, Freud understood that the loss of the first love object, namely the mother, and the quest for its replacement were crucial unconscious aspects of human love. Finally, in his third theory, "love and object loss," Freud realized that human love is also an attempt to regain the lost objects of one's earlier life, especially one's mother and one's father.

It is obvious from the many words for love in our various languages and for the many gods of love in our different religions that there are many different forms, types, and qualities of human love—infantile, mature, narcissistic, altruistic, maternal, paternal, filial, fraternal, sexual, spiritual, as well as what we call "divine love." Freud believed that one's emotional health was measured by one's capacity to love (and to work). Other psychoanalysts have spoken of inner harmony, the absence of pathological defenses, and sound ego boundaries. Love has remained one of the major subjects of psychoanalytic investigation, yet few psychoanalysts have written a cohesive text on it.

Bergmann studied Freud's three theories of love and their later development and expansion by other psychoanalysts. Reviewing Freud's theories of love, Bergmann believed that Freud never integrated his three views of love into one coherent theory. In subsequent psychoanalytic theories, however, each of those views was developed further and in different directions (Abraham 1926; Waelder 1930; Reik 1944; Fenichel 1945; Balint 1948, 1952, 1956; Fairbairn 1952; Fromm 1956; Winnicott 1965; Mahler et al. 1975; Bergmann 1971, 1980, 1982, 1988; Bak 1973; Binstock 1973; Kernberg 1975; Arlow 1980; Bach 1980).

DEVELOPING AND EXPANDING FREUD'S THEORIES

Michael Balint (born Mihály Maurice Bergmann, 1896–1970), an important Hungarian-British Jewish-born Freudian psychoanalyst, placed a great emphasis on what he called "primary love." As the official synopsis of his book says, one of the eternal problems of mankind is that of love and hate. Why and how does it happen that we love this one of our fellow men, feel safe in his affection, expect satisfactions of our needs from him, and are attracted to him, while we hate and avoid others? Ever since the publication of Freud's first works, one of the main objects of psychoanalytic research has been the study of these powerful currents of the human mind.

Balint contributed several important papers on this subject. The first half of his book was a collection of all his papers on this topic. "Psycho-sexual Parallels to the Fundamental Law of Biogenetics" was an attempt to trace the development of the "erotic instincts" from their earliest biological beginnings in unicellular organisms to their highest manifestations in human beings. Other papers deal with the problems of "Genital Love," "Transference of Emotions," "Love and Hate," and so on. Balint thought that the complexities of human love and hate can be better understood if they are considered as derivatives of a very primitive relation such as the one that exists between mother and child or between two lovers, and which he describes as "primitive love" or "primary love."

Perhaps the most important field of research where this peculiar form of human relation called "love" can be studied is the psychoanalytical situation, the emotional relation between the patient and his analyst. This relation is the central problem of psychoanalytic technique and Balint's ideas made many old problems appear in a new light, but also gave rise to many intriguing new ones. It is well known that theories about the true nature of the infantile mind, theories about the development of a child's sentiments toward his early love objects, and the theories of psychoanalytic technique are closely interrelated. The second half of his book contained Balint's contributions to other issues of psychoanalytic technique.

Martin Bergmann discussed the history of the psychoanalytic controversy on the "genital character," the relation between love and gender identity, between love and narcissism, the hierarchical structure of the capacity to love, and the crucial relation between love and object loss. He also discussed the impact of psychoanalytic concepts such as *symbiosis* and *rapprochement* (Mahler et al. 1975; Shane and Shane 1989) on the understanding of conflicts in loving. Bergmann thought that while the differences in emphasis made it difficult to build a coherent psychoanalytic theory of love, it is productive to bring divergent views together. He suggested a unified theory of love based on accumulated psychoanalytic observations (Bergmann 1988).

Bergmann cited the English poetess Elizabeth Barrett Browning (1806–1861), whose misleadingly named *Sonnets from the Portuguese* include her most famous poem, *How do I love thee? Let me count the ways* (Sonnet XLIII):

> How do I love thee? Let me count the ways.
> I love thee to the depth and breadth and height
> My soul can reach, when feeling out of sight
> For the ends of Being and ideal Grace.
> I love thee to the level of everyday's
> Most quiet need, by sun and candle-light.
> I love thee freely, as men strive for Right;
> I love thee purely, as they turn from Praise.
> I love thee with a passion put to use
> In my old griefs, and with my childhood's faith.
> I love thee with a love I seemed to lose
> With my lost saints,—I love thee with the breath,
> Smiles, tears, of all my life!—and, if God choose,
> I shall but love thee better after death.

Bergmann ended his article by humbly comparing Browning's many ways of loving with his mere four aspects of love. "One of the best-known love poems in the English language, by Elizabeth Browning, opens with: 'How do I love thee, let me count the ways.' My own counting, less extravagant, is: *refinding, hoping to find what was denied, idealization, and integration.* I have stressed the connection between refinding and integration. I must now acknowledge the insight as a debt" (Bergmann 1988, p. 671).

Two years after Bergmann, the American psychoanalytic philosopher Jonathan Lear studied Freud's psychoanalytic interpretation of love (Lear 1990).

Lear believed that Freud had posited love or "libido" as a basic force in nature, one that makes individuation—the condition for psychological health and development—possible. Lear thought that love was active and important not only in the development of the individual but also in individual psychoanalysis and indeed in the development of psychoanalysis itself. After reviewing the history of the philosophical conceptions of love, nature, and mind, Lear argued that love could cure human suffering because it is the force that makes us human.

LOVE, HATE, RAGE, AND DEPRESSION

In some ways, violent terror and the *narcissistic rage* that underlies it (Kohut 1972) are defenses against depression. Depression often masks murderous rage. If you feel enraged, you cannot feel depressed at the same time. Therefore, it is important for us to examine human depression and its psychodynamics so that we may understand why terrorists need to defend themselves against it.

Karl Abraham (1877–1925) was a brilliant German Jewish psychoanalyst and a pupil of Sigmund Freud. He had many original ideas, often preceding Freud's own, and one of them was the intimate relationship between love and hate in "melancholia," which we now call "depression," and which usually develops when we lose a person who was very close to us, whom we both loved and hated at the same time, and whose death we cannot mourn. For melancholia to occur, the "object relationship" must be ambivalent: hate and love must be in contention. Once love for the object has taken refuge in "narcissistic identification," hatred can function against the part of the ego identified with that object. There it obtains "sadistic satisfaction," as reflected in the melancholic individual's suicidal wishes. Such desires result in hatred of the object being redirected back upon the self.

One of the key psychological issues here is the *ambivalence,* the mixture of love and hate for the same person, constitutional or associated with the circumstance of loss, which leads to *love and hate doing battle against one another* in the unconscious psyche until love escapes into the ego to preserve itself and hate leads to melancholia which finds expression in the typical form we are familiar with. This confrontation always ends in exhaustion, whether the unrelenting struggle with the lost object stops on its own or the object is abandoned because it is without value (Abraham 1927). If we are able to tolerate our ambivalence and integrate our good and bad feelings toward the same person or "object" whom we have lost, then normal development may occur. If not, we may get stuck in a *splitting* process, where first we split our mother into an all-good one (fairy) and an all-bad one (witch), and later we also split our whole world into an all-good part and an all-bad part, as in George Bush's "axis of evil" and "axis of good." Depression often begins after we are abandoned by our loved (and hated) "object" who "dies on us." This abandonment provokes deep *narcissistic rage* (Kohut 1972), however irrational, often because it repeats much earlier abandonments and other hurts from that object. This leads to regression, the loss of self-love and self-esteem, guilt feelings, self-accusation for the death of the loved one, need for self-punishment, suicidal ideation, and internal emotional pain.

In his classic paper on "melancholia," Karl Abraham investigated the relation between depressive states and the "pre-genital stages of libidinal organization" meaning Freud's oral and anal stages in the development of love, hate, and the psyche (Abraham 1927). Despite the obvious fact that depressed people exhibit all the symptoms of *oral* deprivation, including loss of appetite and anorexia, others overeating to fill their inner void, or a longing for the mother's long-lost breast, Abraham strangely attributed the hostility, aggression, or anger hidden in the depression to Freud's *anal* stage of development. He divided the anal-sadistic phase into two periods. In the earliest period, the "drives" obtain satisfaction by rejecting and destroying the object. During this period, the libido of the melancholic individual begins to regress. The "libidinal" regression does not end with the first period, however, but continues through the "oral-cannibalistic" stage by introjecting the lost object (the mother). This is accompanied by a refusal to eat (anorexia), a key indicator of melancholic depression.

Abraham concluded his analysis by listing five factors whose "interaction causes the specific clinical manifestations of melancholia": the constitutional reinforcement of *oral* eroticism in melancholics, the fixation of the libido on the *oral* phase of its development, *the injury to infantile narcissism caused by disappointment in love from the maternal object,* the overcoming of this injury prior to the control of Oedipal desires, and *the repetition of this primary disappointment later in the life of the subject.* While Abraham's insights were brilliant, his mistake in focusing on the "anal-sadistic" phase in depressive patients was due to the prevailing state of psychoanalytic knowledge and theory in his time. As the psychoanalyst Willard Gaylin put it, "at that time the libido theory offered only one explanation for hostility—anal sadism" (Gaylin 1968, p. 6).

In the 1920s, when Karl Abraham studied human depression, oral rage and sadism were not yet recognized and understood by psychoanalysts. They would be discovered some years later by Melanie Klein and her followers. Nonetheless, it is clear from Karl Abraham's formulations that he intuitively understood the deep oral rage underlying the "anal-sadistic" phase that he focused upon. Karl Abraham, however, later modified his own theory on depression. He realized that the depressed person had an "oral predisposition," was stuck or fixated in the oral stage of development, had suffered an early loss of love, rejection, *narcissistic injury* or disappointment before resolving his Oedipal conflict, and that this disappointment, injury, loss of love, or abandonment was repeated later in life, bringing about the depression. Narcissistic injury, which may encompass rejection, shame, humiliation, and other painful injuries to the self, produces *narcissistic rage* (Kohut 1972), which is boundless, and may be turned against the self. As it is true that adult love often repeats the early loves of our life for our parents, so it may be true that the loss of love through death or abandonment may repeat an earlier loss of love and cause deep depression. In this sense, love is the essence of life: receiving love from one's mother or caretaker at the outset of our life gives us the inner strength to go through life and its hardships. Losing that love at an early stage leaves us more vulnerable to be traumatized by later losses (Gaylin 1968, p. 10). In fact, *losing one's mother's love, or not having a good-enough mother to begin with, can cause the infant panic and terror—which may eventually lead him or her to acts of terror, repeating the terror that he or she had experienced within.*

THE MOTHER'S BREAST AS THE ORIGIN OF LOVE, HATE, AND TERROR

Melanie Klein was a psychoanalytic visionary and revolutionary. She discovered the all-important hidden emotions of our very early infancy and psychoanalyzed very little children. Klein believed that our adult life, which we believe to be rational and logical, is often irrational, having its emotional roots in our infancy. While her own personal life was tragic in many ways, including several depressions and estrangement from her daughter, she was able to sublimate her personal suffering into deep psychological insights (Segal 1981; Grosskurth 1986).

Melanie Klein was born an unwanted child and named Melanie Reizes, the youngest of four children, to a Viennese Jewish dental surgeon and his wife in Vienna. As a young woman she studied medicine, but in 1902 she abandoned her medical studies to marry at the age of twenty-one. Her unhappy marriage produced three children. Klein became interested in psychoanalysis when she was in Budapest around 1910. Due to her inner torment, she sought analysis and was psychoanalyzed by Sándor Ferenczi (1873–1933), the Hungarian follower of Sigmund Freud who later "deviated" from Freud's theories and broke with him (Grosskurth 1986).

Sándor Ferenczi was a controversial psychoanalyst, as he advocated the actual love of the analyst for the patient, and often blurred the lines between psychoanalysis, love, and sexual love. He analyzed the daughter of his mistress and fell in love with her. Unlike Freud, Ferenczi came to believe that his patients' accounts of sexual abuse by their parents as children were truthful, having verified those accounts through other patients in the same family. This, among other reasons, resulted in his break with Sigmund Freud (Rudnytsky et al. 1996; Rachman 1997). In any event, Ferenczi urged the young Melanie Klein to study the psychoanalysis of young children, and in 1919 she produced her first paper in the field. Klein later specialized in the psychoanalysis of children, becoming an expert on this subject. In 1921 Melanie Klein was invited by Karl Abraham to join the Berlin Psychoanalytic Institute, remaining there until 1926. She then came to London at the invitation of Alfred Ernest Jones (1879–1958), the founder of the British Psycho-Analytical Society and of the International Journal of Psycho-Analysis, and a former president of the International Psychoanalytic Association, who had been analyzed by Freud in Vienna (Grosskurth 1986).

As with most people who take up psychiatry, psychology, or psychoanalysis, Melanie Klein had deep personal emotional reasons for becoming a psychoanalyst. Her personal life was tragic. She was an unwanted and unloved child.

Both her parents showed little affection to her. Her much loved elder sister died when she was only four years old. Melanie was made to feel guilty for her brother's death. Her studies were interrupted by marriage and children. Her marriage failed. Her son died. Her only daughter, the well-known psychoanalyst Melitta Schmideberg (1904–1983), was very angry at her mother and hated her. She fought with her mother openly and histrionically in the British Psycho-Analytic Society and then left for America. She neither reconciled with her mother nor attended her funeral. Melanie Klein was clinically depressed at various times. She suffered greatly. She was also at odds with Anna Freud and the psychoanalytic establishment (Grosskurth 1986).

However, like Freud himself, it was precisely out of her personal misery that Melanie Klein gained her invaluable insights into human emotions and their formation in the earliest stages of our infantile development (Klein 1932, 1937). Children have numerous fears and anxieties, beginning with the infant's experience of birth itself, which can also be traumatic (Rank 1929). Klein believed children's play to be a symbolic way of controlling their early anxiety. She observed free play with toys as a means of determining the feelings and ideas associated with the early years of life. Her "object relations" theory related ego development during this period to the experience of various "drive objects," physical objects that were associated with psychic drives. *In early development, she found, a child relates to parts of its parent rather than to complete objects—* for example, *to the mother's breast rather than to the whole mother.* This she called a *"partial object."* This early, unstable, and primitive mode of identification with the mother's breast was termed by Klein the "paranoid-schizoid position." The word "schizoid" comes from a Greek verb meaning to cut, sever, or slice. In modern psychoanalysis, a "schizoid" person is one who cuts himself off from normal, satisfactory human relationships.

Melanie Klein thought that the next development phase in the infant's relationship to its mother's breast was the "depressive position," in which the infant comes to relate to whole objects, such as the mother or father, rather than to partial objects, like the mother's breast. This phase is marked by the infant's recognition of the ambivalence of his feelings toward objects, his love and hate for the same object (such as the mother's breast), and thus the moderation of his internal conflicts about them. For Klein, there was no really happier phase in this early "oral" stage, when the infant is actually entirely happy with its mother or her breast. Ambivalence was the best outcome to hope for.

Two psychoanalytic scholars have used Melanie Klein's theories of love and hate to help explain Islamic terrorism:

> the pressures of revenge, humiliation, inferiority or illegitimacy lose their power to intimidate, once ordinary Muslims gain a voice. They intend to show that there is a strong reparative streak in Islam even at a time when the jihadist mentality appears to be on the ascendancy. We would suggest that this dilemma is related to attempts to overcome, as well as to continually resist, the state of inner conflict which

Melanie Klein has called: the depressive position. The term denotes the point in human development when people begin to integrate feelings of love and hate. The alternative is to maintain a near total division between subjective states of love and hate, and the focus of such states: the "hated object" and the "idealized object." This *splitting* is accomplished by the psychological mechanisms of *denial* and *projection* and/or projective identification (Berke and Schneider 2006; italics added).

Melanie Klein thought that what we call "love" and "hate" begins in our earliest mother-infant relationship. The infant's first "love object" is not its whole mother but its mother's "good breast," the nourishing, milk-giving, life-giving, "loving" breast, which is the prototype of all human love. So is the mother's love for its baby. Similarly, hate originates in the infant when the mother's breast is frustrating, withholding, hurting, or felt as "bad." As Klein herself put it,

Feelings of love and gratitude arise directly and spontaneously in the baby in response to the love and care of his mother. The power of love—which is the manifestation of the forces which tend to preserve life—is there in the baby as well as the destructive impulses, and finds its first fundamental expression in the baby's attachment to his mother's breast, which develops into love for her as a person. My psycho-analytic work has convinced me that when in the baby's mind the conflicts between love and hate arise, and the fears of losing the loved one become active, a very important step is made in development. These feelings of guilt and distress now enter as a new element into the emotion of love. They become an inherent part of love, and influence it profoundly both in quality and quantity (Klein 1937, p. 311).

Melanie Klein believed that the infant moves from the splitting "paranoid-schizoid position" into the integrating "depressive position" in relation to its all-important "object," which is the mother's breast. Klein thought that the infant develops a "projective identification" in which it was not the impulse only, but parts of the self and bodily products that were in fantasy projected into the object. When pain came, she said, one would "put the pain on someone else" who was then felt as the persecutor. The aims of projective identification could be getting rid of an unwanted part of oneself, a greedy possession and scooping out of the object, and control of the object. One of the results was identification of the object with the projected part of the self.

The "depressive position" was more developed, when the infant realized that the mother that one hated was also the mother that one loved. The depressive position took place when one integrated the mother as a whole object rather than as a part object: not only her breast but her whole body and her whole personality. One would inhibit the need to attack, and contain the feeling into oneself. This led to the capacity for taking in and tolerating more pain. Klein's theory was also deeply linked to ambivalence; one could love and hate the mother or any other person and still have a relationship. In fact, *ambivalence, a mixture of love and hate, may be the most common condition in our human relationships.* The fixation on breasts in our mass culture and communication media as "sex symbols" is well known. Some people, both men and women, unwittingly search for the good breast that they never had all their lives, at times with unexpected and even disastrous consequences.

LOVE VERSUS HATE

Three years after the publication of Melanie Klein's book on children, an unorthodox Scottish psychiatrist named Ian Dishart Suttie (1889–1935) published a book on the origins of love and hate which took issue with Freud's theories and did not mention Melanie Klein (Suttie 1935). The book was in press when the forty-six-year-old Suttie died of a perforated duodenal ulcer. Suttie believed that the infant mind was dominated by the innate need not to lose the mother, which was the motivation that powered all future growth. He thought that love originated in the baby's good, warm, nurturing relationship with the mother, whereas hate originated in the frustration by the mother of the baby's needs for her affection, milk, and warmth (Suttie 1935, New Edition, 1988, p. 15).

One can sum up Suttie's ideas as follows: The human infant starts out in a state of nonsexual union with the mother. That is the paradigm of love. The great challenge of psychic development is the infant's separation from the mother. The trauma of badly negotiated separation from the love object gives rise to hate. The main task of early childhood is coming to terms with independence. Coming to terms with genital sexuality is not a task of early childhood and the "Oedipus Complex" notion of sexual rivalry with the father is a fiction, a construction put on the jealousy of the child confronted with another person who makes claims upon the mother. The great range of human activities including religion, science, and culture can be seen as autonomous activities and not derivatives or sublimations of the sexual impulse.

Suttie disputed Freud's ideas, and his *Origins of Love and Hate* divided psychoanalysts. Like the other "deviationists," Sándor Ferenczi and James Arthur Hadfield, who wrote the Preface to Suttie's book, Suttie made one of the most passionate pleas for a psychotherapeutic practice based on the physician's love for the deeply deprived patient. He also advocated a view of human nature congruent with the findings of modern biology, a more optimistic vision than that of "pessimistic" traditional Freudian psychology. Suttie's book was a powerful and early critique of Freud's "dual instinct theory" of psychoanalysis—*eros* and *thanatos*. One serious problem with Suttie's theories, however, is his apparent denial of anger, rage, and hate as normal human infantile emotions. Suttie thought that such "bad" emotions could be eliminated if only the mother could give the infant the good feeling of loving security. He ignored Melanie Klein's writings on the subject five years earlier, in which she found that hate was as natural as love in the infant (Klein 1930; Gordon 2002, pp. 117–119).

Suttie's ideas were unorthodox within psychoanalysis, and were rejected by most psychoanalysts. Yet fifty-three years later, in 1988, the British psychoanalytic developmental psychologist John Bowlby (1907–1990) wrote a foreword to a new edition of Suttie's book. In another book on a similar subject still later, the psychotherapist David Mann called psychotherapy "an erotic relationship" because of the powerful "transference" and "countertransfrence" feelings that develop between the patient and the therapist (Mann 1997). The word "erotic," however, in our culture usually connotes sexual love, whereas the feelings that each of the two participants unconsciously "transfers" to the other, the deepest unconscious emotions that he harbors within himself since his early life, are not necessarily sexual, not even necessarily love. A few years later, Mann put some order into the psychoanalytic theories of love and hate (Mann 2002).

This brief account of Melanie Klein's important psychoanalytic theories of love and hate and Ian Suttie's "counter-theories" was meant to throw some light on some of the most important emotional issues in the human mind. Unlike Suttie's, Klein's theories inspired a new and important school in psychoanalysis, the so-called "Object Relations" school, which was pioneered by the British psychoanalysts William Ronald Dodds Fairbairn, Donald Woods Winnicott, Harry Guntrip, and others. As in many organized societies and religions, this "heresy" initially led to a schism within the psychoanalytic movement. Some psychoanalysts could not accept the idea that infants were capable of the emotions observed by Klein. The chief issue is that infantile sensations and emotions are preverbal, they are not conceptual, and it is not easy (if not impossible) for any of us to recall how we felt as babies, or to put ourselves in that place again. Our recollections of our infancy may be the way we feel as adults when we suffer from anxiety, depression, panic, terror, rage, or when we fall in love. Over the decades, however, the schisms healed, as many formerly "Freudian" psychoanalysts were able to accept the insights of Melanie Klein and their other "Kleinian' and "Object Relations" colleagues.

"ORAL" LOVE, HATE, AND TERROR

Freud conceived of the "oral" phase of development as the primary stage in which the infant's emotional world was centered on his mouth: sucking his mother's breast, biting it, and so on. One of Melanie Klein's early followers and colleagues in psychoanalytic Object Relations theory was the Scottish-born psychoanalyst William Ronald Dodds Fairbairn (1889–1964). Fairbairn used Freud's term of "libido," which for Freud denoted sexual love, in a different sense and from an alternative viewpoint. The original Latin word *libido* meant sexual lust or desire, but the word derived from *libere,* meaning to please. Whereas Freud assumed that the human libido was pleasure-seeking, Fairbairn thought of the libido as object-seeking.

In other words, Fairbairn thought that the human libido was not primarily aimed at sexual or physical pleasure but at making *satisfying emotional relationships with others.* The first connections a child makes are with his parents and, more specifically, the infant's first "libido" is for its mother. Through diverse forms of contact between the child and his parents, an emotional bond between them is formed, and the child becomes strongly attached to his parents. This early relationship shapes the emotional life of the child in such a strong way that it determines the emotional experiences that the child will have later on in life, because the early "libidinal" objects become the prototypes for all later experience of connection with others. The kind of love that Fairbairn was discussing is called "object love" in modern psychoanalysis. This love (and its reverse, hate) arises already in infancy, in what Freud called "the oral phase," when the baby is sucking at its mother's breast. There, a love-hate relationship develops that is crucial to the rest of one's life. Sucking alternates with biting, loving the breast with hating it:

> [...] the early oral phase and [...] the late oral phase, when the biting tendency emerges and takes its place side by side with the sucking tendency. In the late oral phase there occurs a differentiation between oral love, associated with sucking, and oral hate, associated with biting (Fairbairn 1952, p. 24).

Indeed, in our adult life, these earliest infantile modes of loving and hating are "sublimated" into higher or culturally accepted interpersonal interactions: thus "biting irony" may be a sublimated form of the angry and hateful biting of the breast, whereas "sucking someone dry" or depleting someone with "love" may be an adult form of infantile oral sucking and oral needfulness. Following Melanie Klein, Fairbairn discussed "object relationships" when the earliest "object" was the mother's breast or nipple:

> the emotional conflict which arises in relation to object relationships during the early oral phase takes the form of the alternative, "to suck or not to suck", i.e. "to love or not to love." This is the conflict underlying the *schizoid* state. On the other hand, the conflict which characterizes the late oral phase resolves itself into the alternative, "to suck or to bite", i.e. "to love or to hate." This is the conflict underlying the *depressive* state. It will be seen, accordingly, that the great problem of the schizoid individual is how to love without destroying by love, whereas the great problem of the depressive individual is how to love without destroying by hate (Fairbairn 1952, p. 49).

It is noteworthy that, like Melanie Klein, Fairbairn spoke of schizoid and depressive individuals, but not of say social, aggressive, or happy ones. With the mother's breast as the earliest love and hate "object," Fairbairn noted that, in the late oral phase, "The object may be bitten in so far as it presents itself as bad. This means that differentiated aggression, as well as libido, may be directed towards the object. Hence the appearance of the *ambivalence* which characterizes the late oral phase" (Fairbairn 1952, p. 49). He discussed the great psychological importance of ambivalence, that mixture of love and hate which begins in this earliest phase of our development but persists into our adult life:

> the great problem which confronts the individual in the late oral phase is *how to love the object without destroying it by hate.* Accordingly, since the depressive reaction has its roots in the late oral phase, it is the disposal of his hate, rather than the disposal of his love, that constitutes the great difficulty of the depressive individual. Formidable as this difficulty is, *the depressive is at any rate spared the*

devastating experience of feeling that his love is bad. Since his love at any rate seems good, he remains inherently capable of a libidinal relationship with outer objects in a sense in which the schizoid is not. His difficulty in maintaining such a relationship arises out of his ambivalence. This ambivalence in turn arises out of the fact that, during the late oral phase, he was more successful than the schizoid in substituting direct aggression (biting) for simple rejection of the object [...] *the depressive individual readily establishes libidinal contacts with others; and, if his libidinal contacts are satisfactory to him, his progress through life may appear fairly smooth.* Nevertheless the inner situation is always present; and it is readily reactivated if his libidinal relationships become disturbed. Any such disturbance immediately calls into operation the hating element in his ambivalent attitude; and, when his hate becomes directed towards the internalized object, a depressive reaction supervenes (Fairbairn 1952, pp. 54–55; italics added).

Fairbairn's work on "object relations" is important because it makes us aware of how deeply our love and hate relationships are rooted in our earliest life experiences, and that we cannot truly understand adult love and hate without becoming aware of their infantile origins. As we shall see, neither can we understand terror without understanding the infantile origins of love and hate. The earliest terror is that of losing the mother.

LOVE AND HATE IN TRANSITION

Born seven years after Ronald Fairbairn, the British psychoanalyst Donald Woods Winnicott (1896–1971) can be said to have founded modern child psychiatry, even though he was not himself a psychiatrist but a pediatrician. While he made errors of judgment and at times also breached professional ethics (Rodman 2003), Winnicott was a great psychoanalytic innovator and had a deep understanding of the human psyche. In his twenties, Winnicott had a personal emotional crisis and began his own psychoanalysis with James Strachey (1887–1967), who had himself been psychoanalyzed by Sigmund Freud in Vienna and would later translate Freud's works from German into English. Winnicott's personal analysis and his great sensitivity helped him understand the crucial importance of maternal love and the earliest mother-child relationship to the development of mature love in the child-turned-adult. His writings emphasized empathy, imagination, and love, or, in the words of Martha Nussbaum, "the highly particular transactions that constitute love between two imperfect people" (Winnicott 1965, 1971, 1989; Nussbaum 2003).

One of Winnicott's chief contributions to psychoanalysis was the notion of the "transitional object." By "transition" Winnicott meant an intermediate space between internal and external reality. In this "transitional space," we can find the "transitional object." In the process of separation and individuation, when the toddler begins to separate the "me" from the "not-me" and evolves from complete dependence on its mother to a stage of relative independence, it uses transitional objects, such as a security blanket or a teddy bear.

An infant experiences himself and the mother as a single united whole. In this phase, the mother "brings the world" to the infant without delay, which gives him the omnipotent illusion that his own wish creates the object of his desire, which brings with it a sense of satisfaction. Winnicott called this "subjective omnipotence." Alongside the subjective omnipotence of a child lies an objective reality, which constitutes the child's awareness of the separateness between himself and his desired objects. While the subjective omnipotence experience is one in which the child feels that his desires create satisfaction, the objective reality experience is one in which the child independently strives to seek out the objects of its desire (Winnicott 1965, 1971, 1989).

Later on the child painfully comes to realize that the mother is separate from him, through which it appears that the child has lost something. The child realizes that he is dependent on others and thus he loses the idea that he is independent, a realization which creates a difficult period and brings frustration and anxiety with it. It is at this stage that love may turn into hate, and that the infant may be overcome with terror. The crucial issue now is how the child deals with these painful feelings. After all, it is impossible that the mother be always there to "bring the world" to the baby, a realization which has a powerful, painful, but hopefully constructive impact on the child. Through his fantasies about the object of his wishes the child will find comfort. A "transitional object" can be used in this process. The transitional object is often the first "not-me" possession that really belongs to the child. These could be real objects like a blanket or a teddy bear, but other "objects," such as a melody or a word, can play this role as well.

This "transitional" object represents all components of "mothering," and it means that the child himself is able to create what he needs as well. It enables the child to have a fantasized bond with the mother when she gradually separates for increasingly longer periods of time. The transitional object is important at the time of going to sleep and as a defense against anxiety. In a later stage of the development, the child no longer needs the transitional object. He is able to make a distinction between "me" and "not-me," and keeping inside and outside apart and yet interrelated. This development leads to the use of illusion, symbols, and objects later on in life (Winnicott 1965, 1971, 1989). The psychoanalytic theories of separation and individuation were further developed by Margaret Mahler and her colleagues (Mahler et al. 1975).

Donald Woods Winnicott reportedly complained to his former patient, close friend, and colleague Marion Blackett Milner (1900–1998), who had also been in love with him, that he had been "weaned early because his mother could not stand her own [sexual] excitement during breast feeding" (Milner 1934, 1937, 1987; Nussbaum 2003; Rodman 2003, p. 14; Sayers 2004). Actually, there may have been other physical and emotional reasons for Donald's being weaned early—if in fact he *had* been—such as his mother's inability to give, a postpartum depression, her narcissistic wish to keep her breasts beautiful, her unconscious rejection of her baby, the pain of mastitis or other pain in nursing, or perhaps the fact that the little baby Donald bit her breast and hurt her. Winnicott's complaint to Milner may also have been an unconscious accusation against *her* that *she* had not given him enough. She, in turn, before her death, complained to Linda Hopkins that Winnicott had failed her in not analyzing her profound rage (at him). Was he aware of his own rage?

Be that as it may, Winnicott could not forget what he remembered as his deep emotional hurt by his mother. Eight years before his death, he returned to this subject in a moving poem about Jesus Christ and his mother Mary (Rodman 2003, pp. 289–291). On a deeper level, the poem is about Winnicott himself and his own mother. The Hebrew-Aramaic phrase *Eloi, Eloi, lama sabachthani?* near the end of the poem is a corruption of the original language of the famous New Testament verse, *My God, My God, why hast thou forsaken me?* (Matthew 27:46).

Winnicott's heart-rending poem expresses the despair of the infant son who has a grieving, depressed, and weeping mother, who cannot give him the "good-enough" mothering that he so vitally needs. "I learned to make her smile, to stem her tears, to undo her guilt, to cure her inward death, To enliven her was my living." With such a mother, the mother-infant roles are reversed, and the child must mother its own mother. This may later become a template for the male adult's love relations with women, in which case the love will not be adult and mature but infantile, and is likely to end in tragedy. It is noteworthy that Winnicott nowhere mentioned anger or rage in this sad poem.

THE SCHIZOID FEAR OF LOVE

The British psychoanalyst Harry Guntrip (1901–1975) was especially inter-ested in how "schizoid" people shut themselves up and avoid contact with others because of their profound fear of painful, damaging, and hurtful "love" (Guntrip 1961, 1968, 1971, 1994). This fear of love is due to their being stuck in what Melanie Klein called the "paranoid-schizoid position" in their earliest relationship to their mother's "bad breast." Guntrip believed that "therapeutic love could cure the schizoid patient."

Like some other psychoanalysts, Guntrip himself had a very hard life emotion-ally. He was a minister in the Salem Congregational Church in Leeds. All his life he had been plagued by "nerves," meaning emotional illness. He overworked mercilessly, then went into periods of depression, anxiety, or collapse. He real-ized that he just had to get help. Reading endless books about psychoanalysis did not cure him. He began regular sessions with the Scottish psychoanalyst Ronald Fairbairn, and later in London with Donald Woods Winnicott. By this time, Guntrip was himself in practice as a psychotherapist. He taught psycho-therapy in Leeds University (a rare thing in itself) and wrote some outstanding texts on psychoanalysis. He never forgot that he had to struggle to understand himself first, "the most important patient on the analyst's list" as Freud had insisted. It is indeed vital for a psychotherapist to first understand himself in order to understand his patients and not to cause them emotional damage: *primum non nocere* (above all do no damage).

Guntrip's writing cited and integrated the work of Melanie Klein, Ronald Fairbairn, and Donald Woods Winnicott. He also advanced his own original ideas, in which he criticized Freud for being too biology-oriented. He argued that the regressed ego exerts a powerful effect on life and understood the "schizoid" sense of emptiness as reflecting the withdrawal of energy from the real world into a world of internal object relations. He worked extensively with "schizoid" patients, people who are detached, withdrawn, and unable to form real emotional human relations. Long before Heinz Kohut, who made the "self" his key theoretical concept, Guntrip came to regard the *self* as the fundamental psychological concept, psychoanalysis as the study of its growth, and psychoanalytic therapy as a means of providing a personal relationship in which the alienated, withdrawn, or "schizoid" self is given an opportunity for healthy growth and development, and finally putting it in touch with other persons and objects as part of the healing process.

Guntrip was preoccupied by the "schizoid process." He described how the person is driven into hiding by fear and then experiences a deep, sequestered loneliness that drives him or her out of hiding back into an adaptive interface with the world. Such a person is constantly caught in the struggle between hiding or connecting to others, but in an adaptive way. Guntrip defined the psychotherapy of the schizoid process as the provision of a reliable and understanding human relationship by the therapist to the patient, of a kind that makes contact with the deeply repressed traumatized child in the patient, in a way that enables one to become steadily more able to live, in the security of a new, real relationship, with the traumatic legacy of the earliest formative years, as it seeps through or erupts into consciousness. It is a process of interaction, the function of two variables, the personalities of the two people working together toward free spontaneous growth (Guntrip 1994). Implied in this was an unconditional acceptance and love for the patient, similar to what Ian Suttie had written about.

A very different approach to the psychology of love was taken by the German-Jewish psychologist, sociologist, and philosopher Erich Fromm (1900–1980), who had been trained at the University of Frankfurt's *Institut für Sozialforschung* (the Frankfurt School). He was the former husband of the German-Jewish psychoanalyst Frieda Fromm-Reichmann (1889–1957), at whose "psychoanalytic sanatorium" in Heidelberg he was trained during the 1920s. In *The Art of Loving,* Fromm proposed his own theories of brotherly love, motherly love, erotic love, self-love, and love of God, and examined "love's disintegration in contemporary Western culture" (Fromm 1956, pp. 77–98).

Fromm thought that because modern man is alienated from himself, from his fellow men, and from nature, we seek refuge from our aloneness in the concepts of love and marriage. However, Fromm believed that "real love" was "not a sentiment which can be easily indulged in by anyone." It is only through developing one's total personality to the capacity of loving one's neighbor with "true humility, courage, faith and discipline" that one attains the capacity to experience real love. This should be considered a rare achievement (Fromm 1956, p. vii). The active character of true love, Fromm observed, involves the basic elements of care, responsibility, respect, and knowledge. Fromm did not have much to say about hate, perhaps denying it in some manner, like Ian Suttie before him.

NARCISSISM, LOVE, AND THE SELF

It has long been recognized by psychoanalysts that in addition to love and hate of others, there are also self-love and self-hate. Self-love is also known as *narcissism* due to the ancient Greek myth of the beautiful young Narcissus, who fell in love with his own image in the water, thinking that it was another beautiful young man, and not knowing that it was himself. The Austrian-born American-Jewish psychoanalyst Heinz Kohut, the founder of "self-psychology," revolutionized psychoanalysis by centering his theories of the human mind around the notion of *narcissism* and the *self* rather than around Freud's drives or affects.

Falling in love and being in love invariably involves an idealization of the love object. This idealization resembles that which the infant and child have for their parents. Idealization may be a defense (involving repression, reaction formation, or denial) against unconscious hostility, rage, and aggression. Being in love often has a narcissistic function. The person who is in love sees himself or herself unconsciously in the idealized love object. Freud considered love a form of transference, by which early love feelings for one's mother or father are unconsciously transferred to the current love object. To Kohut, both infantile incestuous and mature love were always accompanied by "aim-inhibited exhibitionism, heightened self-esteem and overestimation of the love object."

Kohut distinguished between two kinds of transference both in the psychoanalytic relationship and in love relationships: the "idealizing transference" and the "mirroring transference" (Kohut 1971, p. 174). Kohut wrote in a footnote: "I have no hesitation in claiming that there is no mature love in which the love object is not also a self-object [...] there is no love relationship without mutual (self-esteem enhancing) mirroring and idealization" (Kohut 1977, p. 122, n. 12). Kohut rejected Suttie's idea that a psychoanalyst should love his patient "not only because it is not essential but because it is to my understanding a faulty, unempathic response" (Kohut 1978, p. 929).

Kohut did not have much to say about hate, but he had much to say about *rage,* especially what he called "narcissistic rage." Referring to the German Nazis and their mass murders, he wrote: "Human aggression is most dangerous when it is attached to the two great absolutarian [sic] psychological constellations: the grandiose self and the archaic omnipotent object. And *the most gruesome human destructiveness is encountered [...] in the form of orderly and organized activities in which the perpetrators' destructiveness is alloyed with absolute conviction about their greatness and with their devotion to archaic omnipotent figures"* (Kohut 1978, p. 635). This is very important to keep in mind when we try to understand the behavior of Islamic terrorists.

Kohut linked narcissistic rage directly to narcissistic injury: "Narcissistic rage occurs in many forms; they all share, however, a specific psychological flavor which gives them a distinct position within the wide realm of human aggressions. *The need for revenge, for righting a wrong, for undoing a hurt by whatever means, and a deeply anchored, unrelenting compulsion in the pursuit of all these aims, which gives no rest to those who have suffered a narcissistic injury*—these are the characteristic features of narcissistic rage in all its forms and which set it apart from other kinds of aggression" (Kohut 1978, pp. 637–638; italics added). If we think of Osama bin Laden, *al-Qaïda,* and the September 11, 2001 suicide murderers, we can well appreciate the correctness of Kohut's observations (Falk 2001b). It is safe to say that each and every one of the "terrorists" suffered from deep narcissistic injury and boundless narcissistic rage.

LOVE AS SELF-EXPANSION

When we study love and hate, and their relation to terror, we often wish to know whether opposites attract, as the saying goes, or do we rather fall in love with those who are like us? The Swiss psychiatrist Carl Gustav Jung (1875–1961) thought that he had the answer. Rather than a clearly formulated theory of love, however, Jung gave us aphorisms like, "Where love rules, there is no will to power; and where power predominates, there love is lacking. The one is the shadow of the other." Jung saw "love at first sight" as "anima, the shadow of the animus." Jung, and who during Adolf Hitler's rule in Germany (1933–1945) willingly collaborated with Hitler's Nazis, told his Chilean friend Miguel Joaquín Diego del Carmen Serrano Fernández (born 1917), the self-styled "esoteric Hitlerist," that "nothing is possible without love, not even the processes of alchemy, for love puts one in a mood to risk everything and not to withhold elements" (Serrano 1966; Noll 1994, 1997).

In 1909, at the Burghölzli, the cantonal psychiatric university hospital and clinic of Zurich, the thirty-four-year-old Carl Gustav Jung had fallen in love with one of his female patients, the twenty-three-year-old Russian Jewish medical student Sabina Spielrein (1885–1941), and made her his mistress. Paul Eugen Bleuler (1857–1940), the Burghölzli director, found out about this breach of professional ethics and dismissed Jung from his job. Jung's relationship with Sabina, however, lasted until 1912. Sabina saw Sigmund Freud in Vienna. The young Jung had become Freud's disciple and heir apparent, but fell out with his mentor in 1913. Jung had a serious emotional crisis (a depression or psychotic episode), and founded his own "Jungian school" of psychoanalysis (Freud and Jung 1974). Tragically, in 1941 Sabina Spielrein was murdered by Hitler's Nazis, with whom Jung collaborated (Loewenberg 1995, pp. 71–76).

To replace Freud's concept of the "unconscious," Jung had coined the term "shadow." The Jungian "shadow" is the diametrical opposite of the conscious self, everything that it does not wish to acknowledge about itself. A person who sees himself as kind has a shadow that is unkind. Conversely, an individual who is brutal has a kind shadow. The shadow of persons who are convinced that they are ugly appears to be beautiful. The Jungian "shadow" is neither good nor bad. It is meant to counterbalance our one-sided "character traits." Jung emphasized the importance of being aware of one's shadow and incorporating it into one's conscious awareness, to avoid unconsciously projecting these attributes onto others. The shadow in dreams is often represented by dark figures of the same gender as the dreamer, such as gangsters, prostitutes, beggars, or liars.

In the mid-1980s, the American-Jewish philosopher Irving Singer published a three-volume history of the Western philosophy of love (Singer 1984–1987). At the same time, two American-Jewish psychologists, Arthur and Elaine Aron, published a "Jungian" theory of love as "the expansion of the self" (Aron and Aron 1986). In fact, their theory drew on Freud's ideas about the connection between love and narcissism. The Arons believed that the need for "self-expansion" was the basic motivation for human behavior so that people are attracted to others in whom they see the opportunity for self-expansion. Aron and Aron believed that their theory could clarify some issues related to human sexual attraction. For example, similarity had been identified by researchers as a major predictor of attraction, but how do we explain the apparent contradiction between the idea that "birds of a feather flock together" and the notion that "opposites attract"?

The Arons believed that these seeming contradictions reflected the roles that similarity plays in different phases of a love relationship. At first, similarity is the key factor: it serves as a "precondition variable," that is, it decides whether a love relationship is at all possible. After the perceived possibility of the love relationship is affirmed by both sides, however, it is the opposite of this "precondition variable" that determines the development of the love relationship. At this point, dissimilarity is decisive: it makes the lover believe that the love relationship offers an opportunity for self-expansion and that it is worth maintaining (Aron and Aron 1986).

The "highly sensitive" Elaine Aron (her own description of herself) later wrote "how to" books for highly sensitive persons, telling them how to manage their love life (Aron 1996, 2000). She defined "highly sensitive persons" as people who "pick up on subtleties, reflect deeply and therefore are easily overwhelmed." Drawing on the findings of modern neuropsychology, Aron saw the cause of this "innate temperament" of the "highly sensitive person" as his or her strong "pause-to-check system," involving the cerebral neurotransmitter serotonin. The result, she thought, was "a major, normal, inherited difference in how the entire nervous system functions [and affects] every aspect of life" for the 15–20 percent of the population who are "highly sensitive people."

Elaine Aron also identified other people as "high sensation seekers" who had the "inherited traits" of love for change and bold risk-taking, spurred by high levels of the neurotransmitter dopamine. She thought it possible for one person to be a "highly sensitive person" and a "high sensation seeker" at the same time, or to be non-sensitive and non-sensation seeker, or any combination of the two. She offered self-tests to help her readers assess themselves and their partners in both areas. Based on her research as a psychotherapist, hundreds of personal interviews with individuals and couples, and some recent controlled studies done by others, Aron describes the various possible "personality combinations," the reasons for their attraction to one another, and the potential areas of conflict in love relationships. She offered "a fresh way of perceiving the diversity and complexity of human personality that will help readers better understand themselves, their partners and the dynamics of interaction" (Aron 2000). Despite the fascinating new science of neuro-psychoanalysis (Solms 1997; Kaplan-Solms and Solms 2000; Solms and Turnbull 2002; Peled 2008), however, the activity of two neurotransmitters cannot explain the vast complexity of human love (or hate).

LOVE AND ATTACHMENT

Melanie Klein had written of "the baby's attachment to his mother's breast, which develops into love for her as a person" (Klein 1937, p. 311). The attachment view of love is both a developmental and an evolutionary view. The emotional bond between infants and their mothers is evident in both humans and primates. When an infant needs its mother and she is unavailable, such as in the case of separation, the infant is extremely agitated, distracted, and engaged in protest and active searching to regain her presence. If such searching fails, the infant becomes sad or depressed, and eventually enters a state of defensive disregard for and avoidance of the mother if she returns.

"Attachment" was the term introduced by the British psychoanalytic developmental psychologist John Bowlby (1907–1990) for a set of behavioral actions (crying, smiling, clinging, moving, looking, etc.) that function together to achieve proximity to the primary caregiver, who is normally the mother, and establish a mutual love relationship with her (Bowlby 1969–1980; Rholes and Simpson 2006; Grossmann et al. 2006). The breaking of this attachment may lead to unhappy consequences. Bowlby himself had deep personal reasons for developing this "attachment" theory. He was the fourth of six children and was raised by a nanny, rather than by his mother, in the traditional British fashion of his class, feeling abandoned by his mother. His father, Sir Anthony Bowlby, the first Baronet Bowlby, was the surgeon to the King's Household. Sir Anthony had lost his own father at the age of five.

As a child, John Bowlby saw his mother only one hour a day after teatime, though during the summer she was more available. She had thought that spoiling her children was dangerous so that attention and affection was the opposite of what was required with a child. When Bowlby was almost four years old, his beloved nanny, who was actually his primary caretaker in his early years, left the family. This loss deeply traumatized him. Later, he was to consider this loss as tragic as the loss of a mother. At the age of seven, he was sent off to boarding school. His later books, *Separation: Anxiety and Anger* and *Loss: Sadness and Depression* (Bowlby 1969–1980, vols. 2 and 3), revealed that he regarded it as a terrible time for him. Because of such experiences as a child, he displayed an unusual sensitivity to children's suffering throughout his life.

Bowlby's "attachment theory" argued that the "biological" purpose of such an innate behavioral system is to keep the infant close to the mother and protect it during its early and most vulnerable years. This notion draws on Ian Suttie's statement that the infant's primary need is to retain its mother (Suttie 1935, New Edition, 1988, p. 15). An infant's attachment experience with the mother or other primary caregiver is so profound that the infant develops "internal working models" of attachment (i.e., mental representations of self and the way others relate to the self), which will guide a person's expectations of and behavior in relationships throughout life. Toward the end of his life, Bowlby wrote a foreword to a new edition of Ian Suttie's theories on love and hate, which had challenged traditional Freudian theories (Bowlby 1988).

Intrigued by Bowlby's theories, researchers began to investigate individual differences in attachment style. Mary Ainsworth and her colleagues identified three major attachment patterns based on infants' behavior in a reunion with the mother after a brief separation. "Secure" infants, in the mother's presence, explore actively and use the mother as a "secure base" for their adventures. They are upset when separated from the mother, and seek bodily contact and comfort when reunited. "Anxious/ambivalent" infants, upon the mother's return, show desire for proximity, but also anger and resistance. They display an intense emotional protest and an inability to be comforted into normal play. "Avoidant" infants ignore and avoid interaction with the mother by turning away to other things such as playing with toys. Ainsworth and her colleagues have also found sets of parental behaviors that correspond to the infants' attachment styles. The secure mothers are sensitive and responsive. The anxious mothers are inconsistent, unpredictable, and intrusive. The avoidant mothers are rejecting and rebuffing (Ainsworth et al. 1978).

Adult romantic love can be viewed as a continuation of Bowlby's attachment process, according to Shaver, Hazanet, and Bradshaw (1988). They applied Ainsworth and her colleagues' three-category system to the study of adult romantic love by translating it into an adult romantic attachment measure. The results from their empirical studies generally support the notion that characteristics of parent-child relationships identified as probable causes of differences in infant attachment styles are also among the determinants of adult romantic attachment styles. First of all, the proportion of the three attachment styles is roughly the same in adulthood as in infancy when measured by their romantic attachment questionnaire (e.g., 55 percent secure, 25 percent avoidant, and 20 percent anxious/ambivalent). Also, differences in adult attachment styles are found to be related to differences in most significant love experiences, mental models of self and relationships, attachment history (memories of childhood relationships with parents), vulnerability to loneliness, and feelings related to work, such as feelings toward relationships with coworkers and using work to avoid social contacts. The latter finding is in line with Bowlby and Ainsworth's concept of the relation between the "attachment system" and the "exploration behavioral system."

Shaver, Hazanet, and Bradshaw (1988) further conceptualized love as an integration of three biologically based behavioral systems: attachment, caregiving, and sexuality. Each has its own set of distinct behaviors and functions. All three behavioral systems can be distorted by "non-optimal social-learning experiences." And they may take on different time courses, which may be the reason for love's different subtypes and developmental stages, as they are identified by other researchers. For example, Hatfield and Walster's "companionate love" includes attachment and caregiving but not necessarily sexuality, whereas "passionate love" emphasizes only sexual attraction (Hatfield and Walster 1978). In recent years, several hundred articles and edited-book chapters on the subject of human attachment have been written by scholars. Attachment theory has become one of the most popular perspectives currently influencing research in close relationships (Cassidy and Shaver 1999).

Bowlby viewed the early separation from the mother as the cause of *anxiety and anger,* and the loss of the mother as the source of *sadness and depression.* He believed that unpleasant stimuli like darkness, noise, strangeness, being alone, or sudden approach were anxiety-provoking, and that the child reacts to such anxiety with "biologically-inherited" behavior such as flight and avoidance. The Canadian psychoanalyst Charles Hanly disagreed with what he called Bowlby's "ethological" theory of anxiety, arguing that "the factors identified by Bowlby play a secondary role to psychodynamic factors in the causation of phobias," that we need to consider the patterns of "object relations" in anxiety reactions, and "the regulatory work of the ego's mechanisms of defense which provide for the autonomous regulation of anxiety" (Hanly 1978, pp. 377–378).

Bowlby also has a non-psychoanalytic critic in the developmental psychologist Judith Rich Harris. Bowlby had laid a great emphasis on the quality of the child's early relationship with its mother. Harris believed that nature matters more than nurture. Most people assume that kind, honest, and respectful parents will have kind, honest, and respectful children and parents that are rude, liars, and disrespectful will have children that are the same way. This, however, may not be the case, Harris thought. Parents do not entirely shape their child's personality or character. A child's peers have more influence on them than their parents. Children whose parents were immigrants can continue to speak their parent's native language at home, but can learn their new language and speak it without an accent, while the parent's accent remains. Children learn these things from their peers because they want to fit in with their peer group (J.R. Harris 1998, 2006). But Harris seems to have missed the child's hunger for the parents' love and the vicissitudes of their relationships.

SUMMARY: LOVE AND HATE IN "WESTERN" SOCIETY

All the psychoanalytic theories of love and hate agree that they are vastly complex emotions with deep roots in our infancy and in our unconscious mind. Our earliest physical and emotional experiences with our mother deeply affect the kind of people we fall in love with, what people we hate, how love may turn into hate, the kind of attachments we form with people, and the healthy or unhealthy nature of our love and hate relationships. Love and hate have to do with our sexuality, our narcissism, our early loss of our fusion with our mother, and our quest for its restoration, re-finding the lost object, idealization, and integration. They fulfill our deepest needs and can cause us our most tragic troubles if our conflicts about our early love and hate objects have not been resolved.

The single most important psychoanalytic notion for our understanding of terrorism seems to be Heinz Kohut's notion of *narcissistic rage*. I shall repeat it here before moving on to the study of Islamic terrorism: "*The need for revenge, for righting a wrong, for undoing a hurt by whatever means, and a deeply anchored, unrelenting compulsion in the pursuit of all these aims, which gives no rest to those who have suffered a narcissistic injury*—these are the characteristic features of narcissistic rage in all its forms and which set it apart from other kinds of aggression" (Kohut 1978, pp. 637–638). This boundless rage, together with many other unconscious factors, which we shall discuss below, such as longing for love, longing for fusion, splitting, projection, and the dynamics of the fundamentalist Muslim family, may help us solve the psychological riddle of Islamic terrorism, including the suicidal type.

A few years ago, the British psychotherapist David Mann edited a learned book on the psychoanalytic theories of love and hate, or rather about love and hate in psychoanalysis (Mann 2002). Those theories, however, developed in what we call "Western" society, in the late nineteenth and twentieth centuries. Are they valid for Muslim society in the twenty-first century, both in the Muslim countries and in the Western countries with Muslim minorities? The second part of this book will try to answer these questions.

Two years after the tragic Oklahoma City bombing of 1995, in which hundreds were killed and injured, an American scholar published a psychoanalytic study of its unconscious motivations (Carr 1997). He believed that we need to go beyond a reading of the passionate convictions, the "rational" rhetoric, and ideological arguments in trying to understand this act of terrorism and the aftermath reactions. In the highly emotionally charged and anxiety-producing environments of social conflict, one can also expect to encounter a number of unconscious processes—such as projection, projective identification, splitting, idealization, stereotyping, narcissistic desire for the ego ideal (or group ideal), denial, and other defense mechanisms. Carr cited a representative text from the reporting of the Oklahoma bombing and its aftermath which he then read through the conceptual lens of psychoanalytic theory. He highlighted the issues and behaviors that seem typically to arise in such disaster situations.

The American literary and psychoanalytic scholar Elaine Hoffman Baruch thought that psychoanalysis was vital for understanding terrorism in general and of Islamic terrorism in particular (Baruch 2003). She believed that the tragedy of September 11, 2001 had injected new life into psychoanalysis, both by serving therapeutic needs and by illuminating the causes of terrorism. Baruch felt that "the traumatic separation of the sexes in Islamic societies," which prevented a normal expression of sexual feelings, was a major cause of Muslim fundamentalism, and that the fanatical Islamic search for violent political activity and suicide bombing was but "one result of hating one's own sexual impulses." She thought that of all the scientific disciplines, psychoanalysis was best able to deal with the irrational aspects of terrorism. Although psychoanalysis "shapes the way people in the West look at the world," not all of its principles are universal, and it should give more attention to the Islamic world in the hopes of developing a "global talking cure." Baruch's hopes, however, seem unrealistic when the world is facing a fanatical Islamic government, that of Iran, which may soon possess nuclear weapons and other weapons of mass destruction.

Unlike Baruch, the American-born Israeli psychologist Israel Charny, an international expert on genocide, is not psychoanalytically oriented. Charny proposed a psychological way of fighting suicide bombing (Charny 2006). Like the former chief of staff of the Israeli army, General Moshe Ya'alon, he thought that suicide bombings and terror were the opening salvos of the "Third World War." Charny sought to understand the psychology of suicide bombers and the Muslim culture from which they came. From this understanding of "human evil," he proposed a "hawkish" campaign that ultimately emphasized peace rather than irrational fear. Since suicide bombing and Islamic terrorism have psychological causes, Charny proposed a psychological weapon in the war against them—a war that he believed would only escalate without "drastic action." In contrast to the fanatical Islamic preachers' cry "we love death," Charny called for a "worldwide campaign for life" led by religious and secular leaders—including Muslim ones—across the globe. As with Baruch, however, in view of the experts' pessimism about the success of the "war on terror," and the Iranian situation, one wonders whether Charny's optimism was founded.

A psychoanalytic study of *Islamic* terrorism, which involves love, hate, terror, and rage in the Muslim family and society, begs the questions of how that society is different from "Western" society, including religion *and* politics, and whether love and hate develop differently in those societies. As Reveron and Murer have pointed out, there are many kinds of Muslim societies: Arab and non-Arab, nomadic and sedentary, rural and urban, fanatically religious and relatively "secular," Sunni and Shiite, Wahhabi, Sufi, majority and minority, "Westernized" and "non-Westernized," and so on (Reveron and Murer 2006). It is as hard to generalize about child-rearing practices, family dynamics, and the development of love and hate in such varied Muslim societies as it is in supposedly uniform "Western" society.

Moreover, the geographical terms "East" and "West" are psychological notions, and there is indeed a special discipline in applied psychoanalysis called "psycho-geography" (Stein and Niederland 1989). "Western" society and Muslim society are not completely-distinct entities, but have some overlap. Present-day Europe, for example, has a large Muslim population, and there are serious problems between the majority Christians and the minority Muslims, especially in France. When we try to study love and hate in those two societies, we need to try to avoid splitting, black-and-white thinking, and oversimplification. We are dealing with very complex phenomena, both on the individual and on the collective level.

To see how easy it is to oversimplify the problem, one may contrast the journalistic view of Islamic terror with the psychoanalytic one. After the tragic 2001 destruction of New York's World Trade Center and the suicide murder of thousands of innocent people, the Italian journalist Oriana Fallaci (1929–2006), the "warrior reporter" who was then in New York and was as traumatized by the tragedy as many other people, published a book denouncing Muslim society as a whole (Fallaci 2002). At the same time, the psychoanalyst Ruth Stein published a study that sought to understand it (Stein 2002).

Fallaci argued that Islamist terrorism was nothing new, but only the most recent manifestation of an ominous reality that has existed for one thousand four hundred years. She believed that most Muslims all over the world were happy with *al-Qaïda*'s attacks on America, with some of the most radical terrorist sympathizers living in European capitals, advocating *jihad* on the free societies that have given them succor. Muslims, she argued, are incompatible with European culture and society, and cannot be assimilated. Fallaci attacked "pampered" Italians who disdain manual labor and refuse to have children, thus making Muslim immigration necessary, and resented the "vulgar and anti-social habits" that many Islamic immigrants have brought into Europe (especially their high-handed and abusive treatment of women). Fallaci's book did not help understand or resolve the problem, and was considered by many Muslims inflammatory, racist, and biased. Her approach was very different from that of Ruth Stein, also then in New York, who sought to understand the unconscious emotional roots of Islamic terrorism (Stein 2002). We shall discuss Stein's study in the final chapter of this book, where the case studies will be presented.

At about the same time as Stein's article was published, her French Canadian colleagues Dianne Casoni and Louis Brunet published a study on the psychodynamics of terrorism (Casoni and Brunet 2002). They traced a parallel between the intrapsychic phenomena provoked in the witnesses of terrorist acts and the psychodynamics present in the authors of such acts. Casoni and Brunet suggested that terrorists unconsciously wish to draw witnesses into a psychic realm similar to their own. Through complex processes of identification, the fact of witnessing terrorist acts is understood as triggering a regressive pull toward the use of splitting and projective identification in order to defend oneself against despair. The intrapsychic differences between witnesses and terrorists were outlined, and a clinical case study was presented to illustrate the propositions presented.

Also at about the same time, the American military psychiatrist Emmanuel Cassimatis published another psychoanalytic study of terrorism (Cassimatis 2002). He began with a personal recollection of September 11, 2001, and then went on to share some thoughts about terrorism from the vantage point of a citizen who retired from active military duty a little over a year ago. He then speculated about a possible psychoanalytic understanding of terrorists and their motivation while acknowledging that terrorists too are individuals, and that no hypothesis can apply to an entire group, across the border. To illustrate his points, the author shared some vignettes from literature, biography, and philosophy. He then reflected on the post–September 11 roles of American psychoanalysts or psychodynamic psychiatrists, both as clinicians and as Americans.

The Psychological Role of the Mass Communication Media

We have repeatedly witnessed the important role played by our mass communication media in fighting or abetting Islamic terrorism. Some of our mass communication media report Islamic terrorist activity by giving us as much blood and gore as possible, quenching (and perhaps augmenting) the public thirst for such sensations. Television stations show us horror videos of massacres, executions, and atrocities which they euphemistically call "disturbing images." Yet the true horror of terrorist savagery is at times concealed from us by these very media, which euphemistically and even sympathetically call those murderous terrorists "activists," "militants" and "freedom fighters."

An example of the latter distortion occurred on September 20, 2004, in Iraq, when the American building contractor Eugene Armstrong (1953–2004), who had been kidnaped by the Islamic fanatics of *Jama'at al-Tawhid wal-Jihad* (the Community of Monotheism and Holy Struggle), led by the Jordanian-born master terrorist Abu Musab al-Zarqawi (1966–2006), was savagely beheaded by the latter. The actual scene of decapitation, filmed by the assassins themselves, was not telecast by most "Western" television chains. The American scholar David Livingston Smith, who was of Armstrong's age, thought that we prefer to deny the horrors: "Like many terrible things," he wrote, "it is something that we do not want to think about too much if we can help it" (Smith 2007).

Ostensibly to counterbalance the denial of the U.S. mass communication media, Smith did the opposite: he deliberately described the censored video of Armstrong's decapitation in its gruesome detail: "The long knife sliced through

Armstrong's flesh. He screamed. Blood gushed from his neck. His body shud-dered and became limp. The executioner placed the dripping, severed head on the back of Armstrong's lifeless body [...] Armstrong's execution was an act of war, and war is terrible" (Smith 2007). Was this gory description really neces-sary? The American critic Abram Bergen thought that "though [this video is] very disturbing, Smith believes it would perhaps have been better for our media to show it, rather than stopping short before any blood was drawn" (Bergen 2007). In fact, one wonders whether Smith did not use this horrific description to sell his own work to a public thirsting for sensational news of a sexual and violent nature.

In the summer of 2007, the American television news channel Cable News Network, better known as CNN, aired a three-chapter, six-hour documentary on religious terrorism, made by its forty-nine-year-old chief international corre-spondent, the Iranian-British-born Christiane Amanpour, entitled *God's Warriors*. This documentary dealt with religious terrorism in the world's three monotheistic religions, devoting a two-hour chapter to each. Amanpour's stated intention was to describe Jewish, Muslim, and Christian religious fundamentalism as rising, dangerous political forces. The three chapters were accordingly titled *God's Jewish Warriors, God's Muslim Warriors,* and *God's Christian Warriors.* The documentary was filmed in the United States, Europe, and the Middle East.

The six-hour CNN documentary was ostensibly evenhanded, purporting to give equal time and equal importance to fundamentalist violence in the three religions it covered. The first chapter focused on the Jewish underground movement in Israel, the murder of the Israeli Prime Minister Yitzhak Rabin, the Israeli settlements in the Palestinian territories, and the fund-raising in the United States that supported them. The second chapter presented the rise of radical Islamic groups in Arab and Muslim countries. The third chapter focused on the United States and on the political influence of fundamentalist Christian religious leaders.

CNN's documentary *God's Warriors* was supposed to be serious and to tran-scend the usual superficial coverage of television news. Mark Nelson, a senior CNN executive, proudly proclaimed, *"God's Warriors* is an investigation of reli-gion, at a time when religious activism is a signature cultural phenomenon of our times. This project's global scope is ideally suited for the skills of someone with as impressive of a journalistic pedigree as our own Christiane Amanpour." In her documentary, Christiane Amanpour declared that during the past thirty years, each of the three monotheistic faiths had produced extremist factions that became powerful political forces, comprising followers who share a dissatisfaction with modern society and a determination to place God and religion back into daily life and into the seats of power. "There are millions of people around the world who feel that their faith is being ignored—pushed aside—and they are certain they know how to make the world right," she said. "We cannot and should not ignore them. And, with this report, we've tried to explain them." She presented videos of the most violent acts of the most extreme fanatics in each of the three religions and interviews with some of their victims and perpetrators.

Unfortunately, the CNN documentary was not quite as objective or even-handed as it purported to be. Many people and groups were deeply unhappy with it. The Committee for Accuracy in Middle East Reporting in America, also known as CAMERA, took out a large newspaper advertisement angrily accusing the documentary of "equating the extremely rare cases of religiously-inspired violence on the part of Christians and Jews with radical Islam's global, often state-supported, campaigns of mass killing" and of "presenting highly controversial critics of Israel and the so-called Israel lobby and doing so without challenge." Dan Abrams, a senior person at CNN's rival, Microsoft's National Broadcasting Corporation, better known as MSNBC, called the CNN documentary "the worst type of moral relativism" and described it as "shameful advocacy masked as journalism." Rabbi Marvin Hier, the dean of the Simon Wiesenthal Center, named after the Polish-Jewish "Nazi hunter," pointed out that while the vast majority of the Israeli Jewish population condemns Jewish terrorism, a sizable part of the Arab population applauds Islamic terrorism. He called the CNN documentary preposterous, ludicrous and unforgivable.

The world's mass communication media, especially television, play an obvious psychological role in Islamic terrorism, inflaming our passions—and those of the terrorists—with their violent sound a fury, while often taking sides for or against the terrorists. Those who call the murderous terrorists "activists," "militants" or "freedom fighters" take a pro-terrorist stand by their very use of those terms to describe them. Those who equate Jewish and Christian terrorism with Islamic terrorism make false and invalid comparisons, since the former are nowhere as important, dangerous, or popular in their own societies as the latter. One useful thing that Christiane Amanpour's documentary did do was to show how religious fanaticism and terror has nothing to do with reality and everything to do with irrational, rigid, fervent, and unshakable religious belief.

Some Arab and Muslim mass communication media are sympathetic to the Islamic terrorists, while others, heavily censored by their governments, condemn them. One Arab television station in particular, Qatar's *al-Jazeera,* has a special role in the Arab world. Qatar is one of the few Arab countries with ties to Israel. It is an Arab emirate in Southwest Asia, occupying the small Qatar Peninsula on the northeasterly coast of the larger Arabian Peninsula. Qatar is bordered by Saudi Arabia to the south; otherwise the Persian Gulf surrounds the state. The Arabic name *al-Jazeera* means "the peninsula," and it refers both to the Qatar Peninsula and to the larger Arabian Peninsula of which it is a part.

The original *al-Jazeera* television channel was created in 1996 by the Emir of Qatar, Sheikh Hamad bin Khalifa, and it was joined by many former staff members of the Arabic-language service of BBC World who had lost their jobs when their service was shut down under Saudi Arabian pressure. *Al-Jazeera's* television broadcasts quickly became available via satellite throughout the Middle East, thoroughly changing the television landscape of the region. Due to heavy censorship by their authoritarian regimes, many Arab Middle Easterners had been unable to watch "Western" television channels or any channels other than their own state-censored national stations. *Al-Jazeera* introduced a freedom of speech on television that had been unheard of in many of these Arab countries. It presented controversial views regarding the governments of many Arab Gulf or Persian Gulf states, including Saudi Arabia, Kuwait, Bahrain, even Qatar itself. It also presented controversial views about Syria's relationship with Lebanon, and the Egyptian judiciary.

Critics have accused *al-Jazeera* of using sensationalism to increase its audience share, a common practice among television stations. Some of *al-Jazeera*'s broadcasts have resulted in drastic action: on January 27, 1999, *al-Jazeera* interviewed critics of the Algerian government on its program *Al-Itidjah al-Mouakass* (The Opposite Direction). To prevent the program from being viewed by its citizens, the Algerian government cut the electric supply to large parts of its capital Algiers and possibly to large parts of the country. At that time, *al-Jazeera* was not well known in the "Western" world, but where it was known, the opinion about it was often favorable and *al-Jazeera* claimed to be the only politically-independent television station in the Middle East.

Al-Jazeera's coverage of the Lebanese Civil War in 2000–2001 boosted its viewer ratings throughout the Middle East. In late 2001, *al-Jazeera* achieved worldwide fame when it broadcast video statements by Osama bin Laden and other *al-Qaïda* leaders following their September 11 destruction of New York's World Trade Center. In 2006 *al-Jazeera* launched its English-language sister channel, *Al-Jazeera English,* broadcasting from Doha, Kuala Lumpur, London, and Washington, which has made it better known in the "Western" world. Whether or not *al-Jazeera* is "objective," or what effect it may have on Islamic terrorists, is another question. The U.S. government, while generally applauding freedom of speech, has criticized *al-Jazeera*'s stand against its war in Iraq, and the U.S. Air Force has allegedly bombed *al-Jazeera*'s offices in Afghanistan and in Iraq, killing its employees. *Al-Jazeera* has also been banned from the New York Stock Exchange.

Terrorism and Anxiety

In a panel on terrorism organized by psychoanalysts in 2004, Ronald Ruskin, the moderator, noted that *terror is a normative element of anxiety, often present in children's literature.* In exploring terrorism in our time, Ruskin called for a dialogue between psychoanalysts, members of other disciplines, and the whole community. The first panelist, Marcelo Viñar, emphasized the importance of studying terrorism at the intersection of individual pathology and collective culture "to deepen the understanding of the dynamics between the individual and collective mind, of the functioning of the mind in solitude and in a crowd." His paper, "An allegation for the enemy's humanity," postulated that when people's identities are threatened by external forces such as globalization, they can develop a terrorist mind, because of the fear of "otherness"—that is, "the temptation to transform somebody different into an enemy, and to deal with this enemy through destruction and extermination" (Elmendorf and Ruskin 2004).

The psychoanalysts Salman Akhtar, Stuart Twemlow, and Frank Sacco have argued that psychoanalysis had much to offer to an understanding of terrorism in two primary domains: the collective social context and group dynamics of terrorism, and the understanding of the individual psychopathology of the terrorist. Twemlow argued that the terrorist label is always assigned to the other person; it is never a self-assigned role. The term is applicable to individuals. For example, the FBI has classified the school shooters as domestic or anarchic terrorists. Terrorists usually consider themselves the victims of humiliation by the enemy with incompatible political, religious, or personal ideologies. The definition of terrorism is influenced by the political and social mores of the time (Akhtar 1999; Twemlow and Sacco 2002; Twemlow 2005). In any event, as we have seen, early feelings of anxiety, panic, and terror are very often found in violent terrorists.

Self-Knowledge and Understanding Others

The ancient Greek adage "Know Thyself" was reportedly inscribed in golden letters at the lintel of the entrance to the Temple of Apollo at Delphi, where people came to seek self-knowledge and fortune-telling from the Pythiae. The phrase has been attributed to at least five ancient Greek sages: Chilon of Sparta, Thales of Miletus, Socrates, Pythagoras, and Solon of Athens, as well as to the mythical poetess Phemonoe, a daughter of the god Apollo, the first Pythia and the inventor of the hexameter. According to Juvenal, the precept descended from heaven.

Indeed, we cannot hope to understand others without first understanding ourselves. This is also a basic principle of becoming a psychoanalyst or psychotherapist: one must first undergo a rigorous psychoanalysis or psychotherapy with an elder or senior colleague for several years. Similarly, in order to understand Islamic terrorism and the origins of love and hate in Muslim society, we need to look at love and hate in our own society first. Self-knowledge, however, is no easy task. It is acquired at the heavy cost of emotional pain, time, money, effort, and battle with one's inner demons. As the Lebanese-born American Arab sociologist Sania Hamady put it, "to know oneself is a painful process" (Hamady 1960, Foreword).

The psychoanalytic view of love, hate, terror, and rage pays special attention to their unconscious aspects, which are conveyed, among other things, by the words that we use for these complex emotions and by their related meanings. As for love, the Arabic language has eight different words for love as a noun and seven as a verb. The modern Hebrew language has one word for love—*ahavah,* two words for sexual desire—*kheshek* and *tshukah,* and another word for affection—*hibah*. On the difference between love and sexual desire, see Bader (2002) and Akhtar (2005a, 2005b).

The Greek language has three different words for love—*agape* for spiritual love, *eros* for sexual love, and *philia* for other kinds of love. The Sanskrit language has *rasa* for love in general and *kama* for sexual love, but the Sanskrit noun *rasa* also has numerous other meanings such as affection, emotion, flavor, taste, condiment, sauce, spice, seasoning, desire, charm, pleasure, delight, nectar, essence, sap, juice, marrow, liquor, drink, syrup, drought, elixir, potion, butter, milk, soup, broth, serum, sperm, semen, and a mineral, salt, or metal in a state of fusion, while the Sanskrit verb *rasa* means to taste, to have an appetite for life, or to delight in one's existence. In the Pāli language, the liturgical language in which the scriptures of Theravada Buddhism (also known as the Pāli Canon or in Pāli the *Tipitaka*) were written down in Sri Lanka in the first century BCE (in the Sinhalese script), the word *metta* means loving-kindness.

Our human languages also distinguish between different types of love. Sanskrit has many words derived from *rasa* such as *shakhyarasa* for friendly love, *shantarasa* for neutral love, *dasyarasa* for servile love, *vatsalyarasa* for parental love, *shrinagararasa* for conjugal or sexual love, *madhuryarasa* for sweet love, as well as special words for fraternal love, happy love, compassionate love, angry love, chivalrous love, fearful love, astonished love, lamenting love, enthusiastic love, even ghastly love. Our religions have different gods of love and sexuality. The Hindu love-god is Kama, but the ancient Greeks had several such gods—Aphrodite, Eros, and the nymphs—while marital love and fidelity were assigned to the goddess Hera, wife of Zeus, "because the Greeks would never have thought of confusing falling in love with the capacity to maintain prolonged marital fidelity" (Bergmann 1988, p. 654). The Greeks had different words derived from *eros* and *philia* such as *paedophilia* (love of children), *necrophilia* (love of the dead), *philanthropia* (love of men), *philhellenia* (love of the Greeks), *erotomania* (love madness), and *nymphomania* (sexual madness).

Languages and religions are only part of the complexity of love and hate. Human love differs from "love" in other mammal species in that fantasy and language play a key role in it. Love is essential to our physical and emotional survival. It has been a major theme in human religions, philosophy, literature, music, drama, visual art, and every other aspect of human imagination and creativity. If we are fortunate, we receive maternal love when we are babies, and our mother receives our infantile love when we suck her breast, kiss her, smile at her, or hug her. Throughout our life, we experience love—or the lack of it—every day. It is easy and perhaps natural to *classify* human love into types such as infantile love, mature love, maternal love, paternal love, fraternal love, "Platonic" love, sexual love, spiritual love, narcissistic love (self-love), and love of God.

As in the case of Islamic terror and other matters, however, theories that *categorize* love do not necessarily *explain* its causes, origins, development, and functions. Psychoanalytic theories, on the other hand, take those issues as their primarily concern. However, the psychoanalytic theories on love are scattered through the psychoanalytic literature. As we shall see, there are few articles and fewer books on the psychoanalysis of love. Moreover, narcissism or self-love is a key issue in psychoanalysis. Some think that it is the primary and healthy love that each of us feel for himself early in his life, while others think that it is "a secondary and pathological state resulting from the frustration in the love relationship" (Gaylin 1968, p. 288). We shall discuss Heinz Kohut's and other theories of narcissism below.

When I was a young psychology student in the 1960s, one of my fellow students complained to me that we were being taught so much about the behavior of rats in mazes but nothing about the most important thing in our lives—love. Four decades later, the American psychotherapist David Mann edited a book on the psychoanalytic theories of love and hate (Mann 2002). This book is an attempt to follow in Mann's footsteps, to redress my fellow student's complaint, to survey the psychoanalytic literature on love, hate, terror, and rage, to offer some new insights into those key aspects of our human existence, and to link all of these insights to the understanding of the scourge of Islamic terror which plagues our world. When the infant or child feels abandoned, abused, or humiliated, its yearning for love, turned into terror, hatred, and rage, may be one of the keys to this deeper understanding.

A Clash of Civilizations?

For all its "strangeness" to the "Western" mind, Islam is one of the world's major religions, with hundreds of millions of believers. The conventional wisdom has it that Islam was created in the seventh century of the Christian era by the man Muslims believe to be the "Last Prophet," Muhammad ibn Abdallah (570–632 CE), "the messenger of Allah," who had "visions" of Allah, the father god of the ancient Arabs, speaking to him and commanding him to create the new religion. Muhammad was the "last prophet" as all the major prophets of Judaism and Christianity had been incorporated into Islam, which sought to present itself as the ultimate religion. There are also "revisionist" theories of the birth of Islam which challenge these facts (Hawting 1999; Ibn Warraq 2000; Nigosian 2004).

Recently, an Iranian-American "clinical neuropsychologist" has sought to "prove" that the Prophet Muhammad's religious visions (or hallucinations), which led to the creation of Islam, were products of epileptic seizures (Sadeghian 2006). In fact, Muhammad may have suffered from psychiatric rather than neurological illness: like some of the Jewish prophets of ancient times (Falk 1996, pp. 179–190), not only did he have hallucinations, but several times during his life he was depressed and attempted suicide (F.E. Peters 1994; Inamdar 2001). Muhammad's alleged suicide attempts are documented in several prominent Islamic texts in Arabic beginning in the ninth century CE: Muhammad ibn Ismail al-Bukhari's *Sahih al-adab al-mufrad lil-Imam al-Bukhari* (the *hadith* or oral tradition of Islam), Ibn Ishaq's *Sirat Rasul Allah* (Chapter of the Messenger of God), later rewritten by Ibn Hisham, Ibn Sa'd's *Kitab al-Tabaqat al-Kabir* (Book of the Major Classes), and al-Tabari's *Ta'rikh al-Rusul wa'l-Muluk* (History of the Messengers and Kings). These books are part of the basis of Islam today.

Al-Bukhari's *Sahih* is considered the second most important text in Islam, following the Qur'an. Ibn Ishaq's is considered to be the earliest biography of Muhammad, and al-Tabari's *History* is the best historical collection on early Islam (Watt 1953; Ibn Hisham 1955; Ibn Sa'd 1967; al-Bukhari 1971; al-Tabari 1985–1999; Ibn Ishaq 1989; F.E. Peters 1994; Inamdar 2001).

Because Muslim culture is so different from "Western" culture, and because Islamic terror gives "Westerners" the feeling that Islam wants to rule the world, in our own time it has become commonplace to speak of an inherent "clash of civilizations" between Christianity and Islam, or between "Western" culture and "Middle Eastern" culture, between which a growing chasm is occurring, no meeting of the minds is possible, and a mounting conflict is unavoidable. This notion was popularized in the early 1990s by the "Western" scholars Bernard Lewis and Samuel Huntington (Lewis 1990; Huntington 1993). The "clash of civilizations" notion is controversial, however. The Palestinian-American Christian scholar Edward William Said (1935–2003) bitterly criticized it as "the clash of ignorance" (Said 2001).

Perhaps because numbers are less painful to recall than actual memories and images of the horrors, many people use the expression *9/11* to refer to the terrible tragedy of Islamic terrorist attack on the twin towers of New York's World Trade Center on September 11, 2001, which cost thousands of lives and dealt a collective trauma to all Americans as well as individual traumas to its survivors. After the tragic event, many scholars dealt with their shock and trauma by writing scholarly books and articles about it. One of them was Daniel Pipes, a neoconservative American historian and "counter-terrorism analyst." Pipes distinguished between the religion of Islam and the ideology of militant Islam or "Islamism," which he believed was incompatible with democracy, freedom, multiculturalism, and other human rights values. Pipes compared militant Islam to the pernicious twentieth-century ideologies of Nazism and Marxism in that it is a radical political ideology that has the stated goal of taking over the world (Pipes 2002).

The neoconservative Japanese-American scholar Yoshihiro Francis Fukuyama (born 1952) thought that the West had already won the "clash of civilizations" against Islam (Fukuyama 1992). Pipes believed that Fukuyama's optimism was premature and that the Islamic threat was still very real. While U.S. President George W. Bush, who tends to see his world in black-and-white, saw his enemies as "evil doers" and declared "the global war on terror," Pipes saw the enemy of the United States as militant Islam. He believed that "if it is true that most Muslims are not Islamist, it is no less true that all Islamists are Muslims." Pipes studied the "peaceful yet insidious" American Muslim groups, such as the Council on American-Islamic Relations, the American Muslim Council, and the Muslim American Society, that use the liberal U.S. judicial system and the tolerant U.S. mass communication media to "get special treatment" and promote their cause, as well as the more visible violent strain of American Islamism. He thought that the tolerance of Islam in America had led to a double standard in American society: while a positive and "sanitized" view of Islam was adopted by U.S. public schools and mass communication media, negative views of Islam were rejected, and at the same time, negative views of Christian and Jewish groups are all too prevalent in U.S. schools and media (Pipes 2002).

While Pipes thought that militant Islam was incompatible with Western culture, he believed that secular and moderate Muslim states like Turkey could coexist with the West and become a good model for other Muslim states. Pipes added, however, that virtually all of the other Muslim states in the Middle East were moving toward Islamic fundamentalism rather than toward Western secularism. The core of the militant Islamist movement, Pipes thought, like most of the World Trade Center airplane hijackers of September 11, 2001, consisted of highly educated and overachieving Westernized Arab Muslims, rather than the abjectly poor Muslims that many people thought were behind this radical movement. Ideology, not poverty, wrote Pipes, was the driving force behind militant Islam. Poverty did not create Muslim radicals. Intelligent radical Muslim ideologues used poverty, intimidation, and brainwashing in the Muslim *madrasas* to help promote their cause (Pipes 2002).

As part of his study of Islamism in America, Pipes focused on two separatist Black American Muslim groups, the Nation of Islam and the National Ummah, and on their leaders. The Nation of Islam had been founded in 1930 by a bizarre mixed-race American named Wallace Dodd Ford, born some time between 1877 and 1893, who changed his name to Wallace Dodd Fard Muhammad and disappeared in 1934. His successor, Elijah Muhammad (born Elija Poole, 1897–1975), of whose childhood little is known, incredibly made Wallace Fard Muhammad into the Muslim god Allah, writing,

> Allah came to us from the Holy City Mecca, Arabia, in 1930. He used the name Wallace D. Fard, often signing it W.D. Fard. In the third year He signed His name W.F. Muhammad, which stands for Wallace Fard Muhammad. He came alone. He began teaching us the knowledge of ourselves, of God and the devil, of the measurement of the earth, of other planets, and of the civilizations of some of the planets other than earth.

Elijah Muhammad was succeeded by Louis Farrakhan (born Louis Eugene Walcott in 1933), a virulent racist and anti-Semite (Pipes 2002).

The National Ummah is one of America's largest Black Muslim groups. It is led by the convicted murderer Jamil Abdullah al-Amin, born Hubert Gerold Brown in Louisiana in 1943 and known in his youth as H. Rap Brown. His activism in the American civil rights movement included the Student Nonviolent Coordinating Committee, of which he was named chairman in 1967. Rap Brown was soon arrested in Maryland and charged with inciting to riot after a fiery speech he had given there. After the Chicago student riots at the Democratic National Convention in 1968, Brown left the Student Nonviolent Coordinating Committee and joined the Black Panthers. After avoiding trial on charges of inciting riot and of carrying a gun across state lines, he made the Federal Bureau of Investigation's Ten Most Wanted List. Rap Brown was arrested after a shoot-out in 1971 in New York. He spent five years in the Attica state prison after a robbery conviction. While in prison he converted to Islam and changed his name to Jamil Abdullah al-Amin. After his release from jail, he opened a grocery store in Atlanta and became a Muslim spiritual leader, preaching against drugs and gambling. He also became a leader of the National Ummah. In 1993 he published a book on his life and theories (al-Amin 1993).

In 2000 Jamil Abdullah al-Amin shot two black policemen, Ricky Leon Kinchen and Aldranon English, who tried to arrest him on charges of driving a stolen vehicle, impersonating a police officer, and failure to appear in court, all charges that stemmed from an earlier traffic stop. Kinchen was killed and English seriously injured, shot in the hip, arm, both legs, and back. One of the bullets ruptured a gas canister he had strapped to his belt, which temporarily blinded him as he tried to return fire. In 2002 the Black Muslim leader was found guilty of murder and sentenced to life imprisonment without parole, and is currently serving his sentence at Georgia State Prison near Reidsville. There is considerable controversy, however, as to whether or not Jamil al-Amin was the shooter. Supporters of Jamil al-Amin have asserted that another man, Otis Jackson, who confessed to the shooting but later recanted, was the real shooter. These supporters assert that the investigation and trial was plagued by irregularities, including the suppression of evidence. Some feel that Jamil al-Amin's conviction was politically motivated.

Pipes believed that radical Islamists in Muslim countries had used Black American Muslim demagogues like Elijah Muhammad and Jamil Abdullah al-Amin to their advantage. He thought that it was important for all Americans to understand militant Islam and to realize that the extremist Black American Muslim groups were not a normal Black reaction to American racism. Al-Amin had written, "the Constitution of the United States [...] its main essence it is diametrically opposed to what Allah has commanded" (al-Amin 1993). Pipes considered this a seditious statement. "These people want to take away your constitution and replace it with the *Qur'an*" (Pipes 2002).

Pipes thought that for moderate Muslims and "the West" to win "the war on terror," the West must not appease "neo-fascists hiding behind a head-dress." He urged Americans to notice that so-called moderate Muslim organizations like the Council on American-Islamic Relations, the American Muslim Council, and the Muslim American Society all defended Jamil al-Amin, a convicted murderer, as a good Muslim, and that this was the least of their sins. Pipes wanted these groups to prove that they did not support anti-American militant Islam by denouncing Jamil al-Amin, Ahmad Adnan Chaudhry (another convicted murderer), and Mohammad Salah (accused of financing aid to *Hamas*). In all these cases, their silence was deafening, said Pipes.

Pipes thought that the "West" should not try to defeat a nebulous "global terrorism" but see who its real enemy is. The first step in fighting Islamic terrorism was for Americans to call their enemy by its name: militant Islam. He urged Americans to see that Islamism was as insidious and dangerous as any strain of Nazism or Fascism that they had witnessed in their lifetime. Pipes thought that the Bush administration was using the vague "terrorist" label so as not to upset the Muslim world. He pointed out that America was at war with *militant Islam* and cited the Prussian General Carl von Clausewitz (1780–1831) to the effect that "contradictory goals in war is a mistake."

Pipes thought that "the chief enemies of Western civilization" were *al-Qaïda,* the Afghan Taliban, and their sympathizers. The "West" had three rings of Muslim enemies. The first ring were Afghanistan's Taliban. The second ring was the larger population of militant Islamic sympathizers in most of the Muslim Arab world and non-Arab Muslim countries like Indonesia, Malaysia, and Bosnia. With one billion Muslims on our planet, Pipes estimated that as many as 150 million fall into this group. The third ring were the non-militant Muslims who were infected with anti-American hate, including leaders like Saddam Hussein of Iraq and Muammar Qadhafi of Libya. Pipes estimated that roughly 500 million Muslims harbor anti-American and anti-Western feelings.

Pipes disagreed with Huntington's notion of the "clash of civilizations." He preferred to call it a clash of ideologies. Pipes believed that militant Muslims regularly killed other Muslims that opposed their program—witness the over 100,000 Muslims killed in Algeria, and many times that number in the Iran-Iraq war. Pipes proposed an updated version of George Kennan's cold war doctrine: "a long term patient but firm and vigilant containment of (its) expansive tendencies." He believed that American fortitude and will would convince the moderate Muslim world that it is worth fighting for Western tolerance and freedom rather than a world of Fascism and chains (Pipes 2002).

If I have dwelt at some length upon Pipes' theories of militant Islam inside and outside America, it is because they represent the views of many well-meaning neoconservative and right-wing American intellectuals. Rather than deal with their painful emotions, evoked by the terrible tragedy of September 11, 2001, and try to understand the convoluted psychology of Islamic terrorists, they take a militant anti-Islamic stance. While Pipes was writing his book, the late psychoanalyst John Mack wrote that "without understanding what breeds them and drives [the terrorists] to do what they do in a particular time and place, we have little chance of preventing further such actions, let alone of 'eradicating terrorism'" (Mack 2002, p. 174).

The North African Muslim historian Abu Zayd Abdur-Rahman bin Muhammad bin Khaldun al-Hadrami (1332–1406), better known as Ibn-Khaldun, was one of the greatest Muslim historians of all time. The Pakistani-born Muslim anthropologist Akbar Ahmed holds the Ibn-Khaldun chair in Islamic Studies at American University in Washington. Ahmed believed that Islam was under siege by Western civilization. "The twenty-first century will be the century of Islam," Ahmed predicted, adding that "the twenty-first century might be a time of war between Islam and other civilizations" (Ahmed 2003). Ahmed thought that we were "living dangerously in a post-honor world" and that the fast pace of social change caused by globalization has left many in traditional societies feeling uncertain and vulnerable.

Religions are not rational, logical, coherent philosophies. They are the irrational products of human conflicts, fantasies, wishes, and emotions. Like every other religion, Islam is fraught with internal contradictions. Ahmed pointed out that Islam is both "exclusivist" and "inclusivist," respectful of women but also mired in cultural traditions that oppress them. Some portions of Ahmed's book are fascinating and engaging, particularly his ethnographic explorations of different pockets of Muslim life. He recounted his difficult personal experiences as a Pakistani scholar who made a controversial film about Pakistan's founder, Muhammad Ali Jinnah (1876–1948), and concluded: "Looking at the breakdown of society for a Muslim scholar is like staring into the face of despair." Ahmed nevertheless communicated his optimism after visiting the inclusive, tolerant, and moderate Muslim community in Toledo, Ohio.

The Ugandan-born American political scientist and anthropologist Mahmood Mamdani, himself a Muslim of Indian origin, has pleaded for "culture talk" instead of a "clash of civilizations." Culture talk "assumes that every culture has a tangible essence that defines it, and it then explains politics as a consequence of that essence" (Mamdani 2004, p. 17). Mamdani believed that political Islam had emerged as the result of a modern encounter with Western power, and that the terrorist movement at the center of Islamist politics is an even more recent phenomenon, one that followed America's embrace of proxy war after its defeat in Vietnam.

Mamdani studied the Reagan years in the United States, during which America embraced the highly ideological (and unconsciously split-off) politics of the "good us" versus the "evil them." Identifying militant nationalist governments as Soviet proxies in countries such as Nicaragua and Afghanistan, the Reagan administration backed terrorist movements in those countries, hailing them as the "moral equivalent" of America's Founding Fathers. Mamdani thought that the era of proxy wars had come to an end with the U.S. invasion of Iraq, and that there, as in Vietnam, America would need to recognize that it is not fighting terrorism but nationalism, a battle that cannot be won by occupation.

The issues of Islamic terror seem to evoke such overwhelming emotions that many scholars cannot separate their feelings from their scholarship. Neoconservative scholars like the British-American author, journalist, and critic Christopher Hitchens, the British-Israeli historian Robert Wistrich, and the American foreign relations expert Walter Russell Mead have decried the Muslim religion as "Islamic Fascism" and "Arabian Fascism" and have used the derogatory term *Islamofascism,* a neologism suggesting an association of the ideological or operational characteristics of modern Islamist movements with the European Fascist movements of the early twentieth century, Neo-Fascist movements, or totalitarianism. The *New Oxford American Dictionary* defines *Islamofascism* as "a controversial term equating some modern Islamic movements with the European fascist movements of the early twentieth century." Critics of the term argue that associating the religion of Islam with political Fascism is as offensive and inaccurate as the term "Judeo-Nazi" coined by an antiestablishment Israeli scholar in the 1970s and still used by Palestinian propaganda (Hitchens 2001; Wistrich 2001; Mead 2004; Burleigh 2006; Safire 2006).

Interestingly enough, the derogatory word *Islamofascism* appears to have been coined by a Muslim scholar, Khalid Duran, a specialist in the history, sociology, and politics of the Islamic world who is based in Germany: "The term seems to have appeared first in the *Washington Times* in a reference to Islamist fundamentalists. Coined by Khalid Duran, a Muslim scholar seeking to explain Islam to Jews, the word was meant as a criticism of hyper-traditionalist clerics—who in turn denounced Duran as a traitor to the faith" (Scardino 2005). Other scholars attribute the invention of the term *Islamofascism* to the American journalist and author Stephen Schwartz, a Jewish convert to Islam, a vocal critic of Islamic terrorism, and the executive director of the Center for Islamic Pluralism, and to Christopher Hitchens, the British anti-religion crusader.

The British historian Michael Burleigh, who is accused by some critics of anti-Muslim and anti-Irish sentiments, has nevertheless called the term *Islamofascist* a dangerous label. Here are his major arguments:

> Clearly there are huge contextual differences [between Islam and Fascism]. Militant Islamists are utterly murderous and viciously anti-semitic, but the heterogeneous ethnic composition of *Al-Qaïda* hardly suggests that visions of racial purity matter to it. In fact, *Al-Qaïda* is doing its best to recruit white and black people in order to outwit authorities looking for Arabs and Pakistanis. Fascism emerged as a form of "anti-politics" designed to bridge endemic conflicts between capital and labour. It favoured corporatist economics, in which employers and workers would be dragooned by the state. These doctrines have little bearing in economies of entrepreneurs and traders. Before his mafia-like Sudanese hosts stole his money in the late 1990s, Bin Laden was a (not very proficient) venture capitalist, ploughing his (modest) fortune into forlorn business endeavours to bankroll terrorism. More insurmountably, the rise of radical Islam since the late 1970s reflects the bankruptcy of the two dominant political creeds in the Arab world, nationalism and socialism, the two western movements that comprised fascism (Burleigh 2006).

Whether or not socialism always "comprised fascism," as it did in its Soviet form, Burleigh's arguments are fairly sound, but, given the general tendency in "the West" to equate Islam with evil, one can only hope that Mamdani's "culture talk" will not be a dialogue of the deaf.

The American national security expert Derek Reveron and the American political scientist Jeffrey Murer thought that Lewis's and Huntington's idea of "clash of civilizations" was based on "failing to differentiate between the Middle East and Islam" (Reveron and Murer 2006, p. xxii). The idea of the "clash of civilizations" may be an oversimplification, an unconscious *splitting,* an attempt to see our complex multicolored world in black and white (Mack 2002, p. 174; Falk 2004, pp. 148–150). For one thing, Arab culture and Muslim culture are not the same. The largest Muslim countries in our world—Indonesia, Bangladesh, and Pakistan—are non-Arab and not even in the Middle East but rather in South Asia.

The French Islamic scholar Olivier Roy thought that his colleagues had over-emphasized the role of Islam in shaping our contemporary societies. He believed that the culturalist approach had been reinforced by recent tragic events, and more precisely by the way in which observers, politicians, and public opinion were trying to cast these events into an intelligible conceptual framework that might explain the incomprehensible (Roy 2004, p. 16). Roy suggested that the important events in the world of Islam were taking place not in the regions we ordinarily think of as Islamic but rather in Europe. He pointed to today's global terrorists, who, he says, are overwhelmingly likely to have studied and lived in Europe (or the United States) and to have embraced radical Islamic ideas there, not in the Muslim countries where they were born.

Roy believed that he could trace contemporary Islamic terrorism to the terror of the German Baader-Meinhof gang and other terrorist Maoist movements of the 1960s and 1970s. Global Islamic terror, for Roy, was not only born of the interaction between Islam and the West, but also reflected the aspiration of displaced Muslims living in Europe to create a transnational Islamic identity, forged in revolution. Noah Feldman, however, thought that "Roy's Eurocentric focus and his impulse to link Islamic terror to Marxist-inspired radicalism obscure the extent to which satellite television and the Internet have spread Western ideas into the Islamic world" (Feldman 2005).

Despite the failure of his policy and his tragedy in Iraq, and the failure of his attempts to institute democracy in Middle Eastern countries lacking any democratic tradition, where the social structure is totally alien to this system of government, President George W. Bush of the United States continues to split his inner and outer world into all-good (us) and all-bad (them) objects and operates on the black-and-white notions of the "clash of civilizations" and the "war on terror." One of the most ominous examples is the current conflict between Iran, Israel, and the United States, which may lead to another tragic war. *Al-Qaïda*'s leaders, those of the Muslim Brotherhood, and President Mahmoud Ahmadinejad of Iran—all wish to wipe Israel (and America) off the face of the Earth and to establish a new Islamic *khilafah* (caliphate, empire, or government) over the world, as they believe it was in the Middle Ages. These cultures seem so different from one another, and the hate and narcissistic rage of fanatical Muslims for America, Israel, and other "emblems" of "evil Western culture" are so great, that we remain puzzled, perplexed, and frightened: do love and hate develop the same way in Muslim culture as they do in "Western" culture? Is Muslim culture so radically different from ours, so that no "culture talk" as proposed by Mamdani may be possible? Let us examine the case of Iran.

Amir Taheri and Iran's Humiliation

As we have seen, dignity and humiliation are central emotional issues to Iran and to its president. One of the controversies surrounding our understanding of Iran is centered around the Iranian-born journalist Amir Taheri who has been mentioned at the beginning of this book, and whose birth date is kept a secret. From 1972 to 1979 Taheri edited *Kayhan,* Iran's main daily, until Iran's king, Mohammad Reza Shah Pahlavi (1919–1980), was toppled by the *ayatollah* Ruhollah Khomeini (1900–1989) (Zonis 1991). Fearing the new Islamic regime's retribution for his support of the Shah, Taheri fled to London, where from 1980 to 1984 he was the Middle East editor for the *Sunday Times.* He has been based in Europe since then.

In 1984, Taheri left the *Sunday Times* and began to work on his *Nest of Spies,* a chronicle of American intelligence operations in Iran during the Shah's rule. Taheri argued that U.S. foreign policy toward Iran had been a failure. Unconsciously projecting his guilt feelings for his contribution to the Shah's repressive regime on the United States, Taheri wrote that the U.S. attempt to foster democracy in a Muslim country and its support of the Shah's "decadent policies" had served the interests of Islamic fundamentalists and led to the Shah's downfall. Taheri had conducted interviews and used official American government and intelligence documents that had been seized by Iranian student nationalists after they seized the American embassy in Teheran in 1979. He argued that America's latest foreign policy failure, the Iran-Contra affair, was due to the lack of congressional interest and concern in foreign affairs, which allowed the State Department and the CIA to operate with little regulation and supervision.

Without proper acknowledgment, Taheri used the work of his predecessors on his subject (B. Rubin 1980; Ramazani 1982; Sick 1985). Two other works on American-Iranian relations were published in the same year as Taheri's (Bill 1988; Cottam 1988). Some critics praised Taheri's *Nest of Spies,* while others denounced its author as an academic fraud. In a scathing review, the Iranian-born American-Jewish Persian Studies scholar Shaul Bakhash detailed numerous inaccuracies, mistaken readings, and references to nonexistent texts or sources. Checking Taheri's footnotes and references like a scholarly detective, Bakhash stated that Taheri "repeatedly refers us to books where the information he cites simply does not exist. Often the documents cannot be found in the volumes to which he attributes them [. . .] [and] repeatedly reads things into the documents that are simply not there" (Bakhash 1989, p. 45). In one case, Bakhash noted, Taheri had cited an earlier article of his own, but offered content that he himself never wrote in that article. Bakhash added that Taheri's *Nest of Spies* was "the sort of book that gives contemporary history a bad name" (p. 46).

Following Bakhash, the American-Jewish journalist Larry Cohler-Esses called Taheri's book "a concoction of nonexistent substances" (Cohler-Esses 2006). In his review of Taheri's book, Bakhash had "detailed case after case in which Taheri cited nonexistent sources, concocted nonexistent substance in cases where the sources existed, and distorted the substance beyond recognition when it was present" (Cohler-Esses 2006). In an angry response published two months later in the same magazine, Taheri accused Bakhash of personal animosity toward him but failed to rebut Bakhash's charges. Cohler-Esses thought that Bakhash had "exposed Taheri as a journalistic felon" (Cohler-Esses 2006).

Taheri had also published a story in the *New York Post* identifying Mohammad Javad Zarif (born 1960), the Iranian permanent representative to the United Nations, as one of the former Iranian students involved in the 1979 seizure of the U.S. Embassy in Tehran (Taheri 2005). The American scholar Dwight Simpson and his Iranian colleague Kaveh Afrasiabi accused Taheri of fabricating false stories, as Zarif had been Simpson's teaching assistant at San Francisco State University and could not have been in Iran at the same time. Javad Zarif left the United Nations after a five-year term in 2007.

In 2006, Taheri had published an article in a Canadian newspaper claiming that the Iranian parliament had passed a law that "envisages separate dress codes for religious minorities, Christians, Jews and Zoroastrians, who will have to adopt distinct colour schemes to make them identifiable in public." The Iranian government claimed that Taheri had taken an Iranian parliament *discussion* on a dress code law that would have Muslims wear garments identifying their religion and falsely reported it as a *law being passed* requiring Jews to wear badges as they had been forced to do under the German Nazis.

In fact, Iranian law does require Jews to identify themselves as such *when they sell food,* but Iran claimed that badges for Jews were not actually under discussion, nor in the law. Taheri stated that his report was correct and that the dress code law has been passed by the Islamic Iranian *Majlis* and would be submitted to the Iranian Council of Guardians. He did not claim that badges for Jews are in the law, but does say that special markers for followers of Judaism, Christianity, and Zoroastrianism were under discussion as a means to implement the law. The Canadian newspaper retracted the story several hours after it was posted online. It blamed Taheri for the falsehood in the article and published a full apology. Taheri stood by his story. Taheri also published several pro-Israeli pieces. In 2007 he visited Israel and spoke at the right-wing Israeli Institute for Contemporary Affairs. While some see Taheri as a courageous Iranian willing to lay down his life to save his country from its fanatical Islamic government, others sees him as a fraudulent journalist fabricating sensational stories. In any event, the Taheri affair is one more example of how "dignity" and "humiliation" play an enormous role in Iran's quest for nuclear weapons and for domination through terrorism. Those who do not feel humiliated do not need to humiliate or dominate others.

The Emotional Structure of Muslim Families

The venerable Arabist scholar Bernard Lewis saw "the roots of Muslim rage" in historical terms. The Muslims had lost their medieval dominance and been shamed and humiliated by the "West." The inferior *dhimmis* had become their masters. The psychoanalytic scholars Joseph Berke and Stanley Schneider agreed with Lewis:

> For the Arab world the end of Islamic ascendancy announced by the enfranchisement of "dhimmis" and rule by foreigners *reversed the proper order of things,* just like the discoveries of Galileo shocked a Catholic Europe. For instance, the Egyptian historian, al-Jabarti, was appalled that: "[...] contrary to ancient custom, that (non-Muslims) wear fine clothes and bear arms, wield authority over Muslims and generally behave in a way which inverts the order of things established by divine law." But this was only one of a series of painful religious, cultural and political upheavals that fuelled a fury rooted in an endemic state of inferiority, especially since *in the Arab mind,* [sic] "most Jews are miserable, cowardly and unclean." The establishment of the State of Israel, in 1948, was a particular blow, for it called into question the preeminent basis of Islamic religion and honor (Berke and Schneider 2006; italics added).

Note that Berke and Schneider used the controversial notion of the "Arab mind" as self-evident, as if they knew the image of the Jew in the minds of all Arabs. It is true that the Palestinian Arabs still view their defeat and losses in 1948 as their *naqba* or catastrophe. One Arab writer wrote: "That a land Arabized by *jihad* should have been lost to a *dhimmi* people by the beneficiaries [sic] of the *dhimmi* condition during thirteen centuries is considered as a catastrophe of cosmic dimensions" (O'Brien 1986, p. 340). The Muslims, for whom the use of slaves captured in East Africa was common, do indeed regard the second-class *dhimmi* as "beneficiaries" of their humiliating condition because they were "free" rather than slaves. The *Palestine-Israel Journal* devoted a whole issue to this subject (Abu-Zayyad 2002; Tamari 2002).

MUSLIM SOCIETY AND THE MUSLIM FAMILY

In view of Kohut's notions of "narcissistic rage," could the roots of Muslim rage at the West also be in the Islamic family? What kind of love (or hate) do Muslim infants and children receive in their families? What might be the causes of boundless narcissistic rage within the Muslim family? Some "Westerners" ask "Why do the Muslims hate us so?" and find their answer in the Qur'an, where Allah is said to hate the infidel. But all Muslims do not really hate "us" so, and for those who do, the fanatical Islamists, the causes are much more complex.

Like the Qur'an and the religion of Islam itself, the origins of Muslim rage (and terror) may indeed lie in the Muslim family. The question of the particular psychological structure of Muslim families and their effect on Muslim society have preoccupied many scholars. Some scholars have attempted to explain the special emotional makeup of the Arabs and Muslims as arising from the way of life of the original desert Arab nomads or Beduin (the word comes from the Arabic *badaween* meaning "men of the desert"). The *Beduin* valued sons vastly more than daughters because men can fight other tribes for survival, avenge humiliations, and thereby save the tribe from shame and humiliation, whereas women can do none of these things. The desert Arabs used to bury some of their female children alive in the sand.

Iraq is a mixed society of Muslim Arab Shiites, Sunnis and non-Arab Kurds. The respected Iraqi Shiite historian and sociologist Ali Hassan al-Wardi, a Muslim critic of Beduin culture, Arabic literature, and Arab sexual ethics, found an *izdiwaj* or "split personality" among Iraqi Arabs: an Iraqi Arab may do something and then turn around and do something else which contradicts his earlier actions. He saw this "duality" as a result of a history of conflict between Beduin nomads and settled people. This in turn created a society of the ruled and the rulers. While the Iraqi dominates those he can, he continually complains about the injustices of others toward him. Al-Wardi also pointed out several other "dualities" in the Iraqi culture: the segregation of men and women, classical Arabic versus the colloquial vernacular, innovation versus tradition, and sincerity versus hypocrisy (al-Wardi 1951, quoted in DeAtkine 2004; Patai 1973, pp. 75, 141, 201–202; Raphaeli 2006).

Al-Wardi found that Iraqi Arabs demand perfection in others while making excuses for themselves. "They call for certain principles they never carry out. They call for goals that they can never achieve. That is why they encourage their leaders to do miracles but when the time comes, they turn their backs giving many excuses and blaming luck." He thought that this "duality" came from traditional Arab child rearing, in which the Arab boy learns early in his life that he must live two different lives: the obedient, perfect son expected by his father, as well as the irresponsible street kid that he is most of his time. His school discipline and the expectations of his family run in opposition to the neighborhood values of the boys of his sectarian community, whether Shiite, Sunni, Kurdish, or other, which al-Wardi thought was about violence, power, and control. As a result "the Iraqi individual grows up with an extreme tendency toward sectarianism, knowing nothing about his religion." This problem has been exacerbated by the constant wars, executions, and relocations of ethnic minorities, as well as the exodus from countryside to the cities. There are many young Arab men who are street people, without fathers or a family relationship. Many of these are drawn into various terrorist organizations for money or prestige (al-Wardi 1951, quoted in DeAtkine 2004 and Raphaeli 2006).

As for the linguistic duality, al-Wardi thought that Iraqis have been "cursed with the huge difference between classical Arabic and the Iraqi dialect." This requires a "dualistic system of thought patterns" which emphasizes "poetic rhymes and grammatical decoration," producing orators who are admired for "unique synonyms" instead of speaking to the ills of their society (al-Wardi 1951, quoted in DeAtkine 2004; Patai 1973, p. 202; Raphaeli 2006). Al-Wardi believed that the Iraqi character in particular and Arab character in general were heavily influenced by Beduin culture, which is characterized by tribalism, aggression, and chivalry, and which entails permanent warfare (al-Wardi 1969–1976). The chief "Western" proponent of the view that the modern Arab character derived from the old Beduin culture was the psychoanthropologist Raphael Patai (1910–1996), a Hungarian-born Jewish scholar who lived in Palestine after Hitler came to power in 1933, left Palestine for Mexico in 1947 and later settled in the United States (Patai 1973). His book, *The Arab Mind,* however, is controversial. We shall discuss this below.

The Structure of Muslim Society

To understand Muslim society, we need to look at basic interpersonal issues such as trust and mistrust in that society. The German-American psychoanalyst Erik Homburger Erikson (1902–1994) thought that "basic trust" versus "basic distrust" was the basic conflict of the first of the eight "ages of men" or stages of development. The infant must develop basic trust in its mother to grow normally and healthily. Erikson's analysis of "trust" and the consequences of early injuries of basic trust (narcissistic injuries) is still valid. He stressed that the regaining of basic trust is a necessary condition for a meaningful psychotherapy with those who have been damaged in this way. Erikson's older colleague Karen Danielsen Horney (1885–1952) had also used similar terms (Horney 1939; Erikson 1950; Stensson 1999).

Like Horney and Erikson, the Turkish-Cypriot-born American psychoanalyst Vamık Volkan found that basic trust in his early mother and father was an all-important element in the development of a child into a psychologically healthy adult (Volkan 2004, pp. 73–74). One of the questions in the psychoanalysis of Muslim families is to what extent that basic trust exists in these families, and how well the parents are capable of giving this vital sense of trust to their children. The Indian-born American psychoanalyst Salman Akhtar has edited a book about psychoanalysis and Islam in which some of the chapters deal with this question (Akhtar 2008).

THE TRADITIONAL MUSLIM FAMILY

The human family, such as we know it, is the key social element or unit in every human society, and in Muslim society it has its special structure and dynamics. Moreover, society structures itself around the family and the clan. The traditional Muslim family, rising from the nomadic Arab family of the Arabian desert, is tight-knit, patriarchal, hierarchical, and autocratic, and has less psychological differentiation and individuation among its members that exists in "Western" families. In fact, traditional Arabs are organized into *clans,* which include many families, and at times even whole tribes. What one member of the family or clan does, his success or failure, his honor or his shame, reflects on the whole family or clan, as if the others and he were one and the same.

The *blood feud* has been well known throughout recorded human history, and is common among Arabs and Muslims. A blood feud is a long-running argument or fight between parties—groups of people, especially families or clans. Blood feuds tend to begin because one party (correctly or incorrectly) perceives itself to have been attacked, insulted, humiliated, or wronged by another. A long-running cycle of retaliation, often involving the original parties' family members and/or associates, then ensues. Blood feuds can last for generations. In areas, or among groups, without strong central government, the blood feud can be the only way to seek justice between and within communities. Blood feuds existed in early Greece (Treston 1923).

Among the Arabs and Muslims, *blood vengeance,* the obligation to kill in retribution for the murder of a member of one's family or tribe, is one key way of maintaining *honor* in their society. The Israeli Arab scholar Alean al-Krenawi and his Canadian colleague John Graham have shown that the practice of blood vengeance, though illegal in most countries of the world, is a key part of many traditional cultures in which maintaining honor is crucial (al-Krenawi and Graham 1997). They outlined the cultural and historical contexts of the practice of blood vengeance among the Bedouin of the Negev desert of Israel, considered the consequences for the targeted family and detailed the coping strategies adopted by the family, especially the children, under conditions of extreme social, emotional, and economic deprivation, and discussed social work intervention.

Equally well known in Muslim and Arab culture are the "honor crime" and the practice of "honor killing." This occurs when a girl's "crime" of having had sexual relations before marriage is thought to bring shame not only on her but on the whole family or clan, and this shame can only be erased by killing her. This must be done by her brother, father, or uncle. The mother can do nothing to save her daughter. The American feminist scholar Phyllis Chesler raged against the tragic and, to us, horrific Muslim practice of "honor killing": a girl who becomes pregnant out of wedlock must be killed by her brother, father, or uncle to preserve the honor of the family:

> Little girls live their lives under a communal death threat—the honor killing. Both male and female infants and children are brought up by mothers, too often debased and traumatized women. As such, children are forever psychologically "contaminated" by the humiliated yet all-powerful mother. *Arab and Muslim boys must disassociate themselves from her, too often in spectacularly savage ways.* But, on a

deep unconscious level, they may also wish to remain merged with the source of contamination, a conflict that suicide bombers both act out and resolve when they manfully kill but also merge their blood eternally with that of their presumably most hated enemies, the Israeli Jews. Israeli Jews may actually function as substitutes or scapegoats for an even more primal, hated/loved enemy: woman (Chesler 2004a; italics added).

Woman, in this case, is the early mother, the source of milk, life, love, nourishment, warmth but also potentially the source of deprivation, rejection, and loss, especially if she herself had been abused, humiliated, and traumatized, as Chesler thinks that she is in Muslim society. Carrying her argument to extremes, Chesler made the extravagant claim that, in the whole Muslim world, "widespread sexual abuse leads to paranoid, highly traumatized and revenge-seeking adults." Based on Patai (1973), she also claimed that there were

> barbarous family and clan dynamics in which children, both girls and boys, are routinely sexually abused by male relatives, infant males are sometimes over stimulated by being masturbated, boys between the ages of seven to twelve are publicly and traumatically circumcised, many girls are forced to undergo cliterodectomy [actually, female genital mutilation, the excision or tissue removal of any part of the female genitalia for cultural, religious or other non-medical reasons] [...] and women are seen as the source of all shame and dishonor and treated accordingly: very, very badly (Chesler 2004a).

Unfortunately, Chesler's firebrand anti-Arab feminism is accompanied by a rather loose methodology. Psychoanalysis is a science with a methodology. To claim a solid foundation for a psychoanalytical theory of Muslim terrorists, she needs to produce significant data. Instead, she cited only a few unverified allegations. Chesler did not produce any statistics of sexual abuse in Muslim countries, nor a psychological profile of terrorists (obtained directly during a followed psychoanalysis, for instance, just as Freud used such cases to build his theory) that confirms that they have been sexually abused, nor did she spell out the mental process which leads a sexually abused person in the context of the Muslim world to terrorist attack (recognition by the father is not quite enough for such a process). There are unconscious reasons to suicide bombing but, to unveil them, one needs to be free of obvious political and personal bias. Moreover, the situation of women in Muslim cultures varies considerably, as Suad Joseph and his colleagues have shown (Joseph et al. 2003–2007).

Another practice in the traditional Arab and Muslim family is that parents who have a firstborn son first name him and then change their own names to reflect their parentage of him. If the son's name is Jihad, then the father's name becomes Abu-Jihad and the mother's name Umm-Jihad (Barakat 1993, p. 98). While the Arab scholar thought that this is an expression of the "commitment and self-denial" of the parents, one might also see it as if the identity of the *parent* is more important to him or her than their previous identity, and this ties the firstborn son to his parents in a very firm and hard-to-individuate manner.

The two Arabic words for "family," *'aila* and *usra,* come from Arabic roots meaning "support." The Arab family is a support unit. The question is, who supports whom? There is some linguistic and psychological evidence that the parents expect support from their children. The father is the *janna* (provider) and the mother is the *banna* (homemaker), but children who begin as *'iyal* (dependents) change to *sanad* (supporters), and some parents call their children *sanadi* (my support) at an early age (Barakat 1993, p. 98). This would seem to reverse the traditional roles, and put a psychological burden on the child.

The "Arab Mind"?

Is there such a thing as a collective psychology of the Arabs, what some scholars have called an "Arab mind"? (Patai 1973; Laffin 1974). Several scholars of Arab psychology, both Arab and non-Arab, thought that severe emotional blows normally befall the Arab boy at a tender age, when he ceases to be the object of the love and adulation of his mother and sisters and becomes the direct object of his father's aggression, including shame and humiliation (Hamady 1960; Glidden 1972). Two scholars, one Jewish, the other Christian, whose books bear the same title, stressed the fact that in Arab culture the son, unlike the daughter, enjoys an overindulgence of his wishes and is spoiled by the women of his family (Patai 1973; Laffin 1974, 1979, 1985).

Despite their good intentions and the efforts that they put into researching and writing them, Patai's and Laffin's books have offended Arab and Muslim scholars, who see them as oversimplified generalizations and even as racist stereotyping and "Orientalism" (Said 1978). Since 2001, when the United States in the name of its "global war on terror" invaded Afghanistan and Iraq, Patai's book has become popular among many American neoconservatives but also controversial among "liberal" and leftist American scholars, some of whom call it "the bible of the United States neoconservatives."

Patai wrote that while the crying of baby girls is "routinely" ignored, male infants are picked up immediately and soothed by female relatives, and that this comforting and soothing of the baby boy often takes the form of handling his genitals, a tactic that was also used simply to make him smile. Of the Arab mother-son relationship, Patai wrote, the mother's breast, the son's greatest source of pleasure and gratification, was his for the asking. The father, meanwhile, must toughen up his pleasure-centered, hedonistic infant son, who savors the bitter taste of the father's heavy hand, the rod, the strap, and, at least among the most tradition-bound Beduin tribes, the saber and the dagger whose cut or stab will traumatize and harden him for life. Once this has happened, Patai writes, the boy will have assumed "the typical male Arab personality."

The French anthropologist Germaine Tillion, an expert on Berber Muslim culture in North Africa, believed that the key traits of what northern Europeans take to be those of Muslim or Arab society—the seclusion of women, endogamy, male circumcision, and the prohibition against eating pork—were fragments of an ancient Mediterranean culture underlying current Muslim, Christian, and Jewish cultures (Tillion 1983). Tillion argued that child-rearing practices in southern Italy and France had much in common with North African mores. Her views, however, are not widely shared by her colleagues. Some scholars have dismissed Patai's work as unfounded generalizations or even as an arrogant "Orientalism" in which a non-Arab *pretends* to understand Arab family and social culture, or as "the new crusades" (Said 1978, 2001; Barakat 1993; Qureshi and Sells 2003). The notion of "Orientalism," however, is itself controversial (Falk 2004, pp. 144–148).

Some scholars have shown that "distortions" of other cultures than one's own occurs on all sides, including the Arab one (Buruma and Margalit 2004). These scholars argue that a reciprocal negative "Occidentalist" stereotype of "the West" has arisen in the Arab and Muslim world, one that considers "the West" licentious, amoral, hypersexualized, aggressive, and engaged in a "new crusade" against Islam. Buruma and Margalit traced this "Occidentalist" stereotype back to the thinkers of the Western counter-Enlightenment. Some Arab and Muslim scholars counter that the abuse of Iraqi Arab prisoners at the Abu Ghraib prison in Iraq, in which American soldiers reportedly raped Muslim prisoners, humiliated them, and forced them to eat pork and drink alcohol, suggest that the seemingly biased Muslim "Occidentalist" worldview has real sources in the actual experience of the domination and humiliation of Muslims by "Westerners." In the wake of the Iraq war, it would seem, mutually reinforcing Occidentalist and Orientalist stereotypes have contributed to the fear, mistrust, and suspicion that divide Islam from the West and feed the "war on terror."

The American personality psychologist Gary Gregg, an expert on identity and self-representation, took a comprehensive approach to the subject of the "Arab mind," or rather Middle Eastern culture (Gregg 2005). Using autobiographies, literary works, ethnographic accounts, and life-history interviews, in English, Arabic, and French, Gregg reviewed psychological writings on the region by psychologists, anthropologists, and sociologists. Rejecting the stereotypical descriptions of the "Arab mind" or "Muslim mentality," Gregg used a life-span-development framework, examining influences on development in infancy, early childhood, late childhood, and adolescence, as well as on identity formation in early and mature adulthood.

Gregg viewed Middle Eastern patterns of development in the context of cultural psychology, and compared Middle Eastern patterns less with "Western" middle-class norms than with those described for the region's cultural neighbors: the Indian subcontinent, sub-Saharan Africa, and the Mediterranean shore of Europe. Gregg concluded that the region's perennial strife stems much less from a stubborn adherence to tradition and resistance to modernity than from widespread frustration with broken promises of modernization—with the slow and halting pace of economic progress and democratization. Gregg described the lives, families, and social relationships of Middle Easterners as they struggle to reconcile the lure of Westernized lifestyles with traditional Arab or Muslim values. His book was essentially different from Patai's, however, in that no psychoanalytic interpretation of unconscious emotions was attempted.

The Egyptian Arab scholar Tarek Heggy thought that Arab psychological defects were culturally induced. Heggy believed that these defects developed over time as a combination of cultural attributes deriving from historical, political, economic, social, and educational factors which, like any acquired attributes, were amenable to change (Heggy 1991, 2003). Heggy's first book was published in Arabic, but has not been translated into any European language. There are some English summaries on the Internet. Heggy wrote, "I now believe that another step should precede the acceptance and practice of criticism, namely, the dismantling of the wall of denial behind which we have sequestered ourselves for the last few decades. For it is clear that we cannot embark on a process of constructive criticism of our mistakes and shortcomings before we overcome our insistence on denying their existence in the first place" (Heggy 2005). One of his readers thought that while the unhealthy denial of reality was widespread among the Arabs, the fatalistic Arab concept of *inshallah* (Allah willing) was even more pernicious (Heggy 2005; cf. Mannes 2002–2003).

The Muslim Child's Ambivalence Toward Its Parents

Traditional Muslim religious faith idealizes the family. The structure of the Muslim family is considered to rest on four "pillars" or "values" that are much better than "Western" family practices. They are based on Qur'anic regulations and the traditions or *hadith* from the life of the Prophet Muhammad, handed down from generation to generation. Those four "pillars" are: (1) Family life as a cradle of human society providing a secure, healthy, and encouraging home for parents and the growing children. (2) Family life as guardian of the natural erotic desires of men and women, leading this powerful urge into wholesome channels. (3) Family life as the very breeding place for human virtues like love, kindness, and mercy. (4) Family life as the most secure refuge against inward and outward troubles. The strength of these four pillars is made up by the Muslim social system, and the benefits of family life are extended not only to blood relations but encompass also the worldwide "family" of Muslims, the Islamic brotherhood, or the *ummah* (the nation of Islam), a word derived from *umm* (mother). So much for the idealized view of the Muslim family (Martin 2004).

During the 1970s and 1980s, the American anthropologist Andrea Rugh lived in an Egyptian Arab village and later in a Syrian Arab village to write a book on Egyptian Arab village life (Rugh 1984). She was struck by the village life and culture, and later published her observations on some of the differences between Muslim Arab and "Western" society (Rugh 1997). During her eight months there, she became involved in the domestic life of her landlord's family. Rugh reported on the personalities and activities she encountered and analyzed them.

She delineated the premises of family life both in the unnamed village and in the author's sophisticated American circles. She concluded that Muslim Middle Easterners see their lifetime interests "best served through long-term commitment to *families,*" while Americans believe the key to happiness lies in *individuals* who can "cope on their own outside the parental family" (Pipes 1997).

To illustrate this difference dramatically, Rugh cited a Western reporter asking an elderly Egyptian Arab woman whether she has realized her full potential (as a woman), to which came this uncomprehending reply: "I am a daughter, wife, mother, sister, aunt, grandmother. What else do you want me to tell you?" This difference has wide implications. American parents go to great lengths to help their children form friendships outside the family, and this leads kids to find a "powerful base" in non-family groups that deeply shapes their values. In contrast, Syrian Arab families discourage contact outside the family unit, not trusting the little ones to handle the "subtleties" of these intricate and somewhat adversarial relations; better they should stay within the safe familial confines. As a result, Rugh suggests, Americans cope better with change, while "Arabs have no problem with adolescent rebellion." The American scholar Daniel Pipes thought that "non-Western" peoples may adopt other facets of Western life but that Rugh rightly conclude that "as yet there is no revolutionary worldwide convergence toward anything like a single family type." The differences she describes here are likely to persist, perhaps even deepen (Pipes 1997). Indeed they have.

If we study the Muslim family, however, the real source of Muslim love, hate, and terror, we see a striking psychological dynamic. Normally, at first the son receives much loving care from his mother, who is grateful to her son for being born, in a society that values a woman who has sons much more than one who has daughters. When the son reaches a certain age, however—usually seven— he is suddenly and abruptly forced to be self-sufficient, to support his parents, to work, to serve, to give, to obey his father, to submit to him, and to keep silent in his father's presence. To add insult to injury, the Muslim boy is circumcised some time between the age of seven and the age of thirteen, the time decided by his father. This violent circumcision, a direct attack on his sexual organ, is a traumatic event, psychologically akin to castration. Sigmund Freud considered it an unconscious substitute for castration.

If the mother herself had been abused or traumatized by her parents, brothers, or husband, which is not uncommon in Muslim society (Haj-Yahia 2000; Chesler 2004a), and could not give the son the maternal love he requires, the son feels betrayed, rejected, or abandoned, by her, his love for her is tinged with mistrust, anger, and hate. This profound *ambivalence* toward the mother may be unconsciously displaced toward "America." In a psychobiographical study of Osama bin Laden, whom "Westerners" consider "the world's worst Muslim terrorist," I have shown how his hatred for "America" grew out of his rage at his mother for abandoning him at an early age, and how this hatred for "America" was nonetheless tinged with love, admiration, and idealization, so that his feelings for America were deeply ambivalent. Unable to integrate his good and bad feelings for his mother, however, he *split* them unconsciously so that the Muslim *ummah* became the all-good mother for him and "America" the all-bad one (Falk 2001b).

Losing the protection and care of his mother, passing under the harsh control of his rival father, and being circumcised by the latter may constitute a sharp, traumatic turn of events in the life of the Muslim boy, even in the best of cases. The young boy then harbors a deep feeling of narcissistic rage against his father. This can become even worse if a furious Muslim father beats up his son when the latter does not obey him or does not respect his honor as the father wishes. Father and son become chronically enraged at each other, but the son must repress his rage, while the father may give vent to it physically. In still worse cases, the son suffers narcissistic injuries from his mother as well. The mother, whose social standing in Arab society is low, may herself feel hurt or oppressed, and may not be able to give her son the love, warmth, understanding, and separate existence that he so badly needs. If the son receives poor mothering, his narcissistic injury and boundless narcissistic rage may lead him to terrorism.

Terror, Basic Mistrust, and the Lack of Object Constancy

For its healthy development, it is essential for the infant and child to sense and perceive the mother as a constant, available, dependable, unchanging, reliable, loving, and trustworthy "object." The *basic trust* that psychoanalysts like Horney, Erikson, and Volkan wrote about must be there. If the mother leaves him, he must know that she will soon come back rather than feel abandoned. She can be trusted to give him all the supplies that he needs to survive and to thrive—milk, love, food, warmth, caring, empathy, and understanding. During the "separation-individuation" phase of infant development, and perhaps even earlier, the child achieves this soothing inner sense of "object constancy" which helps him choose a good mate and build good relationships with others throughout life (Mahler et al. 1975; D.N. Stern 1985).

However, if the mother cannot give her baby these feelings of being a constant, unchanging, reliable, loving, and trustworthy "object," then he will develop the unhappy and painful feelings of terror, panic, *boundless narcissistic rage,* and the *lack of object constancy.* He will not be able to trust people, he will not perceive them as they are but rather either idealize them or denigrate them in succession, and he will be surprised to see them "changed" when they had never really been as he had thought they were.

The lack of object constancy is a very serious psychological problem related to psychopathology, as well as to narcissistic and borderline personality disorders. The American psychoanalyst Harold P. Blum studied the pathogenesis of paranoia and the different forms of paranoid psychopathology (Blum 1981).

He emphasized the mental representation of the persecutor and certain features of the paranoid persecutory system. The paranoid personality tends to misperceive and distort reality in selected areas. Persistent fantasies of outer or inner danger coexist with unreasonable expectation and exaggeration of hostile threat and hypersensitivity to minor mishaps and injuries. Affection and commitment are unreliable, and disappointments in relationships are regarded as potentially menacing or malevolent. Expectations or conviction of infidelity, betrayal, and conspiracy appear, with narcissistic rage and hate directed at "disappointing" love objects or their disguised, symbolic representation (Kohut 1972; Masterson 1981, 2000; Blum 1981; Kernberg 1975, 2002).

In this connection, it is important to cite a study by the political scientists Marvin Zonis and Craig Joseph on conspiracy thinking in the Middle East (Zonis and Joseph 1994). The authors observed that suspicious, paranoid "conspiracy thinking" is more developed in the Middle East than it is in "Western" societies. Arab, Iranian, and Muslim societies in the Middle East tended to attribute their failures and disasters to conspiracies by the Western powers, Jews, Zionists, Israelis, and other "enemies" of their societies. While pointing out that conspiracy thinking has many causes, including the psychological, historical, cultural, social structural, and political, Zonis and Joseph reviewed the psychoanalytic theories of the paranoid process, based on *passivity, regression,* and unconscious *projection,* and explained that Middle Eastern societies, which had been dominated by others, react to stress and anxiety with conspiracy thinking (Zonis and Joseph 1994, p. 453).

Sheikh Ibrahim Mudayris is a prominent Palestinian Arab Muslim preacher in Gaza who regularly exhorts his believers to the destruction of Israel. He has screamed, for example,

> Allah has tormented us with the people most hostile to the believers—the Jews [...] With the establishment of the State of Israel, the entire Islamic nation was lost, because Israel is a cancer spreading through the body of the Islamic nation, and because Jews are a virus resembling AIDS, from which the entire world suffers [...] You will find that the Jews are behind all the civil strife in this world. The Jews are behind the suffering of the nations [...] Listen to the Prophet Muhammad, who tells you about the evil end that awaits Jews. The stones and trees will want the Muslims to finish off every Jew [...] We have ruled the world before, and by Allah, the day will come when we rule the world again (Sutton and Vertigans 2005, pp. 12, 204).

This is not an atypical battle cry among fanatical Islamists. In the summer of 2005, Sheikh Mudayris gave the world an example of his hatred. Drawing his sword from its sheath, the preacher cried in a televised sermon:

> "The Jews are a virus similar to AIDS, from which the entire world is suffering," Mudayris said. "You'll find that Jews are behind every conflict on earth. The suffering of nations? The Jews are behind it! [...] Don't ask Germany what it did to the Jews, since the Jews are the ones who provoked the Nazis. "Hundreds of verses about them came down [from 'heaven'] and appeared in the *Kor'an,*" he continued.

"And in them it is told of their corruption and evil intentions." Palestinian Media Watch named one of those *Kor'anic* verses that curse the Jews: "Indeed you will find that of all mankind, those with the strongest hatred of the believers, are the Jews and the pagans." (*al-Maada*: 82). Mudayris also refers to the following *hadith* (oral traditions relating to the words and deeds of the Moslem prophet Mohammed): "The hour [of resurrection] will not come until the Moslems make war against the Jews and kill them, and until a Jew hides behind a rock and tree, and the rock and tree will say, 'Moslem, servant of Allah, there is a Jew behind me, come and kill him!'" [Here Mudayris drew his sword and waved it in the air]. Mudayris also preached the fall of the Western powers. "Allah willing, He will get rid of the USA," he said. "He will do it [...] [Muslims] have ruled the world [in the past] and a day will come, by Allah, and we shall rule the world [again]. The day will come and we shall rule America, Britain, we shall rule the entire world, except the Jews. Jews will not agree to live under our rule since they have been treacherous throughout history" (Sutton and Vertigans 2005, pp. 12, 204).

Two Jewish psychoanalysts have pointed out the powerful role of unconscious *splitting, denial,* and *projection* in such jihadist outbursts:

Whether unconsciously determined or not, in order to gain or maintain political power, the belief systems of the *jihadists* seem to exemplify these mechanisms. Thus, on one hand, they widely disseminate the *Protocols of the Elders of Zion* [a Russian antisemitic fabrication of 1905 "proving" that the Jews conspire to rule the world], in order to "prove" a Jewish conspiracy to take-over the world. And, on the other hand, Sheikh Mudayris, among others, publicly asserts: "(Moslems) have ruled the world before, and, by Allah, the day will come when we will rule [...] America, Britain, and the entire world." In considering these words, one must not underestimate the power of projective processes (Berke and Schneider 2006).

However, sermons full of projective traits, like those of *Sheikh* Mudayris, are still being preached every Friday in hundreds of thousands of mosques, not only in Gaza or Palestine, but all over the Islamic world.

The Abuse of Women and Children in Muslim Society

Do Muslim mothers provide their children with psychological security and "object constancy"? Can they do it? Do they have those inner qualities and forces themselves? While modern scholars emphasize the wide variety of roles and relations enjoyed by women in "modern" Muslim society, the situation in reality is quite complicated and not quite so rosy. Thus, the venerable *Encyclopaedia Britannica* says,

> For [Muslim] women, modernization is especially problematic. Urged on the one hand to be liberated from Islām and thereby become modern, they are told by others to be liberated from being Western through being self-consciously Muslim. There is little information on the situation of ordinary women in premodern Islāmdom, but evidence from the modern period underscores the enormous variety of settings in which Muslim women live and work, as well as *the inability of the stereotype of meek, submissive, veiled passivity to reflect the quality of their lives.* As always, Muslim women live in cities, towns, villages, and among migratory pastoral tribes; some work outside the home, some inside, some not at all; some wear concealing clothing in public, most do not; for some, movement outside the home is restricted, for most not; and, for many, public modesty is common, as it is for many Muslim men. For many [Muslim women], the private home and the public bath continue to be the centres of social interaction; for others, the world of employment and city life is an option. As always, few live in polygamous families. Strict adherence to the Sharī'ah's provision for women to hold their property in their own right has produced Muslim women of great wealth, in the past as well as today. Clearly,

any simple description of the lives of Muslim women is misleading (Islāmic world, in *Encyclopædia Britannica 2006 Ultimate Reference Suite DVD;* italics added).

In reality, however, Muslim women are often abused by males in their family—their fathers, brothers, or husbands. The Israeli Arab scholar Muhammad Haj-Yahia has studied wife and child abuse in Arab society, which had already been observed by Patai and Laffin (Haj-Yahia 1999, 2000). Wife abuse and child abuse are connected. *Abused and traumatized wives do not make good-enough mothers. They in turn traumatize, abuse, and enrage their child, whose rage at his mother may later be displaced to his future wife—or to America or Israel.* Not having themselves a sense of inner security and "object constancy," these mothers fail to provide them to their children. The psychoanalysts Adelaide Johnson and S. A. Szurels have shown many years ago that an abused, traumatized mother unconsciously instigates antisocial behavior in her child, as if to vicariously get back at her abusers—the dominant males in her family and society (Johnson and Szurels 1952).

In the fundamentalist Muslim family, then, an endless and tragic vicious cycle of women-and-child abuse often exists, communicated and passed on from one generation to the next. Abused children often become abusive parents. The child is not only abused by his father but, perhaps unconsciously, also by his mother. Wife abuse is a common psychological problem in the Arab and Muslim family and society. The abuse of wives is not only a social phenomenon, as a way of asserting the husband's dominance, but also a psychological one: the rage at his mother, whom the son cannot beat or abuse, may be unconsciously displaced to his wife, whom he can beat and abuse when he becomes her husband and "owns her"—or to "America."

The Swiss-American-Jewish psychoanalyst Leon Wurmser, an expert on the feeling of shame and its vicissitudes (Wurmser 1981), reviewed eight books on the subjects of 9/11, terrorism, and genocidal prejudice. Here is some of what Wurmser had to say about the connection between child abuse, shame, rage, and terrorism in Islamic society:

> Severe historical trauma lives on in the cultural memory of a people, is transmitted from generation to generation, mostly in the form of survivor guilt and shame that must be expiated. This leads directly to the background of terrorism: *A culture that abuses its children and inculcates blind obedience to authority creates suicide bombers.* It continually re-creates new trauma, but is itself rooted in historical trauma. *It deflects the rage created by incessant shaming (and reinforced by historical grievances) onto an outward enemy* who symbolizes values antithetical to all that the culture claims to honor; there is a deep sense of humiliating deficiency (Wurmser 2004, p. 924; italics added).

Wurmser went on to analyze the psychodynamics of shame and humiliation within the fundamentalist or traditional Muslim family and its relation to terrorism. This analysis is very important for our understanding of the unconscious roots of Islamic terrorism:

From a psychoanalytic point of view, *the pathology of an archaic, shame-oriented superego, rooted in severe physical or emotional traumatization, is as important as historical injustices, economic deprivations, religious fanaticism, or the threat posed by modernity.* On the one side, *the shamed part of the self is projected onto the victim; it needs to be tortured and destroyed as a symbol of one's own image of weakness and victimhood.* On the other side, *a harsh superego—a punishing and absolving, absolute authority—is projected onto leaders, terrorist groups, and above all onto "God."* Terrorism can thus be understood as an externalization of inner conflict with an archaic superego. This conflict is guided by *pervasive resentment*—"inner" here meaning within the individual, as well as within family, group, and large community. Terrorism's history is a tale of shame and resentment and their exploitation for power and profit (Wurmser 2004, p. 924; italics added).

Wurmser's "pervasive resentment" is shorthand for "boundless narcissistic rage." Indeed, feelings of shame and impotent rage at both parents often overwhelm the Arab boy from a very young age. The Arab boy's rage at his mother for abandoning him at the age of seven, or even much earlier, psychologically, if she is traumatized and abused, may consolidate and crystallize his earlier infantile rage at the mother for her earlier psychological abandonments. The rage at his father for shaming or abusing him physically and emotionally fuels the inner volcano. In the best of cases, the Arab boy unconsciously channels his rage into constructive or creative avenues. In the worst cases, he may unconsciously displace them onto the American or Israeli enemy who, as he thinks and feels, has robbed him of his fatherland or motherland—the symbolic mother, or at America, the "Great Bad Mother."

The Israeli Arab scholar Muhammad Haj-Yahia has also been studying child abuse in the Arab family. He noted the dearth of public knowledge about the problem of child maltreatment in Arab societies. In the Palestinian West Bank and Gaza Strip, the Arabs are facing the challenge of establishing their own social welfare system. In creating services for families and children, the helping professionals in these areas find that one of the main challenges is to integrate and apply knowledge accumulated in Western countries into a different sociocultural context. Another challenge is to develop knowledge on this subject congruent with their own cultural background (Haj-Yahia and Shor 1995).

Because of this lack of knowledge, a study was conducted among students in the helping professions in the West Bank. The scholars examined the students' perceptions of situations of child maltreatment; their awareness of signs of maltreated children; their awareness of risk factors which could be related to this problem; and their willingness to report cases of child maltreatment. The results indicated a high level of agreement among students in viewing situations of abuse as well as neglect as maltreatment. Differences were found in their willingness to report situations of maltreatment. A higher tendency was found to report situations of abuse rather than neglect. An inclination was found among students to minimize social and cultural factors as risk factors and to disregard signs that did not contain explicit signals of danger as characteristics of maltreated children. Implications for the development of services in Arab societies are discussed. In any event, it was clear that child abuse was prevalent in Arab society (Haj-Yahia and Shor 1995).

In a further study, Haj-Yahia and a female colleague found that sexual abuse exists in Palestinian society, and that sexual abuse has a strong psychological impact on victims, including psychosis, hostility, anxiety, somatization, phobic anxiety, paranoid ideation, depression, obsessive-compulsiveness, and psychological distress. The scholars pleaded for further research into different aspects and dimensions of the problem in Arab societies (Haj-Yahia and Tamish 2001). Safa Tamish, who studied human sexuality at NYU, is now a leading expert on Palestinian Arab female sexuality.

THE MUSLIM ABUSE OF WOMEN

Shame and humiliation are very painful emotions which can lead to narcissistic injury and boundless *narcissistic rage.* In the case of the Muslim world, one of the areas where shaming practices are an active subject of scholarly discussion is feminist discourse and women's studies. Among the more strident voices are that of the American-Jewish feminist scholar Phyllis Chesler, author of *Women and Madness* (Chesler 1972), *The New Anti-Semitism* (Chesler 2003), and *The Death of Feminism* (Chesler 2005a), and her feminist "psychoanalyst and Arabist" colleague Nancy Kobrin. In a patently reductionist argument, *Chesler and Kobrin believe that the abuse of women and the hatred of women in Islamic culture are the true and only causes of Islamic terrorism.*

Chesler and Kobrin believe that men who commit mass murder also hate women and blame their crimes on women. Kobrin believes that the "absolute degradation" of Arab and Muslim women by their shame-and-honor society means that Arab sons must perpetually rid themselves of the "contamination" that contact with women represents to them; and that "Arab sons must psychologically abandon their mothers even as they experience abandonment by their mothers. Many such sons are trained to mistrust, police, routinely batter, and sometimes even murder their female relatives. Kobrin believes that such psychological dynamics may play a crucial role in contemporary Islamic terrorism" (Chesler and Kobrin 2006).

As a young woman, Dr. Chesler briefly lived in Kabul as the wife of a Muslim Afghan whom she had met and married in New York City. After a few months of what she described as being "under house arrest in the 10th century," she fled back to the United States. Based on the work of the American-Jewish "psychoanalyst and Arabist" Nancy Kobrin, Chesler claimed that a ferocious misogyny with widespread sexual and other abuses of women were common in Muslim and Arab societies—and that they were the true cause of Islamic terrorism (Chesler 2005a; Chesler and Kobrin 2006). Chesler and Kobrin publish many of their articles in *Front Page Magazine,* an online neoconservative American publication, combining a feminist viewpoint with a right-wing bias.

Kobrin has written a book on Islamic suicide terrorism, to which Chesler wrote the introduction, but it has not been published due to the publisher's fear of a violent "jihadist backlash" against it. In that book, Kobrin mentioned the battle of Khaybar, an oasis some 95 miles to the north of Medina (ancient Yathrib), in what is now Saudi Arabia. Khaybar was inhabited by Jews before the rise of Islam. The battle of Khaybar was fought in 628–629 CE by Muhammad and his Muslim followers against the Khaybar Jews. The sources that scholars have for such events are limited and often inadequate. Muhammad may have moved against Khaybar in order to raise his prestige among his followers, as well as to capture booty to sustain subsequent conquests. The battle ended in his victory, which allowed him to gain sufficient money, weapons, and support from local tribes to capture Mecca eighteen months later. The defeated Jews were reduced to slavery. To the Muslims, the name Khaybar became a symbol of Muslim victory over the "evil" Jews.

On July 28, 2006 Naveed Afsal Haq, a thirty-year-old mentally ill Christian American of Pakistani Muslim origin, took a thirteen-year-old American girl hostage in order to gain entry to the Jewish Federation Building in Seattle, Washington. Haq declared that he was "angry with Israel" and announced that it was a "hostage" situation. He began shooting women, including one who was pregnant. Five Jewish- and Christian-American women were wounded and one, fifty-eight-year-old Pam Waechter, was murdered. Haq shot several of the women in the abdomen. Chesler and Kobrin had this to say about this tragedy:

> While girl- and woman-battering and honor murders are increasingly normalized in Islamic culture, the enemy-outsider, who must also be scapegoated, has been increasingly eroticized. Israel-hatred and Jew-hatred have achieved a level of political-erotic obsession among jihadists that may even surpass that of the Nazi era. Israel is no longer "feminine" and for some, this is its great, existential crime. Israel refuses to absorb the hatred and violence or to forever turn the other cheek. Individual Jewish women, though, may present a particularly tempting target to mentally ill and violent Muslims in a jihadic era. The "Jewess" is the most denigrated female in Islamic ideology. Zaynab bint Al-Harith, the Khaybar "Jewess," is the woman who was falsely accused of having poisoned the prophet Muhammed after having witnessed the beheading of her entire male community in the Battle of Khaybar. Not coincidentally, Hizbullah currently calls its missiles "Khaybar." We have also been told that a new Iranian television station is known as "Khaybar" (Chesler and Kobrin 2006).

As far as I know, there is no television station, Iranian or otherwise, called *Khaybar.* In 2007 Iran's second television station broadcast a 28-episode television series entitled *40 Soldiers* in which the evil Jews of Khaybar are involved, and in which mythical ancient Persian heroes vanquish the United States. Zaynab, daughter of Harith, was the sister of Marhab, the "giant" leader of the Khaybar Jews, and she did lose her father, brother, and husband in the battle. Whether or not she poisoned the Prophet has remained a matter of bitter controversy. After the publisher's decision not to publish Kobrin's book, an indignant Chesler wrote, in the wake of the Pope's mistreatment [by Muslims], they would not be able to provide security for their staff people were her book to inflame the "Muslim street." Dr. Kobrin's book discusses, in depth, the normalization of cruelty and child abuse, including pederasty and daughter-abuse that is pandemic in the Arab Muslim world and how such shame and honor childrearing practices renders adults vulnerable to death-cult temptations and brainwashing. She focuses on the degradation of women in the Islamic world and how that is a crucial factor in suicide terrorism (Chesler 2006).

Needless to say, the "degradation of Islamic women" cannot in itself explain Islamic terror (Joseph et al. 2003–2007; Martin 2004).

MUSLIM FEMINISM

Despite the suppression of women in the Muslim world, or perhaps because of it, an international Muslim feminist movement has grown in the past few years. By 2006 the international movement was founded in the Catalan capital of Barcelona, Spain. Here is a report from a prominent Middle Eastern publication:

International conference on Islamic feminism begins as 400 women participants fight un-Islamic cultural practices. Muslim women from around the world Friday took up the fight against a "macho" interpretation of Islam's Koran at the opening of an international conference on Islamic feminism. "Islamic feminism is necessary for a proper image of women, for their dignity and their place in culture and politics," said Mansur Escurado, president of Spain's Muslim organization *La Junta Islamica,* whose Catalan branch organized the event in Barcelona. "It will come into full force when women are able to make choices in life with their own consent," Escurado said. The three-day conference was called to "support women who are fighting for recognition of their rights in the Islamic world" and rising up "against the long-established supremacy of men," he said. *The Islamic feminist movement has slowly emerged in the Muslim world, which comprises some 29 countries with more than one billion people.* The advocates—mostly well-educated, urban women versed in the Koran—argue that Islam must not be a pretext for cultural practices denigrating women, dictated by men with a monopoly on interpreting Islam's holy book. The Barcelona meeting drew [more] than 400 participants from Pakistan, Iran, Sudan, Tunisia, Algeria and from such European countries as Britain, France, Germany, the Netherlands, Italy, Greece, Norway, as well as Mexico and the United States (*Middle East Online,* November 4–5, 2006; italics added).

One should note that no women came to Barcelona from Syria, Egypt, Saudi Arabia, Lebanon, Iraq, Libya, Morocco, and most other Arab countries. This may not be accidental, as the rulers of these countries would not abide the participation of their women citizens in a conference which they feel would undermine their Muslim traditions and their own autocratic rule:

While some women wore Muslim veils, and others steered away from traditional dress, the participants had in common a desire to listen and share their experiences and bring what they learned to the women back in their homelands. "Nothing can

really begin until women start to talk to other women," said Pilar Vallugera, director of the department on women and rights at city hall in Barcelona. Besides the dis-
approval of some men, the pioneers of Islamic feminism also face the rejection,
incomprehension and anger of some of their Islamic sisters. The meeting, considered part of a "*jihad* for equality of the sexes", will also address such fundamental
topics as codes in Sharia laws, polygamy, sexual rights, as well as "the intellectual
role of women", said Abdennur Prado, one of the organizers of event, which runs
through Sunday. For a young mother from Lahore, Pakistan, the conference in
Spain is a way "to fight the cliches about the conditions of women in the Muslim
world". But for her and most of the Muslim feminists, overcoming stereotypes is
a monumental task. "An enormous number of things must be done in this situation
because the liberation of women is also a fight for all humanity," said the Pakistani
participant. "We live for the most part under rules which were handed down in
Saudi Arabia centuries ago, and there are still too many unenlightened mullahs
who direct our lives" (*Middle East Online,* November 4–5, 2006).

While the stridently feminist activists Phyllis Chesler and Nancy Kobrin may
have applauded the Barcelona meeting, it was nevertheless a very small beginning in the fight against the widespread abuse and suppression of women in traditional Islamic culture, society, and the family. Once again, however, it cannot be
emphasized strongly enough that there are many different conditions of women
in different Muslim families and societies (Samiuddin and Khanam 2002; Joseph
et al. 2003–2007).

Biased Views of Islamic Terrorism

Unfortunately, the feminist, right-wing views of Chesler and Kobrin on Islamic terror are not only reductionist and distorted, they are also strongly biased. They carry their views of woman abuse and child abuse in Arab and Muslim society to extreme lengths, and reduce the complex causes of Islamic terrorism to the simplistic explanation of "the abuse of women." As the Chesler-Kobrin case indicates, one of the crucial problems in academic discourse is how to keep one's personal and political feelings from affecting one's scholarship. Chesler began her career as a leftist, but she turned to the political right in response to what she came to see as the anti-Israeli and anti-Semitic viewpoints increasingly prevalent on the far left of political discourse in the United States, in Europe, and in the academic world. As a Jew, a woman, and a feminist, she has three sources of scholarly bias to overcome. She often confuses "Muslim" with "Islamic fundamentalist," thus aggravating the black-and-white "us and them" mentality, as if the entire Muslim world were of one piece. Black-and-white thinking is dangerous and unrealistic (Mack 2002, p. 174), and the unconscious roots of Islamic rage, terrorism, suicide bombing, and suicide murder are far more complex that Phyllis Chesler and Nancy Kobrin would portray them (Falk 2004, pp. 159–173).

Another biased scholar is Raphael Israeli (not his original name), an extreme-right-wing Moroccan-born Israeli "Orientalist" who, like those who coined *Islamofascism,* coined the neologism *Islamikaze* for Islamic suicide bombers (Israeli 1997, 2003). Israeli got the idea for his neologism from an article published in June 1996, which had originally appeared in the London Arabic-language publication *al-Watan al-Arabi* (the Arab Motherland), was translated into English and cited by the Israeli Hebrew-language newspaper *Ha'aretz,* which also has an English edition. The article mentioned a slogan proudly displayed at the main entrance to an Islamic terrorist-training camp in Afghanistan, which became known as "Kamikaze Barracks." The slogan read: *Jihad—Istishhad— Paradise—Islamic Kamikaze—Human Bombs.* The Arabic word *istishhad* means "act of martyrdom" (Bostom 2003). Israeli combined "Islamic Kamikaze" into *Islamikaze* to signify that the primary goal of suicide bombers is not suicide but the infliction of damage upon the enemy (Israeli 1997, 2003).

The term *Islamikaze* has not been accepted by other scholars, however. It continues to be used in Israeli's own publications and in their reviews. The most prominent usage of the term is in Israeli's own book on the subject. While the neoconservative American scholar Andrew G. Bostom praised this book, the former United States Senator Sam Nunn questioned whether Israeli's concept of "Islamikazes" as motivated by military rather than suicidal goals may be helpful in profiling possible suicide bombers, and the respected scholar Stephen Blackwell criticized Israeli's coinage of "Islamikaze" as a "flippant phrase" that "demonstrates a fundamental ignorance of Islamic culture" (Bostom 2003; Nunn 2004; Blackwell 2005).

TRYING TO SEE THE WHOLE PICTURE

Islamic terrorism is often played out on the background of the Arab-Israeli conflict, which is tragic and seemingly without any hope of resolution (Falk 2004). It is too easy to take a one-sided, partisan viewpoint of this conflict. One might say that both sides are right, but that nothing can be done to undo their grievances. While some extreme right-wing Israeli Jews deny that their country is occupying another people's land, and see their country's occupation of the Palestinian Arab lands as a legitimate Jewish settlement in ancestral Jewish lands, many other Israelis, the Palestinian Arabs themselves, and most of the rest of the world see it as a straightforward military presence in one country by another. To most Palestinian Arabs, this is an illegal and unjust occupation, which they deeply resent and wish to "shake off" (hence the word *intifada*).

Moreover, Palestinian Arab children are deliberately and actively taught to hate Israel and the Jews. Muslims believe that Allah turned Jews into apes and pigs to punish them for not believing in Him (Qur'an 7:166, 2:65, 5:60). Palestinian Arab children are taught songs in which the Jews are called dogs, apes, or pigs, and in which they are allowed to kill the Jews and drink their blood. The Jews are demonized (Shoebat 2005; Darwish 2006; M.A. Gabriel 2006). America, England, and Israel are portrayed to the Palestinian Arab children as their mortal enemies who must literally be exterminated. This helps the little Palestinian Arab children unconsciously *displace* their rage from their parents or siblings to the Israelis, Jews, British, and Americans.

The Palestinian Arab feelings of hatred, rage, and despair have already engendered two major uprisings against Israel. The first Palestinian Arab *intifada* against the Israeli occupation erupted in 1987 and lasted several years. The second Palestinian Arab *intifada* against the Israeli occupation, the so-called *al-Aqsa Intifada*, erupted in the fall of 2000, after what Palestinian Arabs saw as Ariel Sharon's provocative visit to the *Haram ash-Sharif* (the Temple Mount to Jews). Since that time, the radical Islamic groups of *Hamas* and *Islamic Jihad* have used suicide murder, along with rocket attacks on civilians, as their key weapons in their relentless war on Israel, which they hate with a passion and wish to annihilate. So does the Lebanese *Hezbollah*.

While the Palestinian Arab *intifada* has rational emotional causes as well as irrational and unconscious ones, fanatical terrorism, and especially suicide terrorism and murder, is so irrational and tragic that it cries out for a deeper psychological investigation, understanding, and explanation. As we have seen, and shall soon see, this most horrifying brand of terrorism in the Arab-Israeli conflict, and in *al-Qaïda*'s war on "the infidel Crusaders," involves unconscious fusional longings for the early mother, yearning for the love of Father Allah, *displacement* of murderous rage from one's mother or father to one's "oppressor," and the infantile unconscious defensive processes of *splitting, projection,* and *denial.*

One of the first psychological writers to investigate the psychology of terror and terrorists was the Polish-English writer Józef Teodor Konrad Korzeniowski (1857–1924), better known as Joseph Conrad. In his *Heart of Darkness* (Conrad 1902), this insightful author understood that the "sharp" lines separating savagery from civilization can become blurred under extreme psychological circumstances, and that ideological terrorists, who are so fond of citing lofty ideals, unconsciously rationalize their murderous acts as intellectual abstractions. The motif of darkness in the title recurs throughout the book. It reflects the unknown, the "darkness of barbarism" contrasted with the "light of civilization" and the ambiguity of both—the dark motives of "enlightened" civilization and the freedom of "dark barbarism," as well as the "spiritual darkness" of several "civilized" characters. This sense of darkness also lends itself to a related theme of obscurity—again, in various senses, reflecting the ambiguities in the work. Moral issues are not clear-cut or unambiguous. That which ought to be on the side of "light" is in fact mired in darkness, and vice versa. In the same way, in this book, I try to look at the dark, the hidden aspects of Islamic terror and of the "global war" against it.

Religious Extremism, Psychic Regression, and Terror

The belief in Allah as the Great Father in Heaven with whom one unites after one's heroic martyr's death is central to the mind of the Islamic suicidal terrorist. Before analyzing further the psychology of suicidal terrorists, therefore, we need to understand the psychology of religion and that of religious extremism, fanaticism, radicalism, and fundamentalism. The psychoanalytic literature on religion is very large. The founder of psychoanalysis, Sigmund Freud, thought that all religious belief—whether in God, the Devil, angels, demons, or any other supernatural beings—was a neurotic "illusion," comparing it to an individual patient's obsessional neurosis (Freud 1961). The rationalist British ethologist, evolutionary biologist, and scientific popularizer Clinton Richard Dawkins believed that the human idea of God was a "delusion," and that religious beliefs were the cause of all trouble in our world, including terrorism (Dawkins 2006). However, the British literary critic and philosopher Terry Eagleton, who had written about the terror in Northern Ireland, thought that Dawkins was actually obsessed with the idea of God:

> [Dawkins] is like a man who equates socialism with the Gulag. Like the puritan and sex, Dawkins sees God everywhere, even where he is self-evidently absent. He thinks, for example, that the ethno-political conflict in Northern Ireland would evaporate if religion did, which to someone like me, who lives there part of the time, betrays just how little he knows about it. He also thinks rather strangely that the [Northern Irish] terms Loyalist and Nationalist are "euphemisms" for Protestant and Catholic, and clearly doesn't know the difference between a Loyalist and a

Unionist or a Nationalist and a Republican. He also holds, against a good deal of the available evidence, that Islamic terrorism is inspired by religion rather than politics (Eagleton 2006).

In traditional, fundamentalist Islam, nothing separates religion from politics. Allah rules everything, the *Shari'a* is a universal system of just laws, the Islamic *ummah* is ruled by the *khilafah,* which includes the Muslim state, the "Muslim nation," and the Muslim religion in one integral whole. Moreover, both religion and politics are products of the human mind, and psychologically cannot really be separated. The scholarly fields of *psychoanthropology* and *ethnopsychiatry* have discovered how deeply social structures affect individual psychological processes. At least one American psychoanalyst, however, the Cypriot-Turkish-born Vamık Volkan, thought that religious belief in God is part of the normal processes of our human development:

> The image of God incorporates inputs from different sources as the child grows and it is modified according to an individual's own psychology—early identification and unconscious fantasies, for example—as well as socio-cultural experiences, education, and the use of religious symbols. For each individual, the image of God becomes a source of various significant images, such as maternal or paternal images. It also becomes a source of psychological nourishment, anxiety of punishment, omnipotence, hatred, and so on—including, very significantly, the sense of belonging to a family, clan, and/or large group (Volkan 2001a, p. 157).

Whether moderate human religious belief is normal or not, religious extremism, fanaticism, and fundamentalism often involve psychopathological processes. The religious fanatic displays a marked psychological *regression.* Like an anxious and unhappy infant, full of narcissistic rage, he unconsciously denies reality, projects and externalizes the unbearable aspects of his own self upon his enemies, displaces his narcissistic rage from early parental figures to the hated "enemy," and splits his world into all-good and all-bad parts—a black-and-white picture with no shades of gray. Religious extremism and fanaticism have occurred throughout history and in every religion and sect. Scholars have noted "the tendency of some [fanatical] members of traditional religious communities to separate from fellow believers and to define the sacred community in terms of its disciplined opposition to non-believers and 'lukewarm' believers alike" (Marty and Appleby 1995, p. 1). This is how *al-Qaïda*'s fanatical followers distinguish themselves from other Muslims as the "true believers."

While all religious fundamentalists are psychically regressed, there are different kinds and levels of regression. There is in fact a continuum of regressive levels. On a mild and adaptive level of regression, the religious fundamentalist gains comfort from the internal symbolic images of nurturing parents, like Father Allah, and feels like a loved child. He is able to relate to the world realistically. However, on an extreme and malignant level of regression, the fanatical religious fundamentalist is possessed by anxiety, omnipotence, megalomania and uniqueness, and infinite narcissistic rage, and relates to the world only in a distorted fashion. It is those extremely and malignantly regressed fundamentalists that become the dangerous terrorists (Volkan 2004, p. 135). This is what Heinz Kohut had in mind when he spoke of the most dangerous kind of human aggression (Kohut 1978, p. 635).

The British psychoanalyst Wilfred Ruprect Bion (1897–1979) studied small-group psychodynamics. He classified groups into several types. The basic-assumption group is shaped by the unconscious of each group member, and the assumptions play out without the cooperation or even knowledge of individuals. The dependent group seeks an all-powerful leader, the fight-flight group needs an enemy and wants the leader to formulate a defense, and the pairing group looks forward to some promised perfect state in the future. The concept of a pairing group needs some explanation. The metaphor here is that the group allows two of its members to become a couple; these two create a child who becomes the savior of the group. New ideas (the contained) always carry the power to disrupt a basic assumption group (the container) in the process Bion called "catastrophic change." Regressive, primitive, and hostile, basic-assumption groups resist learning. Members of this type of group use language as a weapon of aggression rather than as a tool for exploring ideas (Bion 1961). Human aggression, rage, and hatred can take many forms. One of them is the erotic or sexual. The American psychoanalyst Robert Stoller (1925–1991) called sexual perversions, such as the sadomasochistic ones, "The erotic form of hatred" (Stoller 1975).

The Jewish psychoanalytic scholars Joseph Berke and Stanley Schneider believed that the murderous narcissistic rage of the Islamic terrorist has a powerful "erotic" aspect:

> In our scheme of understanding, the Muslim terrorist, indoctrinated in mosques by imams who preach hate and fundamentalistic ideology, is swept up by an erotic surge of emotion that fuels hostility, murderous rage and a sadistic urge to conquer and be all-powerful. This libidinal excitement is a temptation that hangs in-the-air and becomes transformed and displaced as violent feelings which run amok amid erotic urges which are then expressed as extreme sadistic expressions of terrorism [...] This means that the internal world of the terrorist is replete with persecutory all-bad objects because the good objects have been repressed and displaced by religious and cultural indoctrination [...] (Berke and Schneider 2006).

The trouble with Berke and Schneider's analysis is that it is not the indoctrination by the preachers or recruiters that initially repress or displace the "good objects." In the mind of the Islamic terrorist, the "good objects" have already been displaced long ago, in his early life, by the split-off all-bad "object" of the "bad mother." The indoctrination by his leader only serves to reinforce this early-life displacement: it builds upon it.

Berke and Schneider further analyzed the unconscious defensive processes of the Islamic terrorist, emphasizing his indoctrination. Using a mixture of early-Freudian "instinct theory" and other, more modern psychoanalytic theories, such as those of Bion, Klein, and Stoller, they wrote:

Muslim terrorists, because of the fundamentalistic religious and cultural indoctrination and brainwashing do not have a perceived internal conflict [...] The terrorist, through years of ideological indoctrination, has a collapsing of developmental stages and in a fused primitive mode is pressured by strong *instinctual urges* that become expressed sadistically [...] The indoctrination of fundamentalistic beliefs does not permit a maturation of the *instinctual urges* into a socially modifiable and coherent whole. Rather it fosters a regression back to early pre-oedipal strivings and longings, or to the sadism and envy that Klein described, as well as the *erotic* longings and early *sexual* awakenings Stoller has focused on. In other words, *the victimizer functions at a at a very early, primitive and regressed emotional level.* Bion tries to tie-together all these parts with a micro (individual) vs. macro (society) paradigm. The narcissistic investment in self does not move towards a merger with the group. Rather, it denudes the individual of psychic energy that could and should move him forward. This is the mindset of the terrorist (Berke and Schneider 2006; italics added).

As we shall repeatedly see, the "mind-set" of the Islamic terrorist is much more complicated than this, and indoctrination works on those who are already functioning at a regressed and primitive level as a result of their early-life trauma, "young people whose personal identity is already disturbed," and youths who seek an outer element to internalize in order to stabilize their chaotic and unstable internal world (Volkan 2001b, p. 209).

Fantasies of Rebirth through Violent Death

At this point, we shall make a detour through the psychology of Christian "cults" in order to clarify that of Islamic terrorists. Ruth Stein noted the deep longing for the love of Father Allah and for a union with Him in Heaven in Mohamed Atta, the leader of the *9/11* (September 11, 2001) Islamic suicide murderers (Stein 2002). Religious fanaticism, however, is not limited to Muslims. It is shared by American Christian fundamentalism and many other fundamentalist religious groups. Charles Strozier, a prominent American historian and psychoanalyst, spent five years attending fundamentalist Christian religious services and interviewing apocalyptic fundamentalist Christians who believe in the coming End of Days. His interviewees included an ex-prostitute, a multimillionaire entrepreneur turned missionary, a fiery preacher, and a Wall Street broker. Like George W. Bush, all of them were "born-again Christians" who regarded their past lives as sinful and worthless. Strozier concluded that their born-again experiences represented unconscious attempts to heal their traumatized and fractured selves (Strozier 1994).

The key psychological role of violent fantasies and acts in millennial and messianic movements has been explored (Head and Landes 1992; Robbins and Palmer 1997; Landes 2000; Landes et al. 2003). Fantasies of rebirth—actual or symbolic, peaceful or violent—are common among religious extremists, such as born-again Christians, apocalyptic movements, millenarians, destructive cults and sects, and Islamic terrorists. There is a massive individual and collective psychopathology in these groups. Fantasies of rebirth are often tied to fantasies— or acts—of violent death, including suicide or murder. The anthropologist

Ernest Becker tried to explain human civilization as our unconscious denial of the unbearable idea of our mortality (Becker 1973).

An Israeli Jewish psychologist thought that "rebirth is *always* tied to imagined death and violence" and that "the apocalypse is first the denial of death" (Beit-Hallahmi 2002, pp. 166, 173). To illustrate the connection between the craving for rebirth and the wish for violent death, Beit-Hallahmi cited the extreme examples of the Christian cults of the People's Temple, the Branch Davidians, the Aum Shinrikyo, the Solar Temple Order, and Heaven's Gate cults. The word "cult" may not adequately convey the violent murderous narcissistic rage and the madness of these fanatical religious groups.

Each of those cults had a very disturbed, psychotic or borderline charismatic leader. The People's Temple of Jonestown, Guyana, was led by the borderline Reverend Jim Jones (1931–1978), who drove over nine hundred followers to their suicide (Ulman and Abse 1983; Chidester 1988). The Branch Davidians of Waco, Texas, were led by the psychotic Vernon Wayne Howell (1959–1993), who called himself "David Koresh" after the Biblical Hebrew names of King David and King Cyrus, thought of himself as God, and led dozens of his followers to their violent death (Volkan 2004, pp. 113–122). The Aum Shinrikyo cult of Japan was led by the paranoid Chizuo Matsumoto, who called himself "Shoko Asahara" and killed many innocent people by sarin gas poisoning. In each case, the charismatic leader owed his charisma, at least partly, to some physical defect or foreignness that evoked the infantile fantasies of his followers (Schiffer 1973).

The French-speaking *Ordre du Temple Solaire* was led by a bizarre Italian-Canadian named Joseph di Mambro (1924–1994) and his equally bizarre but much younger Belgian partner Luc Jouret (1948–1994). They were a psychotic couple, a *folie-à-deux* "father-and-son" team who murdered their followers and committed suicide. Thirteen additional members of the cult killed themselves the following year. The Heaven's Gate cult of the United States was led by another psychotic couple, Bonnie Lu Trousdale Nettles (1927–1985), who called herself Ti and Peep, and Marshall Herff Applewhite (1932–1997), who called himself Do and Bo. In yet another case of *folie-à-deux,* this psychotic couple believed that they were the two End Times witnesses in Chapter 11 of the New Testament book of the Revelation or Apocalypse. It was their job to bring about the End Times and the Messiah.

By eschatological fundamentalist Christian belief, the End Times are a time of tribulation that will precede the coming of a Messiah figure in many world religions. The term End Times has evolved from use around a group of Christian millennial beliefs. These beliefs typically include the ideas that the biblical apocalypse in Revelation 11 is imminent and that various signs in current events are omens of Armageddon, the ultimate war between Good and Evil. These beliefs have been widely held in one form, by the Adventist movement, by Jehovah's Witnesses, and in another form by the Dispensational Premillennialists. The Heaven's Gate leaders attracted a few dozen very disturbed individuals who kept moving, designed Internet Web sites, and believed in aliens from outer space. In 1997, thirty-nine Heaven's Gate members committed suicide in the serious belief that a spaceship following the tail of the Hale-Bopp comet was about to take them to a better life on another planet.

Jessica Stern, an international expert on terrorism, thought that the painful feeling of alienation can cause people to join extremist cults (Stern 2003). She studied the violent Christian cult of "The Covenant, the Sword, and the Arm of the Lord," based in Elijah, Arkansas. After their leader received a "revelation" that the End Times had begun, the cult began "fusing together in one body" as directed by a prophetess living on the compound. Psychologically, they were like infants fusing with their mother (the group). They burned family photographs, sold their wedding rings, pooled their earnings, and destroyed televisions and other "reminders of the outside world's propaganda." They also began stockpiling weapons to prepare for the "enemy's" anticipated invasion, the enemy being the U.S. government. But the Apocalypse—and the battle between good and evil forces—failed to materialize on the appointed hour. Each failed prophecy was followed by a revised forecast. Instead of giving in to despair that their dream of the End Times might not materialize, cult members' confidence grew stronger. They intensified their military training, acquired more powerful weapons, and purified themselves to prepare to vanquish the forces of evil. Fortunately, in 1985 the cult ended bloodlessly after its members surrendered to U.S. troops. Stern thought that "Religious terrorism arises from pain and loss and from impatience with a God who is slow to respond to our plight, who doesn't answer."

CHRISTIAN CULTS AND ISLAMIC TERROR

Here we have a psychological link between the extremist Christian fundamentalist cults and the fanatical Islamic terrorists. Religious madness and the yearning for rebirth is not restricted to fanatical Christian apocalyptics. The quest for rebirth through violent death and a new good self or identity to replace the painful *bad self* or *negative identity* (Knutson 1981) also characterizes Islamic fanatics. Like other scholars, the Swiss psychoanalyst Arno Gruen thought that Islamic culture forces blind submission to Islamic rules and authority (Gruen 2002), and his Swiss-American colleague Leon Wurmser stressed the problem of the self:

> The true self is hated and persecuted in the stranger. Identification with a totalitarian authority—merger of the ego in an archaic, *resentment* laden superego figure dictating the necessity of a false self—replaces genuine identity (Wurmser 2004, p. 919).

Indeed, the problem of the self, including self-worth, self-esteem, self-denigration, the grandiose self, self-rage, and other aspects of one's relation to oneself, is crucial to the understanding of terrorism. As in traditional Islam, fundamentalist Muslim culture, in fact, does encourage blind submission to authority, from that of Allah to that of his Prophet and messenger Muhammad to that of the Father. Some scholars think that Islam has been "hijacked" by fanatics.

The Pakistani Muslim scholar Eqbal Ahmad (1932–1999) thought that Islamic fanatics were obsessed with controlling other people's personal behavior, seeking "an Islamic order reduced to a penal code, stripped of its humanism, aesthetics, intellectual quests, and spiritual devotion" (E. Ahmad 1999, 2000, quoted in Said 2001, p. 13). They try to enforce "an absolute assertion of one, generally de-contextualized, aspect of [Muslim] religion and a total disregard of another. The phenomenon distorts religion, debases tradition, and twists the political process wherever it unfolds" (E. Ahmad 1999, 2000, quoted in Said 2001, p. 13). This respected Pakistani Muslim scholar thought that fundamentalist Islamists were concerned with power, not with the soul, and that they sought to exploit people for their political ends, rather than alleviate their sufferings (E. Ahmad 1999, 2000, quoted in Said 2001, p. 13).

The Cypriot-Turkish-born American psychoanalyst Vamık Volkan, an expert on large-group psychological processes, religious fanaticism, and group terrorism, thought that the identity of religious extremists involved "the regressive use of religious beliefs and feelings." This collective regression includes an absolute belief that one is the true believer, the only one in possession of the only true divine text or rule; needing a supreme leader as the sole interpreter of the divine text; the exhibition of magical beliefs; a pessimistic attitude to the world, with paradoxically coexisting contradictory feelings of victimization, helplessness, and omnipotence; the construction of psychological (and sometimes physical) barricades between the group and the rest of the world; the expectation of threat or danger from people and things outside the group's borders; altered gender, family, child rearing, and sexual norms, often including the degradation of women; a changed group morality, which may accept the destruction of monuments, buildings, or other symbols perceived as threatening to the group's beliefs; and attempts at mass suicide or mass murder in order to enhance or protect the large group identity (Volkan 2001a, p. 157).

These regressive collective psychopathological processes occur in fanatical religious "cults" led by deeply disturbed and often psychotic charismatic leaders, as well as in large religious groups. They can be found in all major religions. These processes also occur in modern fanatical Muslim groups like the Afghan Taliban, whose charismatic and paranoid leader, *Mullah* Mohammed Omar, in an unconscious Oedipal act, donned "the sacred cloak of the Prophet Muhammad," and whose followers display clear signs of collective psychic regression (Volkan 2001a, 158–160). It is important to note that the longing for the love of Father Allah detected by Ruth Stein in the *9/11* (September 11, 2001) suicide murder leader Mohamed Atta was also regressive, and that so was his hatred for "America" as the bad mother (Stein 2002).

History's First Islamic Terrorists?

One of the most terrible offspring of fanatical Islamic extremism, suicidal murder and terror, was not invented by Islamic fanatics. The ancient Celts reportedly staged suicidal hunger strikes at the doors of their enemies to shame them. In the eleventh century of the Christian era, the Muslim Abbasid caliphate was based in Baghdad (its original Persian name means "God's Gift"), which in the eighth century of the Christian era the Abbasid Caliph al-Mansur had made into his capital city and renamed *Madinat as-Salaam* (city of peace). It was occupied by the Turkish Seljuks in 1055.

By the eleventh century of the Christian era, Islam had developed many sects, including the Sunnis, Shi'ites, Sufis, and Isma'ilis, a branch of Islam that is the second largest part of the Shi'ite community after the *Ithna'ashariya* (Twelvers). Though there are several subgroupings within the Isma'ilis, the term in today's vernacular generally refers to the Nizaris, a sub-sect of the Isma'ilis who are followers of the Aga Khan and are the only Shi'ite community with a continuing line of *al-Imāma* or "Imamate." The concept of *al-Imāma* in the Shi'ite sense differs greatly from the Sunni understanding.

In 1090 of the Christian era, a fanatical young Nizari Isma'ili leader named Hassan-i Sabbah (died 1124 CE), the leader of the *hashshashin,* who had studied in Egypt and claimed royal descent from the Himyarite kings of Arabia, seized the mountain fortress of Alamut in the Seljuk province of Daylam, on the southern shore of the Caspian Sea in Iran, and launched a campaign of suicide terror against his enemies. Hassan-i Sabbah established a power base among the outer tribes and mountain people, far from the centers of established Islamic political and economic power. Hassan-i Sabbah made himself into a Muslim *imam* and founded the fanatical Islamic sect of the Nizari Ismailites, who used suicide terror against their enemies. According to Western sources, their methods including self-drugging with hashish (cannabis), a practice which the late-medieval travelogue by Marco Polo (1254–1324), who visited Alamut in 1273, introduced into Italian and other European languages in the word "assassin" (Polo 1928; Falk 1996, pp. 381, 476).

The word "assassin" is commonly believed to be a corruption or mutation of the Arabic word *hashshashin* meaning "hashish-eaters." However, some scholars dispute this etymology, arguing that "assassin" is a misnomer originating from Marco Polo's account of his visit to Alamut in which he confused another drug, whose effects are more like those of alcohol, with what we call *hashish* or cannabis (Pollan 2001). Some writers think that "assassin" means "followers of Hassan" (that is, Hassan-i Sabbah). Others suggest that since hashish-eaters were ostracized in the Muslim middle ages, the word *hashshashin* had become a common synonym for "outlaws." The use of this term for Hassan's Isma'ili sect is not necessarily a clue to their *hashish* usage. Some common accounts of their connection with *hashish* are that these "assassins" took *hashish* before missions in order to calm themselves; others say that it helped to boost their strength, and turned them into madmen in battle. Yet other accounts state it was used in their initiation rites in order to show the neophyte the sensual pleasures awaiting him in the afterlife. The connection between their mysticism and *hashish*, however, is not verifiable by reliable and consistent historical accounts; this is not surprising given their secrecy and infamy.

The Anglo-Jewish scholar Bernard Lewis called the Nizari Isma'ilis "history's first terrorists" (Lewis 1967). This is a rather curious characterization in view of the numerous acts of terror in ancient times. In the first century of the Christian era, during the Jewish revolt against the Romans, Jewish zealots called *sicarii* terrorized their political opponents by murdering them with short daggers called *sica* (Falk 1996, pp. 287, 301). Lewis's Anglo-Iranian colleague Farhad Daftary believed that Marco Polo's story about the Isma'ili Nizaris using *hashish* to carry out their killings was a myth, and that the "assassins" would not have been so effective in their deadly and often patient work had they been high on drugs of any kind (Daftary 1994). While Daftary's account is biased in favor of the Isma'ilis, Western accounts since Marco Polo had been biased against them. It would seem that, as with beauty, an assassin is in the eye of the beholder.

Like a medieval *ayatollah,* the fanatical and autocratic *imam* Hassan-i Sabbah led an ascetic existence and imposed a puritanical Islamic regime from Alamut. When one of his sons was accused of murder and the other of drunkenness, he had them both executed. After Hassan-i Sabbah died in 1124 CE, he was succeeded by one of his lieutenants, Dai Kiya Buzurg Ummid, who came from a peasant family in the district of Rudbar, near Alamut. Buzurg Ummid's grandson, also named Hassan, became the *imam* of Alamut in 1162 CE. He seems to have been a paranoid megalomaniac. Two years after Hassan's ascension to the imamate of Alamut, he assembled all of the religious leaders of the area and announced "to all demons, angels, and men" that their salvation lay in obeying his commands and that the religious law of Islam was hereby abrogated. He then made two bows signifying the premature end of *Ramadan* and celebrated by drinking and feasting and holding a festival to mark the shattering of the sacred law. On the door of his library were the words, "With the aid of Allah, the ruler of the universe destroyed the fetters of the law."

Suicide murder was renewed in the twentieth century of the Christian era, during World War II (1939–1945), when Japanese military commanders used suicide pilots, whom they called *kamikaze,* to fly their planes into the American enemy's ships. The Japanese word *kamikaze* means "divine wind." The term harked back to a "miraculous" Japanese victory against the invading Mongols in 1281, which the Japanese attributed to a divine typhoon that sank the Mongolian ships. The Americans, however, used the word *kamikaze* to describe the reckless and suicidal behavior of Japanese fighter pilots.

On the other hand, in our own time, the European mass communication media, especially the French ones, have used the word *kamikaze* to refer to the modern Muslim Arab suicide bombers, often with respect and admiration. Using the Arabic term *dhimmi* for the subservient status of non-Muslims under Islamic rule, an Egyptian-born Jewish scholar has called this submissive European attitude to the Muslims "psychological dhimmitude" (Bat Ye'or 1996, 2002, 2005). Others have warned Europe against ignoring the peril of Islamic terror and even of Muslim culture itself, which threatens to take over the world.

Suicidal murder and terror are widespread. In Sri Lanka, the Buddhist Sinhala are the majority and the Hindu Tamils are the minority. Most Tamils live in peace with the Sinhala, but some are full of narcissistic rage and hate. The Liberation Tigers of Tamil Eelam, one of the world's most sophisticated and tightly organized terrorist groups, have used suicide terror against the governments of Sri Lanka and India. In 1991 a Tamil Tiger suicide bomber killed India's Prime Minister Rajiv Gandhi (1944–1991). In 1993 another Tamil Tiger blew himself up together with the Sri Lankan President Ranasinghe Premadasa (1924–1993) a few days after his chief opponent, Lalith Athulathmudali (whom I had personally met in the 1960s when he was a student in Israel), had been murdered by unidentified gunmen. His assassination was attributed to the Tamil Tigers, who hotly disputed this charge.

The Sanskrit word *singha* means "lion" (hence the name Singapore, village of lions). The Buddhist Sri Lankan Sinhala—also called Sinhalese or Singhalese—named themselves after the Sanskrit word *simhala,* meaning "dwelling place of the lions." The Arabic name for Sri Lanka, *Serendib* or *Sarandib,* the source of the English word "serendipity," is a corruption of the Sanskrit name *Simhaladvipa* (island of the lions). The Arabs borrowed the name from Indians with whom they traded. This, however, is not known to the Tamil Tigers, whose main interest is the destruction of the hated Sinhala, and who seethe with narcissistic rage.

A specialized Tamil Tiger unit called the Black Tigers carries out the suicide attacks on the Sinhalese. If faced with capture by the Sri Lankan authorities, the

Black Tigers commit suicide by swallowing the cyanide capsules that they wear around their necks. The ruthless and overweight Tamil Tiger leader, Velupillai Prabhakaran (born 1954), has been addicted to violence—and food—since his childhood. His psychologically fusional mother was "deeply religious and very fond of him" (Goertzel 2002a, p. 104), while his father was a strict and punitive disciplinarian who demanded absolute obedience from his children and was also clinging and intrusive. It is not hard to imagine the murderous narcissistic rage in Velupillai's unconscious mind (Swamy 1994, pp. 49–69).

In 2000 the Palestinian leaders of the fundamentalist Islamic groups *Hamas* and *Islamic Jihad* began copying the effective suicide murder methods of the Tamil Tigers. The leaders of these fanatical religious groups, who blindly worship Allah and hate the "occupying infidel" with a murderous passion, often recruit a disturbed late-adolescent young man who has failed in his studies, in his work, or in his personal life, indoctrinate him to become a *shaheed* (glorious martyr) and to sacrifice himself in the war of liberation against the hated infidel. One psychoanalyst found that the typical recruits were "unmarried males aged 17 to 23 (sometimes younger). Scouts often choose youths who have been hurt by ethnic conflict: those who have been beaten up by soldiers or police or who have lost a father or brother in demonstrations; those who have not successfully completed their adolescent transformation and are alienated and without much hope for the future in existing political and economic conditions" (Volkan 1997, p. 165). Despite the Muslim prohibition on suicide, these young men (and women) are told that they will become holy martyrs to Allah by carrying out suicide bombings against the hated oppressors, the "infidel" Israelis.

The prospective *shaheed* is told that after his death he will enjoy the love of Father Allah and the sexual favors of 72 *houris* (angelic virgins) in Heaven. His mentors dress him up in black martyr's garb with a green headband carrying key verses from the Qur'an, such as "Think not of those who are slain in Allah's way as dead. Nay, they live, finding their sustenance in the presence of their Lord." They take a video clip of the young man reading the appropriate declaration for Allah and against Israel (unconsciously the Bad Mother), and then send him on his mission to blow himself up among as many Israelis as he possibly can kill while dying as a martyr for Allah (the Good Father) and for Palestine (the Good Mother). However, there have also been atypical cases of women and older men becoming suicide bombers. I shall discuss the psychological literature on the suicide bombers and attempt to link it with what we know of the psychoanalysis of borderline personality disorder and collective psychopathology (Masterson 1981, 2000; Kernberg 2002).

Suicide Murder as Unconscious Fusion with the Mother

In my study of political assassination, I attempted to show that in the person of the political leader whom he murders the political assassin unconsciously seeks to kill his bad early mother and to fuse with her at the same time (Falk 2001a). Nancy Kobrin, the right-wing feminist American-Jewish psychoanalyst, thought that suicide bombers, as well as yearning for death and rebirth, unconsciously seek the deeply coveted fusion with the early mother, which she called "the maternal fusion." Because the suicide bomber dies along with his victims, he desires fusion with them. Rather than wish to kill the sadistic father, she wrote, "the assassin wishes to kill the sadistic pre-Oedipal mother" (Kobrin 2002, p. 182). Like Phyllis Chesler, this scholar simplistically attributed Islamic terrorism to the abuse of women in Muslim society.

One of the ways scholars deal with complex material that provokes their anxiety, and makes its study painful for them, is to divide or classify the subject they are studying into manageable entities. Marvin Zonis and Daniel Offer stipulated three models for the Arab-Israeli conflict—the national-character model, the psychopathology model, and the self-system model (Zonis and Offer 1985, pp. 268–287); John Mack distinguished three levels of causation for suicidal terrorism—the immediate, proximate, and deeper levels (Mack 2002, p. 174); and an American scholar and her Arab collaborators, in an attempt to reconcile the seemingly contradictory studies of suicide bombers, outlined four different models or conceptual frameworks for understanding this tragic phenomenon: the psychological, sociological, psychiatric, and religious models (Fields et al. 2002, p. 219).

The *psychological* model proposed by these scholars focuses on the suicide bombers' personality profiles; the *sociological* model on their marginality, unemployment, and poverty; the *psychiatric* model on their psychopathology; and the *religious* model on their religious belief system. Claiming that none of these models was sufficient to explain the phenomenon, these scholars proposed a "multilevel ecological/dynamic" and a "transactional/ecological" model. As they put it, "the sociopolitical matrix interacting with gender identity and personal and interpersonal loss, with religious sentiment fed by symbolic gratification, and the death of optimism as [a] result of the political situation all must be considered as operational factors in the phenomenon of the Palestinian suicide bomber." These scholars attempted to present their "multilevel, ecological, dynamic and transactional" model in a later study (Fields et al. 2004).

Because Muslim culture is so different from our own, it is very hard for us to understand the thoughts, concepts, and emotions of the Islamic terrorists. The collective psychology of the suicide bombers is just as complex and intriguing as their individual psychology. The Cypriot-Turkish-born American psychoanalyst Vamık Volkan believed that terrorist groups were like any other youth group: "The mechanisms that pull together a football team or boy scout group are similar to those used to create a terrorist group, but in the latter, secrecy binds the recruits" (Volkan 1997, p. 165). Nevertheless, some group dynamics are specific to Muslim Arab culture and even more so to extreme fanatical Islamic groups that carry out murderous terror acts:

> According to fundamentalist Islamic tradition and corresponding cultural norms, most of these teenagers suppress their sexual desires; some even refrain from watching television to avoid sexual temptation. Indoctrination creates a severe—but external—superego, which demands adherence to restricted ways of thinking and behaving. But as a counterweight—or incentive—there is the suggestion of unlimited pleasures in heaven, where their stomachs will be filled with scrumptious food and they will receive the love of houris (angels). After the death of a suicide bomber, members of a terrorist group actually hold a celebration (despite the family members' genuine grief) and speak of a martyr's death as a "wedding." With the examples of those who died before, recruits are given hope and a belief in immortality, as well as assurances that after their demise their parents and siblings will be well taken care of by the terrorist group. In fact, relatives receive compensation (Volkan 1997, p. 166).

As we have seen, the leaders of these fanatical Islamic groups, who blindly worship Allah and hate the "occupying infidel" with a murderous passion, typically recruit a troubled late-adolescent youth who has failed in his studies, his work, or his personal life, and "brainwash" him to become a *shaheed* (glorious martyr), to sacrifice himself for Allah in the war of liberation against the hated infidel. There have also been a few atypical cases of women and older men becoming suicide bombers. Volkan described this process as consisting of two stages:

> The typical technique of creating Middle Eastern Muslim suicide bombers includes two basic steps (Volkan 1997): first, the "trainers" find *young people whose personal*

identity is already disturbed [italics added] and who are [unconsciously] seeking an outer "element" to internalize so they can stabilize their internal world. Second, they develop a "teaching method" that "forces" the large-group identity—ethnic and/or religious—into the "cracks" of the person's damaged or subjugated individual identity. Once people become candidates to be suicide bombers-in-training, normal rules of behavior and individual psychology no longer fully apply to their patterns of thought and action. The future suicide bomber is now an agent of the large-group identity—which is perceived as threatened—and will attempt to repair it for himself or herself and for other members of the large group. Killing one's self (and one's personal identity) and "others" (enemies) does not matter. What matters is that the act of bombing (terrorism) brings self-esteem and attention to the large-group identity (Volkan 2001b, p. 209).

As we have also seen, the prospective *shaheed* is told that he will not only join his Father Allah in Heaven but also enjoy the sexual favors of the 72 *houris* (angelic maidens) in Heaven. There are many Muslim myths and legends about these *houris*. The Qur'an says, "In the Gardens of Paradise will be fair *houris*, good, beautiful [...] restrained (as to their glances), in (goodly) pavilions [...] Whom no man or demon before them has touched" (*Sura* 55). The fourteenth-century Muslim scholar Ibn Kathir, in his *tafsir* (commentary) on *Sura* 55, quoted the Prophet Muhammad as saying, "The smallest reward for the people of paradise is an abode where there are 80,000 servants and 72 wives, over which stands a dome decorated with pearls, aquamarine, and ruby, as wide as the distance from al-Jabiyyah [Syria] to Sana'a [Yemen]."

In the unconscious mind of the prospective *shaheed,* the imaginary *houris* are projections of his idealized mother, virginal, untouched, the fulfillment of an Oedipal dream. His murderous narcissistic rage at his split-off, denigrated, bad mother is displaced to Israel or America. This fulfillment, however, comes at the terrible price of "castration" and death, which brings us to the collective psychopathology of extreme terrorist groups:

Meanwhile, the "teachers" also interfere with the "real world" affairs of the students, mainly by cutting off meaningful communication and other ties to students' families and by forbidding things such as music and television, on the grounds that they may be sexually stimulating. Sex and women can be obtained only after a passage to adulthood. In the case of the suicide bombers, however, the "passage" is killing one-self, not a symbolic castration. The oedipal triumph is allowed only after death. Allah—who is presented as a strict and primitive superego against the derivatives of libidinal drive and a force to be obeyed while the youngster is alive—allows the satisfaction of the libidinal wishes by *houris* (angels) in paradise. Using the Prophet Muhammad's instructions to his followers during the Battle of Badr (624 C.E.) as justification, the "teachers" convince their students that by carrying out the suicide attack, they will gain immortality. In what some consider one of the earliest exam-ples of "war propaganda," Muhammad told his followers that they would continue to "live" in Paradise if they died during the battle. The bomber candidates are told that life continues in paradise. The death of a suicide bomber is celebrated as a "wedding ceremony," a gathering where friends and family rejoice in their belief that the dead terrorist is in the loving hands of angels in heaven (Volkan 2001b, pp. 210–211).

Denial is a common unconscious process or defense among the Arabs (Patai 1973; Heggy 2005). While Muhammad's new Muslims had defeated the Meccan Qureishis at the Battle of Badr in 624 CE, they also lost another battle to the same enemies the following year at Uhud. However, with an infinite capacity for denying reality, the Prophet Muhammad reportedly declared to his followers that their defeat at Uhud was really a victory, and that their seventy "martyrs" had gone to Heaven, while the twenty-two enemy dead were in Hell. The Arabs used this kind of denial when they were defeated in the Arab-Israeli wars of 1948, 1956, 1967, and 1973.

In the same way, the fanatical leaders of extreme Palestinian Islamic groups like *Hamas* and *Islamic Jihad* assure their young recruits that their deaths will really be the beginning of new lives. It is the very fantasy of rebirth through violent death that we have seen in extremist Christian cults. As we have seen, the mentors of the prospective *shaheed* dress him up in black martyr's garb with a green headband carrying Qur'anic verses from *Sura* 3 such as, "Think not of those who are slain in Allah's way as dead. Nay, they live, finding their sustenance in the presence of their Lord." The denial of reality implied in this verse is ignored. They take a video clip of the future *shaheed* reading the appropriate declaration for Allah and against Israel, and then send him on his "sacred" mission to blow himself up among as many Israelis as possible, dying as a martyr for Allah (unconsciously the Good Father) and for Palestine (the Good Mother).

Due to the widespread wife abuse and child abuse in the traditional Muslim family, in many cases the physical and emotional abuse of the Muslim boy causes him to harbor murderous narcissistic rage at his parents, which seeks an avenue of release through *displacement.* The traumatized young Muslim Arab boy will then join the Islamic terrorist organizations, hurl rocks and firebombs at Israeli soldiers, and even become a suicide bomber, being promised instant martyrdom with a guaranteed seat in Heaven and 72 *houris* for his pleasure. The murderous rage of the young Arab terrorist is thus unconsciously *displaced* from the original object, the abusive father or the frustrating mother, onto the Jews, or onto Israel.

Just as the Iranian *mullahs* and *ayatollahs* genuinely believe that the United States is the Great Satan, so the fanatical Arab terrorist is genuinely convinced that Israel, the Little Satan, is the embodiment of Evil. As we have seen, in my psychobiographical study of Osama bin Laden, the leader of the *al-Qaïda* terrorist group that has destroyed so many lives, I have attempted to show that this man's murderous narcissistic rage at America was unconsciously displaced from a profound murderous fury at his own mother, who had abandoned him at an early age (Falk 2001b). The displacement and transference are unconscious to ward off the anxiety associated with feelings of murderous rage toward one's parents.

The Swiss-American-Jewish psychoanalyst Leon Wurmser thought that terrorists unconsciously project and externalize the unbearable aspects of themselves upon those who are not like them (Wurmser 2004, p. 926). As we have seen, and as Zonis had pointed out, Wurmser's "resentment" is an understatement for "boundless narcissistic rage." Thus, the suicide murder is an attempt both to kill the mother and to merge with her forever.

The Roots of Muslim Rage

It is a common observation in the "West" that many Muslims, not only Islamic fanatics or terrorists, are enraged at us. The eminent Anglo-Jewish Arabist Bernard Lewis studied what he called "The Roots of Muslim Rage" from a historical viewpoint (Lewis 1990). Lewis focused on the public and conscious sphere. In my psychoanalytic study of the Arab-Israeli conflict, I discussed some of the personal and unconscious roots of Muslim rage and terrorism in the emotional structure of the Arab family (Falk 2004). The psychology and culture of the "Oriental" Arabs are still a matter of intense controversy between Muslim, Arab, Jewish, Christian, and other scholars (W.I. Cohen 1983; Lewis 1990, 1998, 2002, 2003; A. Ahmad 1991; Heggy 2005; Landes 2007).

The subject naturally stirs deep and powerful emotions among scholars. The American feminist scholars Phyllis Chesler and Nancy Kobrin have suggested that the roots of Islamic rage lie in the fundamentalist Muslim abuse of women, and that Islamic terror was the product of "an Islamic culture that denigrates women in general and a jihadist culture that denigrates all life [sic], including Muslim life, and which seeks to oppress and destroy all living beings. For example, many Islamic suicide killers will purposely target pregnant women or women with small children before they blow themselves up" (Chesler and Kobrin 2006).

It should be pointed out that Islam itself does not "denigrate all life" nor does it "celebrate death." It is true that extremist jihadists like Sheikh Hassan Nasrallah (his name means Allah's victory), the *Hezbollah* leader, has said, "We have discovered how to hit the Jews where they are the most vulnerable. The Jews love life, so that is what we shall take away from them. We are going to win because they love life and *we love death*" (Dershowitz 2008; italics added). But after the beheading of the American hostage Nicholas Berg in Iraq in 2004 by the fanatical Abu Musab al-Zarqawi (who was later killed by U.S. forces), the Lebanese *Daily Star* described the murder as an abhorrent savagery. It is important to distinguish mainstream Islam from the murderous fundamentalism and fanaticism of Islamic *jihadis:*

> The region's kings, princes, and presidents need to learn a valuable lesson from *this abhorrent incident:* that fractured societies produce real-life theaters of shame like the Berg murder in a systemic manner, and that similar fractures are infecting their own societies. If the Berg beheading does not catapult the region's leaders from the world of lethargy to the world of vigorous action to establish law and order in their own societies—and beginning with themselves—then they will be considerably weakened [. . .] What more is needed to galvanize Arab leaders into action? Today, a man named Berg was put to the sword; tomorrow, it could be the Arab nation torn asunder by the same *savagery* (Khouri 2004; italics added).

Three prominent scholars have debated "the cultural clash between Islam and the West" and the powerful emotions of rage, envy, hatred, and also fascination and attraction found in the Muslim world toward America and "the West" in general. One was the Anglo-Jewish Arabist Bernard Lewis, who, in seeking "the roots of Muslim rage" toward "the West," coined the phrase "clash of civilizations." The other was the American political scientist Samuel P. Huntington, who borrowed the phrase "clash of civilizations" from Lewis and made it the basis of his own fame. Lewis and Huntington were bitterly attacked by the Palestinian-American scholar Edward William Said, who called their theories "the clash of ignorance" (Lewis 1990; Huntington 1993, 1996; Said 2001).

Two well-meaning Jewish psychoanalysts thought otherwise. They wrote that "the clash we are witnessing around the world is not a clash of religions, nor a clash of civilizations. It is a clash between two opposites, between two eras. It is a clash between a mentality that belongs in the Middle Ages and another mentality that belongs to the twenty-first century. It is a clash between civilization and backwardness, between the civilized and the primitive, between barbarity and rationality" (Berke and Schneider 2006). Unfortunately, Berke and Schneider took a pro-Israeli and anti-Muslim position, while at the same time purporting to be nonjudgmental and impartial and to look at Islamic terrorism psychoanalytically. We have seen this problem in Phyllis Chesler and Nancy Kobrin, whose feminist and anti-Muslim bias may obscure their vision of this extremely complicated problem. It is indeed hard to keep one's political views and emotions separate from one's scholarship.

The eminent Anglo-Jewish Arabist Bernard Lewis thought that the Muslims are enraged at "the West" for the shame and humiliations that it has inflicted upon them:

> For a long time now there has been a rising tide of rebellion against this western paramountcy, and a desire to reassert Muslim values and restore Muslim greatness.

The Muslim has suffered successive stages of defeat. The first was his loss of domination in the world, to the advancing power of Russia and the West. The second was the undermining of his authority in his own country, through an invasion of foreign ideas and laws and ways of life and sometimes even foreign rulers or settlers, and the enfranchisement of native non-Muslim elements. The third—the last straw—was the challenge to his mastery in his own house, from emancipated women and rebellious children. It was too much to endure, and the outbreak of rage against these alien, infidel, and incomprehensible forces that had subverted his dominance, disrupted his society, and finally violated the sanctuary of his home was inevitable. It was also natural that this rage should be directed primarily against the millennial enemy and should draw its strength from ancient beliefs and loyalties (Lewis 1990, p. 49).

Lewis thought that the Muslims have an endless list of grievances and accusations against "the West"—its colonialism, racism, imperialism, slavery, secularism, and sexism, its exploitation of their oil, its violation of their culture, its disrespect for their wives and daughters (as we have seen in the recent American occupation of Iraq), and, above all, its support of Israel, the principal enemy of the Arabs. Yet the Anglo-Jewish scholar thought that each of the "crimes" with which the Arabs accuse "the West" has an even worse parallel in the Arab world itself. The Western treatment of women, however unequal and oppressive, was vastly better than "the rule of polygamy and concubinage that has otherwise been the almost universal lot of womankind on this planet." Slavery was much more widespread and cruel among the Muslim Arabs than in the West. And, irrationally, Muslim hostility to "Western" imperialism is much deeper and stronger than to Russian imperialism, even though Russia "still rules, with no light hand, over many millions of reluctant Muslim subjects and over ancient Muslim cities and countries" (Lewis 1990, p. 54). Lewis was referring to Chechnya and to the former Soviet Muslim republics of Uzbekistan, Kazakhstan, Turkmenistan, Azerbaijan, Kyrgyzstan, and Tajikistan, which in 1991 became separate countries.

This Anglo-Jewish Arabist thought that while the Muslims at first responded to the advent of "Western" civilization with immense admiration and emulation, in our own time these feelings have turned into their opposite—rage, hostility, and rejection (Lewis 1990, pp. 56, 59). Fanatical Muslim fundamentalists fight against what they see as their two chief enemies: Western secularism and modernism. Lewis called this struggle "a clash of civilizations." His phrase was borrowed three years later by an American political scientist named Samuel Huntington, who at once became famous for this notion.

Muslim Love, Hate, and Rage, from the Family to the Political

The Canadian poet and psychiatrist Ron Charach has studied the complex relationships between love, hate, rage, and shame in Islamic violence which included some of the material in this book. Are the critics of "Western" society correct when they blame extremist Islamist violence against America, Israel, or Europe on unfair Western foreign policy, globalization, exploitation, colonialism, imperialism, or poverty? Or might something more elemental, emotional, and unconscious explain the suppressive and tyrannical governments available to the fundamentalist Islamic nations of the Middle East? Could there be something in the fundamentalist upbringing of Muslim males that sets the stage for them, as adults, to blindly follow destructive charismatic leaders who play on wounded pride and humiliation and stir boundless and blind rage against a vilified Other, while putting their blind trust in their fanatical leaders? (Charach 2006).

The Cypriot-Turkish-born American psychoanalyst Vamık Volkan had answered those questions in his book *Blind Trust*. Who is that vilified Other? Who is that dehumanized enemy? In the case of the "war on terror," and in the case of the fanatical Islamist war on the "Crusaders," that Other, that enemy, is the projective personification of all the bad, devalued, dangerous, and unacceptable aspects of the self. It is then impossible for us to have empathy for the enemy's losses or suffering (Volkan 2004, p. 108). Volkan's colleague Leon Wurmser connected dehumanization with "resentment," his term for boundless narcissistic rage (Wurmser 2004, p. 925).

As Marvin Zonis had argued, Wurmser's "resentment" is an understatement for Kohut's "boundless narcissistic rage." This rage is unconsciously displaced from the father and mother to "America," Israel, and other entities that have deep symbolic value as the bad parents.

The Canadian political scientist Thomas Homer-Dixon has warned against the "folly" of looking for a single psychological factor to explain Islamic terrorism, such as wife abuse or child abuse, endorsing the need for more investigation into its multiple causes. "Such mudslinging over the relative merits of single-cause explanations of terrorism is utterly pointless. It gets us nowhere, because complex social events are never caused by one thing. Any particular event—whether a war, economic recession, treaty negotiation, or instance of terrorism—is always the product of the combined influence of an incalculable number of factors. The influence of any one factor will depend on the specific constellation of other factors operating in that case" (Homer-Dixon 2006a).

Homer-Dixon was psychologically perceptive. *"Participants in terror,"* he wrote, *"tend to be men in their twenties or thirties who are ferociously angry because of powerful feelings of humiliation"* (italics added). He identified a few potential sources of such humiliation, such as a lack of political and economic opportunity (rather than by the father in the family), then added that terrorists strongly identify with a group, society, or culture they perceive as oppressed or exploited. "Extremist leaders then inflame and manipulate these feelings of humiliation, partly by defining the 'enemy'—the group or society that's responsible for all problems and that should be the target for attack," Homer-Dixon wrote. In most cases, the enemy is "America, the big Satan" or "Europe, the Crusader" or "Israel, the little Satan" (Homer-Dixon 2006a).

Psychologically, however, the Islamic terrorist's deep feelings of humiliation and rage due to "lack of political and economic opportunity" are the tip of the iceberg. The iceberg itself is not the later humiliations as adults but the early humiliations as children. Do Arab or Muslim families cause such powerful feelings of shame and humiliation in their children, which in turn produce this ferocious, boundless, murderous narcissistic rage, which in turn is displaced to their new "oppressors"? Charach thought that there had to be some early psychological trauma in their families that lead some young fanatical Muslim people to become so "ferociously angry" and have "powerful feelings of humiliation" (Charach 2006).

Charach examined the psychological differences between the emotions of shame and guilt, the bad feelings that accompany loss of love, rejection, and other early "narcissistic injuries." Developmentally, shame is an earlier, more basic emotion than guilt, shame being tied to the very early phases in the formation of a cohesive sense of self, such as the "oral" and "anal" stages. Guilt feelings are developed later as the product of a more fully formed conscience, an achievement that only occurs once the child has given up intense "libidinal" (love) and "aggressive" (hate) ties to its early parenting figures. Guilt feelings develop in the genital or Oedipal phase of psychosexual development.

Interference with normal child development through abuse, rejection, with-drawal of love, criticism, punishment, double messages, shaming, blaming, and other forms of unhealthy parenting may cause in the child a failure to neutralize these powerful bonds, a persistence of infantile narcissism, and a later tendency to experience heightened shame and narcissistic rage. Such interference may result from trauma with or without the early loss of parents, overindulgence, or overstimulation of the child by the parents, or excessive use of punishment and other abusive *shaming* techniques in child rearing.

Shame is an excessively painful feeling, and it is prevalent in Muslim culture, which is a "shame-based culture" (Hamady 1960). In a classic chicken-and-egg dilemma, it is hard to say whether the "culture of shame" has caused shaming child-rearing practices or vice versa. It may be a vicious cycle. What the Palestin-ian Arabs see as their *naqba* (catastrophe) of 1948 is to them a perennial shame, humiliation and need for vengeance. Understanding the Arab notions of *sharaf* (male honor), *ird* or *ard* (female sexual honor), *wajh* (face saving), and shame is crucial to understanding Arab culture and society. To most Arabs and Muslims, preserving their honor is indispensable, while the feeling of shame is unbearable (Patai 1973, pp. 106, 120–123; Laffin 1975).

In explaining the "socialization" or child rearing in the Muslim family, the American Middle East scholar Elizabeth Warnock Fernea has observed that

> Socialization of the child took place primarily within the home, and the father and mother were ultimately responsible for their offspring. However, grandparents, aunts, uncles, and cousins were also expected to participate in a child's rearing and usually did so, by acting as disciplinarians if parents were seen to be neglecting the child's progress toward becoming *mu'addab*(a) or by acting as affectionate supportive figures if parents were seen as being too harsh. This varied according to class. In the homes of the elite, servants and nannies, often poor relatives, helped socialize the children. In both rural and urban areas, neighbors also became involved in the child's socialization, as did the Quranic schoolteachers. Thus many adults were participants in the discipline and development of the child, reinforcing each other and providing alternate role models and sources of support for the child as it grew to maturity (Fernea 1995).

Fernea did not seem to realize that so many adults around him or her might pro-vide confusing or conflicting role models and identification figures for the Arab child so that his sense of self or ego identity are not clearly defined. She noted the enormous difference between Arab culture and "Western" culture:

> *In this general and idealized picture* there is little evidence of the idea of carefree childhood or indeed of childhood as an important stage in itself. According to [Hamid] Ammar, *"in adult eyes, the period of childhood is a nuisance, and child-hood activities, especially play, are a waste of time"* [Ammar 1954, p. 126]. This does not mean that children did not play, but that play was the child's business; for adults the emphasis was on the serious business of preparing children for their roles in the world of adulthood. In this system, then, childhood was not seen as a specific bounded time period, and adolescence, as perceived in western modern

thought, scarcely existed. One moved from babyhood through childhood to puberty and adulthood. Adult privileges and social status may be assumed with marriage and childbearing, but adult economic responsibilities might begin at any age past infancy, an attitude not very different from that depicted by Charles Dickens in the novels of Victorian England (Fernea 1995; italics added).

Is this what we call "child abuse" or "child neglect" in Western culture? Muhammad Haj-Yahia thought so. In explaining the differences between the Arabic *sharaf* (male honor) and *ird* or *ard* (female honor), Fernea observed:

Marriage, which took place after puberty, marked the end of childhood and the assumption of adult responsibility for the beginning of another family group, with its own children to socialize. Marriage was the significant moment when family honor was tested, a concept that might be defined as the reputation of the group for morality, courage, religiosity, and hospitality. However, honor was defined differently for boys and girls: a boy's honor, *sharaf* concerned all the above issues, as did that of a girl, but for the girl, honor had a further, crucial meaning. A girl's honor, or *'ard,* was defined as her chastity before marriage and her sexual fidelity after marriage. A man's honor, once lost, could be regained. A girl's honor could not. The woman therefore had a greater burden of honor to protect, and was said to carry the honor of the group with her. *Any breath of gossip impugning a girl's sexual behavior was cause for her to be severely punished and ultimately could result in her death* (Fernea 1995; italics added).

This is only part of the great emotional burden placed on girls and women in Muslim society, which Phyllis Chesler has complained about so bitterly.

In Muslim and Arab societies, truth is not a great value, lying is not necessarily bad, neither is abuse of power, nor hurting others. Shame and humiliation are the unbearable feelings. Guilt feelings are not prevalent: shame feelings are. What is really bad is shame, loss of face, loss of honor. Over four decades ago, the Lebanese-born Arab-American sociologist Sania Hamady called her culture "the culture of shame" (Hamady 1960). Hamady was aware that her book would upset her fellow Arabs:

I am fully aware that (1) *no person (and by the same token, no group—be it religious, national, or other) submits to self-analysis except reluctantly. To know oneself is a painful process. Many rationalizations and defences of one's self-concept for the protection of his self-esteem must first be abandoned.* Facts that, so far, had remained unknown to himself or were repressed or deliberately ignored must be made conscious. It is not pleasant to destroy illusions and change attitudes toward oneself that hitherto have served to shield him from reality—sometimes unbearable; (2) that *no one enjoys being analyzed in public, although he rejoices in seeing his commendable characteristics revealed and praised. But having his failings and disagreeable qualities laid bare obviously would delight no one;* (3) that *individuals do not relish being thought of in terms of categories, to be classified as Americans, Arabs, etc., unless it is flattering or advantageous.* When it is a question of defects in one's groups, everyone begins to think of himself as separate, unique and different from the rest. But Time makes it imperative for the Arabs to submit to this critical self-analysis which, I know, would be somewhat agonizing for any group. They are facing acute and rapid change in certain spheres of their "material culture," in the way they were governed and in their way of living. They ought, however, to realize that aspects in their "value culture" would not change with technological or political development, unless, through social leadership, the lag in "value culture" change could be minimized (Hamady 1960, Foreword; italics added).

Indeed, many Arabs did not like Hamady's analysis of their culture and attacked it severely. They kept denying their own psychological problems. Hamady found that shame was the worst and most painful feeling for an Arab, and that the overwhelming need to erase one's shame, to preserve one's own honor and the honor of one's family, clan, and tribe—in other people's eyes as well as in one's own—is psychologically crucial. Any injury, real or imaginary, to one's honor causes the Arab an unbearable feeling of shame that must be wiped out or repaired by an act of revenge that injures those who have damaged one's honor. This code of honor can lead to interminable "blood revenge" and blood feuds between Arab clans, and to the "honor killing" of one's own daughter or sister if she has "dishonored her family" by losing her virginity out of wedlock. Hamady thought that the Arabs lived in fantasies of their glorious past rather than in their painful present, that they had no compunction about lying to achieve their goals. If they wished to survive and prosper, they needed to wake up to reality. The contemporary Egyptian scholar Tarek Heggy has been saying very similar things.

Why have the Arabs lost most of their wars against tiny, outnumbered Israel? Hamady thought that it was their fear of facing their painful reality that caused their defeats. To lessen the burning pain of what they felt to be their shaming and humiliation by the Jews, the Arabs of Palestine, Syria, Jordan, Egypt, Iraq, and Lebanon have talked themselves into believing that it was not the "weak" Israelis who had defeated them but the "mighty" Americans. Many Muslim Arabs believed that the Israelis were the "New Crusaders" and would last no longer than the Crusaders' Kingdom of Jerusalem, set up in 1099, defeated by the Kurdish Muslim leader Salah ad-Din al-Ayyubi (Saladin) in 1187 and finally dismantled by the Mamluks in 1291.

Muslim Arab culture is fraught with contradictions. While Arab society is authoritarian and patriarchal, requiring absolute obedience, a key part of the Arab concept of *sharaf* (honor) is the freedom from being ruled or humiliated by others. An Arab proverb says that nothing is more humiliating than being under another man's authority. At the same time, in the traditional Muslim Arab family, the father has absolute authority, and the son must submit to him, even if he is abused by his father. Can this be the reason the Arabs hate government so badly? The harsh rule of the father at home may cause the son to rebel and to displace his patricidal rage onto political authority figures. On the other hand, the father's honor depends on his ability to maintain his authority in the family. What about the son's honor? Can the son take "revenge" on his father to restore his honor? (Hamady 1960; Patai 1973; Laffin 1975).

From a psychoanalytic viewpoint, the painful feeling of shame begins at an early stage in our development, during the second year of our life, when we must wrestle with the issues of separation, individuation, and differentiation from our mother and develop a sense of autonomy, separateness, and self. Our toilet training may cause us to feel shame when we soil ourselves with feces or wet ourselves with urine. The sense of lack of autonomy is tied in with the feeling of shame. Honor, pride, and *amour propre* are aspects of narcissism, the maintenance of self-worth, self-respect, and self-love. The painful feelings of shame and humiliation are not limited to Arab culture; they have led politicians to fateful and even tragic decisions (Kaufman 1989; Steinberg 1996). Shame and humiliation, and the resulting "boundless narcissistic rage," are crucial to our understanding of the mind of the terrorist (Twemlow 2005, pp. 958–959).

SHAME, RAGE, AND SELF-ESTEEM

If a child is repeatedly overwhelmed by shame and narcissistic rage, he or she will have trouble with his own self-esteem, will have a hard time setting up abstract ideals and may, in order to shore up their sense of well-being as an adult, opt to serve idealized parent-like figures; they become a version of those fervent men and women cheering at mass rallies in which hyperbole and blind allegiance are the norm. A psychologically vulnerable person, who has been traumatized with shame and humiliation, may create in his fantasy an idealized version of his or her own self, in order to maintain internal balance. Such grandiosity typically requires a reviled Other onto which one can unconsciously *project* one's personal deficiencies—members of a rival sect, women, men, homosexuals, or members of other races. For many fanatical Muslims who are filled with "ferocious hatred" and "boundless narcissistic rage" against the "oppressors," these are America, Europe, Israel, "the West," or "the Crusaders."

Ron Charach cited Heinz Kohut, the founder of the "self-psychology" school of psychoanalysis and psychotherapy, whom we have discussed above, and who had extensively explored the origins of shame and narcissistic rage in the human psyche (Charach 2006). His theories are useful in understanding and treating narcissistic personality disturbances. To Kohut, *the development of a cohesive sense of self is a lifelong project,* one that relies on a child receiving accurate empathy and "love" from his or her parents—a sense of being accurately "mirrored." This early empathy and mirroring are crucial to the development of adult love. Their absence can cause lifelong rage and hatred. This is no less true in Muslim society than in Western ones (Kohut 1971).

Many fundamentalist religions and sects, like fanatical Islam, with their emphasis on suppressing the sexual drive and their elevation of the afterlife over life itself, are repressive in nature and resort to shaming people to keep them in line (Davis 2005). They give strict directions at the expense of empathic understanding. The parents can provide their children with a coherent narrative but also with a "groupthink" that can lead to sanctioning the persecution of select groups that challenge that narrative (Charach 2006).

The intellectual rigidity and "closed mind" of religious fanatics are an uncon-scious defense against painful emotions (Rokeach 1960). Islamic fundamentalists are not alone in having a psychology fraught with painful emotions and unhealthy beliefs. As we have seen, the American psychoanalyst and historian Charles Strozier found that, just like Roman Catholics believe in papal infallibility, American Christian fundamentalists share four basic and immutable beliefs: the inerrancy of the Bible, or biblical literalism, the belief that every word of the Bible is to be taken literally as the word of God; born-again conversion or the experience of being reborn in Christ; evangelicalism or the duty of the saved to spread the gospel to others; and apocalypticism or Endism, the rigid belief that *The Book of Revelations* describes the terrible events and the End Times that must come to pass for God's plan to be fulfilled (Strozier 1994).

Fundamentalist literalism is a symptom of black-and-white thinking, which is the infantile process of *splitting* the world into all-good and all-bad parts, as a baby does its mother. A decade later, the eminent American scholar Walter A. Davis exposed the dangers of the literalism, the obsession with the apocalypse, and the troubled antisexual attitudes of the Christian fundamentalist right, and how these have dovetailed with many of the blind spots of the Bush administration in the United States (Davis 2005, 2006).

Ron Charach pointed out that the tragic shame-rage cycle is painful to contem-plate, but that we ignore it at our peril. Often, after the outbursts of mass killings by young people that traumatize our society, we repeatedly hear that the young perpetrator "seemed depressed," that he was a "loner," that he had been "abused by a parent," or that he had been "repeatedly taunted by his peers." We keep hearing that "he had a need to get even" with a particular group. These people are overwhelmed by their own "ferocious and boundless narcissistic rage" which is the product of very deep narcissistic injury. Shame, humiliation, and rage play a key role in such events. Unfortunately, the shaming practices in fundamentalist societies are not widely discussed (Charach 2006).

Charach believed that, like fundamentalist Christians in the United States, many rigidly patriarchal orthodox Jewish families share some psychological features with their fundamentalist Muslim brethren. In all three cases, males are overvalued relative to females. They are raised mainly by their mothers and then turned over to the tutelage and scrutiny of stern male teachers who are powerful father figures. If those teachers encourage in them a kind of compensatory group narcissism, telling them that their religion or the particular branch of their reli-gion is the only true way, the tragic results are predictable. It is an agonizing fact that the assassin of the late peacemaking prime minister Yitzhak Rabin came from a fundamentalist Jewish background (Falk 2001a). James Charles Kopp (born 1954), who in 1998 murdered Dr. Barnett Slepian, an American gynecolo-gist who practiced abortion legally, was a devout Roman Catholic with links to fundamentalist Christian sects (Charach 2006).

Nevertheless, Charach agreed with Phyllis Chesler that the shaming and abusive child-rearing practices of Muslim fundamentalists contribute to an adult propensity for extreme violence. Few journalists and even scholars are willing to see the connection between the abuse or vilification of women, the mistreatment of children, and the deeply pervasive sense of shame-and-rage reactions so readily exploited by fanatical Islamic leaders to recruit suicide bombers and other fanatical Muslims filled with "boundless and ferocious narcissistic rage." To explore, let alone expose, such matters may provoke the very shame reactions that are so dangerously disproportionate. Journalists feel much safer reporting and exposing less psychologically loaded, more proximal and obvious sources of humiliation, such as Israeli checkpoints and regular harassment by soldiers.

Charach, however, thought that such journalists are missing the psychological point. The American self psychologist Donald Nathanson explained how the emotion of shame tends to be maximally generated when a person or group is geared up to have something very good happen, only to find the good feelings shattered by something bad happening instead (Nathanson 1992). Parents have an infinite capacity to disappoint their children. They may set up expectations only to disappoint them. An example of this would be a parent who plans an elaborate family outing for his child, then cancels it at the last moment without explanation or excuse. For more global examples, consider what happens when the Iraqi people are expecting liberation from a very dangerous dictator, Saddam Hussein, only to find themselves thrown out of work by a nondemocratic transitional government in Iraq hastily appointed and led by an American governor (Charach 2006).

Taking for granted the validity of the assumptions of Bernard Lewis and Samuel Huntington about the "clash of civilizations," Charach thought that the current "clash of civilizations" unfolding in the Middle East was in part a collision between an individualistic, guilt-based "Judeo-Christian" tradition and a collectivist, honor-based Muslim culture that regards the shame of humiliation as the ultimate injustice. In Muslim society, shame and humiliation provoke infinite rage and must be avenged and undone at all cost, including life itself. It is also a clash between religious fundamentalism and modernity, and religiously persecuted people everywhere, including women and gays, have a vital stake in it. It is a bitter irony that the deposed Saddam regime was largely secular in nature, as are the governments of Syria, Lebanon, and Israel (Charach 2006).

Muslim men sensitized to shame by mistreatment and abuse at the hands of their parents and teachers are more likely to react with boundless narcissistic rage of psychotic proportions when they feel shamed in their adult lives. In the Middle East especially, there is no shortage of provocations around which to rationalize and justify extreme emotional responses, nor any shortage of targets to which to displace infantile rage at one's abusive parents. The magnifying effects of television ensure that every time an American or an Israeli bomb misses its mark, the horrific results in innocent civilian deaths are piped into millions of Arab homes. Images such as those that came out of the Abu Ghraib prison in Iraq or "the Hezbollah-Israel war waged on the backs of the Lebanese civilians" add to the collection of images likely to evoke shame and produce endless rage

(Charach 2006). Charach does not seem to have realized that this war also made refugees of hundreds of thousands of Israelis and killed many of them.

Does this "boundless narcissistic rage" lead to suicide bombing or to the development of nuclear weapons? As I have shown in my psychoanalytic study of the Arab-Israeli conflict, there are many different causes for people becoming suicide bombers, and they begin in the family, but are later augmented by social and cultural forces (Falk 2004, pp. 159–173). Charach also thought that narcissistic rage was a necessary contributor to suicide bombings, but not a sufficient one. Murder-suicides are highly orchestrated group events and often involve coercion and manipulation by the recruiters. The members of fanatical Christian religious cults have fantasies of rebirth through violent death. We have long known the catastrophic results of mixing extreme religious views with idealized suicide— as in the mass suicides of Jimmy Jones' People's Church in Guyana and the cult religions of the Heaven's Gate and Solar Temple.

THE MUSLIM LOVE OF DEATH

Sheikh Hassan Nasrallah (born 1960), the Lebanese Hezbollah leader who had sent his own son to die in the battle with Israel, has said, "The Jews love life, so that is what we shall take away from them. *We are going to win, because they love life and we love death." Why do fanatical Muslims love death?* Why do they not wish to live for Allah rather than to die for him? Some scholars think that the early Islamic concept of the love of death originated at the Battle of al-Qadisiyyah in the year 636 CE—the decisive engagement between the Muslim army and the Sassanid Persian Zoroastrian army during the first period of Muslim expansion, which resulted in the Islamic conquest of Persia—when the commander of the Muslim Arab forces sent an emissary with a message from Caliph Abu Bakr to the Persian shah. The message stated: "You should convert to Islam, and then you will be safe, for if you don't, you should know that I have come to you with an army of men that love death, as you love life." This account is often recited in today's Muslim sermons, newspapers, and textbooks. It is an ominous statement for life-loving "Westerners" to hear.

The Israel-Hezbollah war of 2006 indeed brought death and destruction to many Jews and Arabs and destroyed the lives of many families on both sides. Ron Charach thought that the first step in being able to manage powerful and painful emotions like shame and rage is to accurately identify them. He found hope in a recent *Hamas* newspaper editorial, in which Editor Ghazi Hamad, amid escalating violence in Gaza since Israel's withdrawal, called for the Palestinians to examine their own behavior rather than blaming Israel for all their problems. He stressed "self-criticism and self-evaluation," two character traits of which the entire Middle East is in urgent need. It has indeed been quite characteristic of the Arabs to blame "the West" for all the ills and woes.

Charach thought that both America and Israel would do well to avoid "pushing the Muslims' shame button" as much as possible, and to avoid shaming responses to injured Muslim pride (narcissistic injuries). And they should be aware that obstinate pride and a lack of self-awareness afflict both East and West. The Edifice Complex still afflicts governments suffering for megalomania. When Charach learned of the 1,776-foot-tall Freedom Tower soon to occupy the former World Trade Center site in New York City, his first thought was, "Where do they intend to paint the bull's-eye?" (Charach 2006)

Such thoughts may seem pessimistic, but they show a psychological understanding of *the boundless narcissistic rage among fanatical Muslims* and of the great difficulty of changing the emotional and political structure of Muslim society. While some of Charach's observations may be correct, to me the big question is whether the "war on terror" in Iraq, in Afghanistan, and in Pakistan, and the looming and ominous war in Iran, can solve the psychological problems that gives rise to such terror. Even finding, arresting, or killing *al-Qaïda*'s leaders in the remote Pakistani tribal regions of Waziristan will not do the trick. Like everything else in human affairs, the roots of love and hate are in the family. You cannot impose democracy on a hierarchical, patriarchal, and autocratic Muslim society so long as the basic family and social structure remains unchanged.

Like the magical "surge" in the war in Iraq, which is supposed to win the war against the Iraqi terrorists, the "global war on terror" that U.S. President George W. Bush sees as a struggle between "those fanatical terrorists who wish to impose fear and tyranny on the world" and "we who love freedom" is a self-defeating, irrational, split-off, infantile, oversimplified view of our reality. It ignores the psychological roots of terror, narcissistic rage, the borderline personality of terrorists, and the infantile roots of love and hate. The psychoanalyst Ruth Stein discovered that a deep longing for the love of "Father Allah" played no less a psychological role in the motivations of the "holy martyrs" who killed thousands of innocent people in New York's Twin Towers than did their deep hatred of "Bad Mother America" (Stein 2002). The Middle East scholar Marvin Zonis knew that "boundless narcissistic rage" motivates suicidal terrorists, and the psychoanalyst Vamık Volkan observed that "killing one's self" (and one's personal identity) and "others" (enemies) does not matter (Volkan 2001b, p. 209; Zonis 2003). What matters is that the act of bombing (terrorism) brings self-esteem and attention to the large-group identity. Such extreme and "bizarre" motivations have their roots in the psychodynamics of parent-child relations in the fundamentalist Muslim family. We need to understand them thoroughly if we are to preserve our human civilization from further destruction.

Case Studies

OSAMA BIN LADEN AND AMERICA: "THE GREAT SATAN" AS A PARENTAL SYMBOL

To most of us, Osama bin Laden (born 1957) is the Saudi Arabian-born Muslim Arab leader of the *al-Qaïda* terrorist network and the author of the worst-ever violent terrorist attacks on the United States of America, beginning with the mass murderous attacks on its embassies in East Africa and culminating in the tragedies in New York and Washington on September 11, 2001. To his fanatical followers and admirers, however, Bin Laden is not a terrorist or an evildoer but a freedom fighter, a holy martyr, a man carrying out his sacred mission of liberating the Islamic and Arab world from domination, humiliation, and exploitation by an evil Western world led by the United States. Millions of people in the Arab and Muslim world—though they are by no means the majority—worship Osama bin Laden as a hero, the *mahdi,* and the savior of Islam, a latter-day Saladin who drives the "crusaders" out of the "holy land" (Falk 2001b).

It is no secret that powerful emotions underlie great intellectual efforts. No scholar can ever be truly objective about his or her subject. As an Israeli, whose country is second only to the United States on Osama bin Laden's most-hated list, I find it hard to assume an objective stance in studying this tragic, fanatical, and charismatic terrorist. Like beauty, charisma is in the eye of the beholder. Bin Laden's charisma had to do with his bizarre masculine-feminine personality, with his being a foreigner, and with unconscious emotions in the immature minds of his followers (Abse and Jessner 1962; Schiffer 1973). Another factor that makes objective study particularly challenging is the limited amount of available sources for Bin Laden's life history. Nevertheless, it is crucial to try to begin to understand how Bin Laden came to be what he is and why so many young Arabs and Muslims admire him and are ready to kill themselves at his bidding.

The subject at hand requires a fair knowledge of Arab and Muslim culture, the psychology of terrorism, and Bin Laden's biography. Some of the recent studies of Arab and Muslim culture are by Ahmed (1988, 1999), Ajami (1981, 1998), Falk (2004), Khashan (2000), Khattab (1987), Laffin (1975), Norval (1999), and Patai (1973). On terrorism, recent texts are by Crenshaw and Armonk (1996), Reich (1990), and J. Stern (1999). The literature on Osama bin Laden has proliferated. The best biography is by Adam Robinson (2001; cf. Goertzel 2002b). There are other studies by AbuKhalil (2002), Alexander and Swetnam (2001), P.L. Bergen (2001), Blanc (2001), Bodansky (1999b), Brisard and Dasquié (2001), Falconi and Sette (2001), the International Crisis Group (2001), Jacquard (2001, 2002), Jacquard and Nasplèzes (1998), Landau (2002), Pohly and Duran (2001), Reeve (1999), Sfar (2002), and Sharma (1999).

Osama bin Laden's father, Mohammed bin Awad bin Laden, came to Saudi Arabia from the Hadramawt (literally Court of Death) in Yemen around 1930. He started his life as a poor porter in the seaport of Jeddah, but did so well he became owner of the largest construction firm in the kingdom and one of the most prominent businessmen in Saudi Arabia, with very close ties to the Saudi royal family—the very people whom his son Osama hates and wishes to over-throw (Public Broadcasting Service 2001). Mohammed bin Laden had as many as ten wives and fifty-four children. Osama was his seventeenth son. Since Islam permits a man to have no more than four wives, Muhammad bin Laden, like others in higher Saudi society, repeatedly divorced his fourth wife and took another in her place. Osama's mother Hamida was one of those "fourth wives" (A. Robinson 2001, p. 39).

In contrast to his father Mohammed, who came from rural Yemeni Arab stock, Osama's "stunningly beautiful" mother, Hamida, came from an urban Syrian Arab family. Her father was a trader who did business with Saudi Arabia (Burke 2001). Little is known of her early life. When she was twenty-two years old, her parents gave—or sold—her to Mohammed bin Awad bin Laden, perhaps as part of a business deal. Perhaps they wanted to get rid of a rebellious and troublesome daughter: "While visiting Damascus, Mohammed had come across her, the daughter of a Syrian family with whom he had business links. Although Mohammed usually married Saudi women, entrenching himself within a society that he always felt looked down on him for his Yemeni roots, Hamida was stunning and her family were happy to marry her off quickly" (A. Robinson 2001, p. 39).

Mohammed's attraction to Hamida also had to do with her name being of the same root as his. In Arabic, *Mohammed* means "praiseworthy," while *Hamida* means "praiseworthy" or "to praise." The near-identity of their names did not help the couple, however. The husband's relationship with his newly acquired young wife was difficult, strained, even explosive. It was a "failed twinship":

after Hamida gave him a son, he soon grew to hate her: "Osama was Hamida's only son to Mohammed. His infatuation had soon worn off. She was beautiful but had her own mind and was not the suppliant, unquestioning sort of woman to which Mohammed had become accustomed [. . .] Married at the relatively late age of 22, she was vivacious and had a strong personality. Life within the tightly controlled walls of Saudi society was a shock to her" (A. Robinson 2001, p. 39).

Things quickly went wrong for Hamida and for her little son, Osama. The entire Bin Laden clan, including all of Mohammed's wives and children, turned the Syrian woman and her son into the black sheep of the family. "Even before Osama was born, a deep rift had opened between his parents that would never heal, and would overshadow the first and most painful chapter in Osama's childhood. By the time he was born, Hamida was isolated and ostracized. Within family circles she was spitefully nicknamed *Al Abeda* (the slave) and Osama was soon cruelly branded *Ibn Al Abeda* (son of the slave). It cut him like a knife" (A. Robinson 2001, p. 39).

In this situation, one might speculate that Hamida, rejected by the rest of the family, had no one but her baby boy to turn to for emotional solace. She clung to the little Osama. When he tried to separate and individuate from her, as part of his normal growing, she reacted with anger and rejection, abandoning him emotionally. For the little boy, this situation was unbearable. His self-esteem, already shaky from his difficult relationship with his mother, sank even lower. He must have felt that his mother was the cause of all his troubles—and she then abandoned him physically as well, when her husband sent her away from Jeddah to Tabuk, a distant place in northern Saudi Arabia where he owned a home. "As he became older, this was a situation that Osama felt deeply, the hurt and anger growing inside him. The youngster came to realize that the affections of a nanny or nurse were hardly the same as the permanent and deep love of a mother. Children being children, his siblings found this Achilles' heel and teased him constantly about his parentage. The taunt '*Ibn Al Abeda*' was bandied around often in Jeddah" (A. Robinson 2001, p. 40).

Osama's abandonment by his mother was not clear-cut, however. She seems to have popped in and out of his life many times. Was the boy Osama enraged at his father for separating him from his mother, at his mother for abandoning him—or both? "Some of the family today explain that Osama came to resent both his father for removing him from his mother, and his mother for not attempting to bridge the gap with his father for his sake. The wounds healed but the scars remained" (A. Robinson 2001, p. 40).

With his own mother far away, the little Osama was adopted by the matriarch of the Bin Laden clan, his father's first wife. Her name—or title—was *Al-Khalifa,* an Arabic word meaning "the Prophet's successor," which is rendered in English as "caliph." Al-Khalifa became Osama's surrogate mother, a woman who reportedly "loved and cared for all of Mohammed's children as her own. Most would remain just as close to Al-Khalifa as they did their own birth mothers" (A. Robinson 2001, p. 40).

A Westerner might think that being the son of a concubine or a "slave" woman made Osama an illegitimate child or a bastard. However, in Muslim Arab culture, this would not be the case. A bastard belongs only to his mother, because a paternal relationship outside marriage is not recognized by Islamic law. However, when a concubine who is not married to her Muslim master bears him a child, that child is considered legitimate.

Nevertheless, a hierarchy of legitimacy as well as of birth order did prevail in the Bin Laden family, as it did in other Arab and Muslim families. Being a concubine's son, as well as considerably younger than some of his half-brothers in a society where firstborn sons are accorded affection and reverence, meant that Osama was looked down upon and discriminated against by his "more legitimate" half-brothers. It made him in many ways feel like the Biblical Ishmael—known to Arabs as Isma'il—who is a major figure in Islam, the mythical ancestor of all Arabs and Muslims.

The story of Isma'il (Ishmael) is well known to every Arab and Muslim child who recites the Qur'an at an early age. Ibrahim (the biblical Abraham) has a child by his concubine or slave woman Hagar, whom he names Isma'il (the biblical Ishmael). Ibrahim's wife, Sarah, has no child, and she is jealous of Hagar. Allah tells Ibrahim to send Hagar and Isma'il away into the desert. There, mother and child nearly die of thirst. At that point Isma'il performs a superhuman feat: by kicking the desert sand with his feet, he makes water gush from the ground, a cool, clear stream that quenches his mother's thirst (Khattab 1987). The little baby Isma'il saves his mother's life as well as his own. The mother is overwhelmed with feelings of gratitude and gives thanks to Allah. This scene is remembered by Muslim pilgrims to Mecca on the *hajj* as they run between the two hills of Safa and Marwa, the hills that they believe Hagar herself ran over in her desperate search for water. As they run, they pray that Allah will provide for them too, as He provided for Hagar and Isma'il (Khattab 1987).

However fantastic this may sound to people raised on the Hebrew bible, Muslims further believe that it was not Isaac at all who was "sacrificed" by Abraham but Isma'il, so that it is the Muslims rather than the Jews who are Allah's chosen people (Falk 1996). It is quite probable that as a little boy Osama was taken to Mecca by his father and shown the well of Isma'il. This may have been around the time of Osama's circumcision. By identifying his mother with Hagar and himself with Isma'il, Osama's infantile omnipotence, narcissism, and feelings of being chosen may have crystallized at an early age, as did his murderous rage at his father and half-brothers, while his murderous rage at his beautiful, narcissistic mother remained mostly unconscious.

Osama's father's personality was described by a source in a 2001 WGBH-TV *Frontline* documentary as having contradictory traits: he was a devoted Muslim, very humble and generous, yet he was so proud of the bag he used when he was a poor porter that he kept it as a trophy in the main reception room in his palace. He forced his sons to manage some of his building projects themselves and was very dominating. He kept all his children in one place under his tight control.

He enforced a tough discipline and tyrannized them all with a strict religious and social code. He maintained a special daily routine which he obliged his children to follow. He dealt with his children as adults and demanded that they show confidence at young age. He did his best not to show any discrimination in his treatment of his children (Public Broadcasting Service 2001). Osama was exposed from an early age to his father's strict discipline, including beatings and floggings when he "misbehaved." At the same time, "just as he was sometimes a bully, Mohammed adored all his children. Releasing himself on occasion from the pressures of politics and business, he would relax by taking his offspring for sailing trips on the Red Sea or Arabian Gulf, while at least once a year the extended family headed into the desert for a camp" (A. Robinson 2001, pp. 38–39).

Osama was ten years old in 1967 when his father died in a helicopter crash in the Saudi Arabian desert (A. Robinson 2001, p. 54). Some sources have claimed that Osama's father died in a crash while piloting his own airplane in 1966, and that his nine-year-old son Osama inherited eighty million dollars. Others have said that Osama was eleven when his father died (Burke 2001). The *Frontline* source and a French biographer said that Osama lost his father when he was thirteen (Jacquard 2001, p. 334). The myth of the father dying while piloting his own plane may be due to his being confused with his eldest son, Salim, who died in that manner in 1988. Another biographer believed that Mohammed bin Laden was still alive in the mid-1970s, and that in 1973 he was "deeply affected spiritually when he rebuilt and refurbished [. . .] two holy mosques, and these changes gradually affected Osama" (Bodansky 1999b, p. 3).

Of the elder Bin Laden's funeral, Robinson writes: "As many as 10,000 men were gathered between the gates of the Bin Laden residence and the nearby cemetery. It was an emotional occasion and greatly affected Osama. A great tide of people swept along with the body. To the side, from inside their homes came the sound of women crying and wailing, a strange backdrop to the silence of the large crowd in the street" (A. Robinson 2001, p. 55).

Osama's abandonment by his father did not enhance his feeling of well-being or self-esteem. Deep down, he might have been enraged at his father for leaving him. The loss of his father may have brought about a deep emotional crisis in the ten-year-old boy and led to his becoming more isolated.

> The events of the day had shattered [Osama], but his grief was deeper than simply the loss of a loved one [. . .] he had long repressed a deep gouge in his psyche caused by the partial loss of his mother and a relationship with his father shared with so many siblings, a handful of wives and the pressures of a vast business empire [. . .] Mohammed's sudden death had robbed the youngster of a chance to enjoy anything other than fleeting moments of [filial] satisfaction. Family members recall him reeling emotionally. In the months following Mohammed's death he drew further into himself (A. Robinson 2001, p. 55).

After Osama's father's death, two men vied for his place in Osama's feelings—and in the Bin Laden clan: Osama's uncle, the father's beloved younger brother,

Abdullah bin Awad bin Laden; and Osama's eldest half-brother, Salim bin Muhammad bin Laden. Abdullah was a mature man, while Salim was only fifteen years old. The large bereft family underwent a profound upheaval. "Gradually, the pool of Mohammed's children was broken up and dispersed elsewhere among the many nooks and crannies that was the extended Bin Laden family" (A. Robinson 2001, p. 55). Osama was sent to live with his natural mother in the northern city of Tabuk.

Osama's uncle Abdullah had taken his dead brother's place as head of the family. It seemed like an auspicious new beginning for Osama. He also regained his mother, who had abandoned him—or been taken away from him—at an early age, and whom he had only seen occasionally at big family gatherings. Rejoining his mother, however, was at the cost of being removed from the bosom of the Bin Laden clan (A. Robinson 2001, p. 56). Osama was deeply hurt by being thrown out of his family home. "Although he cried in his mother's arms, it was not from relief at seeing her, or joy [...] [it was] a child's [sorrowful] reaction to the sudden end of the life he had known and the uncertainty of the unknown. He had only occasionally shared quality time with the woman who now held him so tightly" (A. Robinson 2001, pp. 55–56).

We do not know who made that fateful decision to break up the family. Was it the new family patriarch, Abdullah, or the old family matriarch, Al-Khalifa, Osama's stepmother? In his own mind, however, Osama was the victim of the family breakup: "in the final analysis he came to see that, in the absence of reasonable parental relationships, being surrounded by family was a powerful anchor around which to build a stable life. The loss of this anchor, added to the backdrop of all his other problems, was the scenario that would set him on the road to becoming what could be described—at best—as the black sheep of the family" (A. Robinson 2001, pp. 56–57).

The ten-year-old boy was now alone with his beautiful thirty-two-year-old mother. One may wonder if this reawakened the powerful Oedipal feelings that he had repressed at an earlier age. On a still deeper level, he may have harbored unconscious feelings of murderous rage at his mother for abandoning him. He longed to merge with her, but was mortified by the prospect of being engulfed by her. His only defense against this unbearable conflict of feelings was to become "almost mute in front of his mother" (A. Robinson 2001, p. 57). The situation was also very difficult for Hamida, who had now regained the only son that she had lost ten years earlier. While she wanted to embrace him and cling to him, he shied away from her: "[she] struggled to reach out to her son, [but] their conversations remained brief and hard work. Osama was simply aloof and preferred to remain either in his room, or to have one of the servants follow him as he miserably explored Tabuk" (A. Robinson 2001, p. 57).

After two months, Osama wrote his uncle Abdullah asking to return to Jeddah. The uncle agreed to take him back. Shortly after Osama left her, Hamida remarried. Osama was enraged at his mother for what he felt as yet another betrayal and abandonment. It appears that in Osama's unconscious mind, his mother was split into two mothers. One was the idealized all-good mother, initially the mother who nursed him, later his stepmother Khalifa. The other was the denigrated all-bad mother of his earliest years, the selfish, rejecting, humiliating, all-bad mother, the slave, the concubine, sexually tempting but terrifying and hateful. I believe that this mother was later to be personified in the United States, which Osama thought of as *Amrika* (the Arabic name for America).

The British journalist Jason Burke painted a rosy picture of the fourteen-year-old Osama as a swinging teenager: "In bin Laden's early teens there was little sign of the fanatic he would become. In 1971 the family went on holiday en masse to the small Swedish copper mining town of Falun. A smiling Osama—or 'Sammy' as he sometimes called himself—was pictured, wearing a lime-green top and blue flares, leaning on a Cadillac" (Burke 2001). In fact, this rosy picture of the smiling teenage playboy was deceptive. Inside, Osama was growing unhappy, anxious, depressed, his self-esteem increasingly shakier.

At the age of sixteen, the unhappy Osama began a four-year period of addiction to alcohol and prostitutes in the Lebanese capital of Beirut, which became increasingly self-destructive. At the age of twenty, he was saved "from the brink of self-destruction" (A. Robinson 2001, p. 119) by his eldest half-brother Salim, who turned Osama from a life of dissolution to one of devout Islamic religiosity. But the Bin Laden family saga reads like a Greek tragedy. Like his father before him, Osama's elder half-brother was killed in a plane crash. Salim bin Muhammad bin Laden, who had taken over his father's construction company after the father's death, was killed in 1988 while piloting a plane over San Antonio, Texas (A. Robinson 2001).

The cause of Salim's crash was a mystery. Conspiracy theorists believe that Salim had been flying a British Aircraft Corporation BAC-111 plane, which had been bought in 1977 by Prince Mohammed bin Fahd of Saudi Arabia. The plane's flight plans had been at the center of several U.S. investigations. According to one of the plane's American pilots, it had been used in October 1980 during secret Paris meetings between U.S. and Iranian agents. Nothing was ever proven, but Salim bin Laden's accidental death revived some speculation that he might have been "eliminated" as an embarrassing witness to those meetings. An official inquiry was held to determine the exact circumstances of the accident, but its conclusions were not divulged. However, the *Frontline* editors disputed the accuracy of this conspiracy theory: "Salim bin Laden was piloting a light aircraft, not a BAC-111, when he crashed. As for 'secret Paris meetings between U.S. and Iranian emissaries' in October 1980, such meetings have never been confirmed" (Public Broadcasting Service 2001).

Whatever the reality, the death of his eldest half-brother in 1988 was another emotional blow for Osama. Now Salim was dead. What effect did it have on the young boy? Did he feel guilty for the death of his brother—whom Osama had unconsciously wished dead all along anyway because he was jealous of his more privileged status in the family? The crisis was intensified the following year, 1989, when Osama's beloved teacher, Abdullah Yusuf Azzam (1941–1989), was assassinated in Pakistan. Osama believed that Azzam was killed by the U.S. Central Intelligence Agency (Reeve 1999; Jacquard 2001, p. 35). This trauma may have cemented his violent hatred for *Amrika*. Osama named two of his sons after Abdullah—which was also the name of his uncle.

We may surmise that after his father's death, which, because of Osama's early abandonment by his mother, he could not mourn properly, Osama was, consciously or not, in a constant quest for a surrogate father. His initial surrogate father was his paternal uncle, Abdullah. However, Osama was not Abdullah's son, and the uncle sent his troubled nephew away to his natural mother Hamida, which must have damaged Osama's attachment to him. When he went to college at the University of Jeddah, he joined the Muslim Brotherhood, following "the main trend of many educated Muslims at that time" (Public Broadcasting Service 2001). At the University of Jeddah, Osama had two "distinguished" teachers in Islamic studies, which was a compulsory subject in the university (Public Broadcasting Service 2001).

The first of those was Dr. Sheikh Abdullah Yusuf Azzam, "a man whom *Time* magazine called 'the reviver of *jihad* in the twentieth century' who was to become a towering influence on Osama" (A. Robinson 2001, p. 91). Abdullah Azzam was a Palestinian Arab Muslim fanatic, sixteen years Osama's senior, who later became "one of the big names in Afghanistan." The young Osama loved and idealized Abdullah Azzam, but his ambivalent feelings for his dead father continued to torment him. Another Islamic teacher who reportedly influenced the young Osama was Muhammad al-Qutb, brother of the founder of the Muslim Brotherhood, the Egyptian Muslim scholar who wrote dozens of books in Arabic about Islam and then fled to Saudi Arabia, where he became a professor of Islamic studies (Public Broadcasting Service 2001). Apparently, however, he was less important in Osama's emotional life, as he is rarely if ever mentioned by his biographers.

Abdullah Azzam stayed in the United States in the mid-1980s, where he preached *jihad* and delivered fiery condemnations of America in the mosques. Gradually, Sheikh Azzam came to believe that only by means of an organized force would the beloved *ummah* (nation of Islam) ever be able to gain victory. Holy war and armed warfare became his preoccupation: "Jihad and the rifle alone. No negotiation. No meetings. No dialogue. Jihad and the rifle alone," he would tell his audiences. As Fornari has shown, war is the paranoid "elaboration" of unsuccessful mourning (Fornari 1974).

Abdullah Azzam then returned to Afghanistan to wage his holy war against "the infidel." In 1989, on a visit to Peshawar, across the border in Pakistan, Azzam was assassinated by unknown agents. Rumors about the identity of his assassins ranged from his Afghan *mujaheddin* rivals to the American secret services. Most Palestinian Arabs today believe that the American Central Intelligence Agency murdered Abdullah Azzam. Osama bin Laden has not been able to mourn the death of his "adoptive father" any more than he could mourn the death of his real father, he believes that it was the Americans who killed his "adoptive father," and part of his burning vengeance against the United States is due to that feeling. The assassination of Abdullah Azzam added to Osama's murderous rage against *Amrika,* which in turn made him a political assassin himself (cf. Falk 2001b).

Unconsciously, Osama never stopped searching for a father figure. In 1991, when he was thirty-four, he found a new father in the fifty-eight-year-old Hassan Abdullah al-Turabi, the fiery Sudanese Islamic leader. After his uncle and his teacher, Turabi was the third surrogate father named Abdullah in Osama's life. "Dr. Hassan al-Turabi, the charismatic leader of the ruling National Islamic Front (NIF), was a true friend to the [Islamic] cause. He welcomed Osama bin Laden with open arms" (A. Robinson 2001, p. 134). Osama's quest for a father, however, would never end because his internal conflict was never resolved. The charismatic one-eyed Taliban leader, Mullah Mohammed Omar, Osama's father-in-law, may have been another surrogate father to Osama, even though he is two years younger.

At this point in time, one can only hazard some informed psychoanalytic speculation about Osama bin Laden's massacres. What, for instance, could the World Trade Center's Twin Towers have stood for in Osama's unconscious mind? Why did he send two jumbo jets roaring into those twin towers, bringing them down in a horrific inferno? Why was he so preoccupied with "Islam's humiliation by *Amrika*"?

Consciously, Bin Laden thought of America as the symbol of "infidel evil," the sworn enemy of the *ummah.* In his video tape that was broadcast on the Al Jazeera television station in October 2001, he said that America "hated the Arabs and the Muslims with a passion"—an unconscious projection, as it was really he who hated America with a passion. Unconsciously, however, Osama himself was both the greatest defender of the *ummah* and the sworn enemy of his own mother. Did America's twin towers, the symbol of her economic might and plenitude, symbolize his mother's breasts in his unconscious, as some psychoanalysts might think? Did he wish to destroy them as a baby wishes to destroy his mother's "bad breasts"? Did they unconsciously remind him of his father's mighty penis when he was a child? Was he trying to show his brothers what "the son of the slave woman" was capable of?

There is another possible psychological interpretation, however. The way Osama saw it, America had killed both his father and his eldest brother. Father Muhammad was killed when Osama was ten years old, after his American helicopter crashed in the Saudi Arabian desert. Eldest Brother Salim was killed in 1988 when his plane crashed over San Antonio, Texas. Now Osama was going to kill Bad Mother America with its own jumbo planes. When he sent those two jumbo jets crashing into the twin towers of New York's World Trade Center, was Osama unconsciously trying to repeat the terrible traumas of his life, as well as to avenge all his abandonments, rejections, humiliations, and losses?

The issue of shame and humiliation is crucial to understanding Bin Laden's mind and actions. A leading Arabist has noted that "in his pronouncements, bin

Laden makes frequent references to history. One of the most dramatic was his mention, in the October 7th videotape, of the 'humiliation and disgrace' that Islam has suffered for 'more than eighty years' [...] In 1918, the Ottoman sultanate, the last of the great Muslim empires, was finally defeated—its capital, Constantinople, occupied, its sovereign held captive, and much of its territory partitioned between the victorious British and French Empires" (Lewis 2001, p. 1). In his unconscious mind, Bin Laden *was* Islam. He too had suffered "humiliation and disgrace" throughout his early life. To restore his shattered self-esteem, indeed his very sense of self, it was vital for him to avenge these humiliations, and the only way he could do so was to inflict as much humiliation on Bad Mother *Amrika* as he could. The man whose father and eldest brother had been killed by American planes sent America's own planes crashing into her mighty towers, killing thousands of innocent people. In so doing, he unconsciously yearned to unite with America while seeking to destroy her. She, in turn, sought him out and tried to kill him with her bombs.

A WORD OF CAUTION

Psychobiography is at best a risky enterprise (Falk 1985). The foregoing psychobiographical study is only a *sketch* of Osama bin Laden's life and personality. Unfortunately, the paucity of the data does not permit a better-founded analysis at this time. I offer this only as a preliminary venture into the dark territory that is the mind of a man whom Westerners see as the world's most dangerous terrorist and whom he himself and many others in the Arab and Muslim world revered as a hero, martyr, and holy man.

THE CASE OF RAMZI YOUSEF: THE POWER OF NARCISSISTIC RAGE

The Islamic Republic of Pakistan, "the cradle of the ancient Indus Valley civilization," split off from India upon its partition in 1947, first calling itself the Dominion of Pakistan. Its Persian-Urdu name means "Land of the Pure," and its founder was the Indian Muslim leader Muhammad Ali Jinnah (1876–1948), but the name *PAKSTAN* had actually been coined in 1934 as an acronym for its five provinces by Jinnah's colleague Choudhary Rahmat Ali (1897–1951), who published it in his pamphlet *Now or Never: Are we to live or perish forever?* Choudhary wanted his acronym to designate "the lands of the thirty million Muslims" living in the five northern provinces of India—the Punjab, the Afghan North-West Frontier Province, Kashmir, Sindh, and Baluchistan. Since its partition from India, Pakistan's population has grown fivefold, and is now thought to be 165 million, making it the world's sixth most populous country and the second most populous Muslim one (after Indonesia).

In late 2001 and early 2002, when the fanatical *al-Qaïda* and Taliban Islamists were driven from "the Islamic Emirate of Afghanistan" by the U.S. military campaign named "Operation Enduring Freedom," most of them fled across the border to Waziristan and other "tribal areas" in northwestern Pakistan, where the ultraconservative Muslim tribes are sympathetic to them. In October 2007, *al-Qaïda* and Taliban suicide terrorists attempted to assassinate the former Pakistani Prime Minister Benazir Bhutto (1953–2007) upon her return to the Sindh capital of Karachi after eight years in exile. Instead, they killed 136 people and wounded hundreds of others. Two months later, on December 27, Bhutto was assassinated by a suicide gunman. She was a strange mixture of democracy, aristocracy, and autocracy. Benazir Bhutto was the daughter of the former Pakistani President Zulfiqar Ali Bhutto (1928–1979), who had been executed by General Muhammad Zia ul-Haq (1924–1988).

The assassination of Benazir Bhutto may have had the support of Pakistani military and political leaders, intelligence officials, and conservative Islamic political parties, all the way up to then President Pervez Musharraf, all of whom hated her. Pakistan's Inter-Services Intelligence opposed Bhutto's liberal and secular agenda and had backed Islamic terrorist groups in the Indian part of Kashmir and in Afghanistan. Bhutto herself, in a message to Pakistan's president, Pervez Musharraf, had accused three of his associates of conniving in the attempt on her life, including retired Brigadier General Ijaz Shah, a former Inter-Services Intelligence official and the director-general of Pakistan's intelligence bureau, who received intelligence after the Karachi bombing. Musharraf had rejected Bhutto's charges, but his reputation for truth-telling is not perfect. Naturally, Musharraf accused "the terrorists" of Bhutto's assassination.

Pakistan has been a hotbed of Islamic terrorism for three decades (Jalalzai 2002). On February 26, 1993, several Islamic terrorists, including a twenty-five-year-old Pakistani-born Kuwaiti who called himself Ramzi Ahmed Yousef, and who had many other aliases, tried to bomb New York's World Trade Center by using trucks packed with explosives which they planned to set off in the buildings' underground parking lots. Yousef has also used the names Najy Awaita Haddad, Dr. Paul Vijay, Adam Sali, Adam Adel Ali, Adam Khan Baluch, Adel Sabah, Dr. Richard Smith, Azan Muhammed, Adam Ali Qasim, *Armaldo* [sic] Forlani, Muhammad Ali Baloch, Adam Baloch, Kamal Ibraham, Abraham Kamal, Khuram Khan, and other aliases to obscure his identity (Lance 2004, p. 23). Psychologically, the multiplicity of names and identities was not only a ruse to escape arrest but also an indication of Ramzi Ahmed Yousef's *diffuse ego identity and sense of self.* The Italian name he chose, *Armaldo,* was a give-away, as the common Italian name is *Arnaldo.* This may have been part of Ramzi Yousef's self-destructiveness.

In 1995 Ramzi Ahmed Yousef hatched the so-called *Oplan Bojinka,* a planned large-scale attack on international airliners. His uncle, Khalid Shaikh Mohammed, who is only two or three years older than Ramzi, had been a key member of Osama bin Laden's *al-Qaïda,* the international Islamic terror organization then based in the Sudan. The uncle had fought with Muslim fighters in Bosnia and had supported this effort financially. Several U.S. mass communication media claimed that the word *bojinka* meant "loud bang" or "explosion" in Serbo-Croatian. The official report of the U.S. Commission on the events of *9/11* stated that Khalid Shaikh Mohammed had claimed that *bojinka* was *not* Serbo-Croatian for "big bang" but a "nonsense word" that he had adopted for this operation after hearing it on the front lines in Afghanistan. In fact, in Serbo-Croatian, *boj* means "action" or "fight," while *inka* is a grammatical addition to make a concept into an action word, similar to "war" and "warrior." The Serbo-Croatian word *bočnica* translates into English as "boom," and the word *oplan* does not mean much in Croatian, except that the word "plan" means plan or plot, just as it does in English.

In any event, the young uncle obviously had a much greater influence on the younger Ramzi Yousef than his own father did, which tells us something about the relations in the family. The "strict" father may well have been jealous of the uncle and angry at Ramzi for loving his uncle more than him. The term Operation Bojinka can refer to the "airline bombing plot" alone, or that combined with the "Pope assassination plot" and the "CIA plane crash plot." The first refers to a plot to destroy eleven airliners on January 21 and 22, 1995, the second refers to a plan to kill Pope John Paul II on January 15, 1995, and the third refers to a plan to crash a plane into the CIA headquarters in Fairfax County, Virginia and other buildings. *Oplan Bojinka* was prevented in early 1995, but the lessons learned were apparently used by the planners of the horrific September 11, 2001 attacks (more often called *9/11*). The money given to the plotters originated from *al-Qaïda*. Philippine authorities say that Operation Bojinka was hatched by Ramzi Yousef and by his uncle Khalid Shaikh Mohammed while they were in Manila in 1994 and early 1995.

Later in 1995 Ramzi Yousef was arrested at an *al-Qaïda* safe house in Islamabad, Pakistan and extradited to the United States. In 1996 he was tried in a New York City court along with two coconspirators and convicted of planning Operation Bojinka. Ramzi Yousef stated to the court, "Yes, I am a terrorist, and am proud of it as long as it is against the United States government." He was sentenced to life in prison without parole. United States District Court Judge Kevin Duffy self-righteously referred to Yousef as "an apostle of evil" before recommending that the entire sentence be served in solitary confinement. Ramzi Yousef also took on a Palestinian identify, and at least one controversial American journalist claimed that he was an Iraqi agent (Mylroie 1995–1996).

Who is Ramzi Yousef and why did he become such a murderous terrorist? *Could the terror that he inflicted on others be related to a terror, abuse, or victimization that he experienced himself as an infant or child?* As Volkan has pointed out, a child's victimization need not be physical: "it can include being abandoned by a mother at an early age, disappointment over being let down by loved ones, a deep sense of personal failure following parental divorce, or rejection by peer groups" (Volkan 1997, p. 161). However, most terrorism experts do not pay attention to the terrorist's early life, victimization, or abandonment. The *Encyclopaedia Britannica* article on terrorism has sections on definitions, types, and history of terrorism, but none on its psychology. In 1999, in a report to the Federal Research Division of the U.S. Library of Congress entitled *The Sociology and Psychology of Terrorism,* Rex A. Hudson, an American scholar at the Library, had this to say about a dangerous "new breed" of terrorist, namely the Islamic fundamentalist one:

> New breeds of increasingly dangerous religious terrorists emerged in the 1990s. The most dangerous type is the Islamic fundamentalist. A case in point is *Ramzi Yousef,* who brought together a loosely organized, *ad hoc* group, the so-called Liberation Army, apparently for the sole purpose of carrying out the WTC operation on February 26, 1993. Moreover, by acting independently the small self-contained cell led by Yousef prevented authorities from linking it to an established terrorist organization, such as its suspected coordinating group, Osama bin Laden's *al-Qaida,* or a possible state sponsor (Hudson 1999, p. 11).

Hudson's report, however, did not help us understand the mind of Ramzi Yousef, nor has it seemed to help advance the irrational and self-defeating "war on terror" (see below). More horrors are in store for us. Some experts say that the Islamic fanatics are planning "the annihilation of America and the Western world" (Williams 2007). Would it not have been more helpful to know something about the life of Ramzi Yousef, so that we can learn to identify some family dynamics or emotional patterns that mark the future fanatical Islamic terrorist?

Some scholars have defined Ramzi Yousef's "new breed" of terrorism as "the new terrorism" (J. Harris 1983; Laqueur 1999; Simon 2000; Tan and Ramakrishna 2002; Mockaitis 2006). The young British author and television presenter Simon Reeve wrote a book about Ramzi Yousef and his colleagues, but all he could say *psychologically* about Ramzi Yousef was that he was as an "evil genius" who invented new and undetectable kinds of bombs (Reeve 1998). Even after Reeve's book, Ramzi Yousef remains a psychological enigma, a riddle, a tangle of incomprehensible psychological contradictions. Here is an excerpt from a review of Reeve's book by the American scholar Daniel Pipes:

> Mr. Reeve shows that although Yousef has a reputation as an Islamic militant, he had a girlfriend while living in the Philippines and was "gallivanting around Manila's bars, strip-joints and karaoke clubs, flirting with women." From this and other suggestions of loose living, the author finds "scant evidence to support any description of Yousef as a religious warrior." The [United States Federal Bureau of Investigation] agent in charge of investigating Yousef finds that "he hid behind a cloak of Islam." Mr. Reeve concludes that identifying Yousef simply as an Islamic terrorist "is not only inaccurate, it also does an injustice to one of the world's great religions." So, then, what motivated him? Here, Mr. Reeve mistakenly argues that Yousef had no real ideology—"no clear or definable political goals" and a generalized hatred of the United States. This analysis, however, overlooks Mr. Reeve's own plentiful evidence in "The New Jackals" that Yousef, who called himself "Pakistani by birth, Palestinian by choice," made anti-Zionism the core belief of his wretched existence (Pipes 1999).

Pipes pointed out other mistakes and contradictions in Reeve's account of the life of Ramzi Yousef, and thought that he was obsessed with Israel:

> In another note found on his computer, for example, he threatened more attacks on American targets "in response to the [...] assistance given to the Jewish State [...] by the American government." Yousef did have a clear and definable goal: the destruction of Israel. Finding Israeli installations too well defended, he attacked American ones instead. In short, he is a Palestinian terrorist. What makes Yousef's case odd, as again Mr. Reeve notes, is his lack of contact with Israel, never ever having been in that country. "Despite a Pakistani father and a Pakistan passport, despite a secure upbringing [in Kuwait], and several years of education in the West, Yousef chose to affiliate himself with the Palestinians and launch a devastating terrorist war against America on their behalf." Seeking a cause, in other words, he voluntarily took up a Palestinian identity. In this he is far from alone: As *Commentary* magazine recently revealed, Edward Said made this same conceptual leap in the 1970s, just as he took up politics. Before him, Yasir Arafat did likewise in the 1950s; and even earlier, the leading Arab intellectual George Antonius did something similar in the 1930s (Pipes 1999).

Whether or not you agree with the controversial and neoconservative Pipes, the numerous names and multiple identities of Ramzi Yousef, or rather his diffuse identify and sense of self, are striking.

We know precious little of Ramzi Yousef's early life. While his nationality and identity may be disputed (and diffuse), the *Encyclopaedia Britannica* has no entry about him, while the online *Wikipedia* tells us that "Ramzi Ahmed Yousef" is a Kuwaiti of mixed Pakistani and Palestinian descent who was born in 1967 or 1968 in Pakistan and named Abdul Basit Mahmoud Abdul Karim. He later said that he had been born in Kuwait. His father was an immigrant Pakistani engineer who worked for Kuwait Airways, and who came from the Baluchistan province of Pakistan, as did Ramzi Yousef's uncle, Khalid Sheikh Mohammed, the *al-Qaïda* activist. Ramzi's mother was a Palestinian Arab. Ramzi Yousef later said that he was raised in a rural *Palestinian* community in Kuwait. Ramzi excelled in math and science, but *he was treated as a second-class citizen,* "which caused him shame and humiliation, and may have formed his underlying grievance." We are not given any details about who treated Ramzi this way, nor how he may have been shamed or humiliated. While child abuse is not uncommon in traditional Muslim societies, as we shall see below, it is not clear whether he was abused by his father or by his mother, or by the Palestinians, nor whether this "abuse" caused him to feel victimized or terrorized.

The well-known Austrian-American-Jewish psychoanalyst Otto Kernberg is a world authority on narcissistic and borderline personality disorders, which, as we shall see below, may well characterize Ramzi Yousef. A few years ago Kernberg published an important two-part study of "sanctioned social violence" (Kernberg 2003). In the first part, he reviewed the influence on the development of socially sanctioned violence of the hidden psychodynamics of group psychology and mass psychology, the regressive pull of ideologies, personality features of social and political leadership, and historical trauma and social crises. In the second part, Kernberg studied the unconscious process of "dehumanization" in fundamentalist and terrorist groups (Kernberg 2003).

Dehumanization is a very important psychological process to understand, as it enables people like Ramzi Yousef as well as violent groups to carry out acts of terror, murder, and other types of violence without feeling guilt or shame for their actions (Griffith 2002, pp. 37–59; Volkan 2004, pp. 72–73). The "enemy" is viewed as inhuman, and killing him is like killing an animal. It was partly (or perhaps chiefly) this process of dehumanization—viewing the Jews as rats—that enabled the German Nazis to murder six million Jews "in cold blood" during the *Shoah* or Holocaust. The Muslim scriptures often call the Jews pigs, monkeys, or dogs. A similar process (or subprocess) is *demonization*—viewing the enemy as a demon, devil, or monster, the embodiment of evil, and unconsciously projecting upon him all the evil that one has inside one. As Volkan put it, "demonization and dehumanization, of course, set the stage for terrorism, warlike conditions, and wars, and leaders may manipulate this dynamic in order to support their own political decision-making" (Volkan 2004, pp. 107–108).

A fascinating study by the American psychoanalyst Stuart Twemlow on bullying in schools may give us a clue to what the Pakistani-Kuwaiti boy Ramzi Yousef may have suffered in the Palestinian school. Twemlow found that bullying reveals a sadomasochistic ritual that can lead to primitive autistic defenses with *dehumanization* of the victim, exacerbated by a voyeuristic audience of bystanders that is present in the fantasy or the reality of the victimizer. *The manic and triumphant terroristic bullying especially intensifies the humiliation of the victim if there is a bystanding audience, rather than a single person, by increasing the indignity of the humiliation.* Coerciveness, even without words and actions that are clearly humiliating and disrespectful, can lead to a chronic victimized response with debilitating autonomic sequelae (Twemlow 2000; 2005, p. 959).

If this is what Ramzi went through, then he must have carried boundless narcissistic injury and rage within himself. We do know a little more about Ramzi Yousef's life as a young man. Ramzi Yousef spoke Arabic, Baluch, Urdu, and English. He needed to achieve, for in 1985 he left Kuwait for the British city of Swansea, Wales, graduating in 1989 with a degree in engineering from West Glamorgan Institute in Swansea (now the Swansea Institute of Higher Education), where he joined a chapter of the fanatical-Muslim Egyptian Muslim Brotherhood, founded in 1928 by the Egyptian sufi schoolteacher Hassan al-Banna (1906–1949). Some German scholars have found that "many terrorists come from families who exert strong pressure for achievement" (Crenshaw 1986, p. 393). This pressure is often coupled with strong criticism and disparagement, producing in the future terrorist a huge problem of oscillating self-esteem.

Starting in the late 1980s, Ramzi Yousef took spring-break trips from Wales to Pakistan (rather than to Kuwait), where he may have met Islamic fanatics. Following his graduation, Ramzi Yousef went back to Kuwait and was employed as a communications engineer in the National Computer Center of the Kuwaiti

Ministry of Planning. Like Osama bin Laden, at first he saw himself as an international playboy. On August 2, 1990, after Iraq invaded Kuwait, some members of Ramzi's family fled to Pakistan, others to Iran. The self-proclaimed "freedom fighter" for the liberation of the Palestinians allegedly beat his young wives (a common practice among fanatical Muslims) and refused to fast during *Ramadan.*

In the summer of 1993, after the failure of the WTC bombing plot in New York, Ramzi took up a murder contract initiated by members of the Pakistani Sunni terrorist group *Sipah-e-Sahaba Pakistan* to assassinate the female Prime Minister of Pakistan, Benazir Bhutto. The plot failed when Yousef and Abdul Hakim Murad were intercepted by Pakistani police outside Bhutto's residence as they planted the bomb. At this point, Yousef decided to abort the bombing; however, as they attempted to recover it the device blew up, injuring Yousef, who was rushed to the hospital by Murad. In 1994 Yousef reportedly traveled to East Asia and attempted to bomb the Israeli embassy in Bangkok with a device similar to the one he used in New York. En route to delivering the device, the truck carrying the bomb collided with a motorcyclist, causing either Yousef or a coconspirator to flee immediately, leaving the bomb behind.

Ramzi Yousef returned to his native Pakistan, and soon began plotting to fulfill part of his unsuccessful plot. Using the same design as the bombs intended for Operation Bojinka, Yousef planned to conceal the devices inside toy cars and plant them on United Airlines and Northwest Airlines flights out of Bangkok. To carry out the attack, he recruited Istaique Parker, a South African Muslim living in Pakistan. Parker flew to Bangkok with Yousef where they built the devices. Parker got cold feet at the last minute and could not check in the luggage containing the bombs. After returning to Pakistan, Parker became aware of the $2 million bounty being offered by the U.S. government for the capture of Ramzi Yousef. Shortly later Parker contacted the U.S. Embassy in Islamabad and became an informant on Ramzi Yousef.

In late 1994 and early 1995, Ramzi Yousef stayed in the Philippines under an assumed name, plotting his Bojinka Plan. In December 1994, Ramzi boarded a Philippine Airlines Flight 434 in Manila headed to the Philippine city of Cebu en route to Tokyo, Japan. He pretended to be an Italian man named *Armaldo* Forlani. Any Italian speaker would have spotted the false name for *Arnaldo.* Midway through the flight he disappeared into the toilet, took off his shoes to get the batteries and assembled his bomb which he tucked into the life vest under his seat. The plane flew on to Cebu where Yousef got off the plane before the final leg of the flight to Tokyo.

Haruki Ikegami, a twenty-four-year-old Japanese businessman, took Yousef's old seat. Two hours later, the device exploded, killing Ikegami. The blast blew a hole in the floor of the plane and severed the cables that controlled the plane's flaps. The jet's steering was crippled but the captain nonetheless succeeded in making an emergency landing in southern Japan, saving the lives of 272 passengers and 20 crew members. Ramzi Yousef monitored the effects of his "test," then increased the amount of explosive in his devices and began preparing at least a dozen bombs. But just before the Bojinka Plot was due to be launched, in early 1995, a fire started in Ramzi Yousef's Manila flat, in the Doña Josefa Apartments. Philippine police, led by Aida Fariscal, the fifty-five-year-old widow of a slain policeman and herself a policewoman and watch commander in the Manila Police Department in the Philippines, uncovered his plot.

On the night of January 6, 1995, Inspector Aida Fariscal was suspicious about a small fire that went out unassisted at the Doña Josefa Apartments. Her suspicions were augmented by a wave of bombings that hit Metro Manila and Philippine Airlines Flight 434. This led her to uncover the terrorist plot made by alleged *al-Qaïda* agents named Operation Bojinka. She came to the apartment with a police partner, looked around, and left after a telephone rang. She had to ask eleven judges to find one that would grant her a search warrant. She, along with a group of investigators and police, then uncovered evidence, before arresting a suspect who called himself Ahmed Saeed. She refused to let go of a suspect, who turned out to be Abdul Hakim Murad, when he offered her US$2,000 as a bribe. Her decision to investigate the fire saved thousands of lives, including that of Roman Catholic Pope John Paul II and U.S. President Bill Clinton. She received a monetary award of the equivalent of $700 and a trip to Taiwan from the Philippine government. She also won a laminated award from the CIA for her action. The certificate reads, "Awarded to Senior Inspector Aida D. Fariscal, in recognition of your personal outstanding efforts and co-operation."

Does all this give us a better understanding of the unconscious emotional motivation of a terrorist like Ramzi Yousef than does Reeve's book? Certain it is that his sense of self is diffuse, and that he has enough murderous rage in him to want to assassinate unconscious mother figures and father figures in the shape of heads of state and government of both sexes. Our hypothesis, then, is that he felt abused, neglected, abandoned, shamed, and humiliated as a child, that he did not have adequate mothering nor fathering, and that, like many other terrorists, he is a borderline personality who does not know how to handle his narcissistic murderous rage in any way but in violent acts of terror and murder.

TERROR, LOVE, AND HATE: THE CASE OF MOHAMED ATTA

We have examined some basic psychological questions: Where do murderous Islamic fanatical terrorists come from? Why do some Muslim children grow up to become fanatics and suicide bombers while others do not? Why do some people hate others with as much passion as most of us love those who are dear to us? What are the psychological origins of love and hate, and their relation to fear and terror? Are they linked to one another? Do terrorists act out horror scenes from their early life? What is the role of narcissistic rage? Shortly after the 2001 tragedy in New York, the Israeli-American psychoanalyst Ruth Stein published an important study of the terrorists' unconscious emotional motives, which she titled "Evil as Love and Liberation" (Stein 2002). What does murderous evil have to with love, or with liberation, for that matter? Evil, we normally think, is the result of hate rather than love, is it not?

Let us examine this very important question. The New York City horrors of 2001 were indeed committed by a "small minority of fundamentalist terrorists," but they shocked the United States and all mankind, due to the special psychological role of America in our world. They also sparked the study of evil by Ruth Stein, who had moved to New York City, among other reasons, to escape the violence, wars, and suicide bombings in Israel (Uschan 2006). In her fascinating essay, Stein analyzed the final letter of Mohamed Atta, the leader of the suicide murderers who destroyed the twin towers of New York City's World Trade Center, to his followers (Atta 2001).

Who was Mohamed Atta? He was born in 1968 in Kafr el Sheikh, a city in the Nile Delta in Egypt, and also carried a Saudi passport. Was his father a Saudi national? Mohamed grew up in a strict Muslim family in Giza. His authoritarian father wished his children to be all well educated. Since he was a child, Atta spent most of his time staying home and studying. He had an excellent performance and graduated with a degree in architecture from Cairo University. He was apparently not particularly religious during this period. The price he paid for being so good was probably the denial of his inner rage at his strict father or perhaps also at his mother.

In 1993 Mohamed Atta moved to Germany, where he was registered as a student of urban planning at the Technical University of Hamburg from 1993 to 1999. In Hamburg, Atta worked on a thesis exploring the history of Aleppo's urban landscapes and was invited to Aleppo by his professor, Dittmar Machule, for a three-day archeological visit. It explored the general themes of the conflict between Arab civilization and modernity. Mohamed Atta hated how the modern skyscrapers and development projects in Aleppo were disrupting the fabric of that city by blocking community streets and altering the skyline. There were reports that he worked as a car salesman while studying, to help pay for tuition.

In Germany, Atta was registered as a citizen of the United Arab Emirates—his third national identity after Egyptian and Saudi. His German friends describe him as an intelligent man with religious beliefs who often grew angry over the Western policy toward the Middle East, including the Oslo Accords and the Gulf War. MSNBC, in its special program *The Making of the Death Pilots* interviewed his German friend Ralph Bodenstein who traveled, worked, and talked a lot with Mohamed Atta. Bodenstein said, "He was most imbued [sic] actually about Israeli politics in the region and about United States protection of these Israeli politics in the region. And he was to a degree personally suffering from that."

The official report of the U.S. Commission on the tragic events of *9/11* (the terrible tragedy of September 11, 2001) states that "In his interactions with other students [in Germany], Atta voiced virulently anti-Semitic and anti-American opinions, ranging from condemnations of what he described as a global Jewish movement centered in New York City that supposedly controlled the financial world and the mass communication media, to polemics against governments of the Arab world. To him, Saddam Hussein was an American stooge set up to give Washington an excuse to intervene in the Middle East [. . .]" (Kean et al. 2004, p. 161). While in Germany, Atta became more and more Islamically religious, especially after a pilgrimage to Mecca in 1995.

A German Muslim terrorist of Syrian origin, Mohammed Haydar Zammar, claims that he met Atta at this time and recruited him into Osama bin Laden's *al-Qaïda*. Atta started attending an Islamic prayer group at the university, and is thought to have been recruited for fundamentalist causes there. Other students remember him making strident anti-American and anti-Semitic statements. That year he also made an unconditional loan of $25,000 to help a Turkish Muslim immigrant named Muharrem Acar start up a Turkish bakery. In a visit home to Egypt in 1998, his former friends noticed that he had become much more of a religious fundamentalist than he had been before. The rest of the story, Mohamed Atta's leadership of the 2001 tragedy, is well known.

As in the case of Ramzi Yousef, we can see here a young man with diffuse identity, paranoid ideation, and murderous rage at authority figures. However, rather than simply a call to violence, terror, and murder, Ruth Stein found in Atta's letter a deep cry from the heart for the love of Father Allah. This yearning of the son for his imaginary father's love, which he probably could not get from his real, strict father, she found quite poignant. The document was found and released by the FBI and translated from the Arabic for *The New York Times* by the Washington-based international consulting firm Capital Communications Group and by Imad Musa, a translator for the firm. Here are some of the relevant parts of Atta's letter, a four-page document originally written in Arabic:

> Read *al-Tawba* and *Anfal* [traditional war chapters from the Qur'an] and reflect on their meanings and remember all of the things Allah has promised for the *shuhada* [martyrs of Islam] [. . .] Remind your soul to listen and obey [Allah's orders] and remember that you will face decisive situations that might prevent you from 100% obedience, so tame your soul, purify it, convince it, make it understand, and incite it. Allah said: "Obey Allah and His Messenger, and do not fight amongst yourselves or else you will fail. And be patient, for Allah is with the patient." [. . .] Pray during the night and be persistent in asking Allah to give you victory, control and conquest, and that He may make your task easier and not expose us [. . .] Remember Allah frequently, and the best way to do it is to read the Holy Qur'an, according to all scholars, as far as I know. It is enough for us that it [the Qur'an] are the words of [Allah] the Creator of the Earth and the plants, the One that you will meet [on the Day of Judgment] [. . .] You should feel complete tranquility, because the time between you and your marriage [in heaven] is very short. Afterwards begins the happy life, where Allah is satisfied with you, and eternal bliss "in the company of the prophets, the companions, the martyrs and the good people, who are all good company." Ask Allah for his mercy and be optimistic, because [the Prophet], peace be upon him, used to prefer optimism in all his affairs [. . .] Keep in mind that, if you fall into hardship, how will you act and how will you remain steadfast and

remember that you will return to Allah and remember that anything that happens to you could never be avoided, and what did not happen to you could never have happened to you. This test from Almighty Allah is to raise your level [in the levels of heaven] and erase your sins. And be sure that it is a matter of moments, which will then pass, Allah willing, so blessed are those who win the great reward of Allah. Almighty Allah said: "Did you think you could go to heaven before Allah knows whom amongst you have fought for Him and are patient?" [. . .] Remember the words of Almighty Allah: "You were looking to the battle before you engaged in it, and now you see it with your own two eyes." Remember: "How many small groups beat big groups by the will of Allah." And His words: "If Allah gives you victory, no one can beat you. And if He betrays you, who can give you victory without Him? So the faithful put their trust in Allah." [. . .] All of these are worldly things [that humans can do to control their fate, although Allah decrees what will work and what will not] and the rest is left to Allah, the best One to depend on [. . .] Read the words of Allah: "Did you think that We created you for no reason [. . .]" from the *Surat al-Mu'minun* [. . .] (Atta 2001).

When Ruth Stein read this letter, she was deeply moved. While purporting to give practical instructions for an act of terror and mass murder to his followers, Atta's letter spoke again and again about his love for Allah, and about his yearning for Allah's fatherly love for him. Shocked by the tragedy, Stein tried to overcome her trauma actively by analyzing in Freudian psychoanalytic terms the final letter written by Mohamed Atta. Here is the gist of her analysis, where she renders the Arabic name of "Allah" as "God." Allah, to the terrorists, was the all-good father that they longed for but never had:

> The letter has a solemn, serene, even joyful tone that is infused with love of God and a strong desire to please Him [. . .] incessant incantation of prayers and religious sayings while focusing attention on God led to a depersonalized, trancelike state of mind that enabled the terrorists to function competently while dwelling in a euphoric state [. . .] the theme of father-son love is used to explain the ecstatic willingness of the terrorists to do what they saw as God's will and to follow transformations from (self) hate to love (of God), and from anxiety and discontent to a narrowly focused fear of God. Homoerotic bonding and longing, coupled with repudiation of "femininity," are explained as an inability to "kill" the primal murderous father, as the mythological Primal Horde. Freud's description of sons' (group members') hypnotic love for their father leader (which, that when not reciprocated, turns into masochistic submission), seems pertinent for the understanding of the sons' "return" to an archaic, cruel father imago. "Regression" to the father is compared with classical maternal regression (Stein 2002, p. 393).

Stein, who had lived in Iran in her youth and in Israel for most of her life, freely applied Freudian psychoanalytic notions to the Muslim family. Some scholars would question whether the psychological dynamics of the "Western family" studied by Freud are "applicable" to Arab-Muslim culture, while others would defend their "universality." In any event, Stein's "Freudian" analysis of the suicide murderers was her way of dealing with the painful emotions evoked in her personally by the suicidal mass murder. She found entering the mind of the mass murderer a very difficult and painful task:

> Thinking about evil requires a tremendous effort of the imagination and a willing-
> ness to open one's fold to encompass this phenomenon in one's thinking. Getting
> deeply into what it feels like to have a violently disinhibited, super-humanly enti-
> tled, or radically contemptuous and hateful, or utterly despairing, or ecstatically
> numbed, state of mind without trying to repudiate it and to split it off and yet with-
> out completely identifying with it, is no easy task. It may feel alien and disturbing to
> one's usual self-states; pursued deeply, it becomes frightening. *The shocking
> absence of compassion in evildoing feels too discontinuous with what we have
> achieved as a culture in terms of our Western ideals and values of humanism,
> morality, and compassion* (it is by its lack of compassion that religious evil, or *what
> may be called coercive fundamentalism,* distinguishes itself from religious thinking,
> since all religions preach compassion [Armstrong 2000]). Against the psychoana-
> lytic imperative that nothing human shall remain alien to us, stands the effort to
> understand something that is meant precisely to annihilate any understanding as
> well as any physical (or normal) existence (Stein 2002, p. 396; italics added).

Several other analysts have tried to understand religious fundamentalism and to explain the causes of this "shocking of absence of compassion" in religious fanatics (Hiro 1989; Marty and Appleby 1991, 1993, 1995; Strozier 1994; Armstrong 2000; Volkan 2001a; New 2002; Schneider 2002; Weinberg and Pedahzur 2004; Davis 2005). Is their "shocking of absence of compassion" due to an absence of compassion and empathy in their own original families? A per-ceptive psychoanalyst, Stein paid special attention to the love of Father Allah that permeated the terrorist leader's "hate" letter:

> [Mohamed Atta's] letter to the terrorists does not speak of hatred. It is past hatred.
> *Absurdly and perversely, it is about love.* It is about love of God. We can palpably
> sense the confident, intimate discourse of a son close to his father, and the seeking
> of a love that is given as promised and no longer withheld. If this feeling is innerly
> sustained, it does not have to be shown externally; the letter is a reminder: "every-
> where you go, say that prayer and smile and be calm, for God is with the believers.
> And the angels protect you without you feeling anything," it says, and "You should
> feel complete tranquility, because the time between you and your marriage [...] is
> very short" (Stein 2002, pp. 398–399).

Stein thought that the marriage that Atta had in mind was of the sons to their Father Allah, not to the "virgins." Mohamed Atta longed for union with his imaginary All-Good Father, Allah. The infantile *splitting* of one's world into all-good and all-bad parts, which begins when the baby imagines that he has two mothers, an all-good, milk-giving, loving one and an all-bad, withholding, hateful one (Pruyser 1975; Grotstein 1981), is one of the chief unconscious processes in the mind of the fanati-cal Islamic terrorist. The image of Allah as the all-good father permeates the minds of many fundamentalist Muslims, and not only fanatical ones. Allah is loved with all the passion that "America" is hated. The role of the All-Bad Father is assigned to the president of the United States, to the prime minister of Great Britain, or to some other "evil" Western leader. America becomes the denigrated, All-Bad Mother, and the All-Good Mother is one's suffering motherland, or Palestine. Of course, these roles can shift as the unstable mind of the terrorist scans what it takes to be "political reality."

The Swiss-American-Jewish psychoanalyst Leon Wurmser amplified Stein's point about the suicidal terrorist's longing for redemption through fusion with the almighty father figure symbolized by God (Wurmser 2004, p. 925). Wurmser's "inner victimhood" is what produces narcissistic rage. Stein's "liberation" and Wurmser's "redemption" are similar ideas: through his glorious-martyr suicide murder, the Islamic terrorist not only gives vent to his boundless narcissistic rage but also believes that he unites with Allah, liberates himself from his painful feelings of shame, and redeems himself from his unbearable earthly sufferings.

THE GLOBAL WARRIOR ON TERROR: THE CASE OF GEORGE W. BUSH

As we have seen, psychoanalysts have repeatedly found an intimate psychological connection between traumatic terror suffered in one's early life and one's attitude to political or religious terror. As we shall now see, this is not only true of a master terrorist like Osama bin Laden, it is also true of U.S. President George W. Bush and his "global war on terror." The psychological distance between the cop and the criminal is not as great as it may seem. In fact, there is a psychological similarity between them.

On June 1, 2002, in his "commencement" speech to the graduating class of the United States Military Academy at West Point, New York, President Bush chose to unveil new policy guidelines for the United States that included military preemption, showing "strength beyond challenge," taking unilateral action, and extending "democracy, liberty, and security to all regions." Bush announced that the United States and the North Atlantic Treaty Organization would wage "a relentless war on terror." The Turkish-Cypriot-born American psychoanalyst Vamık Volkan has observed that

> from a psychological point of view it is easy to see that these guidelines reflect [fantasies of] omnipotence and entitlement as well as a link between an acute massive shared trauma (the September 11 attacks on American soil) and an ideological response to it [. . .] We can also wonder if the president's personality organization and motivations coming from his internal world influenced these guidelines. In any case, in just a few years' time we would witness the limits of omnipotence and entitlement.

Volkan added,

> I suspect that many books will be written about President Bush's personal motivations for going to Iraq and about his handling of the "war on terrorism." Such a

book written by a psychoanalyst, Justin Frank (2004), a controversial one, already exists. In spite of the interest in this topic, historians, political scientists, and scholars *in general* minimize the role of leaders' personalities when they investigate major world events and the rationale for political leaders' decision-making in relation to such events. This is especially true concerning unconscious aspects.

We shall discuss Frank's book below.

Three years earlier, the American-Jewish journalist Ron Suskind had described the "faith-based" presidency of George W. Bush. Suskind had pointed out the defensive rigidity of Bush's thought and action:

> Bush grew into one of history's most forceful leaders, his admirers will attest, by replacing hesitation and reasonable doubt with faith and clarity. Many more will surely tap this high-voltage connection of fervent faith and bold action. In politics, the saying goes, anything that works must be repeated until it is replaced by something better. The horizon seems clear of competitors. Can the unfinished American experiment in self-governance—sputtering on the watery fuel of illusion and assertion—deal with something as nuanced as the subtleties of one man's faith? What, after all, is the nature of the particular conversation the president feels he has with God—a colloquy upon which the world now precariously turns? (Suskind 2004).

Suskind's poignant questions involve the collective psychology of the United States, with its "superpower syndrome," and the personal psychology of its president, George W. Bush, a former alcoholic who became a "born-again Christian." Three psychoanalytic scholars have dealt with these key questions (Lifton 2003; Frank 2004; Renshon 2004). Robert Jay Lifton observed that both Bush and his appointees had avoided military service in Vietnam. He described the violent aggression with which some people respond to their own "survivor guilt." Their fellow Americans had died, while they had stayed at home. This "survivor guilt" is associated with a low sense of self-esteem and failure in the moment of truth. When such a wound to self-esteem is repressed, it becomes "transformed into impulses toward further violence." This may unconsciously haunt our entire tough-talking Republican leadership who hid out as young men while others died in Vietnam (Lifton 2003).

The American psychiatrist Justin Frank diagnosed President George W. Bush (at a distance) as suffering from "untreated alcoholism," including a narcissistic sense of entitlement, sadomasochistic aggression, "adult attention-deficit hyperactivity disorder," irritability, righteous "judgmentalism," a rigid and unadaptable worldview, and megalomania. Dr. Frank observed that George's little sister Robin died of leukemia at the age of three, when George was seven years old. Frank believed that this traumatic loss, and the way George's parents handled it, had a lasting impact on Bush's psyche. At the time she became ill, Robin was George's only sibling and his favorite playmate (although George's brother Jeb was born before Robin died). George's parents never told him that Robin was sick, although he was told to stop playing with her. Only after Robin's death did they disclose to him her illness, which had lasted longer than doctors expected it to, and had led the Bushes on a frantic quest back to the Eastern United States, to find a specialist who could treat her. These efforts kept them away from their son George for long stretches of time, and he was not present when Robin died, nor at her burial (Frank 2004).

Frank found that the day after the funeral service for Robin, in Connecticut, George's mother Barbara and his father George H.W. Bush quickly returned to Houston. There was no further attempt at closure or a protracted mourning process, in keeping with upper class mores of the time. Frank thought that the apparent abruptness of his little sister's death and the lack of any way to mourn it have had a strong impact on Bush's personal development. Barbara Bush has reportedly said that the way she handled Robin's death with her son was one of the few mistakes she made as a parent. Frank documented several incidents in Bush's life related to Robin's death at various points through Bush's childhood and adolescence (Frank 2004).

Shortly after Robin's death, her mother Barbara and her brother George spent a night at the home of a family friend, Randall Roden. The seven-year-old George had difficulty sleeping, awakening from terrifying nightmares and having to be comforted by his mother. Several months later, when George attended a sporting event with his father and several business associates, he said that he wished that he were Robin. This distressed them, until he said that it was because she had a better view of the game from heaven. Frank thought that his loss of his beloved sister had a lifelong impact on George and that his addiction to alcohol was his reaction to the emptiness and abandonment he felt.

Frank erroneously concluded that George W. Bush had no conscience, no guilt feelings, no emotional suffering, no shame, he says whatever he thinks people want to hear, he does whatever he wants, he lies to us and to himself (denial), and he has a deep fear of failure and humiliation, which he will do anything to avoid. This deep fear helps to explain his relentlessly escalating attacks on others, his bullying, and his use of nicknames to put people down. There is fear of being found out not to be as big in every way as his father. He will not change, because for him change means humiliating collapse. He is fearful of public exposure of his many inadequacies. He has a contempt for truth, a form of self-protection, which helps Bush appear at ease and relaxed. He is and always has been sadistic. He is always sure that he is right. He needs to break and destroy. Finally, Frank thought, it may well be that, unconsciously, the government represents his neglectful parents, and those helped by the government represent the siblings he resents. If George W. Bush wanted to destroy his own family, he could scarcely have done better. Thanks to him, no Bush family member is likely to be elected to high office for generations to come (Frank 2004).

In my view, America is unconsciously the Mother, and it is George W. Bush's mother, Barbara Pierce Bush, who is the key to the understanding of his life and personality. As I have written elsewhere (Falk 2004, pp. 122–123), understanding his early relationship to his mother can help us understand how and why George W. Bush became the severe, rigid, self-righteous, black-and-white-thinking world judge and policeman that he is. Psychologically, those who need to be "born again" may not have been born right to begin with. In 2003 an American news magazine examined Bush's "born-again" religious faith, noting that he was "a quick-to-judge son of a quick-to-judge mother" (Fineman et al. 2003). Shortly thereafter, when Barbara Bush was a guest speaker at Ohio's Ashland University, she said that as she watched her son "guide our country through this very difficult time," she wondered, "Is this the same kid I used to spank?" Did the little George feel terrified when his mother spanked him? *Was George W. Bush's "war on terror" unconsciously motivated by the terror that he had felt in his early relationship to his mother?*

Barbara Bush, of course, was not the only emotional influence in George's life: his father, the former U.S. President George Herbert Walker Bush (born 1924), had a great deal of effect on the son's character as well (Renshon 2004). Yet it was in George's early relationship to his mother that his split-up and projective character was formed. His unconscious Oedipal wish to outdo his father, to take his symbolic "mother"—America—from him, and his conscious wish to avenge his father's "humiliation" by Saddam Hussein—the First President Bush had not completed the Gulf War of 1991 and had almost been assassinated by Saddam—also played a role in George W. Bush's decision to make war on Saddam's Iraq. In fact, Saddam had tried to do to George's father what George himself had unconsciously wished to do to him. At the same time, unlike other alcoholics, George W. Bush had absorbed enough "ego strength" from his mother and father to be able to cure his addiction and to channel his aggressive and self-destructive energies into a presidential campaign that won him the White House (Falk 2004, pp. 122–123).

While Justin Frank's psychological theories about George W. Bush may be plausible, his colleague Irwin Savodnik angrily disputed them, accusing Frank of "a psychoanalytic hatchet job" and claiming that Frank's "diagnoses" were moral and political indictments disguised as "scientific determinations" (Savodnik 2004). More importantly, Frank did not sufficiently consider George's crucial relationship with his mother, Barbara, which affected his entire life and personality. Neither did Stanley Renshon, whose "psychoanalytic" study focused on George W. Bush's relationship to his father. *In my view, Bush's relationship to America mirrors the deepest aspects of his early relationship to his mother: the conscious wish to make her great and the unconscious quest to destroy her, as he actually does with his "global war on terror."*

Renshon's book on Bush is an uneven and unremarkable combination of psychoanalysis and political science. Renshon sought to prove that George W. Bush's presidency was driven by his desire to dramatically change the country in ways that mirror his own personal transformations. In the book's early sections, Renshon traced Bush's difficulties in becoming a mature and successful person within the context of his powerful family. Decades spent as "the black sheep of the family" allowed Bush to develop the ability to "stand apart from others" and the capacity to embrace conflict rather than avoid it. In this section, perhaps, the book offers a balanced and nuanced portrait of a late bloomer, a capable man who nonetheless has been unable to transcend some of the "quirky elements of his psychology." The sections of Renshon's book that deal with George W. Bush's political agenda are partisan and unobjective. Renshon tried hard to refute criticisms of the president and, at one point, grouped all the political groups opposed to Bush's domestic agenda under the single label of "interest-group liberalism." There is even a section of "National Security Questions for Critics." Renshon himself found no fault with Bush's leadership, and he looked forward to a hypothetical future in which Bush will be seen "historically, and appropriately, as a president of the first rank." Needless to say, this rosy view of Bush's personality is not only unrealistic but also at great variance with those of Lifton and Frank.

CONCLUSION

After examining these seemingly very different cases, and after reviewing the theories of Islamic terrorism from the point of view of several disciplines, it seems that the psychoanalytic point of view is indispensable to the understanding of the irrational and highly destructive human phenomenon. *The basic idea is validated: it is those who suffer emotional terror in their very early lives who tend to become terrorists—or leaders of the "global war on terror."* They suffer shame, humiliation, abuse, rejection, abandonment, and feelings of helplessness. They are overwhelmed by their boundless narcissistic rage. They long for the good father (such as Allah) and for the good mother (such as Palestine) that they never had. Splitting their world into all-good and all-bad objects, they unconsciously project upon "the Great Satan" (America) and "the Little Satan" (Israel) the unbearable aspects of their own internalized maternal and parental objects. For all the differences among those various terrorists, their unconscious feelings, motives, and personality organization are much alike.

Bibliography

Abbott, Steve (1989). *Holy Terror.* Freedom, California: Crossing Press.

Abilla, Walter D. (1977). *The Black Muslims in America: An Introduction to the Theory of Commitment.* Kampala, Uganda: East African Literature Bureau.

Abraham, Karl (1926). Character Formation of the Genital Level of Libido-Development. *International Journal of Psycho-Analysis,* vol. 7, pp. 214–222. Reprinted (1927, 1942, 1950). In *Selected Papers of Karl Abraham, M.D.,* with an Introductory Memoir by Ernest Jones, pp. 407–417. London: The Hogarth Press and the Institute of Psycho-Analysis. Reprinted (1953, 1973). New York: Basic Books.

Abraham, Karl (1927). Melancholia and Obsessional Neurosis. In *Selected Papers of Karl Abraham, M.D.,* pp. 422–432. Tr. Douglas Bryan and Alix Strachey. Intr. Ernest Jones. London: Leonard and Virginia Woolf at the Hogarth Press.

Abse, D. Wilfred & Jessner, Lucy (1962). The Psychodynamic Aspects of Leadership. In Graubard, Stephen R. & Holton, Gerald (Eds.) *Excellence and Leadership in a Democracy,* pp. 76–93. New York and London: Columbia University Press.

Abu-Zayyad, Ziad (2002). Was It a Missed Opportunity? *Palestine–Israel Journal of Politics, Economics and Culture,* vol. 9, no. 4, Editorial.

AbuKhalil, As'ad. (2002). *Bin Laden, Islam, and America's New "War on Terrorism."* New York: Seven Stories Press.

Abul-Jobain, Ahmad (1993). *Radical Islamic Terrorism or Political Islam?* Annandale, Virginia: United Association for Studies and Research.

Adorno, Theodor Wiesengrund et al. (1950). *The Authoritarian Personality.* Ed. Max Horkheimer & Samuel H. Flowerman. New York: Harper & Row. New Edition (1952). New York: Harper & Bros. New Edition (1969). New York: W.W. Norton. New Edition (1982). New York: W.W. Norton.

Afary, Janet (2001). Portraits of Two Islamist Women: Escape from Freedom or from Tradition. *The New Left Review,* no. 19, Fall, pp. 46–77.

Ahmad, Aijaz (1991). *Orientalism and After: Ambivalence and Cosmopolitan Location in the Work of Edward Said.* New Delhi: Centre for Contemporary Studies, Nehru Memorial Museum and Library. [Microform].

Ahmad, Eqbal (1999). *Living with Eqbal Ahmad, 1932–1999: A Homage to Academician, Intellectual & Revolutionary.* Lahore, Pakistan: Democratic Commission for Human Development.

Ahmad, Eqbal (2000). *Eqbal Ahmad, Confronting Empire: Interviews with David Barsamian.* Foreword by Edward W. Said. Cambridge, Massachusetts: South End Press.

Ahmad, Eqbal (2001). *Terrorism: Theirs and Ours.* Foreword and interview by David Barsamian. Ed. Greg Ruggiero. New York: Seven Stories Press.

Ahmed, Akbar S. (1988). *Discovering Islam: Making Sense of Muslim History and Society.* London and New York: Routledge. Bristol: Thoemmes Press. Reprinted (1989). London and New York: Routledge.

Ahmed, Akbar S. (1999). *Islam Today: A Short Introduction to the Muslim World.* New York: St. Martin's Press.

Ahmed, Akbar S. (2003). *Islam under Siege: Living Dangerously in a Post-Honor World.* Cambridge: Polity Press. New Delhi: Vistaar.

Ahmed, Akbar S. & Donnan, Hastings (Eds.) (1994). *Islam, Globalization and Postmodernity.* London and New York: Routledge.

Ainsworth, Mary D. Salter et al. (1978). *Patterns of Attachment: A Psychological Study of the Strange Situation.* Hillsdale, New Jersey: Erlbaum.

Ajami, Fouad (1981). *The Arab Predicament: Arab Political Thought and Practice Since 1967.* New Rochelle, New York: Cambridge University Press.

Ajami, Fouad (1998). *The Dream Palace of the Arabs: A Generation's Odyssey.* New York: Pantheon Books.

Akhtar, Salman (1992). *Broken Structures: Severe Personality Disorders and Their Treatment.* Northvale, New Jersey: Jason Aronson. Revised Edition (2002). Northvale, New Jersey: Jason Aronson.

Akhtar, Salman (1999). The Psychodynamic Dimension of Terrorism. *Psychiatric Annals,* vol. 29, pp. 30–35. Reprinted (2002). In Covington, Coline et al. (Eds.) *Terrorism and War: Unconscious Dynamics of Political Violence,* pp. 87–96. London: Karnac Books.

Akhtar, Salman (2002). Forgiveness: Origins, Dynamics, Psychopathology, and Technical Relevance. *The Psychoanalytic Quarterly,* vol. 71, pp. 175–212.

Akhtar, Salman (2005a). *Objects of Our Desire: Exploring Our Intimate Connections with the Things Around Us.* New York: Harmony Books.

Akhtar, Salman (Ed.) (2005b). *Freud Along the Ganges: Psychoanalytic Reflections upon the People and Culture of India.* New York: Other Press.

Akhtar, Salman (Ed.) (2008). *The Crescent and the Couch: Cross-Currents between Islam and Psychoanalysis.* Northvale, New Jersey: Jason Aronson.

Akhtar, Salman & Kramer, Selma (Eds.) (1998). *The Colors of Childhood: Separation-Individuation Across Cultural, Racial, and Ethnic Differences.* Northvale, New Jersey: Jason Aronson.

Akhtar, Salman & Parens, Henri (Eds.) (2001). *Does God Help? Developmental and Clinical Aspects of Religious Belief.* Northvale, New Jersey: Jason Aronson.

Akhtar, Salman et al. (Eds.) (1995). *The Birth of Hatred: Developmental, Clinical, and Technical Aspects of Intense Aggression.* Northvale, New Jersey: Jason Aronson.

Akhtar, Salman et al. (1996). *The Internal Mother: Conceptual and Technical Aspects of Object Constancy.* Northvale, New Jersey: Jason Aronson.

Al-Amin, Jamil Abdullah [H. Rap Brown] (1993).*Revolution by the Book: The Rap Is Live.* Beltsville, Maryland: Writers' Inc. International.

Al-Banna, Hassan (1971). *Al-salam Fi'l'islam.* Jeddah: Al-dar Al-suudiya Li-i-nashr. [Arabic].

Al-Bukhari, Muhammad Ibn Isma'il (1971). *Sahih Al-adab Al-mufrad Lil-imam Al-bukhari.* The Translation of the Meanings of *Sahih Al-bukhari.* Tr. Muhammad Muhsin Khan. Gujranwala, Punjab, Pakistan: Taleem-ul-quran Trust. Third Edition (1976–1979). Eight volumes. Chicago: Kazi Publications. Sixth Edition (1983). Nine volumes. Lahore: Kazi Publications. [Arabic and English].

Al-Bukhari, Muhammad Ibn Isma'il (2005). *Sahih Al-boukhari: Arabe-français.* Traduction et Commentaire De Mokhtar Chakroun. Paris: Al Qalam. [Arabic and French.]

Al-Krenawi, Alean & Graham, John R. (1997). Social Work and Blood Vengeance: The Bedouin-Arab Case. *British Journal of Social Work,* vol. 27, no. 4, pp. 515–528.

Al-Sowayan, Sa'ad (2005). Al-iqtisadiyya (Saudi Arabia) November 15. English Translation: *The Saudi Gazette,* November 17.

Al-Tabari (1985–1999). *The History of Al-tabari.* Thirty-nine volumes. Tr. William Montgomery Watt and M.V. McDonald. Albany, New York: State University of New York Press.

Al-Wardi, Ali (1951). *Shakhsiyat al-Fard al-Iraqi* [The Personality of the Iraqi Individual]. New Edition (2001). London: Dar Layla. [Arabic].

Al-Wardi, Ali (1969–1976). *Lamahat ijtima'iyya min tarikh al-Iraq al-hadith* [Glimpses of the Modern History of Iraq]. Seven volumes. Baghdad: Matba'at al-Irshad. New Edition (1992). *Lamahat ijtima'iyya fi tarikh al-Iraq al-hadith.* London: Dar Fufan. [Arabic].

Alderdice, John Thomas (2002). Introduction. In Covington, Coline et al. (Eds.) *Terrorism and War: Unconscious Dynamics of Political Violence,* pp. 1–17. London: Karnac Books.

Alderman, Geoffrey (2005). Either a Catastrophe or a Conspiracy. The Weekly Review, *The Jewish Chronicle,* June 3, p. 25.

Alexander, Yonah & Gleason, John M. (Eds.) (1981).*Behavioral and Quantitative Perspectives on Terrorism.* New York: Pergamon Press.

Alexander, Yonah & Swetnam, Michael S. (2001). *Usama Bin Laden's Al-Qaida: Profile of a Terrorist Network.* Ardsley, New York: Transnational Publishers.

Allen, James et al. (2000). *Without Sanctuary: Lynching Photography in America.* Santa Fe, New Mexico: Twin Palms Publishers.

Altschuler, Richard (Ed.) (1998). *The Living Legacy of Marx, Durkheim and Weber: Applications and Analyses of Classical Sociological Theory by Modern Social Scientists.* Two volumes. New York: Gordian Knot Books.

American Psychiatric Association (2000). *Diagnostic and Statistical Manual of Mental Disorders: Fourth Edition. Text Revision.* Washington, DC: American Psychiatric Association.

Ammar, Hamid (1954). *Growing up in an Egyptian Village.* London: Routledge & Paul. Reprinted (1966). New York: Octagon Books.

Ansari, Humayun (2004). *The Infidel Within: Muslims in Britain since 1800.* London: Hurst & Co.

Arlow, Jacob A. (1980). Object Concept and Object Choice. *The Psychoanalytic Quarterly,* vol. 44, pp. 109–133.

Armstrong, Karen (1988). *Holy War.* London: Macmillan.

Armstrong, Karen (2000). *The Battle for God: Fundamentalism in Judaism, Christianity and Islam.* New York: Knopf. New York: Harper-Collins. Reprinted (2001). New York: Ballantine Books.

Aron, Elaine (1996). *The Highly Sensitive Person: How to Thrive When the World Overwhelms You.* New York: Carol Publishing Group.

Aron, Elaine (2000). *The Highly Sensitive Person in Love: How Your Relationships Can Thrive When the World Overwhelms You.* New York: Broadway Books.

Aron, Arthur & Aron, Elaine N. (1986). *Love and the Expansion of Self: Understanding Attraction and Satisfaction.* New York: Hemisphere Publish Corporation.

Ashplant, Timothy G. (1987). Fantasy, Narrative, Event: Psychoanalysis and History. *History Workshop Journal,* vol. 23, no. 1, pp. 165–173.

Atran, Scott (2002). *In Gods We Trust: The Evolutionary Landscape of Religion.* Oxford and New York: Oxford University Press.

Atran, Scott (2003). The Genesis of Suicide Terrorism. *Science,* vol. 299, March 7, pp. 1534–1539.

Atran, Scott (2004). Mishandling Suicide Terrorism. *The Washington Quarterly,* vol. 27, no. 3, pp. 67–90.

Atran, Scott (2006). The Moral Logic and Growth of Suicide Terrorism. *The Washington Quarterly,* vol. 29, no. 2, pp. 127–147.

Atta, Mohamed Elamir Awad Al-Sayed (2001). Last Words of a Terrorist. *The Observer,* Sunday, September 30.

Atwan, Abdel Bari (2006). *The Secret History of Al-Qaeda.* Berkeley: University of California Press.

Axell, Albert & Kase, Hideaki (2002). *Kamikaze: Japan's Suicide Gods.* New York: Longman Publishing Group. London: Pearson Education.

Bach, Sheldon (1980). Self-Love and Object-Love: Some Problems of Self and Object Constancy, Differentiation, and Integration. In Lax, Ruth F., Bach, Sheldon & Burland, J. Alexis (Eds.) *Rapprochement: The Critical Subphase of Separation-Individuation.* New York: Jason Aronson.

Bader, Michael J. (2002). *Arousal: The Secret Logic of Sexual Fantasies.* New York: Thomas Dunne Books.

Bak, Robert C. (1973). Being in Love and Object Loss. *International Journal of Psycho-Analysis,* vol. 54, pp. 1–7.

Baker, James A., III et al. (2006). *The Iraq Study Group Report.* New York: Vintage Books.

Bakhash, Shaul (1989). Review of *Nest of Spies: America's Journey to Disaster in Iran* by Amir Taheri. *The New Republic,* vol. 200, no. 20, May 15, pp. 43–46.

Balint, Michael (1948). On Genital Love. *International Journal of Psycho-Analysis,* vol. 29, pp. 34–40. Reprinted (1952). In Balint, Michael, *Primary Love and Psycho-Analytic Technique,* pp. 128–140. The Hogarth Press and the Institute of Psycho-Analysis. Reprinted (1953). New York: Liveright.

Balint, Michael (1952). *Primary Love, and Psycho-Analytic Technique.* London: The Hogarth Press. New Edition (1965). New York: Liveright Publishing.

Balint, Michael (1956). Perversions and Genitality. In Lorand, Sandor (Ed.) *Perversions: Psychodynamics and Theory,* pp. 16–27. New York: Gramercy Books.

Banks, William H., Jr. (1997). *The Black Muslims.* Philadelphia: Chelsea House Publishers.

Barakat, Halim Isber (1993). *The Arab World: Society, Culture, and State.* Berkeley: University of California Press.

Barthes, Roland (1978). *A Lover's Discourse.* New York: Hill & Wang.

Baruch, Elaine Hoffman (1991). *Women, Love, and Power: Literary and Psychoanalytic Perspectives.* New York: New York University Press.

Baruch, Elaine Hoffman (2003). Psychoanalysis and Terrorism: The Need for a Global "Talking Cure." *Psychoanalytic Psychology,* vol. 20, pp. 698–700.

Bat Ye'or (1985). *The Dhimmi: Jews and Christians under Islam.* Pref. Jacques Ellul. Tr. David Maisel, Paul Fenton & David Littman. Madison, New Jersey: Fairleigh Dickinson University Press. Cranbury, New Jersey: Associated University Presses. New Edition (1996). Madison, New Jersey: Fairleigh Dickinson University Press. Cranbury, New Jersey: Associated University Presses.

Bat Ye'or (1996). *The Decline of Eastern Christianity under Islam: From Jihad to Dhimmitude, Seventh to Twentieth Century.* Fwd. Jacques Ellul. Tr. Miriam Kochan & David Littman. Madison, New Jersey: Fairleigh Dickinson University Press. Cranbury, New Jersey: Associated University Presses.

Bat Ye'or (2002). *Islam and Dhimmitude: Where Civilizations Collide.* Tr. Miriam Kochan & David Littman. Madison, New Jersey: Fairleigh Dickinson University Press. Cranbury, New Jersey: Associated University Presses.

Bat Ye'or (2005). *Eurabia: The Euro-Arab Axis.* Madison, New Jersey: Fairleigh Dickinson University Press.

Becker, Ernest (1973). *The Denial of Death.* New York: The Free Press.

Becker, Ernest (1975). *Escape from Evil.* New York: The Free Press.

Beit-Hallahmi, Benjamin (2002). Rebirth and Death: The Violent Potential of Apocalyptic Dreams. In Stout, Chris E. (Ed.) *The Psychology of Terrorism,* Vol. 3, pp. 163–189. Westport, Connecticut: Praeger.

Bellah, Robert Neelly (1970). *Beyond Belief: Essays on Religion in a Post-Traditional World.* New York: Harper and Row. New Edition (1991). Berkeley: University of California Press.

Bender, Bryan (2006). Economists Say Cost of War Could Top $2 Trillion: Tally Exceeds White House Projections. *The Boston Globe,* January 8.

Benjamin, Daniel & Simon, Steven (2002). *The Age of Sacred Terror.* New York: Random House.

Benjamin, Daniel & Simon, Steven (2005). *The Next Attack: The Failure of the War on Terror and a Strategy for Getting It Right.* New York: Times Books.

Benjamin, Jessica (1988). *The Bonds of Love: Psychoanalysis, Feminism, and the Problem of Domination.* New York: Pantheon Books.

Bergen, Abram (2007). Review of *The Most Dangerous Animal: Human Nature and the Origins of War* by David Livingstone [sic] Smith. *Blogcritics Magazine,* September 18.

Bergen, Peter L. (2001). *Holy War, Inc.: Inside the Secret World of Osama bin Laden.* New York: The Free Press. London: Weidenfeld and Nicolson. Reprinted (2002) Waterville, Maine: G.K. Hall and Co.

Bergmann, Martin S. (1971). Psychoanalytic Observations on the Capacity to Love. In McDevitt, John B. & Settlage, Calvin F. (Ed.) *Separation-Individuation: Essays in Honor of Margaret S. Mahler.* New York: International Universities Press.

Bergmann, Martin S. (1980). On the Intrapsychic Function of Falling in Love. *The Psychoanalytic Quarterly*, vol. 49, pp. 56–76.

Bergmann, Martin S. (1982). Platonic Love, Transference Love, and Love in Real Life. *Journal of the American Psychoanalytic Association*, vol. 30, pp. 87–111.

Bergmann, Martin S. (1987). *The Anatomy of Loving: The Story of Man's Quest to Know What Love Is*. New York: Columbia University Press.

Bergmann, Martin S. (1988). Freud's Three Theories of Love in the Light of Later Developments. *Journal of the American Psychoanalytic Association*, vol. 36, pp. 653–672.

Bergmann, Martin S. (Ed.) (2004). *Understanding Dissidence and Controversy in the History of Psychoanalysis*. New York: Other Press.

Berke, Joseph H. (1988). *The Tyranny of Malice: Exploring the Dark Side of Character and Culture*. New York: Summit Books. Reprinted (1989). London: Simon & Schuster.

Berke, Joseph H. (2006). *Malice Through the Looking Glass Reflections and Refractions of Envy, Greed and Jealousy*. London: Teva Publications.

Berke, Joseph H. & Schneider, Stanley (2006). A Psychological Understanding of Muslim Terrorism. *Psychoanalysis and Psychotherapy* online.

Berl, Emmanuel (1924). *The Nature of Love*. Tr. Fred Rothwell. New York: The Macmillan Company.

Berman, Paul (2003). The Philosopher of Islamic Terror. *The New York Times Magazine*, March 23.

Berscheid, Ellen & Walster, Elaine Hatfield (1978). *Interpersonal Attraction*. Reading, Massachusetts: Addison-Wesley.

Bevy, Lawrence J. (Ed.) (2006). *Al-Qaeda: An Organization to Be Reckoned With*. New York: Novinka Books.

Bill, James A. (1988). *The Eagle and the Lion: The Tragedy of American-Iranian Relations*. New Haven: Yale University Press.

Binion, Rudolph (1976). *Hitler among the Germans*. New York: Elsevier. New Edition (1984). Dekalb, Illinois: Northern Illinois University Press.

Binstock, William A. (1973). On the Two Forms of Intimacy. *Journal of the American Psychoanalytic Association*, vol. 21, pp. 93–107.

Bion, Wilfred Ruprecht (1961). *Experiences in Groups, and Other Papers*. New York, Basic Books.

Bion, Wilfred Ruprecht (1963). *Learning from Experience*. New York: Basic Books. Reprinted (1984). London: Karnac Books.

Bion, Wilfred Ruprecht (1970). *Attention and Interpretation*. London: Tavistock Publications.

Bion, Wilfred Ruprecht (1992).*Cogitations*. London: Karnac Books.

Black, David Macleod (1993). What Sort of a Thing Is a Religion? A View from Object-Relations Theory. *International Journal of Psycho-Analysis*, vol. 74, pp. 613–625.

Black, David Macleod (1999). The God I Want. In Stein, Samuel M. (Ed.) *Beyond Belief: Psychotherapy and Religion*. Foreword by Robert D. Hinshelwood. London: Karnac Books.

Black, David Macleod (Ed.) (2006). *Psychoanalysis and Religion in the Twenty-First Century: Competitors or Collaborators?* New York: Routledge.

Blackwell, Stephen (2005). Between Tradition and Transition: State Building, Society and Security in the Old and New Iraq. *Middle Eastern Studies*, vol. 41, no. 3, pp. 445–452.

Blanc, Florent (2001). *Ben Laden et l'Amérique.* Paris: Editions Bayard. [French].

Blass, Rachel B. (2004). Beyond Illusion: Psychoanalysis and the Question of Religious Truth. *International Journal of Psychoanalysis,* vol. 85, no. 3, pp. 615–634.

Blum, Harold P. (1981). Object Inconstancy and Paranoid Conspiracy. *Journal of the American Psychoanalytic Association,* vol. 29, pp. 789–813.

Blum, Harold P. (2004). Separation-Individuation Theory and Attachment Theory. *Journal of the American Psychoanalytic Association,* vol. 52, no. 2, pp. 535–553.

Bodansky, Yossef (1999a). *Islamic Anti-Semitism as a Political Instrument.* Shaarei Tikva, Israel: Ariel Center for Policy Research.

Bodansky, Yossef (1999b). *Bin Laden: The Man Who Declared War on America.* Rocklin, California: Forum Press. Roseville, California: Prima Publishing.

Bongar, Bruce Michael et al. (Eds.) (2006). *Psychology of Terrorism.* Oxford and New York: Oxford University Press.

Borradori, Giovanna (2003). *Philosophy in a Time of Terror: Dialogues with Jürgen Habermas and Jacques Derrida.* Chicago: University of Chicago Press.

Bostom, Andrew G. (2003). Caliphate Dreams. *Front Page Magazine,* December 12.

Bostom, Andrew G. (Ed.) (2005). *The Legacy of Jihad: Islamic Holy War and the Fate of Non-Muslims.* Foreword by Ibn Warraq. Amherst, New York: Prometheus Books.

Bosworth, Clifford Edmund et al. (Eds.) (1980). *Encyclopédie de l'Islam: nouvelle édition établie avec le concours des principaux orientalistes par C. E. Bosworth... sous le patronage de l'Union acadéimique internationale.* New Edition (1989). Six volumes. Eds. E. van Donzel et al. Leiden and New York: E.J. Brill. Paris: G.-P. Maisonneuve & Larose. New Edition (1993–2005). Eleven volumes. Leiden and New York: E.J. Brill. Paris: G.-P. Maisonneuve & Larose. [French].

Boulby, Marion (1999). *The Muslim Brotherhood and the Kings of Jordan, 1945–1993.* Foreword by John O. Voll. Atlanta, Georgia: Scholars Press.

Bowden, Mark Robert (2002). Tales of the Tyrant: What Does Saddam Hussein See in Himself That No One Else in the World Seems to See? The Answer Is Perhaps Best Revealed by the Intimate Details of the Iraqi Leader's Daily Life. *The Atlantic Monthly,* May.

Bowden, Mark Robert (2006). *Guests of the Ayatollah: The First Battle in America's War with Militant Islam.* New York: Atlantic Monthly Press.

Bowlby, John (1969–1980).*Attachment and Loss.* Three volumes. Vol. 1. *Attachment.* Vol. 2. *Separation: Anxiety and Anger.* Vol. 3. *Loss: Sadness and Depression.* London: The Hogarth Press and the Institute of Psycho-Analysis. New York: Basic Books. Second Edition (1999). New York: Basic Books.

Bowlby, John (1988). Foreword to Ian Suttie's *The Origins of Love and Hate.* New Edition. London: Free Association Books.

Boyle, Josephine (1993). *Holy Terror.* London: Piatkus. Reprinted (1995). New York: St. Martin's Press.

Brenman Pick, I. (1985). Working Through in the Counter-Transference. *International Journal of Psycho-Analysis,* vol. 66, pp. 157–166. Reprinted (1988). In Spillius, Elizabeth Bott (Ed.) *Melanie Klein Today: Developments in Theory and Practice,* Vol. 2, pp. 34–47. London and New York: Routledge.

Brewer, Paul (2006). *September 11 and Radical Islamic Terrorism.* Milwaukee, Wisconsin: World Almanac Library.

Brisard, Jean-Charles & Dasquié, Guillaume (2001). *Ben Laden: la vérité interdite.* Paris: Editions Denoël. [French].

Bromberg, Norbert & Small, Verna Volz (1983). *Hitler's Psychopathology.* New York: International Universities Press.

Buchanan, Patrick J. (2004). No End to War: The Frum-Perle Prescription Would Ensnare America in Endless Conflict. Review of *An End to Evil* by David Frum and Richard Perle. *The American Conservative,* March 1.

Buckser, Andrew S. (1992). Lynching as Ritual in the American South. *Berkeley Journal of Sociology,* vol. 37, pp. 11–28.

Bunyan, John (1752). *The Holy War, Made by Shaddai upon Diabolus, for the Regaining of the Metropolis of the World, Or, the Losing and Taking of the Town of Mansoul.* Reprinted (1794). Philadelphia: Mathew Carey.

Burke, Jason (2001). The Making of the World's Most Wanted Man. *The Observer,* October 28.

Burleigh, Michael (2006). Islamofascists: A Dangerous Label. *The Sunday Times,* October 1.

Burrin, Philippe (1994). *Hitler and the Jews: The Genesis of the Holocaust.* Tr. Patsy Southgate. Intr. Saul Friedländer. London: Edward Arnold.

Bursztein, Jean-Gérard (1996). *Hitler, la tyrannie et la psychanalyse: essai sur la destruction de la civilisation.* Aulnay-sous-bois: Nouvelles Études Freudiennes. [French].

Buruma, Ian & Margalit, Avishai (2004). *Occidentalism: The West in the Eyes of its Enemies.* New York: Penguin Press.

Bush, George W. (2005). Remarks by the President at the 20th Anniversary of the National Endowment for Democracy, October 12. Washington, DC: National Endowment for Democracy.

Butcher, Tim (2005). The Moment a Suicide Bombing Mission Failed. *The Daily Telegraph,* June 22.

Byrnes, Joseph F. (1984). *The Psychology of Religion.* New York: The Free Press. London: Collier Macmillan.

Calhoun, Craig et al. (Eds.) (2002). *Understanding September 11.* New York: New Press.

Cancelmo, Joseph A. et al. (Eds.) (2003). *Terrorism and the Psychoanalytic Space: International Perspectives from Ground Zero.* New York: Pace University Press.

Carew, Jan (1988). Columbus and the Origins of Racism in the Americas. *Race and Class,* vol. 29, pp. 1–19 and vol. 30, pp. 33–57.

Carr, Adrian (1997). Terrorism on the Couch: A Psychoanalytic Reading of the Oklahoma Disaster and its Aftermath. *Disaster Prevention and Management,* vol. 6, no. 1, pp. 22–32.

Carter, Michael E. (2005). *Islamic Terrorism in Southeast Asia: An Effects-Based U.S. Regional Strategy Against Jemaah Islamiyah and Abu Sayyaf.* Fort Leavenworth, Kansas: United States Army Command and General Staff College.

Casoni, Dianne & Brunet, Louis (2002). The Psychodynamics of Terrorism. *Canadian Journal of Psychoanalysis,* vol. 10, pp. 5–24.

Cassidy, Jude & Shaver, Phillip R. (Eds.) (1999). *Handbook of Attachment: Theory, Research, and Clinical Applications.* New York: Guilford Press.

Cassimatis, Emmanuel G. (2002). Terrorism, Our World and Our Way of Life. *Journal of American Academy of Psychoanalysis,* vol. 30, pp. 531–543.

Chamberlain, Sigrid (1997). *Adolf Hitler, die Deutsche Mutter und ihr erstes Kind: über zwei NS-Erziehungsbücher.* Mit einem Nachwort von Gregor Dill. Giessen:

Psychosozial-verlag. Second Edition (1998). Giessen: Psychosozial-verlag. Third Edition (2000). Giessen: Psychosozial-verlag. [German].

Chapman, Colin G. (2003). *Cross and Crescent: Responding to the Challenge of Islam.* Downers Grove, Illinois: InterVarsity Press Books.

Charach, Ron (2006). Shame, Rage and Mideast Violence: Are People Raised in Fundamentalist Societies More Apt to Hate Others? *The Toronto Star,* September 17.

Charny, Israel W. (2006). *Fighting Suicide Bombing: A Worldwide Campaign for Life.* Westport, Connecticut: Praeger Security International.

Charteris, Leslie (1932). *The Holy Terror.* London: Hodder and Stoughton. Reprinted (1970). Freeport, New York: Books for Libraries Press.

Chasseguet-Smirgel, Janine (1985). *Creativity and Perversion.* New York: W.W. Norton.

Cheragh, Ali (1977). *A Critical Exposition of the Popular "Jihad": Showing That All the Wars of Mohammad Were Defensive, and That Aggressive War, or Compulsory Conversion, Is Not Allowed in the Koran: With Appendices Providing That the Word "Jihad" Does Not Exegetically Mean "Warfare", and That Slavery Is Not Sanctioned by the Prophet of Islam.* Karachi: Karim Sons.

Chesler, Phyllis (1972). *Women and Madness.* Garden City, New York: Doubleday. 25th Anniversary Edition (1997). New York: Four Walls Eight Windows. New Edition (2005). New York: Palgrave Macmillan.

Chesler, Phyllis (2003). *The New Anti-Semitism: The Current Crisis and What We Must Do about It.* San Francisco: Jossey-Bass.

Chesler, Phyllis (2004a). The Psychoanalytic Roots of Islamic Terrorism. *Front Page Magazine,* May 3.

Chesler, Phyllis (2004b). President Bush and the Little Girl. *Front Page Magazine,* November 1.

Chesler, Phyllis (2005a). *The Death of Feminism: What's Next in the Struggle for Women's Freedom.* New York: Palgrave Macmillan.

Chesler, Phyllis (2005b). Mr. and Mrs. Suicide Bomber. *Front Page Magazine,* November 14.

Chesler, Phyllis (2005c). Serial Political Murderers. *United Press International,* December 5. Reprinted in *Front Page Magazine,* December 6.

Chesler, Phyllis (2005d). The White Moor as Willing Executioner. *Tech Central Station* and *Front Page Magazine,* December 9.

Chesler, Phyllis (2006). Publisher Pulls Book on Muslim Violence. *The Jewish Press,* October 4.

Chesler, Phyllis & Kobrin, Nancy H. (2006). Psychological Roots of Islamic Rage. *The Jewish Press,* August 9.

Chidester, David (1988). *Salvation and Suicide: An Interpretation of Jim Jones, the Peoples Temple, and Jonestown.* Bloomington: Indiana University Press.

Chirot, Daniel & McCauley, Clark (2006). *Why Not Kill Them All? The Logic and Prevention of Mass Political Murder.* Princeton, New Jersey: Princeton University Press.

Choueiri, Youssef M. (1990). *Islamic Fundamentalism.* Boston: Twayne Publishers.

Churchill, Winston S. (1899). On Islam. In *The River War: An Account of the Re-Conquest of the Soudan.* Two volumes. London, New York, and Bombay: Longmans, Green and Co. Reprinted (2000). London: Carroll & Graf Publishers. Reprinted (2006). Mineola, New York: Dover Publications.

Clark, Wesley K. (2003). *Winning Modern Wars: Iraq, Terrorism, and the American Empire.* New York: PublicAffairs. Reprinted (2004). New York: PublicAffairs.

Clarke, Richard A. (2004) *Against All Enemies: Inside America's War on Terror.* New York: The Free Press.

Coates, Susan W. et al. (Eds.) (2003). *September 11: Trauma and Human Bonds.* Hillsdale, New Jersey: The Analytic Press.

Coe, George Albert (1916). *The Psychology of Religion.* Chicago: The University of Chicago Press. New Edition (1979). New York: AMS Press.

Cohen, Ariel (2003). Hizb Ut-tahrir: An Emerging Threat to U.S. Interests in Central Asia. *The Heritage Foundation,* May 30.

Cohen, Warren I. (Ed.) (1983). *Reflections on Orientalism: Edward Said, Roger Besnahan, Surjit Dulai, Edward Graham, and Donald Lammers.* East Lansing, Michigan: Asian Studies Center, Michigan State University.

Cohler-Esses, Larry (2006). Bunkum from Benador. *The Nation,* July 3.

Connell, Raewyn W. (2000). *The Men and the Boys.* Berkeley: University of California Press. London and St. Leonards, NSW, Australia: Allen & Unwin.

Conrad, Joseph (1902). Heart of Darkness. In Conrad's *Youth, a Narrative, and Two Other Stories.* Edinburgh and London: William Blackwoord and Sons.

Conway, Flo & Siegelman, Jim (1982). *Holy Terror: The Fundamentalist War on America's Freedoms in Religion, Politics and Our Private Lives.* Garden City, New York: Doubleday. New Edition (1984). New York, NY: Dell Publications.

Cooley, John K. (1999). *Unholy Wars: Afghanistan, America, and International Terrorism.* London and Sterling, Virginia: Pluto Press.

Corbin, Jane (2002). *Al-Qaeda: In Search of the Terror Network That Threatens the World.* New York: Thunder Mouth Press/Nation Books. New Edition (2003). New York: Thunder Mouth Press/Nation Books.

Cottam, Richard W. (1988). *Iran and the United States: A Cold War Case Study.* Pittsburgh: University of Pittsburgh Press.

Covington, Coline et al. (Eds.) (2002). *Terrorism and War: Unconscious Dynamics of Political Violence.* Intr. Lord Alderdice. London: Karnac Books.

Crenshaw, Martha (1986). The Psychology of Political Terrorism. In Hermann, Margaret G. (Ed.) *Political Psychology: Contemporary Problems and Issues.* San Francisco and London: Jossey-Bass Publishers.

Crenshaw, Martha (1989). *Terrorism and International Cooperation.* New York: Institute for East-West Security Studies.

Crenshaw, Martha (1998). The Logic of Terrorism. In Reich, Walter (Ed.) *Origins of Terrorism: Psychologies, Ideologies, Theologies, States of Mind.* New Edition. Washington: Woodrow Wilson Center Press. Baltimore: Johns Hopkins University Press.

Crenshaw, Martha (2000). The Psychology of Terrorism: An Agenda for the 21st Century. *Political Psychology,* vol. 21, no. 2, pp. 405–420.

Crenshaw, Martha (Ed.) (1983). *Terrorism, Legitimacy, and Power: The Consequences of Political Violence.* Middletown, Connecticut: Wesleyan University Press.

Crenshaw, Martha (Ed.) (1994). *Terrorism in Africa.* Boston: G.K. Hall. Toronto: Maxwell Macmillan Canada.

Crenshaw, Martha (Ed.) (1995). *Terrorism in Context.* University Park: Pennsylvania State University Press.

Crenshaw, Martha & Pimlott, John (Eds.) (1997). *Encyclopedia of World Terrorism.* Three volumes. Armonk, New York: Sharpe Reference.

Cronin, Audrey Kurth (2002–2003). Behind the Curve: Globalization and International Terrorism. *International Security,* vol. 27, pp. 30–58.

Daftary, Farhad (1994). *The Assassin Legends: Myths of the Isma'ilis.* London: I.B. Tauris.

Darwish, Nonie (2006). *Now They Call Me Infidel: Why I Rejected the Jihad for America, Israel, and the War on Terror.* New York: Sentinel.

Davidson, Lawrence (1998). *Islamic Fundamentalism.* Westport, Connecticut: Greenwood Press.

Davis, Walter Albert (2005). The Psychology of Christian Fundamentalism. *Counterpunch,* January 8–9.

Davis, Walter Albert (2006). *Death's Dream Kingdom: The American Psyche since 9-11.* London and Ann Arbor, Michigan: Pluto Press.

Dawkins, Clinton Richard (2006). *The God Delusion.* Boston: Houghton Mifflin Co.

De Boor, Wolfgang (1985). *Hitler: Mensch, Übermensch, Untermensch: eine kriminalpsychologische Studie.* Frankfurt on the Main: R.G. Fischer. [German].

De Rougement, Denis (1940). *Love in the Western World.* Tr. Montgomry Belgion. New York: Harcourt, Brace and Company. New Edition (1956). New York: Pantheon Books. Reprinted (1957). Garden City, New York: Doubleday. New Edition (1983). Princeton, New Jersey: Princeton University Press. Reprinted (1990). New York: Schocken Books.

Dealy, Sam (2006). Terror's Playground. *TIME,* vol. 168, no. 23, November 27.

Dean, Melanie A. (1995). *Borderline Personality Disorder: The Latest Assessment and Treatment Strategies.* Kansas City, Missouri: Compact Clinicals. Second Edition (2001). Kansas City, Missouri: Compact Clinicals. Third Edition (2006). Kansas City, Missouri: Compact Clinicals.

DeAtkine, Norvell B. (2004). Observations and Impressions from Iraq. *American Diplomacy,* March 21.

DeMause, Lloyd (2002). The Childhood Origins of Terrorism. *The Journal of Psychohistory,* vol. 29, pp. 340–349.

DeMause, Lloyd (2006). If I Blow Myself Up and Become a Martyr, I'll Finally Be Loved. *The Journal of Psychohistory,* vol. 33, no. 4, pp. 300–307.

Dershowitz, Alan M. (2002). *Why Terrorism Works: Understanding the Threat, Responding to the Challenge.* New Haven: Yale University Press.

Dershowitz, Alan M. (2008). Worshippers of Death. *The Wall Street Journal,* March 3, p. A17.

Detrick, Douglas W. & Detrick, Susan P. (1989). *Self Psychology: Comparisons and Contrasts.* Hillsdale, New Jersey: The Analytic Press.

Dicks, Henry V. et al. (1967). *Marital Tensions: Clinical Studies Towards a Psychological Theory of Interaction.* New York: Basic Books.

Dietl, Wilhelm (1983). *Heiliger Krieg für Allah: als Augenzeuge bei den geheimen Kommandos des Islam.* Munich: Kindler Verlag.

Dietl, Wilhelm (1984). *Holy War.* Tr. Martha Humphreys. New York: Macmillan.

Diner, Dan (2002). *Feindbild Amerika: über die Beständigkeit eines Ressentiments.* Munich: Propyläen. [German].

Dolan, David P. (1991). *Holy War for the Promised Land: Israel's Struggle to Survive.* Nashville: T. Nelson.

Dresser, Horatio Willis (1929). *Outlines of the Psychology of Religion.* New York: Crowell.

Duran, Khalid & Hechiche, Abdelwahab (2001). *Children of Abraham: An Introduction to Islam for Jews.* Hoboken, New Jersey: Ktav Publishing House.

Dwairy, Marwan (2006). *Counseling and Psychotherapy with Arabs and Muslims.* New York: Teachers College Press.

Eagleton, Terry (2005). *Holy Terror.* Oxford and New York: Oxford University Press.

Eagleton, Terry (2006). Lunging, Flailing, Mispunching: Review of *The God Delusion* by Richard Dawkins. *London Review of Books,* vol. 28, no. 20, October 19.

Elmendorf, Susan A. & Ruskin, Ronald (2004). Trauma, Terrorism: Man's Inhumanity to Man. *International Journal of Psycho-Analysis,* vol. 85, pp. 983–986.

Enders, Walter & Sandler, Todd (2006). Distribution of Transnational Terrorism among Countries by Income Class and Geography after 9/11. *International Studies Quarterly,* vol. 50, no. 2, pp. 367 ff.

Erikson, Erik Homburger (1942). Hitler's Imagery and German Youth. *Psychiatry,* vol. 5, pp. 475–493.

Erikson, Erik Homburger (1950). *Childhood and Society.* New York: W.W. Norton. Second Edition (1964). New York: W.W. Norton. Thirty-fifth Anniversary Edition (1985). New York: W.W. Norton. New Edition (1993). New York: W.W. Norton.

Erikson, Erik Homburger (1963). The Legend of Hitler's Childhood. In Erikson, Erik H. *Childhood and Society,* Second Edition, pp. 326–358. New York: W.W. Norton.

Esposito, John L. (1992). *The Islamic Threat: Myth or Reality?* Oxford and New York: Oxford University Press.

Esposito, John L. (2002). *Unholy War: Terror in the Name of Islam.* Oxford and New York: Oxford University Press.

Esposito, John L. (Ed.) (1999). *The Oxford Illustrated History of Islam.* Oxford and New York: Oxford University Press.

Esposito, John L. (Ed.) (2003). *The Oxford Dictionary of Islam.* Oxford and New York: Oxford University Press.

Faber, Heije (1976). *Psychology of Religion.* Philadelphia: Westminster Press. London: S.C.M. Press.

Fairbairn, William Ronald Dodds (1952). *Psychoanalytic Studies of the Personality.* London: Routledge & Kegan Paul. Reprinted (1952). As *An Object-Relations Theory of Personality.* New York: Basic Books.

Fairbairn, William Ronald Dodds (1994). *From Instinct to Self: Selected Papers of W.R.D. Fairbairn.* Eds. David E. Scharff and Ellinor Fairbairn Birtles. Northvale, New Jersey: Jason Aronson.

Falconi, Fabrizio & Sette, Antonello (2001). *Osama bin Laden: il terrore dell'Occidente.* Rome: Edizioni Fazi. [Italian].

Falk, Avner (1978). Freud and Herzl. *Contemporary Psychoanalysis,* vol. 14, July, pp. 357–387.

Falk, Avner (1985). Aspects of Political Psychobiography. *Political Psychology,* vol. 6, pp. 605–619.

Falk, Avner (1992). Unconscious Aspects of the Arab-Israeli Conflict. *The Psychoanalytic Study of Society,* vol. 17, pp. 213–247.

Falk, Avner (1996). *A Psychoanalytic History of the Jews.* Madison and Teaneck, New Jersey: Fairleigh Dickinson University Press. Cranbury, New Jersey and London: Associated University Presses.

Falk, Avner (2001a). Political Assassination and Personality Disorder: The Cases of Lee Harvey Oswald and Yigal Amir. *Mind and Human Interaction,* vol. 12, no. 1, pp. 2–34.

Falk, Avner (2001b). Osama Bin Laden and America: A Psychobiographical Study. *Mind and Human Interaction,* vol. 12, no. 3, pp. 161–172.

Falk, Avner (2004). *Fratricide on the Holy Land: A Psychoanalytic View of the Arab-Israeli Conflict.* Madison, Wisconsin: University of Wisconsin Press Terrace Books.

Falkenrath, Richard A. et al. (1998). *America's Achilles' Heel: Nuclear, Biological, and Chemical Terrorism and Covert Attack.* Cambridge, Massachusetts: MIT Press.

Fallaci, Oriana (2002). *The Rage and the Pride.* New York: Rizzoli.

Fanon, Frantz (1961). *The Wretched of the Earth.* New York: Grove Press. New Edition (1963). Tr. Constance Farrington. New York: Grove Weidenfeld.

Farlow, Jonathan (2004). *Holy War.* Boone, North Carolina: Parkway Publishers.

Fehr, Beverley (1988). Prototype Analysis of the Concepts of Love and Commitment. *Journal of Personality and Social Psychology,* vol. 55, pp. 557–579.

Fehr, Beverley & Russell, James A. (1992). Concept of Love Viewed from a Prototype Perspective. *Journal of Personality and Social Psychology,* vol. 60, no. 3, pp. 425–438.

Feldman, Noah (2005). Political Islam: Global Warning. *The New York Times Sunday Book Review,* February 6.

Fenichel, Otto (1945). *The Psychoanalytic Theory of Neurosis.* New York: W.W. Norton.

Fernea, Elizabeth Warnock (1995). Childhood in the Muslim Middle East. Introduction to Fernea, Elizabeth Warnock (Ed.) *Children in the Muslim Middle East,* pp. 3–16. Austin: University of Texas Press.

Fernea, Elizabeth Warnock (1998). *In Search of Islamic Feminism: One Woman's Global Journey.* New York: Doubleday.

Fernea, Elizabeth Warnock (2006). *Childhood in the Muslim Middle East.* Online article at http://isc.temple.edu/neighbor/world/muslim-childhood.pdf.

Fields, Rona M. et al. (2002). The Palestinian Suicide Bomber. In Stout, Chris E. (Ed.) *The Psychology of Terrorism,* Vol. 2, pp. 193–223. Westport, Connecticut: Praeger.

Fields, Rona M. et al. (2004). *Martyrdom: The Psychology, Theology, and Politics of Self-Sacrifice.* Westport, Connecticut: Praeger.

Fineman, Howard et al. (2003). Bush and God. *Newsweek,* March 10.

Fischel, Kurt B. & Langer, Audrey R. (1989). *Jihad!* Sherman Oaks, California: New Saga Publishers.

Fisher, Mark (1990). *Personal Love.* London: Gerald Duckworth & Co. Ltd.

Fletcher, Martin (2001). *Bunker-Buster Bombs Blast Bin Laden Caves.* London: *The Times,* November 20.

Forest, James J.F. (Ed.) (2006). *The Making of a Terrorist: Recruitment, Training, and Root Causes.* Three volumes. Westport, Connecticut: Praeger Security International.

Fornari, Franco (1974). *The Psychoanalysis of War.* Tr. Alenka Pfeifer. Garden City, New York: Doubleday Anchor Press. Reprinted (1975). Bloomington: Indiana University Press.

Fradin, Murray S. (1965). *Jihad.* New York: Murray Fradin.

Frank, Justin (2004). *Bush on the Couch: Inside the Mind of the President.* New York: Regan Books.

Freeman, Arthur & Fusco, Gina M. (2004). *Borderline Personality Disorder: A Therapist's Guide to Taking Control.* New York: W.W. Norton.

Freud, Sigmund (1905). *Drei Abhandlungen zur Sexualtheorie.* Leipzig and Vienna: Deuticke. [German].

Freud, Sigmund (1910–1918). Beiträge zur Psychologie des Liebeslebens. In Freud, Sigmund (1906–1922). *Sammlung kleiner Schriften zur Neurosenlehre,* Vol. 4, pp. 200–251. Viernna: Deuticke. [German].

Freud, Sigmund (1914). Zur Einführing des Narzissmus. *Jahrbuch für Psychoanalyse,* vol. 6, pp. 1–24. [German].

Freud, Sigmund (1927). *Die Zukunft einer Illusion.* Leipzig, Vienna and Zurich: Internationaler Psychoanalytischer Verlag. [German].

Freud, Sigmund (1953). Three Essays on the Theory of Sexuality. In Strachey, James et al. (Eds.) *The Standard Edition of the Complete Psychological Works of Sigmund Freud,* Vol. 7, pp. 123–243. London: The Hogarth Press and the Institute of Psycho-Analysis.

Freud, Sigmund (1955). Beyond the Pleasure Principle. In Strachey, James et al. (Eds.) *The Standard Edition of the Complete Psychological Works of Sigmund Freud,* Vol. 18. London: The Hogarth Press and the Institute of Psycho-Analysis.

Freud, Sigmund (1955–1974). *The Standard Edition of the Complete Psychological Works of Sigmund Freud.* Twenty-four volumes. Ed. James Strachey & Al. London: The Hogarth Press and the Institute of Psych-Analysis.

Freud, Sigmund (1957a). Contributions to the Psychology of Love. In Strachey, James et al. (Eds.). *The Standard Edition of the Complete Psychological Works of Sigmund Freud,* Vol. 11, pp. 163–208. London: The Hogarth Press and the Institute of Psycho-Analysis.

Freud, Sigmund (1957b). Instincts and Their Vicissitudes. In Strachey, James et al. (Eds.) *The Standard Edition of the Complete Psychological Works of Sigmund Freud,* Vol. 14. London: The Hogarth Press and the Institute of Psycho-Analysis.

Freud, Sigmund (1957c). Mourning and Melancholia. In Strachey, James et al. (Eds.) *The Standard Edition of the Complete Psychological Works of Sigmund Freud,* Vol. 14. London: The Hogarth Press and the Institute of Psycho-Analysis.

Freud, Sigmund (1957d). On Narcissism: An Introduction. In Strachey, James et al. (Eds.) *The Standard Edition of the Complete Psychological Works of Sigmund Freud,* Vol. 14, pp. 67–102. London: The Hogarth Press and the Institute of Psycho-Analysis.

Freud, Sigmund (1959). Inhibitions, Symptoms and Anxiety. In Strachey, James et al. (Eds.) *The Standard Edition of the Complete Psychological Works of Sigmund Freud,* Vol. 20. London: The Hogarth Press and the Institute of Psycho-Analysis.

Freud, Sigmund (1961). The Future of an Illusion. In Strachey, James et al. (Eds.). *The Standard Edition of the Complete Psychological Works of Sigmund Freud,* vol. 21, pp. 1–56. London: The Hogarth Press and the Institute of Psycho-Analysis.

Freud, Sigmund & Jung, Carl Gustav (1974). *The Freud/Jung Letters: The Correspondence Between Sigmund Freud and Carl Jung.* Tr. Ralph Mannheim and R.F.C. Hall. Ed. William McGuire. Princeton, New Jersey: Princeton University Press.

Friedel, Robert O. (2004). *Borderline Personality Disorder Demystified: An Essential Guide for Understanding and Living with BPD.* Foreword by Perry D. Hoffman, Dixianne Penney & Patricia Woodward. New York: Marlowe & Co.

Friedländer, Saul (1997). *Nazi Germany and the Jews.* New York: Harpercollins.

Fromm, Erich (1950). *Psychoanalysis and Religion.* New Haven, Connecticut: Yale University Press. Reprinted (1951). London: Victor Gollancz.

Fromm, Erich (1956). *The Art of Loving.* New York: Harper.

Fromm, Erich (1967). *The Anatomy of Human Destructiveness.* New York: Holt, Rinehart and Winston.

Frum, David & Perle, Richard Norman (2003). *An End to Evil: How to Win the War on Terror.* New York: Random House.

Fukuyama, Francis (1992). *The End of History and the Last Man.* New York: The Free Press. New York and Toronto: Maxwell Macmillan.

Fusco, Gina M. & Freeman, Arthur (2004). *Borderline Personality Disorder: A Patient's Guide to Taking Control.* New York: W.W. Norton.

Gabbard, Glen O. (1996). *Love and Hate in the Analytic Setting.* Northvale, New Jersey: Jason Aronson.

Gabriel, Brigitte (2006). *Because They Hate: A Survivor of Islamic Terror Warns America.* New York: St. Martin's Press.

Gabriel, Mark A. (2006).*Journey into the Mind of an Islamic Terrorist.* Lake Mary, Florida: Frontline Books.

Gaines, Atwood D. (Ed.) (1992) *Ethnopsychiatry: The Cultural Construction of Professional and Folk Psychiatries.* Albany, New York: State University of New York Press.

Gans, Eric Lawrence (1985). *The End of Culture: Toward a Generative Anthropology.* Berkeley: University of California Press.

Gans, Eric Lawrence (1993). *Originary Thinking: Elements of Generative Anthropology.* Stanford, California: Stanford University Press.

Gaylin, Willard (1968).*The Meaning of Despair: Psychoanalytic Contributions to the Understanding of Depression.* New York: Science House.

Gediman, Helen K. (1995). *Fantasies of Love and Death in Life and Art: A Psychoanalytic Study of the Normal and the Pathological.* New York: New York University Press.

Geertz, Clifford (2003). Which Way to Mecca? Part I and Part II. *The New York Review of Books,* June 12 and July 3.

Glad, Betty (2002). Why Tyrants Go Too Far: Malignant Narcissism and Absolute Power. *Political Psychology,* vol. 23, no. 1, pp. 1–37.

Glass, James M. (1997). *"Life Unworthy of Life": Racial Phobia and Mass Murder in Hitler's Germany.* New York: Basic Books.

Glidden, Harold Walker (1972). The Arab World. *American Journal of Psychiatry,* vol. 128, pp. 984–988.

Goertzel, Ted G. (2002a). Terrorist Beliefs and Terrorist Lives. In Stout, Chris E. (Ed.) *The Psychology of Terrorism,* Vol. 1, pp. 97–112. Westport, Connecticut: Praeger.

Goertzel, Ted G. (2002b). In Search of Bin Laden. *Clio's Psyche,* vol. 8, no. 4, pp. 165, 178–180.

Goldberg, Carl (1996). *Speaking with the Devil: A Dialogue with Evil.* New York: Viking.

Goldberg, Carl (1999). A Psychoanalysis of Love: The Patient with Deadly Longing. *American Journal of Psychotherapy,* vol. 53, no. 4, pp. 437–451.

Gonen, Jay Y. (2000). *The Roots of Nazi Psychology: Hitler's Utopian Barbarism.* Lexington, Kentucky: University Press of Kentucky.

Gonen, Jay Y. (2002). The Impossible Palestinians and Israelis. *Clio's Psyche,* vol. 9, no. 3, pp. 125–127.

Gopin, Marc (2002). *Holy War, Holy Peace: How Religion Can Bring Peace to the Middle East.* New York: Oxford University Press.

Gordon, Sheila (2002). *The Origins of Love and Hate* revisited. In Mann, David (Ed.) *Love and Hate: Psychoanalytic Perspectives,* pp. 111–124. Hove, East Sussex, England, UK and New York: Brunner-Routledge.

Gorenberg, Gershom (2000). *The End of Days: Fundamentalism and the Struggle for the Temple Mount.* New York: The Free Press.

Gorenberg, Gershom (2006). *The Accidental Empire: Israel and the Birth of Settlements, 1967–1977.* New York: Times Books.

Gregg, Gary S. (2005). *The Middle East: A Cultural Psychology.* Foreword by David Matsumoto. Oxford and New York: Oxford University Press.

Grensted, Laurence William (1952). *The Psychology of Religion.* London, New York: Oxford University Press.

Griffith, Lee (2002). *The War on Terrorism and the Terror of God.* Grand Rapids, Michigan: W.B. Eerdmans Publishing Co.

Groebel, Jo & Goldstein, Jeffrey H. (Eds.) (1989). *Terrorism: Psychological Perspectives.* Seville, Spain: Publicaciones de la Universidad de Sevilla.

Grosskurth, Phyllis (1986). *Melanie Klein: Her World and Her Work.* New York: Alfred A. Knopf.

Grossmann, Klaus et al. (Eds.) (2006). *Attachment from Infancy to Adulthood: The Major Longitudinal Studies.* New York: Guilford Press.

Grotstein, James S. (1981). *Splitting and Projective Identification.* New York and London: Jason Aronson. New Edition (1985). New York: Jason Aronson.

Group for the Advancement of Psychiatry (1978). *Self-Involvement in the Middle-East Conflict.* Formulated by the Committee on International Relations, Group for the Advancement of Psychiatry. New York: Group for the Advancement of Psychiatry.

Group for the Advancement of Psychiatry (1987). *Us and Them: The Psychology of Ethnonationalism.* Formulated by the Committee on International Relations, Group for the Advancement of Psychiatry. New York: Brunner/Mazel.

Gruen, Arno (1988). *The Betrayal of the Self: The Fear of Autonomy in Men and Women.* New York: Grove Press.

Gruen, Arno (1992). *The Insanity of Normality: Realism as Sickness: Toward Understanding Human Destructiveness.* Tr. Hildegarde and Hunter Hannum. New York: Grove Weidenfeld.

Gruen, Arno (2002). *Der Kampf um die Demokratie: der Extremismus, die Gewalt und der Terror.* Stuttgart: Klett-cotta. [German].

Guillaume, Alfred (1966).*The Traditions of Islam, an Introduction to the Study of the Hadith Literature.* Beirut: Khayats. Reprinted (1980). New York: Books for Libraries Press.

Gunderson, Cory Gideon (2004). *Islamic Fundamentalism.* Edina, Minnesota: ABDO & Daughters.

Gunderson, John G. (2001). *Borderline Personality Disorder: A Clinical Guide.* Washington, DC: American Psychiatric Press.

Guntrip, Harry J.S. (1961). *Personality Structure and Human Interaction.* London: The Hogarth Press.

Guntrip, Harry J.S. (1968). *Schizoid Phenomena, Object-relations and the Self.* Madison, Connecticut: International Universities Press.

Guntrip, Harry J.S. (1971). *Psychoanalytic Theory, Therapy and the Self.* New York: Basic Books.

Guntrip, Harry J.S. (1994). *Personal Relations Therapy: The Collected Papers of H. J. S. Guntrip.* Ed. J. Hazelll. Northvale, New Jersey: Jason Aronson.

Haj-Yahia, Muhammad M. (1999). Wife Abuse and its Psychological Consequences as Revealed by the First Palestinian National Survey on Violence Against Women. *Journal of Family Psychology,* vol. 13, no. 4, pp. 642–662.

Haj-Yahia, Muhammad M. (2000). Wife Abuse and Battering in the Sociocultural Context of Arab Society. *Family Process,* vol. 39, no. 2, pp. 237–255.

Haj-Yahia, Muhammad M. & Shor, Ron (1995). Child Maltreatment as Perceived by Arab Students of Social Science in the West Bank. *Child Abuse and Neglect,* vol. 19, no. 10, pp. 1209–1219.

Haj-Yahia, Muhammad M. & Tamish, Safa (2001). The Rates of Child Sexual Abuse and its Psychological Consequences as Revealed by a Study among Palestinian University Students. *Child Abuse and Neglect,* vol. 25, no. 10, pp. 1303–1327.

Hallett, Brian (2004). Dishonest Crimes, Dishonest Language: An Argument about Terrorism. In Moghaddam, Fathali M. & Marsella, Anthony J. (Eds.) *Understanding Terrorism: Psychosocial Roots, Consequences, and Interventions.* Washington, DC: American Psychological Association.

Halliday, Fred (1996). *Islam and the Myth of Confrontation: Religion and Politics in the Middle East.* London and New York: I.B. Tauris. New Edition (2003). London and New York: I.B. Tauris.

Hamady, Sania (1960). *Temperament and Character of the Arabs.* New York: Twayne Publishers. New York: Irvington Publishers.

Hamon, Marie-Christine (2000). *Why Do Women Love Men and Not Their Mothers?* Tr. Susan Fairfield. New York: Other Press.

Hanly, Charles (1978). A Critical Evaluation of Bowlby's Ethological Theory of Anxiety. *The Psychoanalytic Quarterly,* vol. 47, pp. 364–380.

Harris, Jonathan (1983). *The New Terrorism: Politics of Violence.* New York: Julian Messner.

Harris, Judith Rich (1998). *The Nurture Assumption: Why Children Turn Out the Way They Do.* New York: The Free Press.

Harris, Judith Rich (2006). *No Two Alike: Human Nature and Human Individuality.* New York: W.W. Norton.

Harris, Lee (2002). Al-Qaeda's Fantasy Ideology. *Policy Review,* no. 114, August–September.

Harris, Lee (2004). *Civilization and its Enemies: The Next Stage in History.* New York: Simon & Schuster.

Hart, Christopher (2007). Review of *God Is Not Great: The Case Against Religion* by Christopher Hitchens. *The Sunday Times,* June 17.

Hatfield, Elaine Catherine & Walster, G. William (1978). *A New Look at Love.* Reading, Massachusetts: Addison-Wesley.

Hawting, Gerald R. (1999). *The Idea of Idolatry and the Emergence of Islam: From Polemic to History.* Cambridge and New York: Cambridge University Press.

Hazan, Cindy & Shaver, Phillip R. (1987). Romantic Love Conceptualized as an Attachment Process. *Journal of Personality and Social Psychology,* vol. 52, pp. 511–524.

Hazan, Cindy & Shaver, Phillip R. (1990). Love and Work: An Attachment-Theoretical Perspective. *Journal of Personality and Social Psychology,* vol. 59, pp. 270–280.

Head, Thomas & Landes, Richard Allen (Eds.) (1992). *The Peace of God: Social Violence and Religious Response in France Around the Year 1000.* Ithaca, New York: Cornell University Press.

Heggy, Tarek (1991). *Egyptian Political Essays.* Cairo: Dar Alshorouk. New Edition (2000). Cairo: Dar Al-Maararef Press.

Heggy, Tarek (2003). *Culture, Civilization and Humanity.* London: Routledge.

Heggy, Tarek (2005). The Arab Mind and the Denial Phenomenon. Online Article Published on *Winds of Change.Net* and other Internet sites, October 4. Reprinted by *The Henry Jackson Society,* October 13 and 23. Reprinted as "The Arab Mind and Denial: Roadblock to Progress." *The One Republic Journal,* November 23.

Hendrick, Clyde & Hendrick, Susan. (1986). Theory and Method of Love. *Journal of Personality and Social Psychology,* vol. 50, pp. 392–402.

Hering, Christopher (1997). Beyond Understanding? Some Thoughts on the Meaning and Function of the Notion of "Evil." *British Journal of Psychotherapy,* vol. 14. no. 2, p. 209.

Hershberg, Eric & Moore, Kevin W. (Eds.) (2002) *Critical Views of September 11: Analyses from Around the World.* New York: New Press.

Hiro, Dilip (1989). *Holy Wars: The Rise of Islamic Fundamentalism.* London and New York: Routledge.

Hitchens, Christopher (1968). Wanton Acts of Usage. *Harper's Magazine,* September.

Hitchens, Christopher (2001). Of Sin, the Left & Islamic Fascism. *The Nation,* October 8.

Hitchens, Christopher (2007). *God Is Not Great: The Case Against Religion.* New York: Warner Twelve.

Hoffman, Bruce (1993). *Holy Terror: The Implications of Terrorism Motivated by a Religious Imperative.* Santa Monica, California: Rand Publications.

Hoffman, Bruce (1998). *Inside Terrorism.* New York: Columbia University Press. New Edition (2006). New York: Columbia University Press.

Hoge, James F. & Rose, Gideon (Eds.). (2001). *How Did This Happen? Terrorism and the New War.* New York: Public Affairs.

Holleman, Jane (1999). *Holy Terror.* New York: Pocket Star Books.

Homer-Dixon, Thomas F. (2006a). Pull Terrorism Up by the Roots. *Toronto Globe and Mail,* September 11.

Homer-Dixon, Thomas F. (2006b). *The Upside of Down: Catastrophe, Creativity, and the Renewal of Civilization.* Washington, DC: Island Press and Shearwater Books.

Honneth, Axel. (1995). *The Struggle for Recognition: The Moral Grammar of Social Conflicts.* Cambridge, Massachusetts: Polity Press.

Hooke, Maria Teresa Savio & Akhtar, Salman (Eds.) (2007). *The Geography of Meanings: Psychoanalytic Reflections upon Land, Space, Place, and Dislocation.* London: International Psychoanalytical Association.

Horgan, John (2005). *The Psychology of Terrorism.* Abingdon and New York: Routledge. New York: Frank Cass.

Horney, Karen (1939). *New Ways in Psychoanalysis.* New York: W.W. Norton.

Houtsma, Martijn Theodoor et al. (Eds.) (1913–1936). *The Encyclopaedia of Islam: A Dictionary of the Geography, Ethnography and Biography of the Muhammadan Peoples, Prepared by a Number of Leading Orientalists. Published under the Patronage of the International Association of the Academies.* Five volumes. Leyden: E.J. Brill. London: Luzac & Co. New Edition (1954). Eleven volumes. Eds. Hamilton Alexander Rosskeen

Gibb et al. Leiden: E.J. Brill. New Edition (1987) *E. J. Brill's First Encyclopaedia of Islam 1913–1936.* Nine volumes. Eds. M.T. Houtsma et al. Leiden and New York: E. J. Brill. New Edition (1989). Six volumes. Eds. E. van Donzel et al. Leiden: E.J. Brill.

Hudson, Rex A. (1999). *The Sociology and Psychology of Terrorism: Who Becomes a Terrorist and Why?* A Report Prepared under an Interagency Agreement by the Federal Research Division, Library of Congress, September 1999. Washington, DC: Federal Research Division, Library of Congress. Reprinted (2002). As *Who Becomes a Terrorist and Why: The 1999 Government Report on Profiling Terrorists.* Guilford, Connecticut: The Lyons Press. Reprinted (2005). As *The Sociology and Psychology of Terrorism: Who Becomes a Terrorist and Why?* Honolulu: Hawaii. University Press of the Pacific.

Huff, Toby E. & Schluchter, Wolfgang (Eds.) (1999). *Max Weber and Islam.* New Brunswick, New Jersey: Transaction Publishers.

Hundley, Tom. (2002). Islamic Radicalism Festers in Europe. *The Chicago Tribune,* February 25.

Huntington, Samuel P. (1993). The Clash of Civilizations? *Foreign Affairs,* vol. 72, no. 3, Summer, pp. 22–28.

Huntington, Samuel P. (1996).*The Clash of Civilizations and the Remaking of World Order.* Washington: Council on Foreign Relations. New York: Simon & Schuster.

Ibn Hisham, Abu Muhammad 'Abd Al-Malik (1955). *The Life of Muhammad: A Translation of Ishaq's Sirat Rasul Allah.* Tr. Intr & Ed. Alfred Guillaume. London and New York: Oxford University Press. Reprinted (2001). Karachi and New York: Oxford University Press.

Ibn Ishaq, Muhammad (1989).*The Making of the Last Prophet: A Reconstruction of the Earliest Biography of Muhammad.* Tr. & Ed. Gordon Darnell Newby. Columbia, South Carolina: University of South Carolina Press.

Ibn Qutyba (1900–1908). *Uyun Al-akhbar.* Ed. Carl Brockelmann. Berlin: Georg Olms.

Ibn Sa'd, Muhammad (1967). *Kitab Al-tabaqat Al-kabir.* (Book of the Major Classes). Tr. S. Moinul Haq and H.K. Ghazanfar. Karachi: Pakistan Historical Society.

Ibn Warraq (Ed. & Tr.) (2000). *The Quest for the Historical Muhammad.* Amherst, New York: Prometheus Books.

Ibn Warraq (Ed. & Tr.) (2002). *What the Koran Really Says: Language, Text and Commentary.* Amherst, New York: Prometheus Books.

Ibrahim, Raymond (Ed.) (2007). *The Al-Qaeda Reader.* Intr. Victor Davis Hanson. New York: Doubleday.

Ignatius, David (2006). Misreading the Enemy. *The Washington Post,* April 28.

Inamdar, Subhash C. (2001). *Muhammad and the Rise of Islam: The Creation of Group Identity.* Madison, Connecticut: Psychosocial Press.

International Crisis Group (2001). *Bin Laden and the Balkans: The Politics of Anti-Terrorism.* ICG Balkans Report # 119. Belgrade, Podgorica, Pristina, Sarajevo, Skopje, Tirana and Brussels: International Crisis Group.

Israeli, Raphael (1997). Islamikaze and Their Significance. *Terrorism and Political Violence,* vol. 9, no. 3, pp. 96–121.

Israeli, Raphael (2003). *Islamikaze: Manifestations of Islamic Martyrology.* London: Frank Cass.

Jacquard, Roland (2001). *Au nom d'Oussama ben Laden...dossier secret sur le terroriste le plus recherché du monde.* Paris: Jean Picollec. [French].

Jacquard, Roland (2002). *In the Name of Osama bin Laden: Global Terrorism and the Bin Laden Brotherhood.* Samia Serageldin, consulting editor. George Holoch, translator. Durham, North Carolina: Duke University Press.

Jacquard, Roland & Nasplèzes, Dominique (1998). *Fatwa contre l'occident.* Paris: Albin Michel. [French].

Jalalzai, Musa Khan (2002). *The Holy Terror: Islam, Violence and Terrorism in Pakistan.* Lahore: Dua Publications. Revised Edition (2002).*The Holy Terror: Al-Qaeda, Taliban and its Roots in Pakistan and Afghanistan.* Lahore: Dua Publications.

James, William (1902). *The Varieties of Religious Experience: A Study in Human Nature, Being the Gifford Lectures on Natural Religion Delivered at Edinburgh in 1901–1902.* New York and London: Longmans, Green, and Co. New Edition (2004). Intr. Reinhold Niebuhr. New York: Simon & Schuster.

Jenkins, John Philip (2000). *Mystics and Messiahs: Cults and New Religions in American History.* Oxford and New York: Oxford University Press.

Johnson, Adelaide M. & Szurels, S.A. (1952). The Genesis of Antisocial Acting Out in Children and Adults. *The Psychoanalytic Quarterly,* vol. 21, pp. 323–343.

Johnson, James Turner (1997). *The Holy War Idea in Western and Islamic Traditions.* University Park, Pennsylvania: Pennsylvania State University Press.

Johnson, Paul Emanuel (1945). *Psychology of Religion.* New York: Abingdon-Cokesbury Press. New Edition (1959). New York: Abingdon Press.

Johnson, Phillip W. & Feldmann, Theodore B. (1992). Personality Types and Terrorism: Self-Psychology Perspectives. *Forensic Reports,* vol. 5, no. 4, pp. 293–303.

Johnson, Reed (2006). His Beautiful Britain: In His Writing, Including the Upcoming "Venus," Hanif Kureishi Chronicles a Nation's Harsh, Ugly Cultural Angst—With Copious Sex and Humor. *The Los Angeles Times,* November 12.

Jones, James W. (1993). *Contemporary Psychoanalysis and Religion: Transference and Transcendence.* New Haven, Connecticut: Yale University Press.

Jones, James W. (2002). *Terror and Transformation: The Ambiguity of Religion in Psychoanalytic Perspective.* East Sussex and New York: Brunner-Routledge.

Joseph, Suad et al. (Eds.) (2003–2007). *Encyclopedia of Women & Islamic Cultures.* Five volumes. Leiden and Boston: Brill.

Josey, Charles Conant (1927). *The Psychology of Religion.* New York: The Macmillan Co.

Juergensmeyer, Mark (2000). *Terror in the Mind of God: The Global Rise of Religious Violence.* Berkeley: University of California Press. Second Edition (2001). Berkeley: University of California Press. Third Edition (2003). Berkeley: University of California Press.

Kakutani, Michiko (2004). Books of the Times: A Confident Prescription for Foiling the Terrorists. Review of *An End to Evil* by David Frum and Richard Norman Perle. *The New York Times,* January 13.

Kakutani, Michiko (2006). Books of the Times: A Portrait of the President as the Victim of His Own Certitude. Review of *State of Denial* by Bob Woodward. *The New York Times,* September 30.

Kamiya, Gary (2004). "An End to Evil" by David Frum and Richard Perle: Undaunted by the Iraq debacle, uber-hawks David Frum and Richard Perle air their fevered wet dream of a national security superstate that slaps down uppity Muslims, bombs North Korea, slices and dices civil liberties and scatters the Palestinians like birdseed. Online article, *Salon.com,* January 30.

Kaplan-Solms, Karen & Solms, Mark (2000). *Clinical Studies in Neuro-Psychoanalysis: Introduction to a Depth Neuropsychology.* Foreword by Arnold Z. Pfeffer. Madison, Connecticut: International Universities Press.

Karsh, Efraim (1997). *Fabricating Israeli History: The "New Historians."* London and Portland, Oregon: Frank Cass. Second Edition (2000). London and Portland, Oregon: Frank Cass.

Karsh, Efraim (2003). *Arafat's War: The Man and His Battle for Israeli Conquest.* New York: Grove Press.

Karsh, Efraim (2006). *Islamic Imperialism: A History.* New Haven: Yale University Press.

Katz, Adam (2004–2005). Remembering Amalek: 9/11 and Generative Thinking. *Anthropoetics: The Journal of Generative Anthropology,* vol. 10, no. 2.

Kaufman, Gershen (1989). *The Psychology of Shame: Theory and Treatment of Shame-Based Syndromes.* New York: Springer Publishing Co. Second Edition (1996). New York: Springer Publishing Co. Reprinted (2002). New York: Springer Publishing Co.

Kean, Thomas H. et al. (2004). *The 9/11 Commission Report: Final Report of the National Commission on Terrorist Attacks upon the United States.* Washington, DC: National Commission on Terrorist Attacks upon the United States. New York: Norton.

Kedourie, Elie (1966). *Nationalism.* London: Hutchinson & Co.

Kennedy, Paul (2001). Letter to the Editor. *The Wall Street Journal,* October 6.

Kepel, Gilles (1994). *The Revenge of God: The Resurgence of Islam, Christianity and Judaism in the Modern World.* University Park, Pennsylvania: Pennsylvania State University Press.

Kepel, Gilles (2002). *Jihad: The Trail of Political Islam.* Cambridge: Harvard University Press. Reprinted (2004). London: I.B. Tauris.

Kepel, Gilles (2004). *The War for Muslim Minds: Islam and the West.* Cambridge, Massachusetts and London: Belknap Press.

Kepel, Gilles (2005). *The Roots of Radical Islam.* London: Saqi.

Kernberg, Otto F. (1975). *Borderline Conditions and Pathological Narcissism.* New York: Jason Aronson. New Edition (1985). New York: Jason Aronson. Expanded Edition (2002). Northvale, New Jersey: Jason Aronson.

Kernberg, Otto F. (1992). *Aggression in Personality Disorders and Perversions.* New Haven: Yale University Press.

Kernberg, Otto F. (1995). *Love Relations: Normality and Pathology.* New Haven: Yale University Press.

Kernberg, Otto F. (2002). *Borderline Conditions and Pathological Narcissism. Expanded Edition.* Northvale, New Jersey: Jason Aronson.

Kernberg, Otto F. (2003). Sanctioned Social Violence: A Psychoanalytic View. Part I: *International Journal of Psycho-Analysis,* vol. 84, no. 3, pp. 683–698. Part II: *International Journal of Psycho-Analysis,* vol. 84, no. 4, pp. 953–968

Kfir, Nira (2002). Understanding Suicidal Terror Through Humanistic and Existential Psychology. In Stout, Chris E. (Ed.) *The Psychology of Terrorism,* vol. 1, pp. 143–157.

Khalidi, Rashid (2006).The Terrorism Trap. *The New York Times,* July 22.

Khashan, Hilal (2000). *Arabs at the Crossroads: Political Identity and Nationalism.* Gainesville: University Press of Florida.

Khattab, Huda (1987). *Stories from the Muslim World.* Illustrated by Robert Geary. Morristown, New Jersey: Silver Burdett Press.

Khouri, Rami G. (2003). Statement to the U.S. Senate Foreign Relations Committee Hearing: "Iraq—Next Steps: How Can Democratic Institutions Succeed in Iraq and the Middle East?" Wednesday, September 24, 2003. Washington, DC: United States Senate.

Khouri, Rami G. (2004). The Murder of Nicholas Berg. *The Daily Star,* Beirut, May 13.

Kimmel, Michael (2000). *The Gendered Society.* Oxford: Oxford University Press.

Kipling, Rudyard (1917). *The Holy War.* Garden City, New York: Doubleday, Page & Co. Reprinted (1981). London: Methuen.

Klein, Melanie (1930). The Importance of Symbol Formation in the Development of the Ego. *International Journal of Psycho-Analysis,* vol. 11, pp. 24–39. Reprinted (1946). In Klein, Melanie, *Contributions to Psycho-Analysis,* pp. 236–250. London: The Hogarth Press and the Institute of Psycho-Analysis. Reprinted (1975). In Klein, Melanie, *The Writings of Melanie Klein,* vol. 1, *Love, Guilt and Reparation & Other Works, 1921–1945.* London: The Hogarth Press and the Institute of Psycho-Analysis.

Klein, Melanie (1932). *The Psycho-Analysis of Children.* Tr. Alix Strachey. London: Leonard and Virginia Woolf at the Hogarth Press and the Institute of Psycho-Analysis. New Edition (1975) in *The Writings of Melanie Klein,* vol. 2. Revised in collaboration with Alix Strachey by H. A. Thorner. London: The Hogarth Press and the Institute of Psycho-Analysis.

Klein, Melanie (1935). A Contribution to the Psychogenesis of Manic-Depressive States. *International Journal of Psych-Analysis,* vol. 16, pp. 145–174. Reprinted (1975) in Klein, Melanie, *The Writings of Melanie Klein,* vol. 1, *Love, Guilt, and Reparation & Other Works, 1921–1945.* London: The Hogarth Press and the Institute of Psycho-Analysis.

Klein, Melanie (1937). *Love, Hate and Reparation: Two Lectures.* London: Leonard and Virginia Woolf at the Hogarth Press and the Institute of Psycho-Analysis. New Edition (1953). London: The Hogarth Press and the Institute of Psycho-Analysis. Reprinted (1975) in Klein, Melanie, *The Writings of Melanie Klein,* vol. 1, *Love, Guilt, and Reparation & Other Works, 1921–1945.* London: The Hogarth Press and the Institute of Psycho-Analysis.

Klein, Melanie (1946a). *Contributions to Psycho-Analysis.* London: The Hogarth Press and the Institute of Psycho-Analysis. Reprinted (1975) in Klein, Melanie, *The Writings of Melanie Klein,* vol. 3, *Envy and Gratitude and Other Works, 1946–1963.* London: The Hogarth Press and the Institute of Psycho-Analysis.

Klein, Melanie (1946b). Notes on Some Schizoid Mechanisms. *International Journal of Psych-Analysis,* vol. 27, pp. 99–110. Reprinted (1975) in Klein, Melanie, *The Writings of Melanie Klein,* vol. 3, *Envy and Gratitude and Other Works, 1946–1963.* London: The Hogarth Press and the Institute of Psycho-Analysis.

Klein, Melanie (1958). On the Development of Mental Functioning. *International Journal of Psycho-Analysis,* vol. 39, pp. 84–90. Reprinted (1975) in Klein, Melanie, *The Writings of Melanie Klein,* vol. 3, *Envy and Gratitude and Other Works, 1946–1963.* London: The Hogarth Press. New York: Delacorte Press and S. Lawrence. New York: The Free Press.

Klein, Melanie (1959). Our Adult World and Its Roots in Infancy. *Human Relations,* vol. 12, pp. 291–303. Reprinted (1963). In Klein, Melanie, *Our Adult World, and Other Essays.* New York: Basic Books. Reprinted (1975) in Klein, Melanie, *The Writings of*

Melanie Klein, vol. 3, *Envy and Gratitude and Other Works, 1946–1963,* pp. 247–263. London: The Hogarth Press and the Institute of Psycho-Analysis.

Klein, Melanie (1975). *The Writings of Melanie Klein.* Four volumes. Vol. 1. *Love, Guilt, and Reparation & Other Works, 1921–1945.* Intr. R.E. Money-Kyrle. Vol. 2. *The Psycho-Analysis of Children (1932).* Vol. 3. *Envy and Gratitude and Other Works, 1946–1963.* Vol. 4. *Narrative of a Child Analysis: The Conduct of the Psycho-Analysis of Children as Seen in the Treatment of a Ten-Year-Old Boy.* London: The Hogarth Press and the Institute of Psycho-Analysis. Reprinted (1975). New York: Delacorte Press and S. Lawrence. New York: The Free Press. Reprinted (1984). New York: The Free Press. New Edition (1985). Ed. Joan Rivière. New York: W.W. Norton.

Klein, Melanie et al. (1952). *Developments in Psycho-Analysis.* Ed. Joan Rivière. Pref. Ernest Jones. London: The Hogarth Press and the Institute of Psycho-Analysis. Reprinted (1983). New York: Da Capo Press.

Klemer, D.J. (1959). *Chinese Love Poems.* Garden City, New York: Hanover House.

Knutson, Jeanne Nicoll (1981). Social and Psychodynamic Pressures Toward a Negative Identity: The Case of an American Revolutionary Terrorist. In Alexander, Yonah & Gleason, John M. (Eds.) *Behavioral and Quantitative Perspectives on Terrorism.* New York: Pergamon Press.

Kobrin, Nancy H. (2002). A Psychoanalytic Approach to Bin Laden, Political Violence and Islamic Suicidal Terrorism. *Clio's Psyche,* vol. 8, no. 4, pp. 181–184.

Kobrin, Nancy H. (2003). Psychoanalytic Explorations of the New Moors: Converts for Jihad. *Clio's Psyche,* vol. 9, no. 4, pp. 157, 172–187.

Koenigsberg, Richard A. (1975). *Hitler's Ideology: A Study in Psychoanalytic Sociology.* New York: Library of Social Science.

Koestler, Arthur (1949). *Promise and Fulfilment: Palestine, 1917–1949.* London: Macmillan.

Kövecses, Zoltán. (1988). *The Language of Love, the Semantics of Passion in Conversational English.* Lewisburg, Pennsylvania: Bucknell University Press.

Kövecses, Zoltán. (1990). *Emotion Concepts.* New York: Springer© Verlag.

Kövecses, Zoltán. (1991). A Linguist's Quest for Love. *Journal of Social and Personal Relationships,* vol. 8, pp. 77–97.

Kohut, Heinz (1971). *The Analysis of the Self: A Systematic Approach to the Psychoanalytic Treatment of Narcissistic Personality Disorders.* New York: International Universities Press.

Kohut, Heinz (1972). Thoughts on Narcissism and Narcissistic Rage. *The Psychoanalytic Study of the Child,* vol. 27, pp. 360–400. Reprinted (1978). In Kohut, Heinz, *The Search for the Self: Selected Writings of Heinz Kohut, 1950–1978,* vol. 2, pp. 615–658. Ed. & Intr. Paul H. Ornstein. New York: International Universities Press.

Kohut, Heinz (1977). *The Restoration of the Self.* New York: International Universities Press.

Kohut, Heinz (1978). *The Search for the Self: Selected Writings of Heinz Kohut, 1950–1978.* Two volumes. Ed. & Intr. Paul H. Ornstein. New York: International Universities Press.

Korinman, Michel & Laughland, John (Eds.) (2007). *Shia Power: Next Target Iran?* London and Portland: Vallentine Mitchell Academic.

Kovel, Joel (1970). *White Racism: A Psychohistory.* New York: Pantheon Books. Reprinted (1988). London: Free Association Books.

Kristeva, Julia (1987). *In the Beginning Was Love: Psychoanalysis and Faith.* Tr. Arthur Goldhammer. Intr. Otto F. Kernberg. New York: Columbia University Press.

Kristol, William (2007). There Is a Way Forward in Iraq: The Just Verdict for Saddam Should Lead Us to Commit to Victory. *TIME,* vol. 169, no. 3.

Küntzel, Matthias (2003). *Djihad und Judenhass: über den neuen antijüdischen Krieg.* Freiburg: Ça Ira Publications. [German].

Küntzel, Matthias (2007). *Jihad and Jew-Hatred: Islamism, Nazism and the Roots of 9/11.* Tr. Colin Meade. New York: Telos Press.

Kuran, Timur (2001). The Islamic Commercial Crisis: Institutional Roots of Economic Underdevelopment in the Middle East. *Journal of Economic History,* vol. 63, June.

Kuran, Timur (2004). *Islam and Mammon: The Economic Predicaments of Islamism.* Princeton, New Jersey: Princeton University Press.

Kureishi, Hanif (1997). *My Son, the Fanatic.* London: Faber and Faber.

Kurth, James (2002). Confronting the Unipolar Moment: The American Empire and Islamic Terrorism. *Current History,* December.

Kushner, Harvey W. (Ed.) (2002). *Essential Readings on Political Terrorism: Analyses of Problems and Prospects for the 21st Century.* New York: Gordian Knot Books.

Kushner, Harvey W. & Davis, Bart (2004). *Holy War on the Home Front: The Secret Islamic Terror Network in the United States.* New York: Sentinel.

Lachkar, Joan (1992).*The Narcissistic/Borderline Couple: A Psychoanalytic Perspective on Marital Treatment.* New York: Brunner/Mazel. Second Edition (2004). New York: Brunner-Routledge.

Lachkar, Joan (1998) *The Many Faces of Abuse: Treating the Emotional Abuse of High-Functioning Women.* Northvale, New Jersey: Jason Aronson.

Lachkar, Joan (2002). The Psychological Make-Up of a Suicide Bomber. *The Journal of Psychohistory,* vol. 29, no. 4, pp. 349–367.

Lachkar, Joan (2006). The Psychopathology of Terrorism: A Cultural V-Spot. *The Journal of Psychohistory,* vol. 34, no. 2.

Laffin, John (1974). *The Arab Mind: A Need for Understanding.* London: Cassell. Reprinted (1975). As *The Arab Mind Considered: A Need for Understanding.* New York: Taplinger.

Laffin, John (1979). *The Dagger of Islam.* London: Sphere.

Laffin, John (1985). *Know the Middle East.* Gloucester: Alan Sutton.

Laffin, John (1988). *Holy War, Islam Fights.* London: Grafton Books.

Laing, Ronald David (1967). *The Politics of Experience and the Bird of Paradise.* Harmondsworth: Penguin Books. New York: Ballantine Books.

Lance, Peter (2004). *1000 Years for Revenge: International Terrorism and the FBI—the Untold Story.* New York: Regan Books.

Landau, Elaine (2002) *Osama bin Laden: A War Against the West.* Breckenridge, Colorado and Brookfield, Connecticut: Twenty First Century Books.

Landes, Richard Allen (Ed.) (2000). *Encyclopedia of Millennialism and Millennial Movements.* New York: Routledge.

Landes, Richard Allen et al. (Eds.) (2003). *The Apocalyptic Year 1000: Religious Expectation and Social Change, 950–1050.* Oxford and New York: Oxford University Press.

Landes, Richard Allen (2007). Edward Said and the Culture of Honor and Shame: Orientalism and Our Misperceptions of the Arab-Israeli Conflict. *Journal of Israel Studies,* vol. 13, no. 4, pp. 844–858.

Langer, Walter Charles (1972). *The Mind of Adolf Hitler: The Secret Wartime Report.* Foreword by William L. Langer. Afterword by Robert G.L. Waite. New York: Basic Books. Reprinted (1985). New York: New American Library.

Langman, Lauren & Kalekin-Fishman, Devorah (Eds.) (2006). *The Evolution of Alienation: Trauma, Promise, and the Millennium.* Lanham, Maryland: Rowman & Littlefield.

Langman, Lauren & Morris, Douglas (2002). Islamic Terrorism: From Retrenchment to Ressentiment and Beyond. In Kushner, Harvey W. (Ed.) *Essential Readings on Political Terrorism: Analyses of Problems and Prospects for the 21st Century.* New York: Gordian Knot Books.

Laqueur, Walter (1999). *The New Terrorism: Fanaticism and the Arms of Mass Destruction.* Oxford and New York: Oxford University Press.

Lawrence, Bruce B. (1989). *Defenders of God: The Fundamentalist Revolt Against the Modern Age.* New York: Harper & Row.

Lear, Jonathan (1990). *Love and its Place in Nature: A Philosophical Interpretation of Freudian Psychoanalysis.* New York: Farrar, Straus & Giroux. New Edition (1998). New Haven, Connecticut: Yale University Press.

Lee, J.A. (1973). *The Color of Love: And Exploration of the Ways of Loving.* Don Mills, Ontario: New Press.

Levi, Iakov (2004). Why Islamic Terror Now. *Matrix,* Fourth new series, vol. 2, no. 6, pp. 1–16.

Levin, Kenneth (2005). *The Oslo Syndrome: Delusions of a People under Siege.* Hanover, New Hampshire: Smith & Kraus.

Levitt, Theodore (1983). The Globalization of Markets. *Harvard Business Review,* May–June issue, May 1.

Levy, Reuben (1930). *An Introduction to the Sociology of Islam.* London: Williams and Norgate.

Levy, Reuben (1957). *The Social Structure of Islam, Being the Second Edition of the Sociology of Islam.* Cambridge: Cambridge University Press. New Edition (2002). London and New York: Routledge.

Levy, Robert I. (1984). The Emotions in Comparative Perspective. In Klaus R. Scherer & Paul Ekman (Eds.) *Approaches to Emotion* (pp. 387–412). Hillsdale, New Jersey: Lawrence Erlbaum.

Lewis, Bernard (1950). *The Arabs in History.* London and New York: Hutchinson's University Library. Fourth Edition (1966). London: Hutchinson. Sixth Edition (1993). Oxford and New York: Oxford University Press.

Lewis, Bernard (1967). *The Assassins: A Radical Sect in Islam.* London: Weidenfeld and Nicolson. New Edition (1987). Oxford and New York: Oxford University Press.

Lewis, Bernard (1990). The Roots of Muslim Rage: Why So Many Muslims Deeply Resent the West, and Why Their Bitterness Will Not Easily Be Mollified. *The Atlantic Monthly,* vol. 266, no. 3, September, pp. 47–60.

Lewis, Bernard (1995). *The Middle East: 2000 Years of History from the Rise of Christianity to the Present Day.* London: Weidenfeld and Nicolson. Reprinted (1995) as *The Middle East: A Brief History of the Last 2,000 Years.* New York: George Scribner & Sons. British Edition Reprinted (1997). London: Phoenix Press. U.S. Edition Reprinted (1997). New York: Touchstone Books.

Lewis, Bernard (1998). *The Multiple Identities of the Middle East.* London: Weidenfeld and Nicolson. Reprinted (1999). New York: Schocken Books. Reprinted (2001). New York: Schocken Books.

Lewis, Bernard (2001). The Revolt of Islam: When Did the Conflict with the West Begin, and How Could It End? *The New Yorker: Fact,* Annals of Religion, November 19.

Lewis, Bernard (2002). *What Went Wrong? The Clash Between Islam and Modernity in the Middle East.* London: Weidenfeld & Nicolson. Reprinted (2002). As *What Went Wrong? Western Impact and Middle Eastern Response.* Oxford and New York: Oxford University Press. Reprinted (2003). As *What Went Wrong? The Clash Between Islam and Modernity in the Middle East.* New York: Perennial Books.

Lewis, Bernard (2003). *The Crisis of Islam: Holy War and Unholy Terror.* London: Weidenfeld and Nicolson. New York: The Modern Library.

Lewis, Thomas et al. (2000). *A General Theory of Love.* New York: Vintage Books.

Lifton, Robert Jay (1999). *Destroying the World to Save It: Aum Shinrikyo, Apocalyptic Violence, and the New Global Terrorism.* New York: Henry Holt and Co.

Lifton, Robert Jay (2003). *The Superpower Syndrome: America's Apocalyptic Confrontation with the World.* New York: Thunder's Mouth Press. New York: Nation Books.

Lincoln, Bruce (2003). *Holy Terrors: Thinking about Religion after September 11.* Chicago University of Chicago Press. Second Edition (2006). Chicago: University of Chicago Press.

Lincoln, Charles Eric (1961). *The Black Muslims in America.* Foreword by Gordon Allport. Boston: Beacon Press. Revised Edition (1982). Westport, Connecticut: Greenwood Press.

Loewenberg, Peter (1995). *Fantasy and Reality in History.* Oxford and New York: Oxford University Press.

Lohbeck, Kurt (1993). *Holy War, Unholy Victory: Eyewitness to the CIA's Secret War in Afghanistan.* Foreword by Dan Rather. Washington, DC: Regnery Gateway.

Lustick, Ian S. (2006). *Trapped in the War on Terror.* Philadelphia: University of Pennsylvania Press.

Mack, John Edward (2002). Looking Beyond Terrorism: Transcending the Mind of Enmity. In Stout, Chris E. (Ed.) *The Psychology of Terrorism,* vol. 1, pp. 173–184. Westport, Connecticut: Praeger.

Mahler, Margaret S. et al. (1975). *The Psychological Birth of the Human Infant: Symbiosis and Individuation.* New York: Basic Books.

Maikovich, Andrea Kohn (2005). A New Understanding of Terrorism Using Cognitive Dissonance Principles. *Journal for the Theory of Social Behaviour,* vol. 35, no. 4, pp. 373–397.

Main, Mary, Kaplan, Nancy & Cassidy, Jude (1985). Security in Infancy, Childhood, and Adulthood: A Move to the Level of Representation. *Monographs of the Society for Research in Child Development,* vol. 50, no. 1 & 2, pp. 66–104.

Maisami, Mona (2003). Islam and Globalization. *The Fountain Magazine,* no. 43.

Mamdani, Mahmood (2004). *Good Muslim, Bad Muslim: America, the Cold War, and the Roots of Terror.* New York: Pantheon Books.

Mann, David (1997). *Psychotherapy, an Erotic Relationship: Transference and Countertransference Passions.* London and New York: Routledge.

Mann, David (Ed.) (2002). *Love and Hate: Psychoanalytic Perspectives.* Hove, East Sussex, England, UK and New York: Brunner-Routledge.

Mannes, Aaron (2002–2003). A Reformer in Egypt: Aaron Mannes on *Egyptian Political Essays* by Tarek Heggy. *Policy Review,* no. 116, December 2002 and January 2003.

Marcinko, Richard & DeFelice, Jim (2006). *Rogue Warrior—Holy Terror.* New York: Atria Books.

Martin, Richard C. (Ed.) (2004). *Encyclopedia of Islam and the Muslim World.* Two volumes. New York: Macmillan Reference.

Marty, Martin (1994). *Accounting for Fundamentalisms: The Dynamic Character of Movements.* Chicago: University of Chicago Press.

Marty, Martin E. & Appleby, R. Scott. (1993) *Fundamentalisms and Society: Reclaiming the Sciences, the Family and Education.* Chicago: University of Chicago Press.

Marty, Martin E. & Appleby, R. Scott (Eds.) (1991). *Fundamentalisms Observed: A Study Conducted by the American Academy of Arts and Sciences.* Chicago: University of Chicago Press.

Marty, Martin E. & Appleby, R. Scott (Eds.) (1995). *Fundamentalisms Comprehended.* Chicago: University of Chicago Press.

Masterson, James F. (1981). *The Narcissistic and Borderline Disorders: An Integrated Developmental Approach.* New York: Brunner/Mazel.

Masterson, James F. (2000). *The Personality Disorders: A New Look at the Developmental Self and Object Relations Approach: Theory, Diagnosis, Treatment.* Phoenix, Arizona: Zeig, Tucker.

Mayer, Jean-François (2004). Hizb Ut-Tahrir—The Next Al-Qaida, Really? *PSIO Occasional Papers,* 4/2004. Geneva: Program for the Study of International Organizations.

Mayhew, Ben (2006). Between Love and Aggression: The Politics of John Bowlby. *History of the Human Sciences,* vol. 19, no. 4, pp. 19–35.

Mazarr, Michael (2004). The Psychological Sources of Islamic Terrorism: Alienation and Identity in the Arab World. *Policy Review,* no. 125, June–July.

Mazzetti, Mark (2006). Spy Agencies Say Iraq War Worsens Terrorism Threat. *The New York Times,* September 24.

Mazzetti, Mark & Rohde, David (2007). Al Qaeda Chiefs Are Seen to Regain Power. *The New York Times,* February 18.

McCarraher, Eugene (2007). Review of *God Is Not Great: How Religion Poisons Everything* by Christopher Hitchens. *Commonweal: A Review of Religion, Politics and Culture,* vol. 134, no. 12, June 15.

McCauley, Clark R. (2002). Psychological Issues in Understanding Terrorism and the Response to Terrorism. In Stout, Chris (Ed.) *The Psychology of Terrorism,* vol. 3, pp. 3–30. Westport, Connecticut: Praeger.

McCauley, Clark R. (Ed.) (1991). *Terrorism Research and Public Policy.* London, England and Portland, Oregon: Frank Cass.

McCauley, Clark R. & Segal, Mary E. (1989). Terrorist Individuals and Terrorist Groups: The Normal Psychology of Extreme Behavior. In Groebel, Jo & Goldstein, Jeffrey H. (Eds.) *Terrorism: Psychological Perspectives,* pp. 41–64. Seville, Spain: Publicaciones de la Universidad de Sevilla.

McFaul, Michael, Milani, Abbas & Diamond, Larry (2006–2007. A Win-Win U.S. Strategy for Dealing with Iran. *The Washington Quarterly,* vol. 30, no. 1, Winter, pp. 121–138.

McNaughton, William (1971). *The Book of Songs.* New York: Twayne Publishers.

Mead, Walter Russell (2004). *Power, Terror, Peace, and War: America's Grand Strategy in a World at Risk.* New York: Knopf. Reprinted (2005). New York: Vintage Books.

Merari, Ariel (1990). The Readiness to Kill and Die: Suicidal Terrorism in the Middle East. In Reich, Walter (Ed.) *Origins of Terrorism: Psychologies, Ideologies, Theologies, States of Mind.* Washington, DC: Woodrow Wilson International Center for Scholars. Cambridge and New York: Cambridge University Press. New Edition (1998). Washington: Woodrow Wilson Center Press. Baltimore: Johns Hopkins University Press.

Miller, Alice (1983). *For Your Own Good: Hidden Cruelty in Child-Rearing and the Roots of Violence.* Tr. Hildegarde and Hunter Hannum. New York: Farrar, Straus and Giroux. Third Edition (1990). New York: Noonday Press. Fourth Edition (2002). New York: Farrar, Straus and Giroux.

Miller, Alice (1998). The Political Consequences of Child Abuse. *The Journal of Psychohistory,* vol. 26, no. 2, pp. 573–585.

Miller, Alice (2005). *The Body Never Lies: The Lingering Effects of Cruel Parenting.* New York: W.W. Norton.

Milner, Marion Blackett [Joanna Field] (1934). *A Life of One's Own.* London: Chatto & Windus. New Edition (1952). Harmondsworth: Pelican Books. New Edition (1981). Los Angeles: J.P. Tarcher.

Milner, Marion Blackett [Joanna Field] (1937). *An Experiment in Leisure: Reflections and Reminiscences.* London: Chatto & Windus. New Edition (1987). Foreword by Gabriele Lusser Rico. Los Angeles: J.P. Tarcher.

Milner, Marion Blackett [Joanna Field] (1987). *Eternity's Sunrise.* London: Virago Books. Los Angeles: J.P. Tarcher.

Mitch, Frank (2002). *Understanding September 11th: Answering Questions about the Attacks on America.* New York: Viking Press.

Mitchell, Stephen A. (2002). *Can Love Last? The Fate of Romance over Time.* New York: W.W. Norton.

Mockaitis, Thomas R. (2006). *The "New" Terrorism: Myths and Reality.* Westport, Connecticut: Praeger Security International.

Modell, Arnold H. (1969). *Object Love and Reality.* London: The Hogarth Press and the Institute of Psycho-Analysis. New York: International Universities Press.

Modood, Tariq (2000). *The Future of Multi-Ethnic Britain: The Parekh Report.* A Report by the Commission on the Future of Multi-Ethnic Britain. London: Runnymede Trust.

Moghaddam, Fathali M. (2005). The Staircase to Terrorism: A Psychological Exploration. *American Psychologist,* vol. 60, pp. 161–169.

Moghaddam, Fathali M. & Marsella, Anthony J. (Eds.) (2004). *Understanding Terrorism: Psychosocial Roots, Consequences, and Interventions.* Washington, DC: American Psychological Association.

Mohamed, Ahmed (2003). *An Islamic Conspiracy for World Conquest.* Napa, California: Lulu Press.

Mohammadi, Ali & Saltford, John (Eds.) (2002). *Islam Encountering Globalization.* London and New York: Routledge.

Morse, Chuck (2003). *The Nazi Connection to Islamic Terrorism: Adolf Hitler and Haj Amin Al-Husseini.* Lincoln, Nebraska: iUniverse.

Muhibbu-Din, M.A. (Ed.) (2006). *Globalization and Terrorism: The Response of Islamic Scholarship.* Abuja: Nigeria Association of Teachers of Arabic and Islamic Studies.

Muñoz, J. (2001). El chico del círculo. *El Correo,* Bilbao, October 10. [Spanish].

Muravchik, Joshua (2007). The Past, Present, and Future of Neoconservatism. *Commentary,* October 1.

Mylroie, Laurie (1995–1996). The World Trade Center Bomb: Who Is Ramzi Yousef? And Why It Matters. *The National Interest,* no. 42, Winter.

Narayan Swamy, M.R. (1994). *Tigers of Lanka: From Boys to Guerrillas.* Delhi: Konark Publishers. New Edition (2002). Delhi: Konark Publishers.

Nassar, Jamal Raji (2005). *Globalization and Terrorism: The Migration of Dreams and Nightmares.* Lanham, Maryland: Rowman & Littlefield.

Nathanson, Donald L. (1992). *Shame and Pride: Affect, Sex, and the Birth of the Self.* New York: W.W. Norton.

Neiwert, David A. (1999). *In God's Country: The Patriot Movement and the Pacific Northwest.* Pullman, Washington: Washington State University Press.

New, David S. (2002). *Holy War: The Rise of Militant Christian, Jewish, and Islamic Fundamentalism.* Jefferson, North Carolina: McFarland & Co.

Niethammer, Lutz (1979). Male Fantasies: An Argument for and with an Important New Study in History and Psychoanalysis. *History Workshop Journal,* vol. 7, no. 1, pp. 176–186.

Nigosian, Solomon Alexander (2004). *Islam: Its History, Teaching, and Practices.* Bloomington, Indiana: Indiana University Press.

Noll, Richard (1994). *The Jung Cult: Origins of a Charismatic Movement.* Princeton, New Jersey: Princeton University Press. Reprinted (1997). New York: The Free Press.

Noll, Richard (1997). *The Aryan Christ: The Secret Life of Carl Jung.* New York: Random House.

Norval, Morgan (1999) *Triumph of Disorder: Islamic Fundamentalism, the New Face of War.* New York: Sligo Press.

Nunn, Sam (2004). Thinking the Inevitable: Suicide Attacks in America and the Design of Effective Public Safety Policies. *Journal of Homeland Security and Emergency Management,* vol. 1, no. 4, Article 401.

Nussbaum, Martha C. (2003). Dr. True Self. A review of *Winnicott: Life and Work* by F. Robert Rodman. *The New Republic,* no. 4632, pp. 34–38.

O'Brien, Conor Cruise (1986). *The Siege: The Saga of Israel and Zionism.* New York: Simon and Schuster.

O'Neill, Bard E. (1990). *Insurgency & Terrorism: Inside Modern Revolutionary Warfare.* Washington, DC: Brassey's.

O'Neill, Bard E. (2005). *Insurgency & Terrorism: From Revolution to Apocalypse.* Washington, DC: Potomac Books.

O'Neill, Bard E. et al. (Eds.) (1980). *Insurgency in the Modern World.* Boulder, Colorado: Westview Press.

O'Sullivan, Noel (Ed.) (1986). *Terrorism, Ideology, and Revolution.* Boulder, Colorado: Westview Press.

Oates, Wayne Edward (1973).*The Psychology of Religion.* Waco, Texas: Word Books.

Ohnuki-Tierney, Emiko (2006). *Kamikaze Diaries: Reflections of Japanese Student Soldiers.* Chicago: University of Chicago Press.

Pagels, Elaine (1995). *The Origins of Satan.* London: Allen Lane. Harmondsworth and New York: Penguin Press.

Palmer, Monte & Princess Palmer (2004). *At the Heart of Terror: Islam, Jihadists, and America's War on Terrorism.* Lanham, Maryland: Rowman & Littlefield.

Palmer, Monte & Princess Palmer (2008). *Islamic Extremism: Causes, Diversity, and Challenges.* Lanham, Maryland: Rowman & Littlefield.

Pape, Robert Anthony (2003). The Strategic Logic of Suicide Terrorism. *American Political Science Review,* vol. 97, pp. 343–361.

Pape, Robert Anthony (2005). *Dying to Win: The Strategic Logic of Suicide Terrorism.* New York: Random House. Reprinted (2006). New York: Random House Trade Paperbacks.

Pappe, Ilan (2006) *The Ethnic Cleansing of Palestine.* London: Oneworld Publishing.

Paris, Joel (1994). *Borderline Personality Disorder: A Multidimensional Approach.* Washington, DC: American Psychiatric Press.

Patai, Raphael (1973). *The Arab Mind.* New York: Charles Scribner's Sons. New Edition (2002). With an Introduction by Norvell B. De Atkine. New York: Hatherleigh Press.

Pedahzur, Ami (Ed.) (2006). *Root Causes of Suicide Terrorism: Globalization of Martyrdom.* New York: Routledge.

Peled, Avi (2008). *NeuroAnalysis: Bridging the Gap between Neuroscience, Psychoanalysis and Psychiatry.* Hove and New York: Routledge.

Pelletiere, Stephen C. (1993). *Islamic Terror and the West: A Question of Priorities.* Carlisle Barracks, Pennsylvania: Strategic Studies Institute, United States Army War College.

Perlman, Diane (2002). Intersubjective Dimension of Terrorism and its Transcendence. In Stout, Chris E. (Ed.). *The Psychology of Terrorism,* vol. 1, pp. 19–49. Westport, Connecticut: Praeger.

Perry, Alex (2007). Saving Somalia: As the U.S. Strikes Al-Qaeda, a New Government Tries to Restore Order. Here's What It Will Take. *TIME,* vol. 169, no. 4.

Person, Ethel Spector (1988). *Dreams of Love and Fateful Encounters: The Power of Romantic Passion.* New York: W.W. Norton.

Peters, Francis E. (1994). *Muhammad and the Origins of Islam.* Albany, New York: State University of New York Press.

Peters, Ralph (2006). *Never Quit the Fight.* Mechanicsburg, Pennsylvania: Stackpole Books.

Phillips, Melanie (2006). *Londonistan: How Britain Is Creating a Terror State Within.* London: Gibson Square. New York: Encounter Books. New Edition (2006) updated with a new preface. New York: Encounter Books.

Phillips, Melanie (2007). Reflections on *Londonistan.* Symposium: Islam, British Society and the Islamic Threat. *Posen Papers in Contemporary Antisemitism,* No. 7, pp. 1–6. Jerusalem: The Vidal Sassoon International Study for the Study of Antisemitism, The Hebrew University of Jerusalem.

Pipes, Daniel (1997). Review of *Within the Circle: Parents and Children in an Arab Village* by Andrea Rugh. *Middle East Quarterly,* December.

Pipes, Daniel (1999). Review of *The New Jackals* by Simon Reeve. *The Washington Times,* December 5.

Pipes, Daniel (2002). *Militant Islam Reaches America.* New York: W. W. Norton.

Piven, Jerry S. (2006). Narcissism, Sexuality, and Psyche in Terrorist Theology. *The Psychoanalytic Review,* vol. 93, no. 2, pp. 231–265.

Pizzey, Erin (1998). *The Emotional Terrorist and the Violence-Prone.* Ottawa: Commoners' Publishing.

Pohly, Michael & Duran, Khalid (2001). *Osama bin Laden und der internationale Terrorismus.* Vorwort von Rolf Tophoven. Munich: Ullstein. [German].

Pollan, Michael (2001). *The Botany of Desire: A Plant's Eye View of the World.* New York: Random House.

Polo, Marco (1928). *Il Milione.* Florence: Leo Samuel Olschki. [Italian].

Post, Jerrold M. (1991). Saddam Hussein of Iraq: A Political Psychology Profile. *Political Psychology,* vol. 12, no. 2, pp. 279–289.

Post, Jerrold M. (1998). Terrorist Psycho-Logic: Terrorist Behavior as a Product of Psychological Forces. In Reich, Walter (Ed.) *Origins of Terrorism: Psychologies, Ideologies, Theologies, States of Mind.* New Edition. Washington: Woodrow Wilson Center Press. Baltimore: Johns Hopkins University Press.

Post, Jerrold M. (Ed.) (2003). *The Psychological Assessment of Political Leaders: With Profiles of Saddam Hussein and Bill Clinton.* Ann Arbor: University of Michigan Press.

Pruyser, Paul W. (1975). What Splits in "Splitting"? A Scrutiny of the Concept of Splitting in Psychoanalysis and Psychiatry. *Bulletin of the Menninger Clinic,* vol. 39, no. 1, pp. 1–46.

Pruyser, Paul W. (1991). *Religion in Psychodynamic Perspective: The Contributions of Paul W. Pruyser.* Eds. H. Newton Malony & Bernard Spilka. Oxford and New York: Oxford University Press.

Public Broadcasting Service (2001). *Frontline—In Search of bin Laden.* Videocassette. Boston: WGBH.

Qureshi, Emran & Sells, Michael A. (Eds.) (2003). *The New Crusades: Constructing the Muslim Enemy.* New York: Columbia University Press.

Qutb, Muhammad al- (1968). *Islam, the Misunderstood Religion.* Delhi: Board of Islamic Publications. Reprinted (1997). Salmiah, Kuwait: International Islamic Book Center.

Qutb, Sayyid al- (1953). *Social Justice in Islam.* Tr. John B. Hardie. Washington: American Council of Learned Societies. Reprinted (1970). New York: Octagon Books.

Qutb, Sayyid al- (1977). *Islam and Universal Peace.* Indianapolis: American Trust Publications. Reprinted (1993). Plainfield, Indiana: American Trust Publications.

Qutb, Sayyid al- (2006). *Basic Principles of the Islamic Worldview.* Tr. Rami David. Preface by Hamid Algar. North Haledon, New Jersey: Islamic Publications International.

Rachman, Arnold William (1997). *Sándor Ferenczi: The Psychotherapist of Tenderness and Passion.* Northvale, New Jersey: Jason Aronson.

Ramazani, Rouhollah K. (1982). *The United States and Iran: The Patterns of Influence.* New York: Praeger.

Rank, Otto (1929). *The Trauma of Birth.* London: Kegan Paul, Trench, Trubner. New York: Harcourt, Brace. New Edition (1952). New York: R. Brunner. New Edition (1993). With a New Introduction by E. James Lieberman. New York: Dover.

Raphaeli, Nimrod (2006). The Revival of Cultural Life in Iraq. *Inquiry and Analysis Series,* The Middle East Media Research Institute, no. 279, June 6.

Redlich, Frederick Carl (1999). *Hitler: Diagnosis of a Destructive Prophet.* New York: Oxford University Press.

Reeve, Simon S. (1998). *The New Jackals: Ramzi Yousef, Osama Bin Laden and the Future of Terrorism.* London: Andre Deutsch. Reprinted (1999). Boston: Northeastern University Press.

Reich, Walter (Ed.) (1990). *Origins of Terrorism: Psychologies, Ideologies, Theologies, States of Mind.* Washington, DC: Woodrow Wilson International Center for Scholars. Cambridge and New York: Cambridge University Press. New Edition (1998). Washington: Woodrow Wilson Center Press. Baltimore: Johns Hopkins University Press.

Reik, Theodor (1944). *A Psychologist Looks at Love.* New York: Farrar & Rinehart.

Reik, Theodor (1949). *Of Love and Lust: On the Psychoanalysis of Romantic and Sexual Emotions.* New York: Farrar, Straus & Giroux.

Renshon, Stanley Allen (2004). *In His Father's Shadow: The Transformations of George W. Bush.* New York: Palgrave Macmillan.

Renshon, Stanley Allen (2006). *Political Psychology* blog online.

Reuter, Christoph (2004). *My Life Is a Weapon: A Modern History of Suicide Bombing.* Tr. Helena Ragg-Kirkby. Princeton, New Jersey: Princeton University Press.

Reveron, Derek S. & Murer. Jeffrey Stevenson (Eds.) (2006). *Flashpoints in the War on Terrorism.* New York and London: Routledge.

Rholes, W. Steven & Simpson, Jeffry A. (Eds.) (2006). *Adult Attachment: Theory, Research, and Clinical Implications.* London: Karnac Books.

Richardson, Louise (2005). Blasts from the Past. London: *Financial Times Magazine,* July 2–3.

Ricks, Thomas E. (2006). *Fiasco: The American Military Adventure in Iraq.* New York: Penguin Press. London: Allen Lane.

Rizzuto, Ana-Maria (1979). *The Birth of the Living God: A Psychoanalytic Study.* Chicago: University of Chicago Press.

Rizzuto, Ana-Maria et al. (2004). *The Dynamics of Human Aggression: Theoretical Foundations, Clinical Applications.* New York: Brunner-Routledge.

Robbins, Thomas & Palmer, Susan J. (Eds.) (1997). *Millennium, Messiahs, and Mayhem: Contemporary Apocalyptic Movements.* London and New York: Routledge.

Robins, Robert S., Post, Jerrold M. (1997). *Political Paranoia: The Psychopolitics of Hatred.* New Haven: Yale University Press.

Robinson, Adam (2001). *Bin Laden: Behind the Mask of The Terrorist.* Edinburgh: Mainstream Publishing Company. Reprinted (2002). New York: Arcade Publishing.

Robinson, Paul (1987). The Women They Feared. Review of *Male Fantasies* by Klaus Theweleit. *The New York Times Book Review,* June 21.

Rodman, F. Robert (2003). *Winnicott: Life and Work.* New York: Perseus Publishing.

Rokeach, Milton (1960). *The Open and the Closed Mind.* New York: Basic Books.

Rosenbaum, Ron (1998). *Explaining Hitler: The Search for the Origins of His Evil.* New York: Random House.

Rosenfeld, Herbert (1971). A Clinical Approach to the Psychoanalytic Theory of the Life and Death Instincts: An Investigation into the Aggressive Aspects of Narcissism. *International Journal of Psycho-Analysis,* vol. 52, pp. 169–178.

Rosenfeld, Herbert (1987). Destructive Narcissism and the Death Instinct. In Rosenfeld, Herbert, *Impasse and Interpretation.* London: Tavistock.

Roy, Olivier (1992). *L'échec de l'islam politique.* Paris: Editions du Seuil. [French].

Roy, Olivier (1994). *The Failure of Political Islam.* Tr. Carol Volk. Cambridge, Massachusetts: Harvard University Press.

Roy, Olivier (2004). *Globalized Islam: The Search for a New Ummah.* New York: Columbia University Press. London: Hurst.

Rubin, Barry (1980). *Paved with Good Intentions: The American Experience and Iran.* New York: Oxford University Press. Reprinted (1981). New York: Viking Press.

Rubin, Zick (1973). *Liking and Loving: An Invitation to Social Psychology.* New York: Holt, Rinehart, and Winston.

Ruby, Charles L. (2002). The Definition of Terrorism; Are Terrorists Mentally Deranged? *Analyses of Social Issues and Public Policy,* vol. 2, no. 1, pp. 9–26.

Rudnytsky, Peter L. et al. (Eds.) (1996). *Ferenczi's Turn in Psychoanalysis.* New York: New York University Press.

Rugh, Andrea B. (1984). *Family in Contemporary Egypt.* Syracuse, New York: Syracuse University Press.

Rugh, Andrea B. (1997). *Within the Circle: Parents and Children in an Arab Village.* New York: Columbia University Press.

Russell, Bertrand (1961). *Has Man a Future?* London: George Allen & Unwin. Reprinted (1962). New York: Simon and Schuster. Reprinted (1984). Westport, Connecticut: Greenwood Press.

Sadeghian, Abbas (2006). *Sword and Seizure: Muhammad's Epilepsy and the Creation of Islam.* Enumclaw, Washington: Annotation Press.

Safire, William (2006). Language: Islamofascism, Anyone? *International Herald Tribune,* Sunday, October 1.

Safouan, Moustapha (2007). *Why Are the Arabs Not Free?* Oxford: Basil Blackwell.

Sageman, Marc (2004). *Understanding Terror Networks.* Philadelphia: University of Pennsylvania Press.

Said, Edward W. (1978). *Orientalism.* New York: Pantheon Books.

Said, Edward W. (2001). The Clash of Ignorance. *The Nation,* October 22, Vol. 273, no. 12, pp. 11–14.

Samiuddin, Abida & Khanam, Rashida (Eds.) (2002). *Muslim Feminism and Feminist Movement.* New Delhi: Global Vision Publishing House.

Savodnik, Irwin (2004). Shrinking the President: A Mind Is a Dangerous Thing to Psychoanalyze. Review of *Bush on the Couch* by Justin Frank. *The Weekly Standard,* vol. 10, no. 3, September 27.

Sayers, Janet (2004). Intersubjective Winnicott. *American Imago,* vol. 61, no. 4, pp. 519–525.

Scardino, Albert (2005). 1-0 in the Propaganda War. *The Guardian,* February 4.

Scherer, Klaus R. & Ekman, Paul (Eds.) (1984). *Approaches to Emotion.* Hillsdale, New Jersey: Lawrence Erlbaum.

Scheff, Thomas (1994). *Bloody Revenge: Emotions, Nationalism, and War.* Boulder, Colorado: Westview Press.

Schiffer, Irvine (1973). *Charisma: A Psychoanalytic Look at Mass Society.* Toronto: University of Toronto Press.

Schneider, Stanley (2002). Fundamentalism and Paranoia in Groups and Society. *Group,* vol. 26, pp. 17–27.

Schneider, Stanley & Weinberg, Haim (Eds.) (2003). *The Large Group Re-Visited: The Herd, Primal Horde, Crowds and Masses.* Foreword by Malcolm Pines. London and New York: Jessica Kingsley.

Schwaab, Edleff H. (1992). *Hitler's Mind: A Plunge into Madness.* Foreword by Peter H. Wolff. New York: Praeger.

Schwartz, Stephen (2002). *The Two Faces of Islam: The House of Sa'ud from Tradition to Terror.* New York: Doubleday.

Schweitzer, Yoram & Shay, Shaul (2003).*The Globalization of Terror: The Al-Qaida Challenge and the Response of the International Community.* New Brunswick, New Jersey: Transaction Books.

Segal, Hanna (1957). Notes on Symbol Formation. *International Journal of Psycho-Analysis,* vol. 38, pp. 391–397. Reprinted in Segal, Hanna (1981). *Melanie Klein,* pp. 49–65. Harmondsworth and New York: Penguin Books.

Segal, Hanna (1981). *Melanie Klein.* Harmondsworth and New York: Penguin Books.

Selbie, William Boothby (1924). *The Psychology of Religion.* Oxford: The Clarendon Press.

Sennett, Richard & Cobb, Jonathan (1972). *The Hidden Injuries of Class.* New York: Knopf.

Serrano, Miguel (1966). *C. G. Jung and Hermann Hesse: A Record of Two Friendships.* Tr. Frank MacShane. New York: Schocken Books.

Sfar, Mondher (2002). *Le spectre du terrorisme: déclarations, interviews et témoignages sur Oussama Ben Laden.* Paris, France: Editions Sfar. [French].

Shaham, Ron (Ed.) (2006). *Law, Custom, and Statute in the Muslim World: Studies in Honor of Aharon Layish.* Leiden and Boston: Brill.

Shane, Estelle & Shane, Morton (1989). Mahler, Kohut, and Infant Research: Some Comparisons. In Detrick, Douglas W. & Detrick, Susan P., *Self Psychology: Comparisons and Contrasts.* Hillsdale, New Jersey: The Analytic Press.

Sharma, Rajeev (1999). *Pak Proxy War: A Story of ISI, Bin Laden, and Kargil.* Foreword by N.C. Suri. New Delhi: Kaveri Books.

Shaver, Phillip R. & Hazan, Cindy (1994). Attachment. In Ann L. Weber & John H. Harvey (Eds.) *Perspectives on Close Relationships,* pp. 110–130. New York: Allyn & Bacon.

Shaver, Phillip R. et al. (1988). Love as Attachment: The Integration of Three Behavioral Systems. In Robert J. Sternberg & Michael L. Barnes (Eds.) *The Psychology of Love.* New Haven, Connecticut: Yale University Press.

Shaver, Phillip R. et al. (1992). Cross-Cultural Similarities and Differences in Emotion and Its Representation: A Prototype Approach. *Review of Personality and Social Psychology,* vol. 13, pp. 175–212. Reprinted (1997) in Jenkins, Jennifer M. et al. (Eds.). *Human Emotions: A Reader.* Oxford, England: Blackwell.

Shaver, Phillip R. et al. (1987). Emotion Knowledge: Further Explorations of a Prototype Approach. *Journal of Personality and Social Psychology,* vol. 52, pp. 1061–1086.

Shay, Shaul (2004). *The Shahids: Islam and Suicide Attacks.* Foreword by Aharon Ze'evi Farkash. Tr. Rachel Liberman. New Brunswick, New Jersey: Transaction Publishers.

Shay, Shaul (2005a). *The Red Sea Terror Triangle: Sudan, Somalia, Yemen, and Islamic Terror.* Tr. Rachel Liberman. New Brunswick, New Jersey: Transaction Publishers.

Shay, Shaul (2005b). *The Axis of Evil: Iran, Hizballah and the Palestinian Terror.* New Brunswick, New Jersey: Transaction Publishers.

Shay, Shaul (2006). *Islamic Terror and the Balkans.* New Brunswick, New Jersey: Transaction Publishers.

Sheftall, Mordecai G. (2005). *Blossoms in the Wind: Human Legacies of the Kamikaze.* New York: NAL Caliber.

Shoebat, Walid (2005). *Why I Left Jihad: The Root of Terrorism and the Rise of Islam.* Ed. June S. Neal. United States: Top Executive Media.

Sick, Gary (1985). *All Fall Down: America's Tragic Encounter with Iran.* New York: Random House. Reprinted (1986). New York: Penguin Books.

Simon, Steven (2000). *The New Terrorism and the Peace Process.* Ramat Gan, Israel: The Begin-Sadat Center for Strategic Studies, Bar-Ilan University.

Simons, Thomas W., Jr. (2003). *Islam in a Globalizing World.* Stanford, California: Stanford University Press.

Singer, Irving (1984–1987). *The Nature of Love.* Three volumes. Chicago: The University of Chicago Press.

Sivan, Emmanuel (1990). *Radical Islam: Medieval Theology and Modern Politics.* New Haven, Connecticut: Yale University Press.

Skaine, Rosemarie (2006). *Female Suicide Bombers.* Jefferson, North Carolina: McFarland & Co.

Smith, David Livingston (2007). *The Most Dangerous Animal: Human Nature and the Origins of War.* New York: St. Martin's Press.

Smith, Joseph H. & Handelman, Susan A. (Eds.) (1989). *Psychoanalysis and Religion.* Baltimore: Johns Hopkins University Press.

Sofsky, Wolfgang. (1999). *The Order of Terror: The Concentration Camp.* Princeton, New Jersey: Princeton University Press.

Solms, Mark (1997). *The Neuropsychology of Dreams: A Clinico-Anatomical Study.* Mahwah, New Jersey: L. Erlbaum Associates.

Solms, Mark & Turnbull, Oliver (2002). *The Brain and the Inner World: An Introduction to the Neuroscience of Subjective Experience.* Foreword by Oliver Sacks. New York: Other Press.

Sonnenberg, Stephen M. (2005). On: The Relevance of Psychoanalysis to an Understanding of Terrorism. *International Journal of Psycho-Analysis,* vol. 86, pp. 1479–1480.

Sonuga-Barke, Edmund et al. (1998). The Mental Health of Muslim Mothers in Extended Families Living in Britain: The Impact of Intergenerational Disagreement on Anxiety and Depression. *British Journal of Clinical Psychology,* vol. 37, pp. 399–408.

Sookhdeo, Patrick (2005). Will London Burn Too? *The Spectator,* November 12.

Spencer, Robert (2003). *Onward Muslim Soldiers: How Jihad Still Threatens America and the West.* Washington, DC: Regnery Publications.

Stapley, Lionel F. (2006a). *Globalization and Terrorism: Death of a Way of Life.* London: Karnac Books.

Stapley, Lionel F. (2006b). *Individuals, Groups, and Organizations Beneath the Surface: An Introduction.* London: Karnac Books.

Starbuck, Edwin Diller (1897). Some Aspects of Religious Growth. *American Journal of Psychology,* vol. 9, no. 1.

Starbuck, Edwin Diller (1901). *The Psychology of Religion: An Empirical Study of the Growth of Religious Consciousness.* London: Walter Scott Publishing Co. New York: Charles Scribner's Sons. Third Edition (1911). *The Psychology of Religion.* London: Walter Scott Publishing Co. New York: Charles Scribner's Sons.

Staub, Ervin (2002). Notes on Terrorism: Origins and Prevention. *Peace and Conflict: Journal of Peace Psychology,* vol. 8, no. 3, pp. 207–214.

Stein, Howard F. & Niederland, William G. (Eds.) (1989). *Maps for the Mind: Readings in Psychogeography.* Norman, Oklahoma: University of Oklahoma Press.

Stein, Ruth (2002). Evil as Love and Liberation: The Mind of a Suicidal Religious Terrorist. *Psychoanalytic Dialogues: A Journal of Relational Perspectives,* vol. 12, no. 3, pp. 393–420. Reprinted (2002). In Piven, Jerry S. et al. (Eds.) *Terror and Apocalypse,* vol. 2 of *Psychological Undercurrents of History.* Lincoln, Nebraska: iUniverse. Reprinted (2003). In Moss, Donald (Ed.) *Hating in the First Person Plural: Psychoanalytic Essays on Racism, Homophobia, Misogyny, and Terror,* pp. 281–310. New York: Other Press. Reprinted (2004). In Piven, Jerry S. et al. (Eds.) *Terrorism, Jihad and Sacred Vengeance.* Giessen: Psychosozial-Verlag.

Stein, Samuel M. (Ed.) (1999). *Beyond Belief: Psychotherapy and Religion.* Foreword by Robert D. Hinshelwood. London: Karnac Books.

Steinberg, Blema S. (1996). *Shame and Humiliation: Presidential Decision Making on Vietnam.* Pittsburgh: University of Pittsburgh Press.

Steiner, John (1987). The Interplay between Pathological Organizations and the Paranoid-Schizoid and Depressive Positions. *International Journal of Psycho-Analysis,* vol. 68, pp. 69–80. Reprinted in Spillius, Elizabeth Bott (Ed.) (1988). *Melanie Klein Today: Developments in Theory and Practice,* vol. 1, pp. 324–342. London and New York: Routledge.

Steiner, John (1994). *Psychic Retreats: Pathological Organizations in Psychotic, Neurotic and Borderline Patients.* London and New York: Routledge.

Stensson, Jan (1999). Trauma and Basic Trust: Editorial. *International Forum of Psycho-Analysis,* vol. 8, no. 1, pp. 1–2.

Stern, Daniel N. (1985). *The Interpersonal World of the Infant: A View from Psychoanalysis and Developmental Psychology.* New York: Basic Books.

Stern, Jessica (1999). *The Ultimate Terrorists.* Cambridge, Massachusetts: Harvard University Press.

Stern, Jessica (2003). *Terror in the Name of God: Why Religious Militants Kill.* New York: Harpercollins.

Stern, Jessica (2004). Holy Avengers. *Financial Times Magazine,* June 12.

Sternberg, Robert J. (1986). A Triangular Theory of Love. *Psychological Review,* vol. 93, pp. 119–135.

Sternberg, Robert J. & Barnes, Michael L. (Eds.) (1988). *The Psychology of Love.* New Haven: Yale University Press.

Stierlin, Helm (1975). *Adolf Hitler: Familienperspektiven.* Frankfurt on the Main: Suhrkamp. [German].

Stierlin, Helm (1977). *Adolf Hitler: Family Perspectives.* New York: The Psychohistory Press.

Stille, Alexander (2002). Radical New Views of Islam and the Origins of the Koran. *The New York Times,* March 2.

Stoller, Robert J. (1975). *Perversion: The Erotic Form of Hatred.* New York: Pantheon Books. Reprinted (1986). Washington, DC: American Psychiatric Press. London: Maresfield.

Stout, Chris E. (Ed.) (2002). *The Psychology of Terrorism.* Four volumes. Vol. 1. *A Public Understanding.* Vol. 2. *Clinical Aspects and Response.* Vol. 3. *Theoretical Understandings and Perspectives.* Vol. 4. *Programs and Practices in Response and Prevention.* Foreword by Klaus Schwab. Westport, Connecticut: Praeger. Condensed Edition (2004). *The Psychology of Terrorism: Coping with the Continuing Threat.* One Volume. Westport, Connecticut: Praeger.

Strozier, Charles B. (1994).*Apocalypse: On the Psychology of Fundamentalism in America.* Boston: Beacon Press.

Sucharov, Mira (2005). *The International Self: Psychoanalysis and the Search for Israeli-Palestinian Peace.* Albany, New York: State University of New York Press.

Suskind, Ron (2004). Faith, Certainty and the Presidency of George W. Bush. *The New York Times Magazine,* October 17.

Sutherland, John D. (1994) *The Autonomous Self: The Work of John D. Sutherland.* Ed. Jill Savege Scharff. Northvale, New Jersey: Jason Aronson. Reprinted (1994). Lanham, Maryland: Rowman and Littlefield.

Sutherland, John D. (2007). *The Psychodynamic Image: John D. Sutherland on Self in Society.* Ed. Jill Savege Scharff. London: Routledge.

Suttie, Ian Dishart (1935). *The Origins of Love and Hate.* London: Kegan Paul, Trench, Trubner. Reprinted (1952). New York: Julian Press. New Edition (1988). Foreword by John Bowlby. Intr. Dorothy Heard. London: Free Association Books. Reprinted (1999). London: Free Association Books.

Sutton, Philip & Vertigans, Stephen (2005). *Resurgent Islam: A Sociological Approach.* Cambridge, England, UK and Malden, Massachusetts: Polity.

Symington, Neville. (1994). *Psychoanalysis and Religion.* New York: Cassell.

Taheri, Amir (1987). *Holy Terror: The Inside Story of Islamic Terrorism.* London: Hutchinson.

Taheri, Amir (1988). *Nest of Spies: America's Journey to Disaster in Iran.* New York: Pantheon Books.

Taheri, Amir (2004). Islam and Democracy: The Impossible Union. *The Sunday Times,* May 23.

Taheri, Amir (2005). The Prez and the Hit Squad. *The New York Post.*

Taheri, Amir (2006). A Colour Code for Iran's "Infidels." *The National Post,* May 19.

Tamari, Salim (2002). Narratives of Exile. *Palestine–Israel Journal of Politics, Economics and Culture,* vol. 9, no. 4, pp. 101–109.

Tan, Andrew & Ramakrishna, Kumar (Eds.) (2002). *The New Terrorism: Anatomy, Trends, and Counter-Strategies.* Singapore: Eastern Universities Press.

Taylor, Charles. (1992). *Multiculturalism and the Politics of Recognition.* Princeton, New Jersey: Princeton University Press.

Taylor, Max & Horgan, John (Eds.) (2000). *The Future of Terrorism.* London and Portland: Frank Cass.

Tenet, George John & Harlow, Bill (2007). *At the Center of the Storm: My Years at the CIA.* New York: HarperCollins.

Theweleit, Klaus (1977–1978). *Männerphantasien.* Frankfurt on the Main: Verlag Roter Stern. [German].

Theweleit, Klaus (1987–1989). *Male Fantasies.* Two volumes. Vol. 1. *Women, Floods, Bodies, History.* Tr. Stephen Conway, Erica Carter and Chris Turner. Foreword by Barbara Ehrenreich. Vol. 2. *Male Bodies: Psychoanalyzing the White Terror.* Ed. & Tr. Chris Turner & Erica Carter. Foreword by Jessica Benjamin and Anson Rabinbach. Minneapolis: University of Minnesota Press.

Thomas, Dominique (2003). *Le Londonistan: la voix du djihad.* Paris: Michalon. New Edition (2005) *Le Londonistan: le djihad au coeur de l'Europe.* Paris: Michalon. [French].

Thomas, Dominique (2005). London Bombs: Focus—London, from Sanctuary to Jihadi Capital. *Adnkronos International,* July 14.

Tibi, Bassam (1998). *The Challenge of Fundamentalism: Political Islam and the New World Disorder.* Berkeley: University of California Press.

Tibi, Bassam (2001). *Islam Between Culture and Politics.* Basingstoke, Hampshire, UK and New York: Palgrave Macmillan. Second Edition (2005). Basingstoke, Hampshire, UK and New York: Palgrave Macmillan in association with the Weatherhead Center for International Affairs at Harvard University.

Tibi, Bassam (2007). *Political Islam, World Politics, and Europe.* London and New York: Routledge.

Tillion, Germaine (1983). *The Republic of Cousins: Women's Oppression in Mediterranean Society.* Tr. Quintin Hoare. London: Al Saqi Books.

Todaro, Lenora (2002). The WEF's Corporate Moguls Debate Their Role as Unelected World Leaders. *The Village Voice*, February 8, 2002.

Treston, Hubert Joseph (1923). *Poine: A Study in Ancient Greek Blood-Vengeance.* London and New York: Longmans, Green and Co.

Tridon, André (1922). *Psychoanalysis and Love.* New York: Brentano's. New Edition (1949). New York: Permabooks.

Tucker, Robert C. (1973). *Stalin as Revolutionary, 1879–1929; a Study in History and Personality.* New York: W.W. Norton.

Tucker, Robert C. (1990). *Stalin in Power: The Revolution from Above, 1928–1941.* New York: W.W. Norton.

Turner, Bryan (1974). *Weber and Islam.* London: Routledge & Kegan Paul.

Twemlow, Stuart W. (2000). The Roots of Violence: Converging Psychoanalytic Explanatory Models for Power Struggles and Violence in Schools. *The Psychoanalytic Quarterly,* vol. 69, pp. 741–785.

Twemlow, Stuart W. (2005). The Relevance of Psychoanalysis to an Understanding of Terrorism. *International Journal of Psycho-Analysis,* vol. 86, pp. 957–962.

Twemlow, Stuart W. & Sacco, Frank C. (2002). Reflections on the Making of a Terrorist. In Covington, Coline et al. (Eds.) *Terrorism and War: Unconscious Dynamics of Political Violence,* pp. 97–125. London: Karnac Books.

Ulman, Richard Barrett & Abse, David Wilfred (1983). The Group Psychology of Mass Madness: Jonestown. *Political Psychology,* vol. 4, no. 4, pp. 637–661.

Updike, John (2006). *Terrorist.* New York: Alfred A. Knopf.

Uschan, Michael V. (2006). *Suicide Bombings in Israel and Palestinian Terrorism.* Milwaukee: World Almanac Library.

Vaknin, Samuel (1999). *Malignant Self Love: Narcissism Revisited.* Ed. Lidija Rangelovska. Skopje: Narcissus Publications. Reprinted (2005). Prague: Narcissus Publications.

Vaknin, Samuel (2001). *After the Rain: How the West Lost the East.* Ed. Lidija Rangelovska. Skopje: Narcissus Publications.

Vaknin, Samuel (2003). *Terrorists and Freedom Fighters.* Skopje: Narcissus Publications.

Van der Waals, H.G. (1965). Problems of Narcissism. *Bulletin of the Menninger Clinic,* vol. 29, pp. 243–274.

Van Evera, Stephen (2006). Israel-Palestine. In Reveron, Derek S. & Murer, Jeffrey Stevenson (Eds.) *Flashpoints in the War on Terrorism,* pp. 1–20. New York and London: Routledge.

Varvin, Sverre & Volkan, Vamık D. (Eds.) (2003). *Violence or Dialogue? Psychoanalytic Insights on Terror and Terrorism.* London: International Psychoanalytical Association.

Victor, George (1998). *Hitler: The Pathology of Evil.* Washington: Brassey's.

Victoroff, Jeff (2005). The Mind of the Terrorist: A Review and Critique of Psychological Approaches. *Journal of Conflict Resolution,* vol. 49, no. 1, pp. 3–42.

Victoroff, Jeff (Ed.) (2006). *Tangled Roots: Social and Psychological Factors in the Genesis of Terrorism.* Amsterdam and Washington, DC: IOS Press.

Vicziany, Marika & Wright-Neville, David (Eds.) (2005). *Terrorism and Islam in Indonesia: Myths and Realities.* Clayton, Victoria, Australia: Monash University Press.

Volkan, Vamık D. (1988). *The Need to Have Enemies and Allies: From Clinical Practice to International Relationships.* Northvale, New Jersey: Jason Aronson.

Volkan, Vamık D. (1997). *Bloodlines: From Ethnic Pride to Ethnic Terrorism.* New York: Farrar, Straus and Giroux.

Volkan, Vamık D. (2001a). Observations on Religious Fundamentalism and the Taliban. *Mind and Human Interaction,* vol. 12, no. 3, pp. 156–160.

Volkan, Vamık D. (2001b). September 11 and Societal Regression. *Mind and Human Interaction,* vol. 12, no. 3, pp. 196–216.

Volkan, Vamık D. (2004). *Blind Trust: Large Groups and Their Leaders in Times of Crisis and Terror.* Charlottesville, Virginia: Pitchstone Publishing.

Volkan, Vamık D. (2006). *Killing in the Name of Identity: Stories of Bloody Conflicts.* Charlottesville, Virginia: Pitchstone Publishing.

Von Rad, Gerhard (1991). *Holy War in Ancient Israel.* Tr. & Ed. Marva J. Dawn. Intr. Ben C. Ollenburger. Grand Rapids, Michigan: W.B. Eerdmans.

Waelder, Robert (1930). The Principle of Multiple Function: Observations on Overdetermination. In Guttman, Samuel A. (Ed.) (1976) *Psychoanalysis: Observation, Theory, Application.* New York: International Universities Press.

Waite, Robert George Leeson (1977). *The Psychopathic God: Adolf Hitler.* New York: Basic Books. Reprinted (1993). New York: Da Capo Press.

Walzer, Michael (2001). Excusing Terror: The Politics of Ideological Apology. *The American Prospect,* vol. 12, no. 18, pp. 16–17 (October 22).

Watt, William Montgomery (1953). *Muhammad at Mecca.* Oxford: Clarendon Press.

Weinberg, Leonard & Pedahzur, Ami (2003). *Political Parties and Terrorist Groups.* New York and London: Routledge.

Weinberg, Leonard & Pedahzur, Ami (Eds.) (2004). *Religious Fundamentalism and Political Extremism.* London and Portland, Oregon: Frank Cass.

Whittaker, David J. (Ed.) (2001). *The Terrorism Reader.* London and New York: Routledge. Second Edition (2003). London and New York: Routledge. Third Edition (2007). Milton Park and New York: Routledge.

Williams, Paul L. (2002). *Al-Qaeda: Brotherhood of Terror.* Parsippany, New Jersey: Alpha Books.

Williams, Paul L. (2004). *Osama's Revenge: The Next 9/11. What the Media and the Government Haven't Told You.* Amherst, New York: Prometheus Books.

Williams, Paul L. (2005). *The Al-Qaeda Connection: International Terrorism, Organized Crime, and the Coming Apocalypse.* Amherst, New York: Prometheus Books.

Williams, Paul L. (2006). *The Dunces of Doomsday: 10 Blunders That Gave Rise to Radical Islam, Terrorist Regimes, and the Threat of an American Hiroshima.* Nashville, Tennessee: WND Books.

Williams, Paul L. (2007). *The Day of Islam: The Annihilation of America and the Western World.* Amherst, New York: Prometheus Books.

Winnicott, Donald Woods (1965). *The Maturational Processes and the Facilitating Environment: Studies in the Theory of Emotional Development.* London: The Hogarth Press. New York: International Universities Press.

Winnicott, Donald Woods (1971). *Playing and Reality.* London: Routledge.

Winnicott, Donald Woods (1989). *Psycho-Analytic Explorations.* Ed. Clare Winnicott et al. Cambridge, Massachusetts: Harvard University Press.

Wistrich, Robert S. (2001). The New Islamic Fascism. *The Jerusalem Post,* November 16.

Wistrich, Robert S. (2004). Islamic Judeophobia: An Existential Threat. In Bukay, David (Ed.) *Muhammad's Monsters.* Green Forest, Arizona: Balfour Books.

Woodward, Bob (2002) *Bush at War*. New York: Simon & Schuster.

Woodward, Bob (2004). *Plan of Attack: Bush at War, Part II*. New York: Simon & Schuster.

Woodward, Bob (2006a). Ford Disagreed with Bush about Invading Iraq. *The Washington Post,* Thursday, December 28, Page A01.

Woodward, Bob (2006b). *State of Denial: Bush at War, Part III*. New York: Simon & Schuster. New Edition (2007). New York: Simon & Schuster.

Wright, Judith (1966). *The Nature of Love*. Melbourne: Sun Books.

Wurmser, Leon (1981). *The Mask of Shame*. Baltimore: Johns Hopkins University Press. Reprinted (1994). Northvale, New Jersey: Jason Aronson.

Wurmser, Leon (2004). Psychoanalytic Reflections on 9/11, Terrorism, and Genocidal Prejudice: Roots and Sequels. Review of Eight Books on These Subjects. *Journal of the American Psychoanalytic Association,* vol. 52, no. 3, pp. 911–926.

Yerushalmi, Yosef Hayim (1991). *Freud's Moses: Judaism Terminable and Interminable*. New Haven, Connecticut: Yale University Press.

Young-Bruehl, Elisabeth (2003). *Where Do We Fall When We Fall in Love?* New York: Other Press.

Zananiri, Mary C. (Ed.) (2005). *Borderline Personality Disorder*. New York: Taylor & Francis.

Zedalis, Debra D. (2004). *Female Suicide Bombers*. Honolulu, Hawaii: University Press of the Pacific.

Zilboorg, Gregory (1962). *Psychoanalysis and Religion*. Ed. & Intr. Margaret Stone Zilboorg. New York: Farrar, Straus and Cudahy. Reprinted (1967). London: Allen & Unwin.

Zinn, Howard (2002). *Terrorism and War*. Ed. Anthony Arnove. New York: Seven Stories Press.

Zonis, Marvin (1991). *Majestic Failure: The Fall of the Shah*. Chicago: University of Chicago Press.

Zonis, Marvin (2003). Values, Narcissistic Wounds, and Violence in the Middle East. Paper delivered at the 26th Annual Conference on the Psychology of the Self, November 6. International Association for Psychoanalytic Self Psychology.

Zonis, Marvin & Brumberg, Daniel (1987).*Khomeini, the Islamic Republic of Iran, and the Arab World*. Cambridge, Massachusetts: Center for Middle Eastern Studies, Harvard University.

Zonis, Marvin & Joseph, Craig M. (1994). Conspiracy Thinking in the Middle East. *Political Psychology,* vol. 15, no. 3, pp. 443–459.

Zonis, Marvin & Offer, Daniel (1985). Leaders and the Arab-Israeli Conflict: A Psychodynamic Interpretation. In Strozier, Charles B. & Offer, Daniel (Eds.) *The Leader: Psychohistorical Essays*. New York: Plenum.

Index

abandonment: for George W. Bush, 207; in Osama bin Laden's life history, 186, 189; in personality development, 38

Abdülmecid (Ottoman sultan), 26

abnormal: determining, 33; society's views of, 32

Abraham, Karl, 87, 88, 89

Abrams, Dan, 111

Abu Ghraib prison, 136, 181

AbuKhalil, A., 185

abuse, and shame-and-rage reactions, 180–81. *See also* child abuse; wife abuse

academic disciplines, religious terror and, 7–12

Acar, Muharrem, 202

Active Endeavor, Operation, 57

"activists," in mass communication media, 109

Adorno, Theodore, 22

adulthood, in Arab society, 176–77

Adventist movement, 159

Afghanistan: overthrow of Taliban in, 57, 193–94; Taliban government in, 20; U.S. invasion of, 77, 135; and "war on terror," 183

Afrasiabi, Kaveh, 126

afterlife, elevation of, 179

aggression, and grandiose self, 99. *See also* violence

Ahmad, Eqbal, 161

Ahmadinejad, Pres. Mahmoud, 65, 67, 70; background of, 68; *Der Spiegel* interview, 68–69; letter to Pres. George W. Bush, 66–67; misreading of, 69; public pronouncement of, 69

Ahmed, Akbar, 121, 122, 185

Ainsworth, Mary, 103

Ajami, Fouad, 185

Akhtar, Salman, 3, 26, 33, 34, 36, 113, 115, 131

Alderdice, John Thomas, 49

Alexander, Yonah, 185

Algeria, media censorship in, 112

Algiers Accords, 76

About the Author

AVNER FALK is an internationally known Israeli clinical psychologist and scholar, an expert in the fields of psychohistory and political psychology. He trained as a clinical psychologist at the Hebrew University of Jerusalem and at Washington University in St. Louis. He practiced psychotherapy for twenty-five years, during which he served as Senior Clinical Psychologist at several Jerusalem mental health centers, before becoming a full-time independent scholar. He has authored seven earlier books, including *Anti-Semitism: A History and Psychology of Contemporary Hatred* (Praeger, 2008), *A Psychoanalytic History of the Jews, Fratricide in the Holy Land: A Psychoanalytic View of the Arab-Israeli Conflict,* and *Napoleon Against Himself: A Psychobiography.*